Hendrik De Smet, Peter Petré and Benedikt Szmrecsanyi (Eds.)

Context, Intent and Variation in Grammaticalization

Trends in Linguistics
Studies and Monographs

Volume 365

Context, Intent and Variation in Grammaticalization

Edited by
Hendrik De Smet, Peter Petré and Benedikt Szmrecsanyi

DE GRUYTER
MOUTON

ISBN 978-3-11-221393-3
e-ISBN (PDF) 978-3-11-075305-9
e-ISBN (EPUB) 978-3-11-075315-8
ISSN 1861-4302

Library of Congress Control Number: 2023930658

Bibliographic information published by the Deutsche Nationalbibliothek
The Deutsche Nationalbibliothek lists this publication in the Deutsche Nationalbibliografie;
detailed bibliographic data are available on the internet at http://dnb.dnb.de.

Typesetting: Integra Software Services Pvt. Ltd.
Printing and binding: CPI books GmbH, Leck

www.degruyter.com

Contents

Peter Petré, Hendrik De Smet and Benedikt Szmrecsanyi

1 General introduction

Context, intent and variation in grammaticalization

Abstract: This general introduction sets the stage for the current volume by discussing the state-of-the-art of research on the role of context, intent, and variation in grammaticalization processes. We specifically discuss proposals that grammaticalization has different (sub)stages, each characterized by different mechanisms, attributes, and parameters. Succinctly put, we argue that context and intent are important in early-stage grammaticalization, while variation is the long-term result of grammaticalization. Subsequently, we briefly contextualize the contributions in the volume as a function of whether they tackle early-stage grammaticalization or late-stage grammaticalization. We end with a résumé of Hubert Cuyckens' career, a scholar dedicated to unraveling grammaticalization and to whom this volume is dedicated in turn, on the occasion of his retirement.

Keywords: Grammaticalization, syntactic variation, extravagance, competition, unidirectionality

1 From the spring to the bog: Grammaticalization and its different stages

For over a century now, the study of how lexical, contentful material develops into more grammatical, procedural material has been a core topic of linguistic research, known as grammaticalization theory. Pioneering work by Meillet (1912) already managed to establish some of the essential underpinnings of the theory, including the concepts of syntactic reanalysis (to which Meillet's term *grammaticalisation* primarily referred) and semantic bleaching and renewal (cf. also Jespersen's cycle, Jespersen 1917). Ever since, grammaticalization theory has kept maturing, with the development of theories of fine-grained semantic and syntactic shifts involving metonymic (Goossens 1999) and analogical processes (Fischer 2007), unidirectionality (Haspelmath 1999, Börjars and Vincent 2011), routinization (Bybee 2006: 715, Schmid 2020) and erosion of phonetic content (Bybee 2006: 720), schematization and shifts in productivity (Traugott and Trousdale 2013: 13ff), among others. Indeed, the list of concepts introduced to describe and explain aspects of grammaticalization by now amounts to the size of a small dictionary in itself. One may wonder if

https://doi.org/10.1515/9783110753059-001

this is a bad sign, showing a fragmentation of the theory into sub-theories that are not well integrated. What is worse, some of the mechanisms[1] underlying grammaticalization proposed in the literature may even seem to contradict one another. This holds in particular for those that describe grammaticalization as a form of reduction (phonetic erosion, loss of independence, semantic loss), a line that was developed early on especially by Lehmann (1985), as contrasted to those characterizing grammaticalization as a form of expansion (increased productivity, combinatorial potential, pragmatic enrichment), a view explicitly taken by for instance Himmelmann 2004 (cf. e.g. Traugott and Trousdale 2013: 113–120 for a more detailed overview of these different viewpoints). However, as has been argued (e.g., Traugott and Trousdale 2013; Cuyckens 2018), the reductive and expansive processes that have been identified are not really contradictory. Instead, they apply to different stages of the grammaticalization process.

A key point in this process arguably is the point where the grammaticalizing construction has emancipated to such an extent that it should be considered no longer an extension of a polysemous source construction, but an independent construction of its own. This shift has been referred to in the past by means of the term 'syntactic reanalysis', but functionalist approaches have shown that the shift cannot be reduced to a formal one alone, and semantics has to be taken into account as well. This is why Traugott and Trousdale have introduced the term of grammatical constructionalization, to refer to this shift in a way that involves both meaning and form (2013: 124). As Cuyckens points out (2018: 193), "the fact that the grammatical constructionalization approach thus adds a chronology to Lehmann's and/or Himmelmann's criteria adds a valuable dimension to grammaticalization research that is certainly worth further investigation." Making this distinction allows us to better see how reduction and expansion operate differently at different stages before and after this tipping point. Some semantic attrition (reduction), for instance, appears to be typical of the stages preceding constructionalization, while an increase in type-productivity (i.e. Himmelmann's 2004 host-class expansion) and syntactic context expansion tends to follow constructionalization. Conversely,

---

1 One may wonder if 'mechanism' is a legitimate term at all. Recently, Walkden (2021: 1) argued that the whole concept of mechanisms of change is flawed, and that, instead, a theory of change "should be entirely derivative of a theory of language in the individual (cognition, acquisition, and use) and ii) a theory of (human) populations, with at least the latter containing no principles or stipulations specific to language". We continue using the term out of convenience, but we should be aware that the reification of cognitive mechanisms in language at the community level is indeed problematic. Language can better be conceptualized as a complex adaptive system, and change in such a system is a matter of continuous self-adjustment of patterns, in response to both functional (e.g., semantic bleaching, functional overload, social indexicality) and formal (e.g., phonetic erosion) stressors at the levels of the individual as well as population dynamics.

pragmatic enrichment through speaker-based implicatures or hearer-based inferences is a form of expansion at the early stages of grammaticalization, while phonetic erosion is a form of reduction in the later stages.

While the different viewpoints found in the literature may therefore not (always) be contradictory, it is important to realize that grammaticalization is not a monolithic process that is identical across its substages. Various attempts have for instance emphasized the importance of distinguishing between the innovation and diffusion stage (see e.g. Croft 2000: 3–5), between primary and secondary grammaticalization, the latter acting on already grammaticalized materials (e.g. Breban 2014; Smirnova 2015), or between consecutive waves of grammaticalization accumulating into a longer-term grammaticalization process (e.g. Petré and Van de Velde 2018: 890). The contributions to the current volume build on these previous attempts to capture the multi-stage nature of grammaticalization, and draw attention to the boundaries between grammaticalization and other types of syntactic shifts. In this vein, this introduction revisits what it means to call grammaticalization a multi-stage process, and situates the different contributions into this broader conceptualization.

Grammaticalization could perhaps be compared to the trajectory of a river. It starts its life as a lively mountain stream going one way down the slope of time, with a clear purpose and intent, clearly guided by the rocky river bedding that is its context. Then, gradually, it expands, gathering more and more water from tributaries. Its pace starts to slow down, and it begins to meander, winding its way through the established grammatical landscape, without the clear guidance it used to have. While growing it has come to contain many more lexical items that, like the fish in that river, also thrive in similar rivers. Also, some fish in the river may not swim along the stream all the time, some may even swim against it. For language users, too, the choice of where to go fishing becomes more muddled. In a similar vein, some lexical items may stop evolving along the grammaticalization stream, or slow down. Ultimately the river may even silt up and only remain as a kind of idiomatic relic in the linguistic landscape.

The idea that the incipient stages of grammaticalization are somehow 'faster' and more straightforward hinges on the observation that these first stages build on contentful source constructions. Change at this point can only go into a limited number of directions. To take the classical example of the English future marker *be going to*: in its initial stages, the combination of *be going* with a *to*-infinitive denotes motion with a purpose. This interpretation invites the inference that what is at stake is the purpose rather than the motion, which recedes into the background, and eventually leads to the establishment of a 'pure' intention reading. Only after the entrenchment of motionless uses can a next step be taken towards a predictive function, and the scope of the grammaticalizing construction may then widen further.

The occurrence of the very first innovations in a grammaticalization process may be motivated in different ways. Some innovations may be emergent below the level of awareness. According to the 'invisible hand' principle (Keller 1994) repeated minimal innovations, hardly more than slips of the tongue, may sneak into fertile contexts, and eventually may lead to the innovation reaching a threshold value after which it starts to diffuse in the community. Yet even though the innovation stage may take place below the level of awareness, it is still functionally driven. Going back to our example of *be going to*, it is generally the case that the most relevant part of the message containing *be going* and a *to*-infinitive is the expression of a purpose or intention, not the motion that is a prerequisite for realizing this intention. A hearer might therefore infer that the message is really about intention instead of motion, according to the Gricean maxim of relevance or relation ('I expect a partner's contribution to be appropriate to the immediate needs at each stage of the transaction'; Grice 1991: 47). In such a view, the first step towards innovation appears to be hearer-driven. However, once a certain inference opens up the way towards innovation, the innovation may be bolstered by more conscious efforts of speakers, for instance by opting for unexpected encodings to make a message stand out. This type of motivation for innovation and potential grammaticalization has been labeled EXTRAVAGANCE in Haspelmath (1999). Both these hearer- and speaker-based processes may cause items to start their way on the grammaticalization cline, meaning that they expand the onomasiological potential for expressing certain procedural relations (such as intention, and, subsequently, future) beyond the original lexical reference of these items.

If successful in the longer term, the expansion into this procedural realm may lead to an ever more schematic construction, with the original lexical semantics fading more and more (cf. Reinöhl and Himmelmann 2017). Such a schematization process increasingly turns the grammaticalizing construction into a competitor with more established grammatical markers. In certain cases, the final result is the replacement of older existing markers, in the way in which English modal verbs virtually replaced the subjunctive. However, such substitutions may not be as common as has been suggested by the focus on them in some of the literature (see De Smet et al. 2018 for an elaborate discussion). Instead of an outgoing and an incoming variant, what grammaticalization often leads up to, is a form of long-term variation. This conclusion was already succinctly drawn by Hopper when he introduced the notion of layering (1991: 22), but recently more systematic attention has gone to the particularities that shape this long-term outcome (a representative Labovian study is Tagliamonte and D'Arcy 2007; Cuyckens et al. 2014 illustrates cognitive research on complementation). Indeed, very often the increased overlap between the older constructions and the newer one leads to a rebalancing of their mutual relationship. This is the point where the river starts to meander, and possibly silt up. While phonetic or lexical variation tends to become socially indexed quite quickly, such variation in the syntactic domain may continue to exist below the level of awareness (cf. Labov 2001: 28). The functional drive that was key to the first stage of grammaticalization is lost. Yet the speech community may start looking for other ways of exploiting the newly emerged variants, for instance in the form of niche formation or stylistic and register variation (see, for instance, the discussion of the contributions by Hundt and by López-Couso and Pérez-Guerra below). From a sociolinguistic perspective, motivations related to style or register constitute a form of indexicalization. Labov's idea that syntactic change typically resides below the level of awareness may therefore not always hold. Buchstaller (2016) thematizes this, relating level of awareness to a scale of salience. While her case study (variation between quotatives) falls somewhat in between lexical and syntactic variation, the contributions by Rohdenburg and Schlüter (on complementation patterns of deceiving verbs) or López-Couso and Pérez-Guerra (on contracted negation) suggest that similar indexicalization mechanisms may be at play with 'pure' syntactic variation.

2 The early functional drive of grammaticalization

While many of the contributions to the current volume pay attention to aspects related to both early and late stages of grammaticalization, four studies contribute especially to our understanding of the earlier stages. These are the chapter by Aijmer, the one by Neels, Hartmann and Ungerer, that by Fonteyn and Manjavacas, and that by López-Couso and Méndez-Naya. The three first offer a case study involving the development of intensifying and/or degree modification functions out of lexical materials. The domains of intensification and degree modification are well-known for their capacity of rapid change. They are particularly sensitive to renewal but also to recycling and long-term variation out of a need to compensate the wear and tear of such emphatic expressions (cf. e.g., Méndez-Naya 2008; Tagliamonte 2008: 362). The fourth study is concerned with happenstance expressions (*maybe, perhaps*), which appear to share this tendency for rapid change, renewal and competition between near-synonymous expressions. As such these case studies form a subcategory of grammaticalizing items, which appears to be commonly subject to change along the lines of speaker-based motivations such as that of the maxim of extravagance. While they are therefore not a representative sample of grammaticalizing constructions more broadly, they are a fine illustration of this clear functional drive for their development early on. Yet as the contributions to this volume show, even at this early stage this drive may be checked by interfering variables.

Aijmer, in *Looking at grammaticalization from the perspective of short-time changes in real time* examines the incipient grammaticalizing process of the expansion of *literally* as an intensifier (e.g., *literally amazing*) in English. The use of *literally* saw a spectacular development over the last two decades, as evident from comparing the 1994 and 2014 editions of the spoken BNC, between which *literally* showed an almost eightfold frequency increase, including further expansion to hyperbolic contexts and the function of a sentence adverbial. This spectacular shift did not go unnoticed by prescriptivists. That it unfolded above the level of awareness is also suggested by Aijmer's findings (and in line with previous case studies like e.g. Tagliamonte 2008), which reveal that social variables such as age and gender, and the social identity related to them are highly relevant, with young female speakers being the leaders of the change. Overall, the study nicely combines internal and external perspectives, showing that the most innovative uses are also associated with the most progressive speakers.

In their chapter *A quantum of salience: reconsidering the role of extravagance in grammaticalization*, Neels, Hartmann and Ungerer reassess the role of extravagance as a driving force in incipient grammaticalization in German. While admitting that not all incipient grammaticalization is necessarily driven by extravagance, they present a case study of quantifier/degree-modification constructions for which they accumulate evidence that extravagance indeed played a role. Their case study illustrates how the initial functional drive may be followed close behind by long-term variation. The functional drive in this case is that of making an expression of quantification/degree modification stand out by using a range of novel nouns as quantifiers (e.g., *ein Fünkchen Hoffnung* 'a spark of hope') or degree modifiers (e.g. *ein Tick besser* 'one tick better') instead of the established expression with *ein bisschen* 'a bit'. Yet the proliferation of such novel expressions very quickly thwarts their natural expansion, and they seem to settle into a more complex relationship of both competition and mutual support, which is further stabilized by the continued existence of the unmarked, older construction with *ein bisschen.*

Fonteyn and Manjavacas, in their chapter entitled *Maximizing the data-drivenness of grammaticalization research*, zoom in on the development of the English prepositional phrase *to death*. Similar to the previous two contributions, *to death* is an example of grammaticalization leading to an intensifying use (*That look of yours frightens me to death*), here out of a (literally lethal) resultative expression. Different from the previous studies, however, theirs focuses on the longitudinal development of the construction rather than just a relatively short time span. Their longitudinal data reveal that the success of an intensifier does not need to be short-lived, but may spread out in the shape of a gradual expansion over several centuries. Beyond this gradual expansion, the study also reveals a sudden increase in schematicity and productivity, associated with advanced stages of grammaticalization, centuries after the first intensifying uses are found. These results potentially call into question the idea that there is a strict divide between early function-driven stages and later stages. However, Fonteyn and Manjavacas are cautious to provide such a functional explanation, especially as this sudden increase appears to coincide with a transition from one corpus resource to another. More generally, the chapter refrains from any claims on the functional drive or motivation of the development. The contribution it wishes to make is primarily a methodological one. In what Fonteyn and Manjavacas call a 'hands-off' method, they combine a number of computational strategies to chart the increase in schematicity and productivity in a fully data-driven fashion with minimal supervision. In doing so, they take the lead in employing more and more advanced quantitative methods to analyze grammaticalization processes, a recent development in the field which we expect to bring further insight into the complexity of this process.[2]

The chapter *From chance to epistemic possibility*, by López-Couso and Méndez-Naya, investigates the grammaticalization of happenstance epistemic adverbs in English from an onomasiological perspective. It shows that repeated grammaticalization along roughly similar pathways, in addition to some blending (presumably) and borrowing, has led to a surprisingly rich inventory of near-synonymous expressions meaning 'maybe' or 'possibly' in English. The chapter intersects with both the study of early stage and late stage grammaticalization. The continuous stream of newcomers in this domain in English is reminiscent of what we see with intensification and degree modification. Similar to the chapter by Aijmer, in dealing with pragmatic markers – in this case, the role of cooptation (i.e., the insertion of a phrasal fragment inside another sentence; cf. Kaltenböck et al. 2011) seems quite obvious. While this is not the focus of the current chapter, it is entirely conceivable that 'freshness' of expression plays a role here. Analogous to intensifiers and degree modifiers, happenstance expressions appear to fulfil a high pragmatic need for the expression of weak possibility. Perhaps it is also the subjectification process of these markers that draws them away from more neutral possibility markers to hedging functions. Yet similar to the conclusions drawn by Neels, Hartmann and Ungerer (see above), it may also be the case that existing markers support each other for a while. And even if in English two markers (*perhaps* and *maybe*) eventually came out victorious, in the several centuries preceding this pruning operation

---

2 Another chapter employing a data-driven approach is that by Los & Lubbers, although theirs tries to combine computational methods with qualitative analysis to tease apart syntactic from stylistic change. We will return to this contribution at the end of the introduction.

grammaticalization somehow seems dysfunctional in being *too* successful – it's grammaticalization in overdrive so to speak. Such a proliferation of grammaticalizing constructions along the same or highly similar pathways possibly calls into question a functional drive related to enhancing expressivity in the communication, though it may still point to a need of variation for the sake of variation.

3 Grammaticalization meandering

We now turn to long-term variation typical of later stages of the grammaticalization process, especially of complementation patterns, which is the topic of most of the remaining chapters. Once a grammaticalizing construction reaches a certain degree of development in terms of schematicity and productivity, this advanced development may also become a burden. The construction becomes more schematic, and its directionality may not be as straightforward anymore. A common outcome is the emergence of long-term variation. Variation can be stable (consider, e.g., the dative alternation in English, which has been around for centuries), but it can also be unstable, with language users looking for novel ways of systematizing and exploiting the co-existing variants (De Smet et al. 2018). Many of the contributions in this volume deal with the factors playing a role in shaping this type of dynamic variation.

Geeraerts, in his chapter *The structured nature of prepositional meaning*, sets the scene for a principled analysis of the complexities of change in the case of already grammaticalized items by focusing on the multidimensional nature of semantic extension. Elaborating his initial response to Cuyckens (1991), Geeraerts revisits the polysemous structure of the Dutch preposition *over* 'over'. In Present-day Dutch, *over* is already a well-established preposition and, in that sense, a later-stage grammatical item. Currently, various extended uses of *over* seem to include a shift from adverbial functions to prepositional complement marking, propelling it further along the grammaticalization cline. However, where the grammaticalization literature likes to present semantic change in terms of a one-dimensional path or trajectory, the Cognitive Linguistics literature tends to represent synchronic semantic representations in terms of more complex two-dimensional networks. Geeraerts' analysis goes further yet in showing how complex semantic representations really are, and criticizes even the two-dimensional nature of traditional radial network visualizations. With this detailed conceptual analysis, the chapter shows that semantic change, often assumed to 'emanate' from the core of a semantic category, may actually have multiple sources, including peripheral ones. It may be assumed that this holds *a fortiori* for later stages of the life of a grammatical marker. As the semantic representations of grammatical markers become more complex, change inherently loses some of its early-stage directionality. Against this backdrop, the contribution encourages historical linguists to think carefully about the dynamics of semantic change, including consequences for grammaticalization research.

The analysis by Geeraerts also serves as a prelude to the chapter by Hundt, *Competition in antagonistic verb complementation*. This chapter shows what happens once prepositions have extended into the domain of complementation by zooming in on the English verbs *fight, oppose* and *protest*. As it turns out, once grammaticalization has reached a sufficiently advanced state in a certain construction, its directionality seems to fade away, possibly because both the grammaticalizing construction and its competitors have lost the expressiveness that could give them an advantage earlier on. For prepositions that grammaticalized into complementation markers, this translates in a century-long competition with regular transitive constructions, where it has not been clear for a long time which construction was gaining the upper hand. Rather than a sweeping replacement, this competition meanders its way through time, with language users exploiting specific aspects of one or the other, resulting in niche-formation. In situations like these, external factors also play a role (a perspective out of the purvey of Geeraerts' contribution). One such factor is that of regional differences, with American English showing a somewhat consistent trend towards more bare complementation over the past two centuries. In contrast, British English shows "stylistic stratification", adopting American English usage in tabloids but not elsewhere (cf. Rohdenburg 2009). Further adding to the meandering nature of this stage of grammaticalization, the developments are very much lexically specific, and the trends observed for the three verbs at scrutiny are not shared by some other verbs where the prepositional complements hold their ground quite well. Retention of prepositional complements does not only apply to specific verbs, but also to niche contexts, which serve as strongholds for conservative patterns. In this case prepositional complements are retained in contexts with intervening material. Overall, the picture that is described is one of grammaticalization bogged down in the complex reality of an evolving grammatical system of a pluricentric language.

The contribution by López-Couso and Pérez-Guerra, *Promoting and inhibiting forces at work*, echoes the findings by Hundt. The case under scrutiny is that of negative contraction in English. Phonetic reduction is of course a traditional hallmark of advanced grammaticalization. It is therefore remarkable again that negative contraction, once established, is no longer primarily driven by language-internal function, nor does it replace non-contracted negation completely. Rather, grammaticalization here again leads to long-term variation, and a sense of things getting bogged down, with external and internal determinants beginning to play on the available variants. According to the authors, external variants take the upper hand here, and it seems that grammaticalization just gives language users that extra option, which they will resort to when it suits them best. At the same time, the contribution again illustrates functional niche-formation, in that a functional division of labour emerges between variants. This underscores that even as variants reflect different degrees of advancement on the grammaticalization cline, they continue to function in a synchronic system. In the case of negative contraction, phonetic reduction created variation that came to be exploited stylistically.

The chapter *Making interpretation redundant*, by Rohdenburg and Schlüter, presents another case of advanced, reductive grammaticalization in English. The authors are specifically concerned with competition in the complementation of English verbs of deceiving (*deceive, delude, fool*). Rohdenburg and Schlüter observe a gradual shift from a more explicit construction type in which a *that*-clause functions as complement of a prepositional phrase (as in *he deceived the public into the belief/into thinking that he would step down*) to a less explicit type without prepositional phrase (as in *he deceived the public Ø that he would step down*). This change shows characteristics of a reductive kind of grammaticalization, creating a novel "ditransitive" argument structure and integrating the superordinate verbs into a more general class of factual and suasive communication verbs (e.g. *advise, convince, inform, let X know, notify, promise, remind, reassure, tell . . .*). This development, in turn, is enabled by the reduced transitivity of the superordinate clauses. There are, then, parallels to the contribution by Hundt (see above), where we likewise see how a very open transitive schema starts to leak, losing members in niche uses to alternative constructions. In their original transitive use the verbs of deceiving under study in Rohdenburg and Schlüter's contribution take an 'interpretator' expressing the mental state (belief/thinking) which the deceiving action aims to cause in the patient (the referent of the direct object expression). Yet such phrases are low in transitivity (in the sense of Hopper and Thompson 1980), as the patient is only weakly affected. Hence, the clause undergoes pragmatic backgrounding and can thus protect constructions with dropped 'interpretators' that are not yet accepted in more exposed discourse positions. This omission proceeds gradually through intermediate stages involving an increased decategorialization and desemanticization of the interpretators, a narrowing of their range of modifiers, and their replacement by (even less modifiable) gerunds. Beyond this general shift, internal factors that further weaken transitivity, such as negation of the superordinate verb, or a reflexive use, are shown to facilitate omission of the 'interpretator' further. As to external determinants, analysis shows that the structural simplification of *deceive*-type sentences is more advanced in British English than in American English, in particular in informal registers (spoken language and fiction). In sum, the neat correlation that the authors establish between the ongoing changes and the functional constraint of weak transitivity may be considered a strong functional motivation for this case of advanced reductive grammaticalization (and eventual omission) of interpretators. On the other hand, it may as well be argued that this case, too, is an example of grammaticalization meandering because of local functional dynamics rather than across-the-board participation in a larger directional trend.

Straddling the syntactic divide, by Rickman and Rudanko, continues the discussion of complementation patterns. The contribution specifically investigates sentential complementation patterns after the matrix verbs *promise* and *threaten*. The point of departure for the study is the customary distinction in generative work between control and raising (NP movement) in the analysis of matrix verbs and adjectives. The point is that typically, a sharp syntactic difference between the two types of constructions is posited. However, as the authors point out, linguistic categories can be permeable and some higher verbs, such as *threaten* and *promise,* actually permit both types of structure. Consider, for example, *Tom promised to take care of the problem* (subject control) versus *Tom promised to be strong of character when grown up* (raising). It is this kind of variation that the authors track over the course of 210 years in recent British English. The focus is on subject control and subject to subject raising constructions after *promise* and *threaten* when a *to*-infinitive complement is present. The analysis shows that the subject control construction is the older and more established syntactic variant for both *promise* and *threaten*. Subject to subject raising after these verbs is a more recent innovation. This is entirely in line with what is known about the development of raising structures, which are a well-known pattern of grammaticalization. Raising is more grammatical, as in such cases the verb (*promise*) is no longer semantically linked to the subject, but instead conveys some kind of epistemic assessment of the future. What is interesting to see here is that the change starts around the same time for the two verbs, but is much slower for *promise* – certain fish appear to swim faster than others, reminding us of the lexical specificities found in Hundt's study (see above). Two plausible motivations are put forward for this asymmetry, frequency effects and pragmatic factors.

All chapters summarized so far deal with the later stages of the grammaticalization process, showing that grammaticalization invariably leads to dynamic longterm variation. However, we should not forget that this kind of research, perhaps more than any other kind of research on language change, faces the challenge of separating 'true' change from variation. This is precisely the topic of the final contribution, by Los and Lubbers, *The development of prose style in English horse manuals*. Los and Lubbers try to tease apart syntactic change from stylistic shifts, at the same time establishing to what extent cases of apparent syntactic change (under which advanced grammaticalization may be subsumed) may be false positives due to imbalances in the corpora used. The authors point out that, very often, the resources used to establish syntactic change are not balanced internally. This may typically happen when different corpora are combined to cover the entire time range investigated, a problem that is for instance acknowledged by Fonteyn and Manjavacas (see above) as potentially distorting their findings. However, the problem may be less obvious in that, even in a corpus balanced across time for genre, genre conventions themselves may change (cf. Biber, Douglas and Finegan 1989), and this may again lead to false positives. To avoid an unwieldy degree of variation in the source material, Los and Lubbers limit their corpus to a single genre that may reasonably be assumed to have remained relatively stable across time, namely that of horse manuals. Applying a data-driven trigram analysis of POS-tags, similar to methods used in stylometry, the analysis uncovers various shifts in the syntactic patterns that are used. The authors then go on to argue that, despite these apparent cases of syntactic change, these shifts can better be explained as changes in the genre conventions. The increase of passives they observe, for instance, is in line with general developments in scientific writing. Similarly, they observe a decrease in end-focus PPs including pronouns and conveying given information. This is related to the trend that authors increasingly strive for old-before-new order, a development in line with a broader shift in the way information structure is managed in English through time. It remains an open question whether such a shift relates purely to a stylistic development (e.g., the establishment of rules for a written language), or whether it does point to a syntactic development, and whether the two are actually mutually exclusive. This question is, however, outside the scope of Los and Lubbers' study, and food for future thought.

4 Dedication

The current volume is dedicated to Hubert Cuyckens, on the occasion of his retirement. The contributions in it capitalize on the line of work taken by Hubert throughout his career, notably within the fields of cognitive linguistics, grammaticalization, complementation and syntactic change more generally. While Hubert has recently been mostly known for his work in historical linguistics, his professional career has known a great many guises. In a way it started even before his university studies, in 1974–1975, when he stayed for a year in Ohio, US as an exchange student within what would become his second family. He brought a General American accent back home, which would inform his English language teaching in his professional career. Pursuing his interest in Germanic languages, Hubert graduated as a Licentiate (roughly the equivalent of an MA) in Germanic Philology (English and Dutch) in 1979. During the academic year following his studies, he combined part-time translating for Janssen Pharmaceutics with teaching at the University of Antwerp, meanwhile preparing his thesis for publication. This thesis, which was a collaboration with fellow linguist Steven Gillis, seems to come from a different universe than the one we associate Hubert with today. Its topic was artificial intelligence and computers in linguistic research. The thesis was well-received, and won Hubert and Steven the IBM Innovation Award, a prize typically awarded to engineers. While not continued in his later academic career, an interest in computational approaches to linguistics remained, lingering in the background, and various of Hubert's later PhD students benefited from his open mind in this regard. After this for the time distinctly exotic adventure he started focusing on what would become his core business: cognitive semantics. He first started a PhD on a postgraduate scholarship in Utrecht in 1980, but returned to his alma mater in 1982, when he obtained a fellowship from the Belgian National Science Foundation. Under the supervision of Georges De Schutter, he embarked on his PhD project, on a cognitive analysis of the semantics of spatial prepositions in Dutch, a position which he started combining with a job as teaching assistant in Business English at the Business Faculty of the University of Antwerp in 1985. He finished his PhD in 1991, after which he was promoted to lecturer of Business English, teaching in Antwerp as well as Kortrijk. Carrying out fundamental research in an applied and teaching-centered position was not straightforward. Hubert managed to publish several papers on cognitive semantics as well as applied linguistics. Yet he also kept applying for more research time, and was successful in 1997 when he was awarded a prestigious Humboldt Research Fellowship.

This key event was soon followed by another. In 1998 he was appointed professor of English linguistics at the University of Leuven. Among his new responsibilities was teaching on the diachrony of the English language. His love for historical linguistics, which had already been looming in the background, now started blooming. It is in 1998 that his first publications on historical linguistics appear, addressing the semantics of the prepositions *to, for* and *by*. One of these is also the first among his publications to contain *grammaticalization* in its title (Cuyckens 1998), a term whose complexities have inspired, haunted almost, Hubert's career up to this very day (Cuyckens et al. 2010; Robbeets and Cuyckens 2013; Cuyckens et al. 2017). A related research topic that starts appearing in Hubert's work from the early 2000s is that of complementation. Against the background of his earlier cognitive linguistic work, Hubert was, and is, particularly fascinated by the complex motivations underlying variation in complementation patterns (De Smet and Cuyckens 2007; Heyvaert and Cuyckens 2010; Cuyckens et al. 2014; Cuyckens et al. 2021). The papers in the current volume combine these long-standing pursuits of Hubert's, centering on variation and grammaticalization, with complementation cropping up time and again.

Complementation and grammaticalization were also, unsurprisingly, the topics dominating his work as supervisor and co-supervisor to a still growing list of PhDs and postdocs, including Lieselotte Brems (as co-supervisor), Hendrik De Smet, An Van linden, Ana Drobnjakovic (as co-supervisor), Peter Petré, Martine Robbeets, Christopher Shank, Vlatko Broz, Nikki van de Pol, Frauke D'Hoedt, Carla Bouzada Jabois, Meili Liu, Chiara Paolini (as co-supervisor) and Eleanor Smith. Meanwhile, Hubert's former PhD students and postdocs are already continuing his legacy at other institutions: Hendrik De Smet is currently a professor of English at KU Leuven, Lieselotte Brems and An Van linden at the University of Liège, Peter Petré at the University of Antwerp, Christopher Shank at Bangor University, and Martine Robbeets at the Max Planck Institute in Jena.

As a supervisor and scholar, Hubert's attention did not just go to academic rigor, but also to networking and service to the community. Highlights include the organization of four international conferences and serving as president of the *Societas Linguistica Europaea* (SLE) from 2009–2011. His editorial commitments deserve special mention. In addition to editing no less than eighteen book volumes and special issues, he also edited, together with Dirk Geeraerts, the widely cited *Oxford handbook of Cognitive Linguistics* (Geeraerts and Cuyckens 2007), as well as having been editor-in-chief of *Folia Linguistica* for half a decennium (2013–2018). Alongside all these activities, Hubert continued to apply for research grants and carry out research on historical syntax. Throughout his career, he published well over a hundred articles and monographs as author or editor. Testifying to his collaborative mindset, these publications feature more than fifty co-authors and co-editors.

In short, Hubert's academic career has been rich, and guided by an exceptional talent of connecting scholars, enabling linguistic research to be taken to the next level. His senior research fellowship at the FRIAS institute in Freiburg (2011) and guest professorships at the University of Gothenburg (2015) are some tokens of recognition for his efforts. The crown on his career, however, was no doubt the Honorary Doctorate he received from the University of Gothenburg in 2016, recognizing his unique and significant contribution to linguistics.

Hubert's collaborative attitude is also mirrored in his synthetic approach to different linguistic traditions. In his work, Hubert Cuyckens has encouraged and contributed to a "fusion of traditions" as the only path towards a "richer and more broadly informed understanding of syntactic change" (Cuyckens 2018: 19). The current volume is to continue and further reify this line of work. It is only by combining the descriptive, conceptual and methodological advances of traditional Historical Linguistics, Cognitive and Structuralist Linguistics and Variationist Linguistics that we can hope to solve the many puzzles of language change.

Acknowledgement: This volume is first and foremost a way of thanking Hubert Cuyckens for the inspiration and support he has offered and continues to offer to us and to the linguistic community. For the production of this volume thanks are due to Ana Drobnjakovic, Beate Hampe, Caroline Gentens, Christian Mair, Daniela Kolbe-Hanna, David Denison, Doris Schönefeld, Ilse Depraetere, Laurel Brinton, Manfred Krug, Mariana Montes, Niki Ritt, Nuria Yanez-Bouza, Olga Fischer, Qingnan Meng and Teresa Fanego for their help with the review process; to Kristin Davidse and Juliette Kayenbergh for helping out with proof-reading and indexing; to Birgit Bartels for her assistance with formatting and layout; to the authors for kindly accepting our invitation to contribute to the volume; and to series editor Daniel Van Olmen and the entire team at De Gruyter, and their associate Sushmitha Ramesh, for their enthusiasm about the volume and their support.

References

Biber, Douglas & Edward Finegan. 1989. Drift and the evolution of English style: a history of three genres. *Language* 65(3). 487–517.

Börjars, Kersti, & Nigel Vincent. 2011. Grammaticalization and directionality. In Bernd Heine & Heiko Narrog (eds.). *The Oxford Handbook of Grammaticalization*. Oxford: Oxford University Press.

Breban, Tine. 2014. What is secondary grammaticalization? Trying to see the wood for the trees in a confusion of interpretations. *Folia Linguistica* 48. 469–502.

Buchstaller, Isabelle. 2016. Investigating the effect of socio-cognitive salience and speaker-based factors in morpho-syntactic life-span change. *Journal of English Linguistics* 44. 199–229.

Bybee, Joan L. 2006. From usage to grammar: the mind's response to repetition. *Language* 82. 711–733.

Croft, William. 2000. *Explaining language change*. London: Longman.

Cuyckens, Hubert. 1991. *The semantics of spatial prepositions in Dutch: A cognitive linguistics exercise*. Ph. D. dissertation, Department of Linguistics, University of Antwerp.

Cuyckens, Hubert. 1998. Grammaticalization in the English prepositions TO and FOR. *C.L.E.A.R. (Cognitive Linguistics: Explorations, Applications, Research)* 28. 1–12.

Cuyckens, Hubert. 2018. Reconciling older and newer approaches to grammaticalization. *Yearbook of the German Cognitive Linguistics Association* 6. 183–196.

Cuyckens, Hubert, Frauke D'hoedt & Benedikt Szmrecsanyi. 2014. Variability in verb complementation in Late Modern English. In Marianne Hundt (ed.), *Late Modern English syntax*, 182–203. Cambridge: Cambridge University Press.

Cuyckens, Hubert, Kristin Davidse & Lieven Vandelanotte. 2010. Introduction. In Davidse, Kristin, Lieven Vandelanotte & Hubert Cuyckens (eds.), *Subjectification, Intersubjectification and Grammaticalization*, 1–26. Berlin/Boston: De Gruyter Mouton.

Cuyckens, Hubert, Lauren Fonteyn, & Peter Petré. 2021. Complexity in complementation. In Gitte Kristiansen, Karlien Franco, Stefano De Pascale, Laura Rosseel & Weiwei Zhang (eds.), *Cognitive sociolinguistics revisited* (Applications of Cognitive Linguistics 48), p. 264–276. Berlin: De Gruyter Mouton.

Cuyckens, Hubert, Lobke Ghesquière & Daniël Van Olmen. 2017. Introduction. In Daniël Van Olmen, Hubert Cuyckens & Lobke Ghesquière (eds.), *Aspects of grammaticalization: (Inter)subjectification and pathways of change*, 1–15. Berlin: De Gruyter Mouton.

De Smet, Hendrik, & Hubert Cuyckens. 2007. Diachronic aspects of complementation: Constructions, entrenchment, and the matching. In Christopher M. Cain & Geoffrey Russom (eds.), *Studies in the history of the English language III: Managing chaos: Strategies for identifying change in English* 3, 187–214. Berlin: Mouton de Gruyter.

De Smet, Hendrik, Frauke D'hoedt, Lauren Fonteyn & Kristel Van Goethem. 2018. The changing functions of competing forms: Attraction and differentiation. *Cognitive Linguistics* 29. 197–234. https://doi.org/10.1515/cog-2016-0025.

Fischer, Olga. 2007. *Morphosyntactic change: Functional and formal perspectives*. Oxford: Oxford University Press.

Geeraerts, Dirk & Hubert Cuyckens (eds.). 2007. *The Oxford handbook of Cognitive Linguistics*. Oxford: Oxford University Press.

Goossens, Louis. 1999. Metonymic bridges in modal shifts. In Klaus-Uwe Panther & Günther Radden (eds), *Metonymy in language and thought*, 193–210. Amsterdam: Benjamins.

Grice, Paul. 1991. *Studies in the way of words*. Cambridge, MA.: Harvard University Press.

Haspelmath, Martin. 1999. Why is grammaticalization irreversible? *Linguistics* 37. 1043–1068.

Heyvaert, Liesbet & Hubert Cuyckens. 2010. Finite and gerundive complementation in Modern and Present-day English: Semantics, variation and change. In Margaret Winters, Heli Tissari & Kathryn Allan (eds.), Historical Cognitive Linguistics, 132–162. Berlin: De Gruyter Mouton.

Himmelmann, Nikolaus P. 2004. Lexicalization and grammaticization: Opposite or orthogonal? In Walter Bisang, Nikolaus P. Himmelmann & Björn Wiemer (eds), *What makes grammaticalization: A look from its components and its fringes*, 21–42. Berlin: Mouton de Gruyter.

Hopper, Paul J. 1991. On some principles of grammaticalization. In Bernd Heine & Elizabeth C. Traugott (eds.), *Approaches to grammaticalization*, Vol. 1, 17–35. Amsterdam: John Benjamins.

Hopper, Paul J., & Sandra A. Thompson. 1980. Transitivity in grammar and discourse. *Language* 56. 251–299.

Jespersen, Otto. 1917. *Negation in English and other languages*. Copenhagen: Høst.

Kaltenböck, Gunther, Bernd Heine, & Tania Kuteva. 2011. On thetical grammar. *Studies in Language* 35. 848–893.

Keller, Rudi. 1994. *On language change: The invisible hand in language*. London: Routledge.

Labov, William. 2001. *Principles of linguistic change. Vol. 2. Social factors*. Oxford: Blackwell.

Lehmann, Christian. 1985. Grammaticalization: Synchronic variation and diachronic change. *Lingua e Stile* 20. 303–318.

Meillet, Antoine. 1912. L'évolution des formes grammaticales. *Scientia* 6. 130–158.

Méndez-Naya, Belén. 2008. Special issue on English intensifiers. *English Language and Linguistics* 12. 213–219.

Petré, Peter & Freek Van de Velde. 2018. The real-time dynamics of the individual and the community in grammaticalization. *Language* 94. 867–901.

Reinöhl, Uta & Nikolaus P. Himmelmann. 2017. Renewal: A figure of speech or a process sui generis? *Language* 93. 381–413.

Robbeets, Martine & Hubert Cuyckens. 2013. Towards a typology of shared grammaticalization. In: Martine Robbeets & Hubert Cuyckens (eds.), *Shared grammaticalization: With special focus on the Transeurasian languages*, 1–20. Amsterdam: John Benjamins.

Rohdenburg, Günter. 2009. Nominal complements. In Günter Rohdenburg & Julia Schlüter (eds.), *One language, two grammars? Differences between British and American English*, 194–211. Cambridge: Cambridge University Press.

Schmid, Hans-Jörg. 2020. *The dynamics of the linguistic system: Usage, conventionalization, and entrenchment.* Oxford: Oxford University Press.

Smirnova, Elena. 2015. When secondary grammaticalization starts: A look from the constructional perspective. *Language Sciences* 47. 215–28.

Tagliamonte, Sali A. 2008. So different and pretty cool! Recycling intensifiers in Toronto, Canada. *English Language & Linguistics* 12. 361–394.

Tagliamonte, Sali A., & Alexandra D'Arcy. 2007. Frequency and variation in the community grammar: Tracking a new change through the generations. *Language Variation and Change* 19. 199–217.

Traugott, Elizabeth Closs, & Graeme Trousdale. 2013. *Constructionalization and constructional changes.* Oxford: Oxford University Press.

Walkden, George. 2021. Against mechanisms: towards a minimal theory of change. *Journal of historical syntax* 5, Article 33. 1–27.

Karin Aijmer

2 Looking at grammaticalization from the perspective of short-time changes in real time

A comparative corpus-based study of *literally*

Abstract: The public media have drawn attention to the increasing frequency of *literally* especially among certain social groups. With that in mind my aim has been to investigate the changes in its frequency and use in present-day English using a comparative corpus-based methodology. The corpora used are the British National Corpus compiled in the 1990s and the Spoken British National Corpus compiled twenty years later. On the basis of the corpora I investigate in what contexts the changes of *literally* occur, the factors licensing the changes and how the shifts are related to the age and gender of the speakers. The findings show that the rise in the frequency of *literally* is due to its grammaticalization to an intensifier in hyperbolic contexts. *Literally* is also spreading to new contexts where it can be analyzed as a pragmatic marker. The changes are driven by young, female speakers who use *literally* for extravagance and to signal group membership.

Keywords: grammaticalization, hyperbole, *literally*, pragmatic marker, Spoken British National Corpus 2014

1 Introduction

Discussion on social media and in newspapers drew my attention to some specific uses of *literally* which have risen in frequency especially among certain groups of people. With that in mind my aim is to investigate whether *literally* is developing in new directions and to describe the changes occurring over a short period of time. It is hypothesized that the short-term changes of *literally* are syntactic, pragmatic and sociolinguistic and that the direction of the changes is towards the performance of an emphasizing or intensifying discourse function. The methodological approach can be described as short-term diachronic comparative spoken corpus linguistics and involves the use of comparable spoken corpora making it possible to trace changes over a short time (cf. Leech et al. 2009). The strength of the corpus methodology is that the observations about the linguistic changes are both quantitative and qualitative. The inspiration to carry out a short-term comparative study of *literally*

https://doi.org/10.1515/9783110753059-002

in present-day English also comes from sociolinguistics (Labov 1994, 2001) and grammaticalization studies.

The research questions guiding this study are:

–   to what extent does *literally* increase in frequency over a short period of time?
–   in what contexts do the changes of *literally* occur?
–   what are the factors licensing the changes?
–   who are the people using *literally* in new ways, and why do they use *literally?*
–   what can we learn about short-term linguistic change from the findings of the study?

The article is structured in the following way. Section 2 deals with previous work where *literally* has been discussed. The short-term comparative corpus-based methodology and the corpora used to study *literally* are introduced in Section 3. In Section 4, I investigate *literally* in respect to its frequency in the corpora. Section 5 tests the hypothesis that *literally* has extended its usage to new contexts over a short period of time on the basis of the corpora used and examines the contexts where *literally* is used as a marker of emphasis and hyperbole. Section 6 contains the concluding discussion.

2 Previous work

Literally has received a great deal of negative attention in the public media because it is frequently used especially by young speakers in contexts where it cannot be interpreted in its original sense. Here are some examples (simplified) from the Spoken British National Corpus (2014):

(1)   I literally suffocate

(2)   It literally made my skin crawl

(3)   That is literally the weirdest thing I've heard in my entire life.

In (1) it is hardly likely that the speaker will suffocate but *literally* is used to signal the speaker's negative emotions. In (2) the speaker uses a metaphor to describe that something is frightening. In (3) the speaker has probably heard many strange things in her life but uses *literally* for extra emphasis.

According to the critics of this use, people "force a 'literally' where the antithetical and more pretentious 'figuratively' would do – would in fact be more literal."

(https://www.theguardian.com/politics/reality-check-with-polly-curtis/2012/mar/12/re
ality-check-literally-wrong-use-word). Despite the arguments about the misuse of
literally this usage is now increasing in frequency and it is mentioned in dictionaries and in grammars (Park, no date).

The properties of *literally* have also been the topic of a great amount of scholarly discussion. The questions concern, for instance, how *literally* is used in present-day English and how its "misuse" should be explained synchronically and
diachronically. It has been claimed that the uses of *literally* described by the mass
media are not a misuse but illustrate a process of subjectification and grammaticalization. In this section I will give an overview of previous approaches to the
analysis of the 'modern' *literally*. Finally, I will show how my methodology and
research questions differ from those approaches.

In present-day English *literally* is an emphasizer and a disjunct. On the basis
of positional criteria, Quirk et al. (1985: 583) defined *literally* as a subjunct with
the function of 'emphasizer' and as a style disjunct expressing "the respect in
which a comment is being judged" (Quirk et al 1985: 615).[1] In the emphasizer function, *literally* emphasizes the speaker's commitment to the truth of the assertion.

> Since it is normally expected that a person intends his hearer to accept what he says as
> true, the addition of the comment or assertion in no way alters, but merely emphasizes the
> truth of the assertion. When these emphasizers are positioned next to a part of the commu-
> nication, without being separated intonationally or by punctuation, their effect is often to
> emphasize that part alone, though there may be ambivalence as to whether the emphasis is
> on the part or the whole (Quirk et al. 1985: 583f.).

Literally as a disjunct appears mainly in initial position with the function of
"making more explicit the respect in which a comment is being 'hedged'" (Quirk
et al. 1985: 616). It belongs to the same family of disjuncts as *figuratively, generally,
metaphorically, personally, strictly*. The emphasizer function is illustrated by (4):

(4)   They literally tore his argument to pieces (Quirk et al. 1985: 584).

Literally emphasizes the truth of the assertion without in any way altering what
has been said.

Quirk et al. (1985) also discuss occurrences of *literally* in contexts where it is
used in new contexts to express hyperbole. An example is:

---

1 In Quirk et al.'s (1985: 566) terminology, subjuncts are adverbials which "have, to a greater or
lesser degree, a subordinate role . . . in comparison with other clause elements". Disjuncts "have
a superior role as compared with the sentence elements; they are syntactically more detached,
and in some respects 'superordinate'"(Quirk et al. 1985: 613).

(5)   The car literally somersaulted off the road. (Quirk et al. 1985: 619)

This use of *literally* is motivated by the speaker's surprise at an unexpected outcome. The authors comment: "It would seem that the speaker wants to emphasize the extraordinary nature of what he is describing – 'Believe it or not!' –, as well as to draw attention to the hyperbolic language used to describe it" (Quirk et al. 1985: 619). Quirk et al. (1985) also mention that "in careless and informal speech, and even indeed in writing, the adverb comes to be used in ways that are 'literally' absurd." One of their examples is (6):

(6)   She literally FLÈW out of the room. (Quirk et al. 1985: 619)

The intended meaning is not that she flew out of the room but that she was in a great hurry.
　　There is a tendency to associate this use with a new function because of its rise in frequency and its use by young speakers. However, the use of *literally* in non-literal contexts is not new as shown by the fact that it is mentioned in the OED. The OED distinguishes three different categories of meaning. The first group (1.a) describes the meaning of *literally* as 'in a literal manner or sense', a literal, exact, or actual sense; not figuratively, allegorically, etc.

(7)   The expression 'class warfare' was meant analogically, not literally, by
　　　Marx and Engels. (2002 M. Desai *Marx's Revenge* (2004) x. 169)

The second group (OED 1.b) describes uses where *literally* is used to "indicate that the following word of phrase must be taken in its literal sense, usually to add emphasis". A modern example is:

(8)   Bloody Dionysian murders..in which a man, said be a 'rapist', is literally
　　　torn into pieces. (2006 *N.Y. Rev. Bks.* 2 Nov. 20/2)

In the third group of uses *literally* has a colloquial sense (OED 1.c) where it is used to indicate that "some (frequently conventional) metaphorical or hyperbolical expression is to be taken in the strongest admissible sense: 'virtually, as good as'; (also) 'completely, utterly, absolutely'". The OED adds: "Now one of the most common uses, although often considered irregular in standard English since it reverses the original sense of *literally* ('not figuratively or metaphorically')."

The colloquial sense is attested as early as 1769:

(9)   He is a fortunate man to be introduced to such a party of fine women at his arrival; it is literally to feed among the lilies. (1769 F. Brooke Hist. Emily Montague IV. CCXVII. 83)

A more recent example is (10):

(10)   'OMG, I literally died when I found out!' No, you figuratively died. Otherwise, you would not be around to relay your pointless anecdote. (2008 Herald-Times (Bloomington, Indiana) 22 Oct. a8/1)

According to Powell (1992), the different meanings of *literally* can be derived from a folk theory of meaning associated with explicitly signaled literal uses of expressions. She draws attention to the function of *literally* to encode "metalinguistic comment and attitudinal perspective on an utterance or on parts of it" and proposes different subcategories of use to describe it (Powell 1992: 335). The most interesting of her subcategories for the current study are the use of *literally* for rhetorical emphasis and its function to reinforce a hyperbolic meaning by means of expressing evaluation (an aesthetic judgement).

Literally as a rhetorical emphasizer is illustrated by examples where *literally* precedes an element denoting an extreme case.

(11)   And I literally hadn't one day without a cigarette in 20 years. (Powell 1992: 341)

Literally is said to be motivated by "a speaker's own astonishment at an outcome or by anticipation that the hearer will be surprised by or doubtful of the extreme case" (Powell 1992: 341).

Powell also gives examples of *literally* in a hyperbolic (metaphorical) context. In (12) where *literally* is paired with a non-literal expression it has the function to encode the speaker's aesthetic judgement.

(12)   The walls were literally paneled with nineteenth-century reproductions and contemporary signals. (Powell 1992: 346)

In the author's judgement *literally paneled* is the best or most appropriate way of describing that the walls were covered with a large number of paintings. Powell remarks that *literally* can also convey that something is interesting and remarkable. This effect can be explained as the result of a conflict between the Maxim of Quality

(Grice 1989) and the Interest Principle (Leech 1983: 146), stating "Say what is unpredictable and hence interesting" (Powell 1992: 346).

It has been argued that *literally* combining with hyperbolic expressions has developed to an intensifier. Synchronically it shares many properties with intensifiers such as the frequent use by young people, capacity for rapid change, and colorfulness (Ito and Tagliamonte 2003). Diachronically, the present-day use of *literally* as an intensifier can be explained as the result of subjectification and grammaticalization. (e.g. Partington 1993; Lorenz 2002; Israel 2002; Nerlich and Chamizo Dominguez 2003).

Partington (1993) states that "a number of lexical items which today have an intensifying function began life with some modal semantic content, through which speakers comment on their assessment of truth" (Partington 1993: 181). Other adverbs taking the same path are *very, truly* and *really.* The changes are assumed take place as the adverbs increase their collocational range with an increase in their frequency as a result. However, Partington does not discuss the developments systematically on the basis of corpora or as an on-going phenomenon.

We are lucky to have some studies of the intensifying uses of *literally* in contemporary English based on authentic corpus data. Calhoun (2015) investigated the syntactic and pragmatic functions of *literally* because she was interested in studying the speakers' attitudes to different uses of *literally.* For her study she analyzed data from public and social media. Based on her data (125 randomly selected tokens of the intensifier) she claimed that *literally* was undergoing pragmatic strengthening and that the process involved grammaticalization (see also Calhoun 2012).

Park (no date) carried out an empirical study of *literally* using the Magazine and Fiction sub-corpora from COHA (Corpus of Historical American English https://www.english-corpora.org/coha/?c=coha&q=8043732) from three different periods (the 1900s, the 1950s and the 2000s) complemented by data from Twitter. It was shown that in the Twitter data, *literally* was an intensifier in 95.33 per cent of the occurrences. She also observed an increase in the occurrences of the intensifier over the last hundred years in the Magazine and Fiction data.

The present study differs from earlier diachronic studies of *literally* since it is restricted to the syntactic, semantic and pragmatic changes which have taken place over a short period of time in present-day English. It is based on large comparable spoken corpora which have been annotated with sociolinguistic metadata making it possible to explore the emergence and rise in frequency of innovative uses of *literally* in present-day English from the perspective of the age and gender of the users. The new uses have a pragmatic meaning which can only be understood in the context of language use. The findings can therefore contribute to the discussion of the factors driving change in the framework of grammaticalization.

3 Methodology and corpora

The methodology is based on the comparison of two matching corpora from different periods of time. We are now in the fortunate position that we can use the Spoken British National Corpus from 2014 as the source for investigating the frequency and use of *literally* in current British English (see Love et al. 2017). The recordings consist of informal conversations involving multiple speakers who are friends or members of the same family. The collection of spoken texts in the corpus amounts to 11.9 million words and can be taken to constitute a representative sample of contemporary spoken British. The Spoken BNC2014 replaces the older British National Corpus which was completed in 1994 as a resource to study present-day English. The traditional British National Corpus has been a rich source for investigating spoken language because it is big and gives sociolinguistic information about the speakers and hearers. However, spoken language is known to change quickly and the traditional British National Corpus can now be regarded as 'historical' and less suitable for the study of present-day English. The current methodology takes advantage of the fact that we can now make detailed comparisons of a particular language phenomenon by using the two corpora for short-term diachronic comparisons.

The corpora which are compared have been collected and designed in similar ways. There are some differences between the corpora in the way the data was collected which should be pointed out (although these do not necessarily affect their comparability). The conversations in the Spoken BNC2014 were recorded by voluntary recruits who used smart-phones to do the recordings whereas for the recordings for the Spoken BNC2014 professional recording equipment was used.

The corpora are comparable with regard to size. However, the traditional BNC consists of a conversational component (the demographically- sampled part) and a context-governed part while the Spoken BNC2014S consists of informal conversations only. The data in the Spoken BNC2014 are therefore comparable only to the demographically-sampled (DS) part of BNC1994. I have therefore used the Spoken BNC2014Sample (Spoken BNC2014S) rather than the whole corpus since it is of roughly the same size as the 4.2 million demographically-sampled part of BNC1994 (BNC1994DS).

Both corpora give sociolinguistic information about the users which makes it possible to relate the changes in the frequency of *literally* to the speaker's age and gender. Six different age groups have been distinguished in the classification of the speakers with respect to age (0–14, 15–24, 25–34, 35–44, 45–49 and 60+).[2]

---

2 There were also a number of 'unknown' speakers (their age and/or gender was unknown). These have not been included in the statistics.

The research was conducted in the following way. All the instances of *literally* were retrieved from the two corpora via the online Corpus Query Processor (CQP) tool (Hardie 2012), exported into a database and further analyzed with respect to sociolinguistic metadata on the users' age and gender, the syntactic context (e.g. whether the collocating item context is a verb or an adjective), the semantic context (whether the collocating element is a metaphor or another hyperbolic item) and function (such as emphasizer or intensifier). For each example of *literally* which is quoted in the text, information is provided about the corpus from which it is taken, the file and number of the line in the corpus. The current speaker in the interaction is identified by a special code preceding the speaker turn.

Raw frequencies of *literally* are given when the two BNC corpora are compared. When sub-corpora are used normalized frequencies of *literally* (number of tokens per million words) have been stated. Log-likelihood tests (LL) have been used to calculate the significance of the results (https://ucrel.lancs.ac.uk/llwizard.html).

4 Frequency of use

The overall rise in the frequency of *literally* which has been noticed by the public media was confirmed by my corpus data. The comparison of the frequency of *literally* in the BNC1994DS and in the Spoken BNC2014S shows that there has been a dramatic increase in the frequency of *literally* over a short period of time. See Table 1.

Table 1: The frequency of *literally* in the BNC1994DS and the Spoken BNC2014S.

Tokens	Number
BNC1994DS	94
BNC2014S	784

The rise in frequency of *literally* over time leads to several questions. Is the increase random or is it the case that a particular function is becoming more frequent? Is there a correlation between the increasing frequency of *literally* and sociolinguistic data such as the age and gender of the speakers? In order to answer these questions the frequency of *literally* will be compared in different contexts of use in BNC1994DS and the Spoken BNC2014S.

As has been shown by sociolinguists (see e.g. Bailey et al. 1991), short-term diachronic changes can be studied both in apparent time and in real time. Changes in apparent time are observed across generations at a specific point of time and can be used to make predictions about changes in real time. From the perspective of apparent time change a peak in frequency is expected to occur among the speakers in the young age group (between 15 and 24 years old) if there is an incipient change. *Literally* undergoes changes both in apparent time and in real time with respect to the age and gender of the language users. Such a frequency peak occurs for example in speech of the 15–24-year-olds in the Spoken BNC2014S. See Table 3.

However, in BNC1994DS there is instead a peak in frequency in the group of speakers between 35 and 44 years old which needs to be explained. See Table 2. A possible explanation is that the peak reveals a change 'from above' (Labov 1990) and that the speakers used *literally* consciously in order to show their emotional involvement.

We get additional evidence for the changes of *literally* over time by comparing its frequency of use among speakers in different age-groups in BNC1994DS and the Spoken BNC2014S. The analysis based on changes taking place in real time shows that *literally* is increasing in frequency among the speakers in all the age-groups. The analysis also demonstrates that the changes are closely associated with young speakers. Both pre-adolescents (0–14-year-olds) and speakers in the 15–24 age group use *literally* more frequently than speakers in the other age groups Table 3).

Table 2: The frequency of *literally* with respect to the age group of the speakers in BNC1994DS.[3]

Age range	Number	Word count	pmw
0–14	6	435,286	13.784
15–24	9	596,113	15.098
25–34	18	816,024	22.058
35–44	30	825,857	36.326
45–59	6	859,736	6.979
60+	6	783,594	7.657

While looking into the ratio female/male speakers using *literally* in the two corpora I could make the observation that it is rising in frequency in female speech. In BNC 1994DS the number of male speakers using *literally* predominates.[4] The comparison with the corresponding data in the Spoken BNC 2014S reveals that the situation has now changed and that female speakers are using *literally* more

---

3 Since the number of speakers differs depending on the age group, normalized frequencies per million words (pmw) have been used.

4 The difference in frequency between male and female speakers is significant (LL 43.38).

Table 3: The frequency of *literally* with respect to the age group of the speakers in the Spoken BNC2014S[3].

Age range	Number	Word count	pmw
0–14	22	69,354	317.21
15–24	355	962,346	368.89
25–34	58	385,311	150.53
35–44	50	662,217	75.50
45–59	38	532,208	71.40
60+	42	940,003	102.78

than males. There were 540 instances of *literally* in female speech in comparison to 244 instances of *literally* in male speech.[5]

Table 4 shows the frequency of *literally* as used by female and male speakers in the BNC1994DS and Table 5 the rates for female and male speakers in the Spoken BNC2014S.

Table 4: The frequency of *literally* with respect to the gender of the speakers in the BNC1994DS.

Gender	Number	Word count	pmw
Female	53	2,940,525	18.02
Male	41	2,054,366	19.98

Table 5: The frequency of *literally* with respect to the gender of the speakers in the Spoken BNC2014S.

Gender	Number	Word count	pmw
Female	540	2,860,739	188.77
Male	244	1,938,045	126.53

There is thus some evidence from the data above that female speakers are propagating the changes of *literally* over time and that the speakers are young. The next stage of the quantitative analysis is to investigate if the rise in frequency is linked to specific syntactic contexts and functions and to inquire whether *literally* is used more by women and by younger people in the new contexts.

---

5 The difference in frequency is significant (LL28.85).

Table 6 shows the distribution of *literally* across syntactic contexts in BNC1994DS and in the Spoken BNC2014S. *Literally* is a modifier of a word or a phrase. It can also be syntactically independent constituent on its own and it is used on its own as a response marker.

Table 6: *Literally* in different syntactic contexts in BNC1994DS and in the Spoken BNC2014S.

	BNC1994DS	Spoken BNC2014S
Verb phrase	44	244
Noun phrase	13	87
Preposition phrase	4	40
Adjective phrase	9	12
Adverb phrase	3	21
Adverbial phrase	–	3
Syntactically independent constituent	7	88
Response marker	–	5
Interrupted or unclear	14	113

Literally modifying a verb phrase

(13)   S0144: they 've **literally taken kids off their parents** (BNC1994DS; KLT 798)

Literally modifying a noun phrase

(14)   S0179: but he he does as little as humanly possible without massively upsetting anyone (.) but do you think the courageous stance is **literally the path of least resistance** (Spoken BNC2014S; S37K 759)

Literally modifying a preposition phrase

(15)   S0336: so it 's like I 'm **literally in the house** for twelve hours which is just a bit depressing (Spoken BNC2014S; SG78 1347)

Literally modifying an adjective phrase

(16)   S0448: ah fine but you should want to watch Game of Thrones cos it is **literally amazing** right why are you not wanting to watch it (Spoken BNC2014S; SAG4 307)

Literally modifying an adverb

(17)   S0421: ≫when we had a lounge I **literally never** used it I was always in my
        room (Spoken BNC2014S; SY7T 65)

Literally modifying an adverbial clause

(18)   S0262: ≫cos I left it **literally as I was buying my popcorn** I just left it up at
        the erm (.) at the till (Spoken BNC2014S; SP9F 199)

Literally as a syntactically independent pragmatic marker

(19)   S0439: **literally my birthday is like a magnet for awful things** (Spoken
        BNC2014S; SEZ2 669)

Literally as a stand-alone response marker

(20)   S0444: ≫have you booked where you 're staying yet?
        S0439: **no no no literally** –ANONnameF and –ANONnameM cos they 're
        Australian (Spoken BNC2014S; SV4W 122)

Literally increases in frequency with verb phrases, noun phrases, adjective phrases,
preposition phrases and adverb phrases in the Spoken BNC2014S. The most interesting finding is that *literally* in the Spoken BNC2014S is spreading to new contexts
where it no longer is integrated in the utterance (as in example 19).

I have identified five different functional categories of *literally* in my data
based on collocational features, syntax and the analysis of the extralinguistic context: (i) to be understood precisely or in a literal sense, (ii) emphasising the speaker's
commitment to truth, (iii) rhetorical emphasizing (with metaphors and hyperbole),
(iv) pragmatic marker, (v) response marker. Table 7 provides the frequencies of *literally* in its different meanings in the two data sets.

Table 7: The frequency of *literally* in different senses in BNC1994DS and Spoken BNC2014S.

	BNC1994DS	Spoken BNC2014S
'precisely', 'in a literal sense'	78	161
emphasizer (emphasising truth)	3	165
rhetorical emphasizer (before metaphor and hyperbole)	4	54
pragmatic marker	–	107
response marker	–	5
Interrupted or unclear	–	297

Literally is increasing in frequency as an emphasizer, a rhetorical emphasizer, as a pragmatic marker and as a response marker. 86 per cent of the occurrences of *literally* in the Spoken BNC2014S were of this kind. When *literally* is used as a rhetorical emphasizer (in metaphorical and hyperbolic contexts) it can be assumed to be used in an innovative way since the number of occurrences of *literally* in BNC1994DS is negligible. There were no instances of *literally* as a pragmatic marker in the BNC1994DS suggesting that this is also a new use of *literally*. These new meanings or functions will be described and illustrated in more detail in the following sections and an explanation will be proposed for their emergence in the framework of grammaticalization. *Literally* as a response marker can also be regarded as a new function which is still infrequent.

5 *Literally* in hyperbolic contexts

According to Claridge (2011: 5), a hyperbolic expression "exceeds the (credible) limits of fact in the given context" and contains the pragmatic attribute "more of x", i.e. more or the same thing. Based on this definition, she suggests that the common denominator of hyperbolic uses of language is that there exists a contrast between the hyperbolic expression and the literal or unmarked form (or the representation of this form in the speaker's thought.) The interpretation of what is said as hyperbolic is derived from this contrast by inferencing. The size and type of the mismatch between a possible literal form and the corresponding hyperbolic form may vary, which may affect the ease with which the intended hyperbolic meaning can be inferred. Hyperbole does not depend on the presence of *literally*. However, *literally* can be understood as a trigger or reinforcer of the hyperbolic interpretation.

It is the topic of the next sections to discuss the hyperbolic contexts where *literally* occurs from the perspective of change. However, it is generally difficult to describe the hyperbolic context in such a way that it is suitable for empirical corpus-based research of the hyperbolic use of *literally*. According to Andersen (2001: 232), "[l]ess-than-literal use of language incorporates not only the poetic use of metaphor, hyperbole and other tropes that are found in the literature, but also the more trivial, but highly common, 'figurative' uses of everyday conversation". As to the type of non-literal expression which is strengthened by *literally* a distinction has been made here between metaphorical and (other) hyperbolic expressions. Another question has to do with the types of function that *literally* can perform in hyperbolic contexts. When *literally* is used in hyperbolic contexts it gives rise to conversational implicatures, for example that what is said is remarkable or unbelievable. However, it needs to be pointed out that it is often difficult to distinguish between uses of *literally* in a literal context (where the words it combines with must be taken in a literal sense) and uses where *literally* is used for hyperbole. There were many ambiguous examples where I have chosen what seems to be the most salient interpretation of *literally* in the context.

The examples of *literally* in hyperbolic contexts with a rhetorical function are found mainly in the Spoken BNC2014S. However, a comparison will be made with *literally* in hyperbolic contexts in BNC1994DS when this is relevant. I hypothesize that the new uses will be more frequent in young people's speech and that females will use *literally* more than males. I will test this hypothesis by investigating the occurrences of *literally* in hyperbolic contexts with respect to the age and gender of the speakers. Section 5.1 deals with *literally* before metaphors and Section 5.2 with *literally* with other hyperbolic expressions. Section 5.3 discusses *literally* as a pragmatic marker and a response marker.

5.1 *Literally* with metaphors

Instances where *literally* is used with metaphorical expressions pose a challenge because the speaker is not concerned with emphasizing the truth of what is said but how it is said (see Quirk et al. 1985: 619).

Literally can, for example, be used with innovative metaphors deliberately contradicting people's world knowledge. According to Claridge (2011: 98), such extravagant metaphors are created to "fill a speaker's expressive needs at a given point in time" and "they are semantically, and potentially also formally, deviant or striking in such a way as to impress the audience."

The function of *literally* is to convey that the information conveyed is so remarkable that it can best be conveyed by a metaphor. (21)-(23) illustrate this use:

(21) S0220: >like he 's the first judge **like literally they could get a duck on the shore to do a better job than he could** that 's because he 's a fucking idiot and heS0211: like literally if I got Louis Walsh as a judge I 'd walk out I 'd go find – UNCLEARWORD like I 'd go find another like I 'd I 'd –UNCLEARWORD like (Spoken BNC2014S; S632 1233)

(22) S0450: probably the worst thing being out though so my brother 's got it really bad and he **literally is like coughs and sneeze the house down** and like it 's worse indoors than it is outdoors (Spoken BNC2014S; SZQX 2862)

(23) S0325: I sent a picture to–ANONnameF I remember I sent a picture to her I
was like do you like my omelette?
S0325: it **literally just looked like sick in a tub** (Spoken BNC2014S; S4PF 519)

In (21) it is not actually the case that the job done by the judge could be carried out by a duck. *Literally* serves as a metacomment remarking on the "extraordinary nature of a situation" (Quirk et al. 1985: 619). The metaphor has been chosen by the speaker (a 22-year-old female) for its for its humor and to attract the hearer's attention. In (22), the metaphor (*he coughs and sneezes the house down*) involves the speaker in saying something that cannot be true. The hearer can therefore infer that *literally* should be taken as a comment on the hyperbolic character of what is said. In (23) it cannot be literally true that a picture looks like *sick in a tub* but the speaker uses *literally* because it is the best way in which the speaker can describe her feelings.

The examples given have in common that *literally* is found in contexts where the speaker uses a creative metaphor or says something which is incompatible with the facts of real life. However, from a speaker perspective, there is no real conflict between what she wants to express and the use of the colorful metaphor but the metaphor is the best way of communicating her attitudes or emotions. Moreover, even in cases where *literally* occurs with novel metaphorical expressions the hearer has no problems to make the intended inference based on world knowledge, shared norms and the context.

The metaphors used were also conventional as in (24)-(26).

(24) S0208: and it **literally it gets right under my skin** because I 'm like mum if
you have to change the way that you act to be more like these people they
're not your fucking friends (Spoken BNC2014S; S8RY 56)

(25) S0179: yeah (.) so it 's like but like
S0026 –UNCLEARWORD
S0179: **literally came up with this idea off the er top of my head** (Spoken
BNC2014S; SG3Q 702)

(26) S0084: across the board and my tutor Mister –ANONnameN **would literally
be tearing his hair out** (.) (Spoken BNC2014S; S7SU 2059)

In (24) the metaphoric expression '*it gets under my skin*' is a well-known metaphor meaning that something makes the speaker annoyed. In (25), the speaker describes how he suddenly comes up with a solution to a problem without giving it much thought. In (26), the force of the tutor's despair is described by a conventional metaphor. The tutor did not literally tear his hair out but the metaphor could be regarded as an appropriate way of describing the person's desperation. Powell (2002: 343) discusses similar instances as having a dual interpretation since *literally* calls attention to the literal meaning but the figurative interpretation is always present. In the present study *literally* has been regarded as rhetorical emphasizer in such cases since the metaphor involves a non-literal use of language.

Literally was only used with conventional metaphors in BNC1994DS (three occurrences). (27) is an example where the speaker has used a metaphorical expression.

(27)   PS0FP: She is absolutely petrified of that cat.
       PS0FS: Yeah?
       PS0FP: **Literally petrified**. (BNC1994DS; KCT 1636)

In (27) it is hardly likely that the woman is literally petrified because she is afraid of the cat but the metaphor should be interpreted as a more colorful way of expressing her emotions.

The quantitative sociolinguistic analysis of *literally* with metaphors shows that the speakers were young and that they were female. There were 13 occurrences of *literally* with metaphors in the Spoken BNC2014S mainly used by 15–24-year-olds (in 12 out of 13 examples) and the speakers were female (in all but one example).[6]

5.2 *Literally* in hyperbolic contexts

In hyperbolic contexts (other than metaphor) *literally* stresses one particular element (which can be a single word or a phrase) and exaggerates its extent and the attitude expressed by the speaker.

I have distinguished several sub-categories of hyperbolic contexts depending on the word or phrase which is emphasized.

5.2.1 *Literally* as a rhetorical emphasizer before hyperbolic adjectives and verbs

Literally can be can be utilized rhetorically before an adjective (or a noun phrase containing an adjective) indicating the extent or degree of a property at the

---

6 The figure includes both non-conventional and conventional metaphors.

upper extreme end of a scale. In this function *literally* can be replaced by 'abso-lutely' or 'totally'. See (28) and (29):

(28)   S0439: I do love that Google is **literally amazing** Google tells you everything (Spoken BNC2014S; S6A7 397)

(29)   S0208: so there 's been (.) so like **literally wi- a ridiculous amount** less of ac-cidents erm (.) this year (.) (Spoken BNC2014S; S5AA 35)

Other examples contain *literally* followed by an adjectival participles such as *shattered, petrified, gutted, bored to tears* with a hyperbolic meaning. However these occurrences have been analyzed as metaphors.

There were only three occurrences of *literally* emphasizing a hyperbolic or extreme adjective in the Spoken BNC2014S and no clear example in BNC1994DS. The demographic data show that the speakers belonged to the 15–24 age group and that two of the speakers were female. The low frequency of *literally* with hy-perbolic adjectives was unexpected since adverbs with an intensifying meaning have as their main function to modify adjectives.

Literally occurred once followed by the hyperbolic verbs *love (it)*, emphasiz-ing "the extent to which a characteristic holds" (Biber et al 1999: 554).

(30)   S0208: cos er on Skype as well (.) when I spoke and I said thank you prop-erly and stuff he was like you have mm –ANONnameF to thank more than me cos she 's you know organised it all she did everything for me and I just literally sat there and broke down again I was like I 'm surrounded by so many nice people in my life right now
       S0202: oh bless him
       S0208 ≫ **literally loved it it 's so amazing** (Spoken BNC2014S; SGHZ 25)

5.2.2 *Literally* with a hyperbolic use of the superlative in the immediate context

Literally co-occurring with a (hyperbolic) superlative of the adjective (which is part of a noun phrase) can be regarded as an innovative context. There were no instances in BNC1994DS. (31) –(35) illustrate some hyperbolic uses of the superla-tive by young females:

(31)   I had n't showered I was **literally the grimmest you could ever be in your entire life** (Spoken BNC2014S; S2AJ 235)

(32) S0439: it 's like someone 's like waffling on about erm cauliflower based piz-
zas they are **literally the most fucking disgusting things I have ever I had
to** just bin them (Spoken BNC2014S; SEZ2 363)

(33) S0135: Someth- yeah I d- I du n no (.) but **it was literally the most random
thing I 've ever done in my life** (.) what happened is we all got – (Spoken
BNC2014S; SVR6 1796)

(34) S0439: she is literally **the shittiest estate agent person I have ever met in my
entire life** (Spoken BNC2014S; SPXV 200)

(35) S0202: but she were fucking amazing **literally the best psychic ever** (Spoken BNC2014S; SMC2 289)

In (31), the speaker describes herself as *the grimmest you could ever be in your
entire life* with a hyperbolic interpretation. In (32) it is obvious that the way the
cauliflower pizza is referred to should be taken as an exaggeration. In (33) the
speaker is using the superlative to describe a military exercise she participated in
using exaggeration because it best expresses her negative evaluation and in (30)
the speaker uses the superlative to express her negative judgement of the estate
agent. All the examples contain *ever* with an indefinite time reference. This usage
was found only in the Spoken BNC2014S.The sociolinguistic analysis confirms the
hypothesis that the speakers who are responsible for the development of hyperbolic uses are generally young and that the majority are females. There were 14
occurrences of *literally* with a hyperbolic superlative all found in female speech
(one speaker in the age group 1–14, 12 speakers in the group 15–24, one speaker
age unknown).

5.2.3 *Literally* as a rhetorical emphasizer with a quantifier expression in the immediate context

Literally also occurs with quantifiers (e.g. *every, all*) and negative words such as
never, no used hyperbolically.

(36) S0084: when his daddy abandoned him (.) **literally every single film is
about father**
S0083: yeah
S0084: abandonment (.) close Encounters er Richard Dreyfuss goes off with
the aliens (Spoken BNC 2014S; SNLY 403)

(37) S0202: it 's a pub called a PoundPub and you can **literally get anything** for a pound in there (Spoken BNC 2014S; SMC2 732)

(38) S0018: **literally every day all my waking hours** was working and then at the weekend I 'd be writing the research projects (Spoken BNC 2014S; S6R4 576)

(39) S0208: erm and I did n't really think it through that I would n't have it back in –ANONplace so like Christmas it was really hard I had to f- I 'd like literally tried **every single pillow in the house** now I found one that 's okay (Spoken BNC 2014S; SNLY 401)

(40) S0441: and that 's **like literally just out of nowhere** and I was like yup (Spoken BNC 2014S; 2AJ 162)

Literally always implies emphasis and sometimes exaggeration. In (36) it is hardly the case that every single film is about father abandonment although the film they discuss has this theme. In (37) the PoundPub offers a number of things for a pound but less likely *anything*. In (38) and (39) the most probable interpretation of *literally* is that is used hyperbolically. In (38), the speaker claims to have been working every day all waking hour in order to draw attention to the amount of work she has done, and in (39) the hearer is not expected to understand what is actually said literally but as an exaggeration intended to convey that the speaker misses her favorite pillow. In (40) *literally* is used with the hyperbolic expression *just out of nowhere* to highlight that what happened was completely unexpected.

The quantitative analysis showed that there was one occurrence of *literally* with a quantifier in BNC1994DS and 17 occurrences in the Spoken BNC2014S. The speakers were young (one speaker in the 0–14 age group, 7 speakers in the 15–24 age group, one speaker in the 25–34 age group). The speakers using *literally* in new hyperbolic ways with a quantifier in the immediate context were mainly female (20 out of 22 speakers).

5.2.4 *Literally* as a rhetorical emphasizer before numerical expressions

Numerical expressions can also be interpreted hyperbolically. In (41) and (42) I have interpreted the numerical expression as an exaggeration and *literally* as rhetorical emphasizer.

(41) S0439: did you also know like a few years ago apparently erm bestiality be-
came illegal in Scandinavia
S0441: nice
S0439: I know I know I was just like only a few years ago ? yeah like
S0441: ≫ bit late
S0439: like pretty sure that became illegal in like England a long time ago
S0441: yeah **like literally hundreds of years ago** surely(Spoken BNC2014S;
S38F 190)

(42) S0135: all good condition and everything (.) she goes oh I just bought this for
twenty pounds (.) we 're like oh okay (.) cool (.) **literally within ten minutes
maximum** she sold it for forty (Spoken BNC2014S; SVR 619)

In (41) Speaker S0441 suggests that it must be *like literally hundreds of years ago*
that bestiality became illegal. The speaker uses overstatement to contrast the situation in Britain with the Scandinavian situation. The phrase *literally within ten
minutes maximum* in (42) can arguably also be interpreted as an overstatement.
The person has bought at a car boot sale and now probably exaggerates how long
it took her to sell it again.

The cases of *literally* before a hyperbolic number expression were fairly infrequent in both corpora. There were six occurrences of *literally* in the Spoken
BNC2014S (most frequently in the combination *literally like*).[7]

To sum up the main points of the discussion in Section 5.2, I have demonstrated that the hyperbolic use of *literally* is on the increase in the Spoken
BNC2014S. The new contexts where the shift can take place were metaphors and
other hyperbolic contexts containing an extreme expression. In these contexts, *literally* did not occur in BNC1994DS or only in a few examples. As a reinforcer of
hyperbolic language, *literally* can conversationally implicate that what is said is
unexpected, remarkable or extraordinary. Other inferences have to do with the
degree of the speaker's involvement and subjectivity. *Literally* can also convey
that the speakers want to appear as creative or amusing.

Table 8 summarizes the findings from the preceding discussion about the hyperbolic contexts where *literally* increases over time based on the corpus comparison:

---

7 There were four occurrences of *literally* before a numerical expression in BNC1994DS all with
a literal interpretation.

Table 8: The frequency of *literally* in hyperbolic contexts in BNC1994DS and the Spoken BNC 2014S.

	BNC1994DS	**Spoken BNC2014S**
metaphor	3	17
hyperbolic adjectives, verbs	1	3
hyperbolic superlatives	–	9
quantifiers	1	22
numerical expressions	–	3

The data also confirmed my hypothesis that the speakers responsible for the development of *literally* to hyperbolic contexts were mainly young speakers in the 15–24 age group. Table 9 shows how *literally* is used in the hyperbolic contexts discussed above across different age groups of speakers. Speakers whose age is unknown have not been included.

Table 9: The distribution of *literally* in hyperbolic contexts across speakers with respect to age.

Age range	Number
0–14	3
15–24	38
25–34	1
35–44	–
45–59	–
60+	–

As shown by the table, the speakers using *literally* in hyperbolic contexts are generally young (between 15 and 24 years old). There were also a few instances of *literally* in the pre-adolescent speaker group. Looking at the male/female ratio for the examples of *literally* in the young speaker groups the quantitative analysis shows that the speakers were female in 85 per cent of the cases. The findings therefore strongly suggest that the speakers who are initiating or driving the change of *literally* to hyperbolic contexts are young female speakers.

5.3 *Literally* as a pragmatic marker

Literally is also used outside the actual utterance structure where it can no longer be regarded as an emphasizer. When *literally* is syntactically independent it arguably fulfills the syntactic, semantic and functional criteria of pragmatic markers (Brinton 2017: 9). The syntactic criterion is regarded as the most important diagnostic of pragmatic marker status. However, *literally* also has other characteristic features discussed in more detail by Brinton (2017). It has little or no propositional meaning and can easily be omitted. Moreover *literally* is multifunctional, having a range of pragmatic functions which need to be described in pragmatics rather than in semantics. (43–44) illustrate how *literally* is used as a pragmatic marker:

(43) S0611: **er literally** it 's so funny because doing the same course you 'd think you 'd be as smart as each other but you 're the worst person at all games (Spoken BNC2014S; S2EF 1271)

(44) S0439: I ca n't deal with him as much I do n't find him as funny I 'm not as fan of like
S0450: **literally he cracks me up** like well it 's I think how he says thing it just literally just gets me
S0439: mm
S0450: in in like it 'll just make me laugh and laugh and laugh (Spoken BNC2014S; SZQX 2096)

Literally serves as signal to the hearer that what is said is noteworthy or remarkable. In (43) the speaker finds it extraordinary that she is not as successful at computer games as her friends although they are doing the same university course. The speaker's attitude is further underlined by *it's so funny*. In (44) *literally* is used by the speaker to draw attention to the remarkable way in which the person's jokes make her *laugh and laugh and laugh.*

Importantly, *literally* also has sociolinguistic and stylistic features associated with pragmatic markers and mentioned by Brinton (2017: 9). For example, both as an emphasizer and a pragmatic marker *literally* is frequent in spoken language. Like pragmatic markers in general it is stylistically stigmatized and negatively evaluated. Finally, it is used in different ways by men and women in its innovative uses.

It was apparent from my comparative analysis that *literally* is rapidly becoming frequent as a pragmatic marker. *Literally* as a pragmatic marker was attested in the Spoken BNC2014S in 107 instances which means that it was more frequent in this function than as a hyperbolic intensifier. There were no cases in BNC1994DS. Looking at the age and gender of the speakers using *literally* as a pragmatic marker we find that this use is both age- and gender-specific.

Literally as a pragmatic marker was used in 95 per cent of the cases by speakers in the young age groups (0–14, 15–24, 25–34). 78 per cent of the speakers were between 15–24 years old. The quantitative analysis of the occurrences where *literally* has been defined as a pragmatic marker also shows that the speakers were females in 79 per cent of the occurrences.

The combination of *literally* with other pragmatic markers (*like* and *just*) supports the hypothesis that *literally* is developing in the direction of a pragmatic marker. *Literally like* (*like literally*) and *literally just* (*just literally*) are increasing dramatically in frequency in the Spoken BNC2014S. *Like literally* occurred 62 times in the Spoken BNC2014S (and *literally like* in 45 instances). In BNC1994DS *literally* co-occurred once with *like*. *Just literally* is also becoming more frequent with a pragmatic meaning (*just literally* 39 tokens; *literally just* 88 tokens). *Just literally* (*literally just*) also occurred in BNC 1994DS (5 occurrences). The rise in frequency occurs among young speakers (about 50 per cent of the speakers using a combination of *literally* and *like* were between 15 and 24 years old). The speakers were female in 68 per cent of the examples. The statistics for the combination of *just* and *literally* also show that the combination is first used by young speakers. The majority of speakers were female (78 per cent) and about half of the total number of speakers were between 15–24 years old. (45)-(46) illustrate the new uses of *literally* with *like* and with *just* to indicate pragmatic functions,

(45)   S0003: **like literally** I did n't have my phone for three hours cos it froze and I could n't get in back on and I thought I thought it 's dead (.) and I was like how do I communicate with the world ? (Spoken BNC2014S; S7DT 323)

(46)   they said are you getting rid of the Christmas cracker he said yes but we 're gon na do something for the royal wedding and **it was just literally** let 's ignore than kind of we 're taking this away from you and let 's (Spoken BNC2014S 1040)

In (45), *like literally* is used with intensifying force to strengthen the speaker's frustration when she cannot use her phone. In (46) the speaker uses (*it was*) *just literally* to express more involvement and to increase the interest of what is said. In both examples the literal meaning of *literally* has arguably disappeared.

Literally is also used in clusters together with several other pragmatic markers as in (47):

(47)   S0037: was using some artistic license there but **like literally you know** I can see her in her face it 's just like she wants to like (Spoken BNC2014S; SH2A 496)

Like literally (or *literally like*) is also found in different collocational frames (e.g. *it's literally, that's like literally. I was like literally, he was like literally*) often with the function to introduce a quotation (or to represent what someone is likely to say).

(48)   S0123: she she 's going by herself to Brazil (.) stupid thing (.) and **it's like liter-
       ally** I 'm gon na go travel Brazil on my own (Spoken BNC 2014S; SJNB 750)

(49)   S0256: like and hair but (.) **I'm literally like** do n't you dare be sick on me
       keep your head that way she goes (Spoken BNC 2014S; S3C6 884)

(50)   S0336: you should 've seen it this table and chairs right came in four sepa-
       rate boxes and I mean like giant boxes and er **we were literally like** how
       the hell do we get rid of all of this ? (Spoken BNC 2014S; SG78 584)

Literally (like) is followed by an imitation or interpretation of what someone has
said and implicates that this is interesting and worth telling. In (48) the speaker is
telling the other person that her sister is going to travel to Brazil on her own. This
is a *stupid thing* which the speaker further highlights by envisaging a scene
where her sister is actually saying this. In (49) the speaker is representing in a
dramatic way how the woman says (*she goes*) to her baby *don't you dare to be
sick on me.* In (50) (*we were*) *literally like* highlights the scene where they received
giant boxes containing furniture that they didn't know how to get rid of.

The frequent use of *literally* with or without other pragmatic markers by some
young speakers indicates that it can become a conversational routine which speakers use without being aware of its literal communicative element. In the Spoken
BNC2014S *literally* was, for example, used 23 times by the same speaker (S0037).

There were only five occurrences of *literally* as response marker signaling
that the speaker agrees with the preceding speaker. In this function *literally* is
related to the adverbs *certainly, definitely, absolutely* and *really*, which can have
the function of providing "the conditions for an exchange whose message is potentially both sharable and familiar" (Powell 1992: 349). In (51) *yeah literally* functions as a response marker.

(51)   S0529: ≫yeah
       S0530: that one ? yeah (.) I watched that and whenever I watch stuff like
       that everyone 's just like what is the point ?
       S0529: **yeah literally**
       S0529it just makes you feeling more depressed rather than like wanting to
       change something and just like oh for fuck 's sake
       S0530: ≫it 's like we 're living in a world by co-op founded by (Spoken BNC
       2014S; S4YQ 1343)

The speaker uses *yeah literally* to show her involvement with what has been said
before taking the turn herself.

Summing up the main points of the preceding discussion in this section, I have argued that *literally* has undergone a further shift to a pragmatic marker in the Spoken BNC2014S. As a pragmatic marker *literally* is placed as a disjunct at the beginning of an utterance and it has little or no semantic meaning. It has multiple functions which need to be accounted for in pragmatics. *Literally* has also been regarded as having pragmatic function in combination with *like* and *just*. In the Spoken BNC1994S, *literally* as a pragmatic marker was frequent in the speech of young people and it was more common in female than in male speech. As a pragmatic marker *literally* has features which can be explained in a diachronic perspective. In the next section I will consider the developments of the new functions from the perspective of grammaticalization and change.

6 Discussion and conclusion

Change in language has been described within the framework of grammaticalization as "[t]he change whereby lexical items and constructions come in certain linguistic contexts to serve grammatical functions, and once grammaticalized, continue to develop new grammatical functions" (Hopper and Traugott 2003: xv). *Literally* in the intensifying meaning can be regarded as a case of grammaticalization following the pattern of a large class of intensifiers (such as *really* and *truly)* which have developed new meanings over time (see Section 2). Grammaticalization has the effect that *literally* increases its range of collocations with a weakening of its lexical meaning as the result. As shown by the present study, the spread to new contexts continues and *literally* can develop to a pragmatic marker which has the whole utterance or (a larger piece of discourse) in its scope and has functions in the spoken interaction.

Nevertheless, there is a great deal of information which is not available about the changes because of the lack of comparable data from several periods of time. The advent of spoken (and written) corpora has now created opportunities to study in a detailed way how, when and why the changes of *literally* occur, and the description can complement the larger picture of the type of change we analyze in the framework of grammaticalization by investigating the mechanisms driving the grammaticalization in a certain direction.

Critical to understanding the linguistic mechanisms of language change from this perspective is the idea that change is initiated by speakers in the conversational interaction. New meanings start out as implicatures from meanings which already exist or they emerge in the interaction (Traugott and Dasher 2002: 35). If the implied meanings acquire social value and are used by a large number of speakers this can lead to pragmatic strengthening and to change. The mechanisms of change in this model are extralinguistic. According to Traugott and Dasher (2002: 40), "the mechanisms involve processes of reasoning, mental projection, association, focusing on salient issues . . . none of which are part of the language system, but rather are processes brought to bear on this system in language use."

My hypothesis is that it would not be possible for the innovations of *literally* to occur unless there are strong motives for it, for example that the speakers are young and want to use a lexical expression in a new way to distinguish themselves from adolescents. Especially if the speakers are young the desire to stand out by being trendy may be a reason for using an element in a new way.

Several different mechanisms have been discussed in the context of grammaticalization and change. According to Haspelmath (1999), the reason why speakers use innovations is that they want to fulfil social goals for example to become popular. Social success can be achieved by being extravagant (or expressive) and Haspelmath proposes that this goal is the reason why people use innovations. The argument is that it is not sufficient to refer to general principles such as economy or clarity to explain some linguistic innovations. Haspelmath (1999: 1057) states that "[t]he crucial point [. . .] is that speakers not only want to be clear or "expressive," sometimes they also want their utterance to be imaginative and vivid—they want to be little "extravagant poets" in order to be noticed, at least occasionally." Thus, using *literally* before a hyperbolic expression (to emphasize a contrast between what is said and what could literally be true) is a way for speakers to innovatively use *literally* to draw attention to the remarkable properties of what is said,

We can assume that the rise in frequency of *literally* occurs because speakers are following the Maxim of Extravagance and use *literally* to draw attention to themselves and to what they are saying. However, *literally* is not yet grammaticalized. We would say that grammaticalization of *literally* to a pragmatic marker occurs when many individual speakers separately start using *literally* in a new way with the procedural function to mark an utterance as remarkable or extravagant and when the new uses of *literally* are no longer commented on by the public media. However, there is no special endpoint for the grammaticalization process which is on-going as long as *literally* is spreading to more contexts.

Sociolinguistic factors are important to describe when and to explain why the grammaticalization changes occur. It has been demonstrated there is a link between the age and gender of the speakers and the increase in the frequency of *literally* over time. The speakers using *literally* the most in the new pragmatic functions are young adults the majority of whom are females. They use *literally* to signal that the message is interesting or remarkable and for the purpose of appearing amusing or humorous. By using *literally* in this innovative way they can identify themselves in a positive way as young speakers. It is apparent that *literally* in this use is increasingly becoming a conversational routine which is used by some young people all the time.

References

Andersen, Gisle. 2001. *Pragmatic markers and sociolinguistic variation: A relevance-theoretic approach to the language of adolescents*. Amsterdam & Philadelphia: John Benjamins.

Bailey, Guy, Tom Wikle, Jan Tillery & Lori Sand. 1991. The apparent time construct. *Language Variation and Change* 3. 241–264.

Biber, Douglas, Stig Johansson, Geoffrey Leech, Susan Conrad & Edward Finegan. 1999. *The Longman grammar of spoken and written English*. London: Longman.

Brinton, Laurel J. 2017. *The evolution of pragmatic markers in English. Pathways of change*. Cambridge: Cambridge University Press.

Calhoun, Kendra. 2012. Literally. The misunderstood intensifier. https://prezi.com/x2ype7d0tf9k/literally-the-misunderstood-intensifier/ (accessed February 2022)

Calhoun, Kendra. 2015. "It is the worst of our time": Youth language, language attitudes, and arguments about *literally. Texas Linguistics Forum* (Proceedings of the 23rd Annual Symposium about Language and Society-Austin. April 17–182015) 58.1–10.

Claridge, Claudia. 2011. *Hyperbole in English. A corpus-based study of exaggeration*. Cambridge: Cambridge University Press.

Grice, Paul. 1989. *Studies in the way of words*. Cambridge, Mass. & London: Harvard University Press.

Hardie, Andrew. 2012. CQPweb – combining powers, flexibility and usability in a corpus analysis tool. *International Journal of Corpus Linguistics* 17(3). 380–409.

Haspelmath, Martin. 1999. Why is grammaticalization irreversible? *Linguistics* 37(6). 1043–1068.

Hopper, Paul J. & Elizabeth C. Traugott. 2003. *Grammaticalization*. Cambridge: Cambridge University Press.

Israel, Michael. 2002. *Literally* speaking. *Journal of Pragmatics* 34(4). 423–432.

Ito, Rika & Sali Tagliamonte. 2003. *Well weird, right dodgy, very strange, really cool*: Layering and recycling in English intensifiers. *Language in Society* 32 (2). 257–279.

Labov, William. 1990. The intersection of sex and social class in the course of linguistic change. *Language Variation and Change* 2. 205–254.

Labov, William. 1994. *Principles of linguistic change*. Vol. 1. Oxford: Blackwell.

Labov, William. 2001. *Principles of linguistic change*. Vol. 2. Oxford: Blackwell.

Leech, Geoffrey. 1983. *Principles of pragmatics*. London: Longman.

Leech, Geoffrey, Marianne Hundt, Christian Mair & Nicholas Smith. 2009. *Change in contemporary English. A grammatical study*. Cambridge: Cambridge University Press.

Lorenz, Gunter. 2002. *Really worthwhile* or *not really significant*?: A corpus-based approach to the delexicalization and grammaticalization of intensifiers in Modern English. In Ilse Wischer & Gabriele Diewald (eds.), *New reflections on grammaticalization*, 143–161. Philadelphia: John Benjamins Publishing Company.

Love, Robbie, Claire Dembry, Andrew Hardie, Vaclav Brezina & Tony McEnery. 2017. The Spoken BNC2014. Designing and building a spoken corpus of everyday conversations. *International Journal of Corpus Linguistics* 22(3). 319–344.

Nerlich, Brigitte & Pedro José Chamizo Dominguez. 2003. The use of *literally*. Vice or virtue. *Annual Review of Cognitive Linguistics* 1. 193–206.

Park, Semi. No date. *Literally* does not always mean literally: a corpus-based diachronic study on *literally* as an intensifier. https://s-space.snu.ac.kr/bitstream/10371/138389/1/8_박세미.pdf (accessed February 2022)

Partington, Alan. 1993. Corpus evidence of language change –The case of the intensifier. In Mona Baker, Gill Francis & Elena Tognini-Bonelli (eds.), *Text and technology: In honour of John Sinclair*, 177–192. Philadelphia: John Benjamins.

Powell, Mava Jo. 1992. Folk theories of meaning and principles of conventionality: Encoding literal attitude via stance adverbs. In Adrienne Lehrer & Eva Feder Kittay & Richard Lehrer (eds.), *Frames, fields and contrasts. New essays in semantic and lexical organization*, 333–353. Hilldale, NJ, Hove, London: Lawrence Fellbaum.

OED = Oxford English dictionary. http://www.oed.com/ (accessed October, 2021).

Quirk, Randolph, Sidney Greenbaum, Geoffrey Leech & Jan Svartvik. 1985. *A comprehensive grammar of the English language*. London: Longman.

Traugott, Elizabeth C. & Richard B. Dasher. 2002. *Regularity in semantic change*. Cambridge: Cambridge University Press.

Jakob Neels, Stefan Hartmann and Tobias Ungerer

3 A quantum of salience

Reconsidering the role of extravagance in grammaticalization

Abstract: Extravagance and salience have gained increasing attention in studies of language change, especially in Diachronic Construction Grammar. Nevertheless, the role of extravagance as a driving force in grammaticalization remains debated. We first offer a theoretical discussion of the issue, along with possible explanations for why opinions on extravagance may differ and how some of the conflicting views may be reconciled. We then present a corpus-based case study on the role of extravagance in the development of German quantifier/degree-modifier constructions. In particular, we focus on relatively recent and innovative patterns like *ein Tick* 'a tick', *ein Fünkchen* 'a spark (diminutive)' and *eine Spur* 'a trace', which complement – and compete with – established constructions like *ein bisschen* 'a bit'. The fact that the younger constructions combine with a range of extravagant lexemes, and that they form relatively constrained semantic clusters in a densely populated grammatical domain, suggests that their emergence may be partially motivated by speakers' extravagant ambitions. Since extravagance may lead to the rise of new constructions even in the presence of near-synonyms, we also address the resulting tension among multiple constructions co-existing in a relation of both competition and mutual analogical support.

Keywords: Extravagance, grammaticalization, quantifiers, degree modifiers, Diachronic Cognitive Linguistics

1 Introduction

The concepts of extravagance and salience have become increasingly popular in recent usage-based and constructionist approaches to language and language change (see e.g. Schmid and Günther 2016, Petré 2017, De Wit et al. 2020, Ungerer and

Acknowledgments: We are grateful to two anonymous reviewers for their tremendously helpful comments on a previous draft of this paper. As constructive and insightful as they were, they were of course in no way as painstakingly detailed as the feedback we would have received from Hubert Cuyckens, had he been given the opportunity to comment on this paper before its publication. We would therefore like to seize the opportunity to thank Hubert for all his services to the linguistic community, and especially for his support for early-career scholars like the authors of the present paper.

https://doi.org/10.1515/9783110753059-003

Hartmann 2020). In particular, scholars have explored Haspelmath's (1999) proposal that extravagance, understood as speakers' use of innovative language in order to be noticed, plays a crucial role in grammaticalization processes. Petré (2017) and De Wit et al. (2020), for example, argue that progressives in English, but also in Dutch and French, were used for extravagant purposes in the initial stages of their development. However, the exact role of extravagance in grammaticalization processes is subject to debate and requires a nuanced discussion. This paper aims at contributing to this line of research by providing an overview of the theoretical state of the art and a case study of a constructional family whose members can at least partly be used in extravagant ways, namely quantifier/degree-modifier constructions. In particular, we focus on a set of relatively new quantifier/degree-modifier constructions in German: *ein Tick* 'a tick', *ein Quäntchen* 'a quantum', *eine Handvoll* 'a handful', *ein Tacken/Zacken* 'a spike', *ein Hauch* 'a breeze/whiff', *eine Spur* 'a trace', *ein Fünkchen* 'a spark', and *eine Idee* 'an idea'. These constructions provide an interesting test case for investigating the role of extravagance in language change and grammaticalization since they arguably emerged as creative and highly salient variations of the default quantifier/degree-modifier constructions in German, *ein wenig* 'a little' and *ein bisschen* 'a bit' (Neels and Hartmann 2018, 2022).

The remainder of this paper is structured as follows. In Section 2, we will give an overview of the theoretical concept of extravagance and its relation to salience. Section 3 discusses the role of extravagance in grammaticalization, suggesting a number of ways in which previous debates about the topic could be reconciled. Section 4 is dedicated to our case study. Section 5 concludes the paper and discusses how our findings can inform ongoing research on speakers' changing constructional networks.

2 Extravagance and its relation to salience

The term *extravagance* was introduced by Haspelmath (1999) to describe one of Keller's (1994: 97) "maxims of action" that play a crucial role in Keller's account of language change: "Talk in such a way that you are noticed." Speakers' tendency to use "imaginative and vivid" language in order to present themselves as "little 'extravagant poets'" (Haspelmath 1999: 1057) has since been argued to underlie the development of new expressions in a number of linguistic domains. These include historical changes like French *ne . . . pas*, which started out as an emphatic negation marker and then gradually lost its emphatic pragmatic force (Haspelmath 1999), the development of *BE going to* into an expression of future activity (Petré 2016), and the use of the English progressive in present-tense main clauses (Petré

2017). As such, the concept of extravagance is closely related to the notion of expressivity that had been evoked in the previous literature on grammaticalization (see e.g. Hopper and Traugott 2003: 73). But "expressivity" is ambiguous as it can both refer to the capacity of a language to express a broad array of different meanings (as in Smith et al. 2013) and to more pragmatic aspects, such as the speaker conveying a certain stance towards the situation (Hopper and Traugott 2003: 73). In traditional grammaticalization approaches that discuss expressivity as a key factor, the pragmatic prominence of a newly grammaticalizing expression such as *ne . . . pas* or *BE going to* is often seen as a side effect of the fact that the new expressions tend to be both phonologically and conceptually much richer than extant grammaticalized constructions. Haspelmath (1999: 1057), however, argues that speakers' (intentional) strive to be creative should be considered a major driving force in language change and grammaticalization, and that therefore the term *extravagance* is more fitting than the terms *expressiveness* or *expressivity*.

In their brief review of the literature on extravagance, Ungerer and Hartmann (2020) summarize five prototypical characteristics of extravagant expressions: they (i) stand out, emphasize the message content, and represent it in a vivid and imaginative way; (ii) deviate from linguistic norms or expectations; (iii) signal the speaker's physical or emotional involvement in the message content;[1] (iv) refer to (speakers' perceptions of) non-canonical situations in the real world; and (v) are often redundant, i.e. contain more material than is strictly necessary. These dimensions bring together various definitions from the literature that emphasize different aspects of extravagance. While, for example, Haspelmath's original definition focuses more on the first aspect, Petré's (e.g. 2017) definition of extravagance puts the third aspect center stage, viz. speakers' emotional involvement. As Ungerer and Hartmann note, the five characteristics should not be understood as necessary criteria, but rather as prototypical features that apply in varying degrees to specific extravagant phenomena.

Essentially pragmatic in nature, the concept of extravagance is closely related to, and draws additional support from, the psycholinguistic notion of salience. Salience is a multifaceted concept in linguistics, psychology and neighboring fields (see e.g. Giora 2003, Günther et al. 2016). While stimuli can be salient for a

---

[1] The aspect of speaker involvement in the message content is reminiscent of subjectification (e.g. Traugott 1995), a concept capturing a type of semantic change that is commonly found within grammaticalization. The concepts of subjectification and extravagance can be kept distinct, however. Subjectification is a change towards meanings signalling speakers' modal stance towards the propositions they make. It is thus a process giving rise to "(inter)personal" expressions in the domain of (epistemic) modality. Extravagance, in contrast, is not a direction of semantic change but a pragmatic motivation and effect, essentially at the level of rhetoric.

number of reasons, some of the resulting types of salience are more closely akin to extravagance than others. In particular, salience effects can arise either from the *non-familiarity* of the stimulus or from the *familiarity* of the stimulus (cf. Schmid and Günther 2016). As illustrated in the following, the concept of extravagance overlaps closely with the former type of salience effects but is distinct from the latter type.

Effects of *salience due to non-familiarity* can be observed in language as well as other cognitive domains (cf. Ellis 2017). For example, a stimulus can stand out because of certain physical properties. In human visual perception, this applies to prominent colors such as red and yellow, while linguistic expressions may be salient thanks to remarkable phonetic properties such as reduplication or onomatopoeia. Other items, such as neologisms, may be salient due to their overall novelty, which derives from low usage frequency (either in terms of absolute frequency or in relative comparison to other competing expressions). In addition, some stimuli are salient only in particular contexts in which they are unexpected, as captured by the psycholinguistic notion of surprisal (cf. Jaeger and Weatherholz 2016). Both these context-free and context-dependent effects of salience due to non-familiarity can give rise to instances of extravagant language. This suggests that extravagance as a pragmatic property is either attached to a given construction itself or that it emerges from the ways in which constructions are combined in context (cf. De Wit et al. 2020). That is, individual constructions having a non-canonical form or expressing a vivid concept possess high extravagant potential *per se*, which is evoked by, or even stored in, the form or meaning pole of their symbolic makeup. In other cases, extravagant deviations from linguistic norms or expectations, for example via unnecessary redundancy, are strongly cotext- and context-dependent.

On the other hand, some phenomena display effects of *salience due to familiarity*, which are less closely related, and in fact often opposed, to the notion of extravagance. For example, this type of salience may result from a form being the preferred, prototypical choice compared to other variants. Geeraerts (2016) refers to this as *onomasiological salience* and discusses the example of the lexical pair *trousers* and *pants*: while these can refer to the same piece of clothing, most speakers will treat one of the terms as their preferred variant. Clearly, this type of salience is positively correlated with frequency of use and is therefore likely to conflict with the above notion of salience by novelty (or surprisal).

Finally, some salience effects do not easily fall on either side of the familiarity/non-familiarity distinction. For example, a stimulus may be salient because it carries associations to which humans attribute particular importance or value. Linguistic examples of this type of salience include words pertaining to accomplishment, (in)dignity or sexuality. These expressions may be judged as extravagant or not, depending on their frequency of occurrence and other contextual factors. A similar case can be made for another type of salience found in sociolinguistics, where the notion of socio-cognitive salience describes speakers' awareness of the social indexicalities attached to a given linguistic variant (cf. Buchstaller 2016). While new expressions or meanings may become *socially salient* through their association with a particular group of speakers, this process requires that the new form has become sufficiently entrenched and thus familiar to members of the wider speech community. It is therefore not clear whether this type of salience contributes to the extravagance of linguistic expressions (cf. also Traugott 2017, who keeps the two phenomena apart).

As the above discussion illustrates, the concept of linguistic extravagance receives a firmer psychological grounding by relating it to a specific subtype of salience, which we have summarized under the label of salience due to non-familiarity. This also helps avoid some of the terminological ambiguities that are common in the literature on language change when the role of salience is discussed without clearly differentiating between its components. Based on these clarifications, we can now proceed to outlining the ongoing debate about the role of extravagance in grammaticalization.

3 The role of extravagance in grammaticalization: Five steps towards reconciling the debate

Many approaches see grammaticalization and salience as closely connected, but disagreement remains about what exact role salience by non-familiarity – and, by extension, extravagance – plays at different stages of the process. As we will discuss below, the particular controversy that we are interested in here concerns the role of salience and extravagance *at the onset* of grammaticalization processes. This debate can be separated from a point that most approaches to grammaticalization agree on, namely that the further development of grammaticalizing expressions proceeds along a cline from lexical to grammatical that involves decreasing salience. This tendency plays a role both in language learning and processing and in language change. Ellis (2017) unites both perspectives:

> At the start of a Linguistic Cycle, highly salient, new constructions enter a language. They are psychophysically intense. They are full of meaning. They are unique in their interpretation. Their novelty charms and surprises.
>
> At the end of a cycle, grammatical constructions exit: by dint of frequency, they have shortened and become psychophysically slight; by dint of shortening, they have become homophonous with low contingency between form and function; by dint of habitual overuse, they have become semantically bleached. (Ellis 2017: 92)

Fulfilling abstract procedural (i.e. non-referential, largely language-internal) functions, grammatical constructions are low-level significative units and usually coded accordingly. Grammaticalization, as Harder and Boye (2011: 63) put it, "gives rise to linguistic expressions which are coded as discursively secondary", i.e. that encode "backgrounded" information. Through cognitive automation and socio-communicative ritualization (cf. Haiman 1994; Lehmann 2017), grammaticalization creates efficient solutions for conveying meanings that speakers frequently wish to communicate alongside more contentful, referential elements. Prototypically, only the latter, lexical, elements are coded in ways that allow speakers to give them primary discourse prominence relative to the co-text, i.e. to make them the focus of the discourse. Note that whenever a meaning potentially realized by a grammatical marker is discursively primary, speakers tend to opt for a semantically and formally richer realization; for example, a low-salience plural suffix may be enriched by lexical expressions such as *several* or *a number of*. On their path to ever more bleached and reduced forms (incl. lack of stress), grammaticalizing constructions become less and less likely to exhibit salience as a part of an utterance.

While it is thus fairly clear that, beyond its incipient stages, grammaticalization involves decreasing salience, the role of extravagance for the onset of grammaticalization is being disputed. Some researchers hold that extravagance drives (or at least assists) primary grammaticalization, but there are also arguments suggesting that high salience impedes grammaticalization processes.

According to Haspelmath's (1999) extravagance approach, having available fresh high-salience means of expression is a key motivation for innovating periphrastic constructions (see also Haspelmath 2000). He suggests that many cases of primary grammaticalization arise from speakers' desire to use innovative, vivid expressions. Since grammatical elements are usually not available for conscious manipulation due to their high degree of executive automaticity, speakers construct novel lexical combinations to satisfy their drive for linguistic creativity (cf. the concept of *Formungstrieb* by Gabelentz 2016 [1891]: 380–384). For example, Haspelmath argues that *by means of* emerged through speakers' attempts to find a lexically richer, innovative alternative to the preposition *with*.[2] If such extravagant lexical expressions gain currency and happen to stand in for concepts that are frequently needed in communication, as found in most categories of grammar

---

2 However, as a reviewer correctly points out, it can be debated whether *by means of* can be considered a (clear) case of extravagance without broadening the concept too much. If we follow Haspelmath in regarding "extravagance" simply as a label for Keller's maxim "Take in such a way that you are noticed", we would argue that the longer, more contentful form probably serves this function – but it does so in a very different way than, for instance, some of the quantifier/degree-modifier constructions discussed in the case study presented below.

like negation, tense, modality etc., the new periphrastic constructions may enter a frequency-sensitive cycle of more profound grammaticalization processes. As far as the onset of primary grammaticalization is concerned, however, Haspelmath's model predicts that it is extravagance that sets this process in motion.

Traugott (2017), in contrast, argues that at the onset of the grammaticalization cycle there are non-extravagant expressions. In her account, early grammaticalizing constructions emerge due to the indeterminacy of meaning and structure inherent in discourse, specifically in low-salience contexts. Discursive ambiguities produce various structural variants from the flow of unremarkable constructs (cf. Croft 2010), and some of these variants can undergo constructionalization and subsequent grammaticalization. One of Traugott's examples is the development of the *BE going to* future: in her view, the new 'future' meaning emerged from a gradual reinterpretation of the earlier 'motion with a purpose' meaning (see below for further discussion). Traugott stresses that the enabling factor in changes like these is low salience: "There is nothing exceptional, extravagant or sumptuous about the onset of grammaticalization. Changes at onset are low in pragmatic, cognitive and social salience." (Traugott 2017: 102). At first glance, this view appears to be the direct opposite of Haspelmath's extravagance account.

After this brief outline of the debate, we now turn towards an attempt to reconcile, at least in part, the opposing views about the role of extravagance in grammaticalization. Specifically, we explore reasons for *why* grammaticalization researchers arrive at such conflicting views, and whether a clearer understanding of the areas in which there is disagreement can provide a first step towards reconciling seemingly incompatible interpretations. In the following, we address five such aspects, arguing in each case that some of the disagreement among scholars can be resolved by taking a closer look at how individual instances of grammaticalization differ, where the potential effects of extravagance may be located, and how these effects can be identified. The five aspects we consider are: (i) the variability among cases of grammaticalization depending on the targeted functional domain, (ii) the fuzzy boundary between grammaticalization and lexicalization, (iii) the difference between actuation and diffusion, (iv) the roles of hearers versus speakers, and (v) the corpus-linguistic operationalizability of extravagance.

Concerning the first factor, some of the controversy may derive from the fact that cases of grammaticalization differ, and that extravagance may play a role in some of them but not in others. Although there may be a greater tendency for change to go unnoticed in morphosyntax compared to lexis, our present, limited knowledge on the sociopragmatics of grammaticalization does not warrant the conclusion that all types or stages of grammaticalization operate below the level of conscious awareness. Arguably, the conditions for the emergence of a new sentence negator or a new degree modifier differ greatly from those for the development of a tense marker, for instance. The former two grammaticalization scenarios involve high rates of renewal; consider Jespersen's cycle of negation (Jespersen 1917; Kiparsky and Condoravdi 2006) or the emergence of new quantifiers and intensifying degree modifiers such as *heaps of* and *hella* (cf. Trousdale 2012). The chief reason for this trend seems to be pragmatic in nature. Emphatic, intensifying expressions "wear off"; there is an inflationary effect of rhetorical devaluation (Dahl 2001), which boosts a key process in grammaticalization, namely semantico-pragmatic bleaching. Some communicative tasks or domains are rhetorically more competitive than others in terms of how often speakers wish to make their point with some sort of emphasis or vividness. For example, contradicting someone is rhetorically more competitive in this sense than locating events in time. This might well be what causes the grammaticalization spiral to move faster for negators than for tense markers. For the same reason, competitive domains such as negation, quantification and degree intensification may be more likely to lead to cases of grammaticalization that start out with salient, extravagant source constructions.

As for the second aspect, cases of grammaticalization and lexicalization are sometimes hard to distinguish, not least because some domains of grammar grade into what is traditionally considered part of the lexicon. Such borderline cases, too, contribute to conflicting views about the role of extravagance, considering that for lexical coinages it is not unusual to be extravagant (e.g. *whodunit*, *red herring*). Since its earliest days, the grammaticalization literature has featured examples that could equally, or should preferably, be classified as instances of lexicalization; Meillet (1912), for instance, included the example of Old High German *hiu tagu* '(on) this day' turning into the Modern German adverb *heute* 'today'. Besides adverbs, the emergence of prepositions (e.g. *in light of*) and derivational morphemes (e.g. *-ship* < Germanic root **skap-* 'to create') could be listed as other cases typically leading to divergent analyses in the literature on grammaticalization and lexicalization. Recent construction grammar approaches have reconceptualized this problematic pair of processes, establishing clearer determinants of each type of change, most notably the parameters of schematicity and productivity (esp. Traugott and Trousdale 2013). However, even then, the dividing lines between grammaticalization and lexicalization are not clear-cut. Some constructions exhibit medium degrees of schematicity and productivity, for example [*not the* A-*est* N_1 *in the* N_2] 'not very clever', as in *not the sharpest tool in the shed*, or the construction [*because* X], as in *because reasons*. Moreover, whether an emergent construction will go down the path of prototypical lexicalization or grammaticalization is not predetermined by the first steps of construction formation and change, since lexicalization and grammaticalization are not opposite but "orthogonal" (Himmelmann 2004) processes sharing a number of subprocesses (see Brinton and Traugott 2005: 110).

Thirdly, scrutinizing the debated role of extravagance at the onset of grammaticalization may furthermore require a specification of the concept of "onset". Each increment of innovation in gradual language change involves a dimension of actuation and one of diffusion/propagation. Actuation is typically driven by cognitive or pragmatic factors (see e.g. De Smet 2012), successful diffusion primarily by social factors (cf. Croft 2000; Weinreich et al. 1968). Accordingly, if salience is involved, subtypes of salience will differ depending on the dimension. Cognitively oriented manifestations of salience, such as surprisal, are more relevant to actuation, whereas socially oriented manifestations, such as social indexicalities (e.g. "young", "liberal") attached to a construction, are more relevant to diffusion. Differences in where researchers draw the boundary between actuation and diffusion as well as between different types of salience can lead to conflicting conclusions about the role of extravagance in language change.

As a fourth point, it might be necessary to unpack the onset of grammaticalization also in terms of speaker versus hearer roles. While some mechanisms proposed in the grammaticalization literature, such as analogy, metaphor and metonymy, can take effect in both production and comprehension, others are either production-centered or comprehension-centered. Explanatory concepts like context-induced reinterpretation (Heine et al. 1991) and reanalysis (e.g. Detges and Waltereit 2002), for instance, operate during comprehension, thus ascribing the fist step of actuation to the hearer. Other concepts, such as invited inferencing (e.g. Traugott and Dasher 2002), suggest that speakers make the first step. Like these mechanisms of innovation, levels of extravagance as a potential motivation for innovation can be assumed to differ in hearers and speakers. This aspect surfaces in Traugott's discussion on (non-)salience in grammaticalization as well:

> Salience may [. . .] be higher for the speaker than for the addressee because the speaker intends a certain direction for the discourse and may actively choose to say something novel in the discourse situation, whereas the addressee interprets it in reference to what has already been said in the discourse situation. (Traugott 2017: 95f.)

It is of course also conceivable that a novel structure is born in a hearer in an unremarkable, low-salience critical context (Diewald 2002), as the hearer is filling semantico-pragmatic indeterminacies with their own interpretation. When the same language user takes over this novel structure or meaning into an act of production, will they be aware of the non-conventionality of this novel use? An affirmative answer should not be excluded, particularly at the onset of primary grammaticalization, when constructions are semantically not yet highly bleached, their usage frequencies typically not yet very high, and their execution thus not yet highly automated. Possibly, novel structures in primary grammaticalization could hardly gain enough currency for successful diffusion (esp. in light of existing near-synonymous alternatives) if the structure was not salient for at least some speakers, who deliberately choose a given construction for its extravagant freshness.

A final aspect contributing to disagreement about the role of extravagance in grammaticalization concerns the extent to which researchers assume that extravagance can be operationalized, and potentially quantified, in historical corpus data. This is illustrated by a comparison of Traugott (2017) and Petré (2016), who both examine the grammaticalization of *BE going to* as a future marker (mentioned above), but draw very different conclusions about the role of extravagance in promoting this change. The different outcomes of their analyses seem to stem, at least in part, from their diverging views on what methods are suitable for evaluating the extravagant potential of the construction.

Traugott (2017) expresses doubt that extravagance can be directly "measured" in diachronic data, due to the "impossibility of gaining direct access to speakers of earlier times" (Traugott 2017: 96). In particular, she notes that past speakers' *perceptions* of salient phenomena appear inaccessible to data-driven inquiry. As a result, Traugott resorts to a qualitative analysis of selected examples in her discussion of *BE going to*. From this analysis, she concludes that there is "no evidence" that early adopters of the prospective future meaning "intended to be noticeable or innovative" (Traugott 2017: 103).

Petré (2016) also concedes the difficulty of quantifying extravagance, as "something which seems to be the epitome of the qualitative expression" (Petré 2016: 125). Nevertheless, he proposes an indirect strategy for identifying extravagant expressions in corpora via their contextual properties. Key to this approach is the assumption that speakers use extravagant language in contexts in which they are emotionally more strongly involved (see Section 2, where this was discussed as one characteristic of extravagant expressions). Following this logic, Petré compares *BE going to* with its competitor *GO to* during the critical grammaticalization period in the early 17th century. He finds that the former construction occurred more frequently with contextual markers that express immediate activity, such as adverbs of current time (e.g. *now*), and less frequently in contexts that typically lack emotional involvement (e.g. stage directions). Petré interprets this use of *BE going to* when highlighting the immediacy of the intended action as evidence of its extravagant nature. Moreover, he suggests that the construction underwent a second cycle of extravagant extension during the 17th century, occurring increasingly in non-motion contexts and thus leading to a salient contrast with its original motion sense. Interestingly, however, Traugott (2017) uses the same piece of evidence to argue against the extravagance of *BE going to*, since in her view the non-motion future meaning falls out naturally from the earlier 'motion with a purpose' sense.

As the above example shows, operationalizing extravagance remains a challenging enterprise. Views differ about whether the concept is best assessed via a qualitative analysis guided by the researcher's intuition, or via a quantitative investigation that draws on indirect contextual measures. Each of these approaches comes with its own benefits and limitations. For example, Petré's (2016) quantitative analysis may uncover contextual regularities in the development of *BE going to* that are not amenable to a qualitative assessment. On the other hand, his choice of contextual markers deserves critical scrutiny: for instance, one might question whether the notion of immediate action, as expressed by adverbials of current time, is *per se* emphatic, and to what extent the (stylistically) extravagant nature of *BE going to* can be separated from its core semantics of 'near future'. Moreover, the above discussion shows that the contextual measures are to a large extent construction-specific, which means that different criteria may need to be devised when investigating other construction types.

Given the remaining challenges for the above attempts to identify extravagant expressions, it is worth considering alternative quantitative or qualitative methods. In Section 4, we pursue a different corpus-based approach to explore the role of extravagance in a specific case of grammaticalization. Specifically, we focus on a set of relatively recent (and potentially still ongoing) changes: the emergence of innovative quantifier/degree-modifier constructions in German. The rationale behind this is that given the recency of the phenomenon, we may be able to combine corpus-based techniques that shed light on the semantic profiles of these constructions with our native speaker intuition in order to evaluate the extravagant nature of the changes. Our case study will be informative about three of the five issues discussed in the present section: first, we investigate whether the grammatical domain of quantification and degree modification may be particularly prone to triggering extravagant change; second, we examine a phenomenon that lies at an intermediate point between grammaticalization and lexicalization; and finally, our corpus study contributes to the ongoing debate about how extravagance can be identified and operationalized. We will leave the other two aspects addressed in this section – actuation versus diffusion and hearer versus speaker roles – to future empirical studies, as corpus-linguistic approaches alone are unlikely to provide conclusive answers to these issues.

4 Case study: Extravagant newcomers in a family of quantifier/degree-modifier constructions

In this section, we aim to explore extravagant potentials in early grammaticalization in a corpus-based fashion. Unlike Petré (2016), Traugott (2017) and Haspelmath (1999), however, we not only study individual grammaticalizing expressions with their collocational profiles, but we also examine their network relations to other expressions which together form a large family of constructions with varying degrees of grammaticalization. Our test case is a family of German periphrastic expressions serving as small-size quantifiers and downtoning degree modifiers. Following up on previous diachronic work by Neels and Hartmann (2018, 2022), we now focus on relatively recent additions to this constructional family. The most frequent quantifier/degree-modifier constructions in German, *ein bisschen* 'a bit' and *ein wenig* 'a little', have been complemented by more innovative patterns like *ein Tick* 'a tick', *eine Handvoll* 'a handful', or *ein Fünkchen* 'a spark' over the course of the last few hundred years.[3]

Our key question is what motivates the continued emergence of these new constructions within a "layered" (Hopper 1991) grammatical domain that is already rich in near-synonymous patterns and could therefore be thought of as "saturated". We suggest that extravagance forms one of these motivating factors. The use of new quantifier/degree-modifier constructions may not only be guided by functional need alone, i.e. speakers' desire to encode previously inexpressible meanings (in line with Traugott's [2017] view), but it may also be partially motivated by speakers' attempts to stand out and express already familiar meanings in novel creative ways.

Previous work that has hinted at the role of extravagance in the grammaticalization of quantifier/degree-modifier constructions focused on *ein bisschen* 'a bit',

---

3 To confirm that these low-frequency quantifier/degree modifier constructions are relatively recent developments, we checked their frequencies in the Reference and Newspaper Corpora of the Digital Dictionary of the German Language (DWDS), a collection of historical and contemporary corpora covering the time span from c. 1500 to 2018. The results for *eine Idee* 'an idea', *ein Tick* 'a tick', and *ein Quäntchen* 'a quantum' are also discussed in more detail in Neels & Hartmann (2022). Overall, the corpus data suggest that all nine constructions under discussion are infrequent in the historical data and have only seen a significant rise in frequency during the second half of the 20th century (with the newest constructions, *ein Zacken* and *ein Tacken*, only being attested from the 1980s and 2000s onwards). Based on these facts, we take our data to represent the early stages of grammaticalization, even though we agree with a reviewer that it remains debatable whether they reflect the exact onset or a slightly later stage during the development of some of our constructions.

which is likely to have emerged as a salient alternative to the older *ein wenig* 'a little'. As discussed in Neels and Hartmann (2018), *ein bisschen* developed along a grammaticalization path that shows striking similarities to the development of English *a bit*, as sketched, for example, by Traugott (2008). It first combined with concrete nouns, as can be expected given its original literal meaning 'bite (diminutive)', but then extended to abstract nouns as well as adjectives and verbs. It can reasonably be assumed that the use of *bisschen*, just like the use of English *bit*, in combination with non-food items was perceived as extravagant in the early stages of its development.

We expect that similar pragmatic mechanisms are involved in the development of the more recent quantifier/degree-modifier constructions discussed here. In particular, we investigate three predictions about how the extravagance of these constructions could manifest itself in the corpus data. First, in line with previous definitions of extravagant language (see Section 2), we expect the newer quantifier/degree-modifier constructions to collocate relatively frequently with lexical items that either display vivid and emotionally loaded semantics, thus signaling the speaker's emotional involvement, or which are stylistically unusual, for example by instantiating marked registers (e.g. formal, colloquial), innovative morphological patterns (e.g. multiple compounding) or striking phonology (e.g. onomatopoeia). Second, we hypothesize that the younger quantifier/degree-modifier patterns should have more narrow semantic profiles compared to the prototype *ein bisschen* 'a bit'. They may not grammaticalize much beyond their initial semantic niche if one central purpose of their existence is to be used on pragmatically special occasions. With their less abstract, richer semantics, they lend themselves to a more vivid style of expression. Third, we expect the semantic profiles of the newer quantifier/degree-modifier constructions to partially overlap with each other, in line with the claim that they emerge from speakers' extravagant ambitions rather than (or in addition to) the need to fill distinct functional gaps. That is, speakers' creative use of the extravagant patterns may give rise to a somewhat redundant network of constructions that cluster around similar functional niches.

In the next sections, we investigate these predictions in a largely exploratory fashion, using a combination of quantitative and qualitative corpus methods.

4.1 Data and methods

Present-day German features dozens of small-scale quantifier/degree-modifier constructions. Apart from the by now highly grammaticalized *ein bisschen* (e.g. *ein bisschen Glück* 'a bit of luck'), we analyze nine representative "newcomers": *ein*

Fünkchen 'a spark (diminutive)', *ein Hauch* 'a breeze', *eine Handvoll* 'a handful', *eine Idee* 'an idea', *ein Quäntchen* 'a quantum (diminutive)', *eine Spur* 'a trace', *ein Tacken* 'a spike (lower German)', *ein Zacken* 'a spike (high German)', and *ein Tick* 'a tick'. The data were drawn from DECOW16AX (Schäfer and Bildhauer 2012, Schäfer 2015), a webcorpus comprising c. 20 billion tokens. The large size of the corpus, together with the fact that its composition reflects both standard and non-standard language use (the data are derived from sources as different as online newspapers and discussion forums on all kinds of different topics), makes it ideal for investigating the role of creativity and extravagance among low-frequency phenomena.

The individual constructions investigated in the present study are exemplified in (1).

(1)   a.   Schade, **ein Fünkchen Hoffnung** war ja doch.
              'Pity, there had been **a spark of hope** after all.' (www.behinderte-hunde-forum.de)

        b.   **Eine Handvoll Manager** und ihre politischen Berater verdienen Unsummen
              '**A handful of managers** and their political advisors earn huge sums' (www.predigtpreis.de)

        c.   Ein vollreifer, intensiver Spanier mit betörenden Aromen von dunklen Beeren und **einem Hauch Schokolade**.
              'A fully ripe, intense Spaniard [i.e. Spanish wine] with beguiling aromas of dark berries and **a breeze of chocolate**.' (www.parfuemerie-thiemann.de)

        d.   Dennoch war Johns Geschichte in meinem Augen **eine Idee besser**
              'Still, John's story was **an idea better** in my view' (www.halobase.de)

        e.   Zu guter letzt fehlte dann auch noch **ein Quäntchen Glück**.
              'In the end, what was missing was **a quantum of good luck**.' (www.msvportal.de)

        f.   Die Leser werden immer weniger, denn sie gehen zum Zeitungslesen ins Internet. Dort ist es bequem, gratis und immer um **eine Spur aktueller** als in der herkömmlichen Tageszeitung.
              'The readers are becoming fewer and fewer, as they go on the internet to read newspapers. There it is comfortable, free and always **a trace more up-to-date** than in the conventional daily newspaper.' (www.der-lifestyle.de)

        g.   Liest du sonst auch 11 Freunde? Das Sonderheft ist noch mal **einen Zacken geiler**!
              'Do you generally read *11 Freunde*? The special issue is even **a spike more awesome**!' (www.hsv-forum.de)

h. Angeschlossen über eine Heimkino-Anlage kommt James Bond: Golden Eye 007 noch **einen Tacken besser** rüber
'Connected to a home cinema system, James Bond: Golden Eye 007 gets across **a spike better**' (www.gameradio.de)

i. Alle Teams, die bisher schon Regionalliga gespielt haben, bleiben entweder gleich stark oder werden nochmal **einen Tick stärker** sein.
'All teams that have already been playing in the regional league either remain equally strong or will be **a tick stronger** still.' (forum.tt-news.de)

These quantifier/degree-modifier constructions share a (prototypical) structural template: [*ein* N(*-chen*) 'small unit' X], i.e. the indefinite article *ein*, a noun denoting a small unit such as *Biss* 'bite' or *Funken* 'spark', which is optionally combined with the diminutive suffix *-chen*, and a productive slot. If nouns enter this slot, the respective construction serves as a quantifier (or partitive), whereas adjectives, verbs and other parts of speech are associated with degree-modifier uses. As shown in Table 1, *ein bisschen* occurs roughly equally with nouns and adjectives, while the newer constructions typically lean towards one lexical class. *Eine Handvoll* occurs exclusively with nouns; *ein Fünkchen*, *ein Hauch* and *ein Quäntchen* preferentially combine with nouns but also occur with adjectives; and *eine Idee*, *eine Spur*, *ein Tacken*, *ein Zacken* and *ein Tick* prefer adjectival items, especially in the comparative.

Table 1: Nouns, adjectives, and other parts-of-speech in the quantifier/degree-modifier constructions. The numbers in parentheses in the ADJ column indicate how many instances occur in the comparative form (e.g. *einen Tick besser* 'a tick better') or in the excessive form (e.g. *eine Idee zu viel* 'an idea too much'). The numbers given here are based on the automatic POS annotation available in the corpus data. Note that *ein bisschen* also occurs with verbs; for the present study, however, we focus on adjectives and nouns as modified items, hence we only queried for *ein bisschen* + adjective or noun.

Construction	N	ADJ (comparative / excessive)	Other	Sum
bisschen	258718	290204	–	549022
Fünkchen	2713	156 (76/5)	3	2872
Handvoll	35998	0 (0/0)	0	35998
Idee	72	1106 (814/272)	0	1178
Hauch	11274	5772 (3486/707)	179	17225
Quäntchen	2707	625 (442/68)	39	3371
Spur	3067	14512 (7015/6868)	0	17579
Tacken	30	1042 (853/241)	50	1122
Zacken	40	977 (893/138)	70	1087
Tick	535	22095 (17027/5905)	984	23614

To address our three hypotheses about the extravagance of the younger quantifier/degree-modifier constructions (see above), we combine the well-established method of collostructional analysis, in particular simple collexeme analysis (Stefanowitsch and Gries 2003), with a fairly simple but potentially innovative network analysis. In the simple collexeme analysis, we compute association/dissociation measures for all lexical items that occur in the open slots of our constructions, by comparing their frequency in the construction with their total frequency in the corpus. We use the log-likelihood ratio G^2 as the association measure; the *p*-value of the association is referred to as the collexeme strength. Collostructional analysis can be used to gauge the semantic "territory" a construction covers: for example, Stefanowitsch and Gries (2003) investigate the pattern [N *waiting to happen*], as in *there's an accident waiting to happen*, and show that this construction preferentially combines with nouns with a negative semantic prosody. In our case, we examine the collexemes of our individual constructions in a qualitative fashion to identify whether the younger quantifier/degree-modifier constructions, compared with the "baseline" prototype *ein bisschen*, tend to attract semantically or formally extravagant lexemes (hypothesis 1), and whether they occupy relatively constrained functional niches, displaying only limited productivity in certain semantic domains (hypothesis 2). For the computational implementation of the method, we use Flach's (2021) package *collostructions*. For reasons of space, the collexeme lists are not displayed here – instead, the full lists can be found in the online supplementary material available at https://hartmast.github.io/degreemodifiers/.[4]

We then move beyond considering our ten quantifier/degree-modifier constructions in isolation, and combine them in a network to examine their degree of functional overlap (or difference). For this purpose, we construct a network containing the top 100 collexemes of each construction, shown in Figure 1 in Section 4.2.3. Each node stands for one type, while the links connect each collexeme type to all quantifier/degree-modifier constructions it is attested with. We limit the analysis to the top 100 collexemes of each construction to keep the visualization more readable. For the same reason, Figure 1 does not include the labels for the collexemes, but instead highlights simply how many collexemes the constructions

---

4 It should be noted that collostructional analysis almost necessarily entails a certain amount of noise: For instance, we have manually corrected the lemmas of the modified items in the concordances we worked with. This was of course not possible for the entire multi-billion-word corpus, from which the total corpus frequencies of each lemma is drawn. Thus, a few lemmas are attested in our dataset but not in the full corpus. As this only affects a very small proportion of items, they were discarded from the present analysis. This explains why the total frequencies of each quantifier/degree-modifier construction in the collostructional analysis partly differ from those mentioned elsewhere in the paper or the supplementary material.

share with each other, and how many of their top 100 collexemes are unique to the construction (for a more detailed graph containing the collexeme labels, see https:// hartmast.github.io/degreemodifiers/). By combining the visual impression of the diagram with exact counts of how many collexemes are shared by each pair of constructions, we will test our third hypothesis, namely that the younger quantifier/ degree-modifier constructions cluster in overlapping functional niches while the prototype *ein bisschen* is more evenly linked to the overall constructional network.

Before we turn to the results, note that the present datasets have a number of limitations. While we manually deleted unambiguous false hits from the data for the less frequent quantifier/degree-modifier constructions (but not for *ein bisschen*), we extracted the lemmas of the modified items automatically by using the lemma annotation of the word tagged as noun or adjective immediately following the quantifier/degree modifier in question. This may lead to an overestimation of adjectives when the modified item consists of an adjective-containing noun phrase: for example, *menschlich* 'human' would be falsely identified as the modificandum in *Wo ist da auch nur eine Spur menschlicher Liebe?* 'Where is there just a trace of human love?'. In addition, some results may be skewed because frequently cited proper names are present in the data, for example the film title *Für eine Handvoll Dollar* (German title of "A fistful of dollars"). For a more in-depth analysis in future studies, the lemmatization should therefore be corrected manually.

4.2 Results

We will now discuss the results of the collexeme analysis and the network analysis in more detail, focusing on their implications for the role of extravagance in the use of the quantifier/degree-modifier constructions. Following the three predictions outlined at the beginning of Section 4, we will first examine the slot fillers of the constructions (Section 4.2.1 and 4.2.2), before turning to the network relations within the constructional family (Section 4.2.3).

4.2.1 Extravagant collexemes

The results of the simple collexeme analysis (see the link to the online collexeme lists in Section 4.1) suggest that the younger quantifier/degree-modifier constructions combine with a substantial number of extravagant collexemes. Among the top 100 collexemes of *ein Hauch* 'a breeze', for example, are a range of nouns that imply either a strong degree of emotionality, such as *Tragik* 'tragedy' (rank 79) and *Dramatik* 'dramatics' (95), or that encode other concepts "beyond the ordinary", such as *Glamour*

'glamour' (rank 15), *Exklusivität* 'exclusivity' (20), *Noblesse* 'nobleness' (67) and the noun *Extravaganz* ('extravagance') itself (12). *Noblesse*, for instance, is "exclusive" not only at a conceptual level, but as a French borrowing it is also part of a more elevated register, as is the collexeme *Frivolität* 'frivolity' (44). Moreover, the noun *Exotik* 'exoticism' is the second most strongly attracted collexeme of *ein Hauch*, and the corresponding adjective *exotisch* also belongs to its top collexemes (57). Another unusual adjectival collexeme of *ein Hauch* is the compound *retro-modern* (94).

Similar examples of extravagant collexemes can also be found for the other younger quantifier/degree-modifier constructions. Many of these collexemes fall into the category of evaluative colloquial lexis, such as *geil* 'awesome' (rank 80 for *ein Tacken*, 86 for *ein Tick*), *abgedreht* 'weird' (rank 94 for *ein Tick*), *beschissen* 'shitty' (rank 59 for *ein Zacken*, 86 *for Quäntchen*) and *Hirnschmalz* 'brainpower, lit. brain goo' (rank 87 for *ein Quäntchen*). Others represent the opposite end of the spectrum, instantiating refined concepts and registers, such as *ausgefeilt* 'elaborate' (rank 73 for *ein Tick*), *schillernd* 'iridescent' (rank 44 for *eine Idee*), *salbungsvoll* 'unctuous' (rank 75 for *eine Idee*), *theatralisch* 'theatrical' (rank 22 for *eine Spur*) and *hymnisch* 'hymn-like' (rank 72 for *ein Zacken*). In some instances, the extravagant qualities of the collexemes are additionally enhanced by their morphological complexity (which in turn often expresses semantic richness), as in (*ein Tacken*) *superwissenschaftlich* 'super-scientific', (*ein Quäntchen*) *Extra-Dramaturgie* 'extra-dramaturgy', *(ein Quäntchen) tragisch-schelmenhaft* 'tragic-prankster-like' and *(ein Fünkchen) Gutfilm* 'goody-goody film'.

Moreover, several quantifier/degree-modifier constructions are sometimes combined in the same sentence, suggesting that speakers use them to signal their emotional involvement in multiple creative ways. Consider Example (2), which features *ein Hauch* 'a breeze' alongside *eine Spur* 'a trace' and *eine Idee* 'an idea'.

(2) Ein visuelles Wortspiel, bei dem andersfarbige Buchstaben das Wort "Art" bilden, das ist noch **eine Spur bemühter, eine Idee volkshochschulkreativer**, mithin **einen Hauch bescheuerter** (DECOW)
'a visual play on words, in which differently coloured letters form the word *art*; that's even **a trace more stilted, an idea more community-college-creative**, hence **a breeze more stupid**'

The most extravagant expression in this example is certainly *eine Idee volkshochschulkreativer* 'an idea more community-college-creative' because of the collexeme's nature as an uncommon, highly complex compound. It is uttered in a derogative context, and so are the other two quantifiers/degree modifiers. Their collexemes, *bemühter* 'more stilted' and *bescheuerter* 'more stupid, daft', are instances of evaluative, emotional language.

Naturally, the results of this qualitative analysis illustrate only trends among the younger quantifier/degree-modifier constructions, and not a sharp dividing line that separates them completely from the older prototype *ein bisschen*. Among the top 100 collexemes of *ein bisschen*, there are at least two items that could be regarded as extravagant: *Bammel* (rank 45) and *Schiss* (81), both meaning 'jitters'. Admittedly, not all of the younger constructions are richer in extravagant collexemes; for example, none of the top 100 collexemes of *eine Handvoll* stand out in this regard. Still, the overall data suggest that in expressive, emotionally loaded contexts like the usage event exemplified in (2) above, language users are more likely to select from the younger, infrequent members of the quantifier/degree-modifier family than from the default modifiers, such as *ein bisschen*.

4.2.2 Constrained functional profiles

A second purpose of our collexeme analysis is to identify whether the younger quantifier/degree-modifier constructions are restricted to more narrow semantic niches compared with the highly grammaticalized prototype *ein bisschen*. For the latter, the top 100 collexemes of *ein bisschen* illustrate that the construction covers diverse semantic fields and that it combines at roughly equal frequency with nouns and adjectives (see also Section 4.1), thus displaying the behaviour of a prototypical grammatical marker. None of its top 100 collexemes refer to edible substances, suggesting that present-day speakers retain virtually no associations between the grammaticalized construction and its lexical source *Bisschen* 'little bite' (as also reflected orthographically by the lower-case form *ein bisschen*).

In contrast to *ein bisschen*, the newer quantifier/degree-modifier constructions display much more specific preferences with respect to the semantics of their collexemes. Some of these semantic constraints appear to be related to the lexical source of the grammaticalizing constructions. For example, *ein Hauch*, besides combining with a few abstract concepts, attracts a number of concrete olfactory and gustatory nouns, such as *Vanille* 'vanilla' (rank 1), *Zimt* 'cinnamon' (8) and *Knoblauch* 'garlic' (10). This preference seems connected to the original meaning of *Hauch* as 'breeze', given that the collexemes denote flavours that can be literally transported by a puff of air. Similarly, the top collexemes of *ein Tick* include the temporal adjectives *schnell* 'fast' (rank 2), *langsam* 'slow' (5) and *spät* 'late' (6), which allude to the ticking of a clock as the most likely source concept for the construction. *Eine Handvoll* combines with count nouns, especially those denoting human beings (*Leute* 'people' [rank 1], *Menschen* 'humans' [3], *Überlebende* 'survivors' [12]), and with mass nouns, in particular grained substances from the domains of food and agriculture (*Nüsse* 'nuts' [4], *Erde* 'soil' [5], *Reis* 'rice' [6]). The latter use, at least, can be related to the literal meaning of 'handful' as a measure of substance volume.

Some quantifier/degree-modifier constructions also display preferences in semantic prosody. *Ein Fünkchen* 'a spark (diminutive)', for example, predominantly quantifies abstract positive concepts, especially *Wahrheit* 'truth' (rank 1), *Hoffnung* 'hope' (2) and *Anstand* 'decency' (4). In comparison, *ein Quäntchen* 'a quantum (diminutive)' has a more mixed semantic prosody, combing both with *Wahrheit* 'truth' (rank 2) and *Humor* 'humour' (3), but also with *Ironie* 'irony' (8) and *Naivität* 'naivety' (12). At the same time, both *ein Fünkchen* and *ein Quäntchen* display a particularly strong connection to their top collexeme(s). *Ein Fünkchen Wahrheit* 'truth' and *ein Fünkchen Hoffnung* 'hope' occur 890 and 679 times, respectively, while *Verstand* 'reason' places a distant third. *Ein Quäntchen Glück* 'luck' occurs 955 times, while the second-ranked collexeme *Wahrheit* 'truth' is only attested 193 times. This suggests that the two constructions have developed specific semi-idiomatic extensions, highlighting the fact that the patterns, despite their overall productivity, display quite tightly constrained functional profiles.

In sum, many collexemes of the more recent quantifier/degree-modifier constructions are indicative of the concrete meanings of their lexical source concepts. These constructions hence display strong *persistence* (Hopper 1991), or, in fact, they have retained limited degrees of productivity and grammaticalization in general. This is expected not only based on their young age, but also if their purpose is to serve as conceptually more vivid alternatives to the highly bleached *ein bisschen* (and *ein wenig*) in situations of pragmatic emphasis.

4.2.3 Network analysis of the constructional family

The third part of our analysis extends the view beyond the individual quantifier/degree-modifier constructions and focuses on their relationships in a constructional micro-network. In particular, we examine the extent to which the members of the constructional family overlap in their functional profiles, thus giving rise to a partially redundant network of extravagant patterns.

The network plot in Figure 1 (see Section 4.1 for an explanation of the method) illustrates how many of their top 100 collexemes the ten quantifier/degree-modifier constructions (i.e. the nine more recent ones + *ein bisschen*) share with each other. The closer the constructions are positioned to each other in the network, the more semantically similar they are. The overall visual impression of the diagram highlights two clusters in which several younger quantifier/degree-modifier constructions display a significant overlap among their collexemes. The first cluster covers the right-hand side of the network, which features five rather densely interconnected constructions: *eine Idee* 'an idea', *eine Spur* 'a trace', *ein Zacken* 'a spike', *ein Tick* 'a tick' and *ein Tacken* 'a spike [low German]'. The other cluster consists of the two constructions in the upper left of the diagram: *ein Fünkchen* 'a spark' and *ein Quäntchen* 'a quantum'. These patterns share a considerable number of collexemes with each other, but are less strongly connected to the rest of the network.

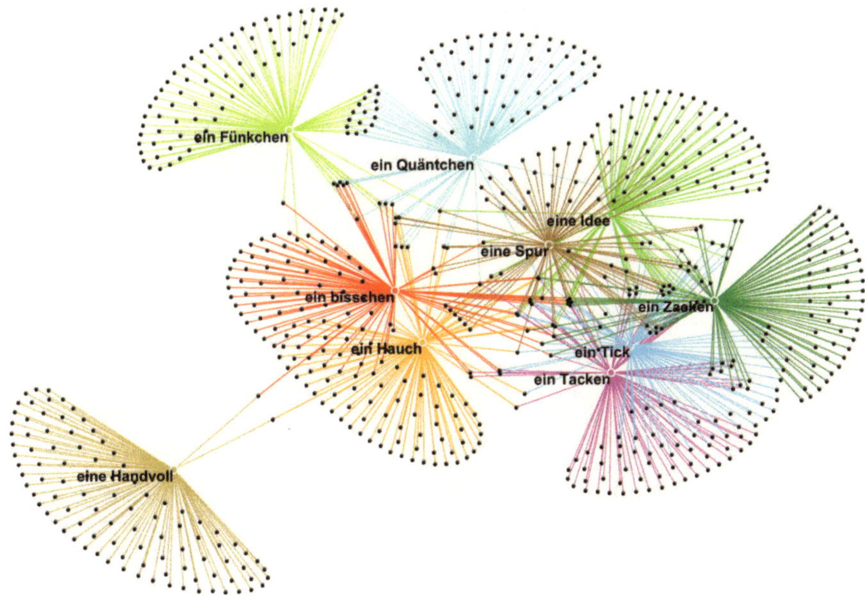

Figure 1: Network of German quantifier/degree-modifier constructions, based on the top 100 collexemes of each modifier.

As far as the remaining constructions are concerned, *eine Handvoll* 'a handful' is only loosely connected to the rest of the network, sharing merely a few of its collexemes with the other constructions. *Ein Hauch* 'a breeze', meanwhile, is linked more flexibly to the other constructions. In line with the fact that the construction combines with both nouns and adjectives, it shares collexemes with several members of the above clusters, including *ein Quäntchen* 'a quantum' but also *eine Spur* 'a trace' and *ein Tick* 'a tick'. Finally, the prototype *ein bisschen* 'a bit', even more so than *ein Hauch*, displays fairly even degrees of overlap with all of the other patterns. As a result, it takes the position of a central "hub" in Figure 1.

To confirm the visual impressions of the network diagram, we can compute exact counts of the number of collexemes that are shared by the quantifier/degree-modifier constructions. This is represented with a heatmap in Figure 2, which uses a colour scheme to indicate how many of their top 100 collexemes the constructions on the x-axis and y-axis share with each other. The heatmap supports our conclusions above: for example, *eine Idee, eine Spur, ein Tacken, ein Tick* and *ein Zacken* overlap in many of their most strongly attracted collexemes (between 18 and 49 out of 100), thus forming a dark-coloured cluster in the lower right corner of the diagram. In contrast, *ein bisschen* shares relatively even numbers of collexemes with all of the newer quantifier/degree-modifier constructions (between 8 and 18), with the exception of *eine Handvoll*, which remains isolated from the rest of the network.[5]

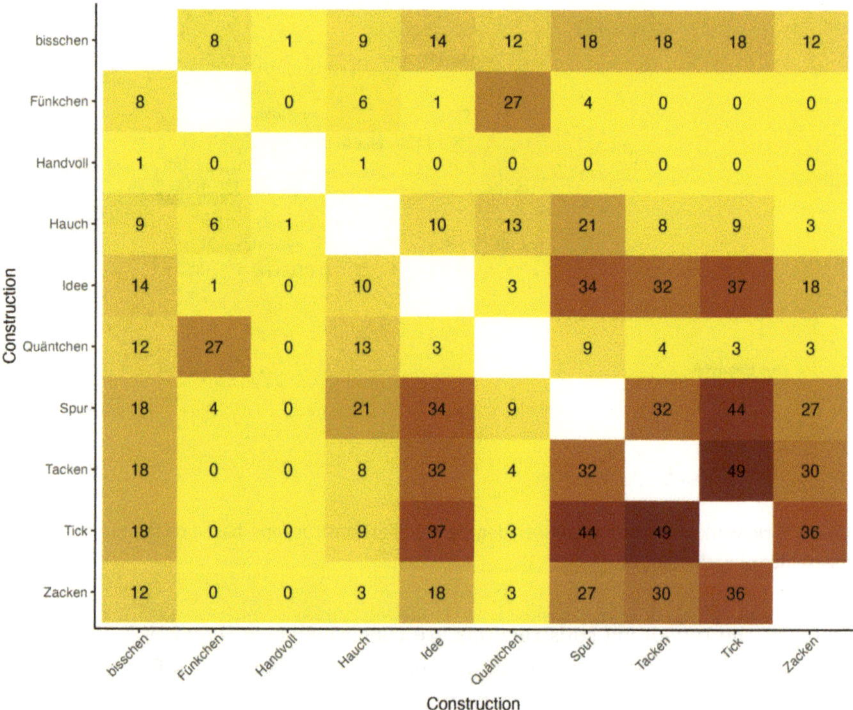

Figure 2: Number of top 100 collexemes that each of the constructions displayed on the y-axis shares with each of the constructions displayed on the x-axis (the darker the color, the higher the relative proportion of collexeme overlap).

---

5 Interestingly, *Tacken* and *Zacken* share fewer collexemes with each other than one might perhaps expect given their formal similarity. One explanation for this might be that they tend to combine with relatively infrequent, often complex adjectives like *feuchtigkeitsspendend* 'moisturising' or *superwissenschaftlich* 'super-scientific'.

In this section, we have pursued a novel (yet simple) network approach to early grammaticalization. Compared to earlier approaches mostly focusing on single constructions, our multi-constructional analysis is more revealing of semantic redundancies, which allow us to infer that the motivations for innovation are probably not so much semantic but stylistic in nature.

4.3 Discussion

The results of our analysis support the view that extravagance has affected the recent development of German quantifier/degree-modifier constructions. Extravagance appears to motivate the current use of the younger members of this constructional family, and since they have gained ground only during the last century, extravagance is likely to have played a role in their emergence as well. As such, our findings can be seen as tentative counter-evidence to the generalizing claim that primary grammaticalization is always triggered by the unintended reinterpretation of non-salient variation (e.g. Traugott 2017, Croft 2010). They provide some new corpus-based support for Haspelmath's (1999, 2000) extravagance-driven "periphrasis-first" account of early grammaticalization.

A first result of our corpus study is that the younger members of the quantifier/degree-modifier family combine with a considerable number of collexemes that can be regarded as extravagant. These collexemes tend to be emotionally loaded (e.g. 'dramatics'), encode otherwise "extraordinary" concepts ('exoticism'), be associated with marked registers ('brain goo'), or instantiate complex morphological patterns ('community-college-creative'). This suggests that speakers may prefer the newer quantifier/degree-modifier constructions over the high-frequency prototype *ein bisschen* 'a bit' when they are emotionally more involved in the situation and/or when they want to attract attention on a stylistic level. Second, our results indicate that the younger quantifier/degree-modifier constructions display relatively constrained functional profiles compared with *ein bisschen.* This is in line with the idea that the newer potentially extravagant constructions are restricted to certain contexts in which they can be used with special pragmatic effect. In particular, the constructions still show signs of persistence (Hopper 1991) of their lexical sources: i.e. they often quantify or modify concepts that belong to the same semantic domain as their source concepts (e.g. airborne substances in the case of *ein Hauch* 'a breeze'). This shows not only that the younger constructions have yet to proceed further along their grammaticalization path, but also that they still retain some of the rich semantics of their lexical sources. As a result, when these constructions are used with collexemes that lie outside their immediate source domain (e.g. *ein Hauch Nostalgie* 'a breeze of nostalgia'), they arguably give rise to more vivid and extravagant descriptions than can be achieved with the semantically bleached prototype *ein bisschen*. Third, our network analysis illustrates that the newer quantifier/degree-modifier constructions display considerable functional overlap with each other and cluster around similar semantic niches. This supports the view that these constructions did not emerge to fill functional gaps in the networks, but that they instead originated as vivid alternatives in a functional domain that was, arguably, already "saturated" with well-established prototypes like *ein bisschen* and *ein wenig*.

On a broader level, our case study has several implications for the discussion points about the role of extravagance in grammaticalization raised in Section 3. First, our findings illustrate the argument made there that cases of grammaticalization may differ in the extent to which they involve extravagance as a motivating factor for diachronic change. In particular, we suggested that some grammatical domains may be rhetorically more "competitive" than others, thus provoking speakers' continuous creation of innovative expressions that stand beside the already existing patterns. The domain of quantification/degree modification may well be one of these competitive domains, given that the concepts denoted by the quantifier/degree-modifier constructions under discussion are inherently deviant from a norm in the sense of being located below a certain baseline on a semantic scale. This creates the communicative need of emphasizing this deviance in creative ways (cf. also Levinson's [2000: 38] famous M[anner]-heuristic: "What's said in an abnormal way isn't normal"). Given that regular use entails conventionalization and, as such, a certain degree of "normalization", innovative quantifier/degree-modifier constructions threaten to "wear off" rather quickly once they are used with sufficient frequency, which leads to a higher demand for new coinages and as such to a higher degree of competition. Previous studies (e.g. Ito and Tagliamonte 2003, Brems 2011) have observed high rates of renewal and recycling especially for intensifying quantifiers and degree modifiers, i.e. expressions such as *heaps of, a hell of a, so, really* and *totally* in English. Inflationary use deprives these intensifiers of their pragmatic value. Conceivably, the high rhetorical competitiveness in the domain of intensifying quantification and degree modification partially extends to related downtoning quantifiers and degree modifiers like those in our case study.

A second aspect we discussed in Section 3 is that the role of extravagance in diachronic change may vary depending on where a phenomenon is situated along the cline between grammaticalization and lexicalization. While the German quantifier/degree-modifier constructions investigated here fall under the scope of grammaticalization, they exhibit shades of what is traditionally classified as lexicalization. Specifically, the borderline status of the constructions under scrutiny becomes apparent when considering the following factors. As typical of grammaticalization phenomena, the development of the constructions generally follows a crosslinguistically attested path: pre-partitive > partitive > quantifier > degree modifier (cf. Traugott 2008, De Clerck and Colleman 2013, Neels and Hartmann 2022). As degree words, these constructions fulfil procedural functions, with increasingly abstract, scalar meanings in particular. From a construction grammar point of view, their nature is best captured as partially schematic constructions with productive slots. Lexicalizing constructions, on the other hand, are typically fully/largely substantive constructions with low productivity and referential functions (cf. Traugott and Trousdale 2013). Still, the German quantifier/degree-modifier constructions pass some tests that Boye and Harder (2012), for instance, point out to be indicative of lexical status as opposed to grammatical status. They partially meet criteria of focalizability and addressability (cf. Traugott 2017: 105f.); and even the most grammaticalized modifiers of this constructional family are still perfectly capable of serving as full utterances in dialogic discourse, as in Example (3).

(3) "Fühlst du dich irgendwie besser?" "**Ein bisschen**. [. . .]" (DECOW)
     "'Do you feel somewhat better?" "**A bit.**"'

Given the theoretical and empirical observations made in this study, it seems reasonable that, in the emergence of new grammatical constructions, symptoms of lexical status increase the likelihood of innovation being driven by conscious extravagant efforts.

A third issue we addressed in Section 3 is whether and how extravagance can be operationalized in a corpus-based way. Our present approach differs in several respects from previous corpus studies (e.g. Petré 2016, 2017); as a result, it has its distinct advantages and limitations, some of which we want to address as a final step. First, we focused on a recent (and potentially still ongoing) case of grammaticalization, in which our speaker intuitions might provide reasonable grounds for judging the (non-)extravagant nature of the collexemes. Analyses of contemporary changes like these may provide proof of concept for the role of extravagance in grammaticalization, without requiring us to speculate about what pragmatic effects a historical development may have had on the speakers of its time. In return, this of course means that the method may not be directly transferable to earlier cases of grammaticalization, in which the effects of extravagance may at best be gleaned from indirect contextual measures (see Section 3 for some discussion).

Second, we used the relatively simple and widely applied tools of collostructional analysis to operationalize the semantics of our constructions. This approach was successful in so far as we found evidence not only of the extravagant collexemes that the younger quantifier/degree-modifier constructions combine with, but also of the semantic niches in which they primarily occur. On the other hand, our study illustrates that quantitative data about frequencies and collocational preferences do not, in themselves, point to the extravagant nature of constructions; instead, characteristics of the collexemes must still be interpreted in a qualitative, and ultimately subjective, fashion. Future studies could examine whether other methods, such as semantic vector space analysis (e.g. Perek 2016), can provide more objective, data-driven ways of characterizing the semantics of the collexemes based on their collocational profiles. One possible application of these methods could be to calculate the dispersion or the average distance among the semantic vectors that represent the collexemes of each quantifier/degree-modifier construction, and check whether these measures support our claim that the younger members of the family have more constrained functional profiles than the prototype.

As a third feature of our approach, we complemented the analyses of the individual constructions with a simple network methodology, which allowed us to explore degrees of functional overlap and differentiation within the constructional family. We believe that extending the scope beyond a single construction and focusing on the interactions between multiple constructions provides a promising avenue for future research on extravagance. Finally, another limitation that our approach shares with other corpus-based work in general is that it does not provide direct evidence of the effects that extravagant expressions have on speakers and hearers. As far as ongoing cases of grammaticalization are concerned, corpus-based approaches could thus be complemented by sociolinguistic questionnaires (e.g. Ungerer and Hartmann 2020), which record speakers' explicit perceptions of extravagant language, or by psycholinguistic experiments (cf. Fine et al. 2013), which measure effects of surprisal via participants' implicit behavioral responses.

5 Conclusion

In this paper, we started out by observing that researchers disagree about the role of extravagance in grammaticalization. We have suggested a number of ways in which the debate can be informed by a more nuanced view of the conditions under which speakers' desire to use noticeable and innovative expressions may drive language change. In Section 2, we argued that the discussion on extravagance can benefit from a clearer characterization of the concept and its relation to the psycholinguistic notion of salience. In Section 3, we addressed five aspects that may help explain why researchers differ in their views on extravagance. Some of these differences may be reconciled by taking into account that extravagance can apply to some cases of grammaticalization more than to others, and that researchers may be focusing on different elements of the process (e.g. actuation versus diffusion, and speaker versus hearer roles). Moreover, the section highlighted some open questions about whether and how extravagant effects can be operationalized, for example in historical corpora. In Section 4, we illustrated some of these theoretical points with a corpus-based case study of recently emerging German quantifier/degree-modifier constructions. Drawing on several explorative methods, we have shown that these innovative quantifier/degree-modifier constructions tend to combine with extravagant collexemes and that they display relatively constrained functional profiles which retain some of the vivid semantics of their lexical source (e.g. *eine Handvoll Menschen* 'a handful of people', which draws on a concrete source domain of 'small objects'). Moreover, our network analysis indicates that the newer constructions occupy overlapping semantic niches in a partially redundant constructional network, suggesting that their emergence was not driven by functional need alone, but also by speakers' desire to express familiar concepts in novel ways.

Despite the limitations mentioned in Section 4, our case study sheds new light on a particularly interesting constructional family that can provide important clues about the factors that drive the grammaticalization of new constructional variants. One intriguing aspect of the constructional family discussed here is that the quantifier/degree-modifier constructions in question seem to co-exist in a relation of both competition and mutual analogical support. On the one hand, they compete with each other, as witnessed by the relatively large number of shared collexemes. Possibly, this competition prevents some of the younger family members from attaining higher usage frequencies. On the other hand, they support each other by forming a densely interlinked constructional family that provides an easily extensible template for coining further [*ein* N(*chen*) X] constructions like *ein Fitzelchen* 'a shred (colloquial/diminutive)', *eine Portion* 'a portion', *ein Häppchen* 'a niblet', and many others. As more and more family members are added and used, the overarching higher-order schema [*ein* N(*chen*) X] gains in strength and productivity (see Neels and Hartmann 2022). This brings us all the way back to the maxims proposed by Keller and entitled "maxim of extravagance" and "maxim of conformity" by Haspelmath (1999). When coining new quantifier/degree-modifier constructions, language users, on the one hand, try to "stand out" by introducing slight modifications to a familiar pattern – on the other hand, however, they also conform to the widespread use of a semi-productive mid-level schema. Innovating new constructions and adding innovative uses to extant constructions are thus no creations ex nihilo but the outcome of affordances within the constructional network.

We hope that our theoretical considerations as well as our case study can contribute not only to the ongoing discussion on extravagance, but also to a reconciliation of different approaches to grammaticalization as sketched by Cuyckens (2018). While some questions have to remain open, we hope to have shown that, in exploring the role of extravagance in grammaticalization, it can prove insightful to go beyond individual patterns and to take families of constructions into account.

References

Boye, Kasper & Peter Harder. 2012. A usage-based theory of grammatical status and grammaticalization. *Language* 88. 1–44.

Brems, Lieselotte. 2011. *Layering of size and type noun constructions in English*. Berlin & Boston: De Gruyter Mouton.

Brinton, Laurel J. & Elizabeth Closs Traugott. 2005. Lexicalization and language change. Cambridge: Cambridge University Press.

Buchstaller, Isabelle. 2016. Investigating the effect of socio-cognitive salience and speaker-based factors in morpho-syntactic life-span change. *Journal of English Linguistics* 44(3). 199–229.

Croft, William. 2000. *Explaining language change: An evolutionary approach*. Harlow: Pearson Longman.

Croft, William. 2010. The origins of grammaticalization in the verbalization of experience. *Linguistics* 48(1). 1–48.

Cuyckens, Hubert. 2018. Reconciling older and newer approaches to grammaticalization. *Yearbook of the German Cognitive Linguistics Association* 6(1). 183–196.

Dahl, Östen. 2001. Inflationary effects in language and elsewhere. In Joan L. Bybee & Paul J. Hopper (eds.), *Frequency and the Emergence of Linguistic Structure*, 471–480. Amsterdam & Philadelphia: John Benjamins.

De Clerck, Bernard & Timothy Colleman. 2013. From noun to intensifier: *massa* and *massa's* in Flemish varieties of Dutch. *Language Sciences* 36. 147–160.

De Smet, Hendrik. 2012. The course of actualization. *Language* 88(3). 601–633.

De Wit, Astrid, Peter Petré & Frank Brisard. 2020. Standing out with the progressive. Journal of Linguistics. 1–36.

Detges, Ulrich & Richard Waltereit. 2002. Grammaticalization vs. reanalysis: a semantic-pragmatic account of functional change in grammar. *Zeitschrift für Sprachwissenschaft* 21(2). 151–195.

Diewald, Gabriele. 2002. A model of relevant types of contexts in grammaticalization. In Ilse Wischer & Gabriele Diewald (eds.), *New reflections on grammaticalization*, 103–120. Amsterdam & Philadelphia: John Benjamins.

Ellis, Nick C. 2017. Salience in language usage, learning and change. In Marianne Hundt, Sandra Mollin & Simone E. Pfenninger (eds.), *The changing English Language: Psycholinguistic perspectives*, 71–92. Cambridge: Cambridge University Press.

Fine, Alex B., T. Florian Jaeger, Thomas A. Farmer & Ting Qian. 2013. Rapid expectation adaptation during syntactic comprehension. *PLOS ONE* 8(10). e77661.

Flach, Susanne. 2021. *collostructions: An R implementation for the family of collostructional methods*. www.bit.ly/sflach.

Gabelentz, Georg von der. 2016 [1891]. *Die Sprachwissenschaft: Ihre Aufgaben, Methoden und bisherigen Ergebnisse*. Berlin: Language Science Press.

Geeraerts, Dirk. 2016. Entrenchment as onomasiological salience. In Hans-Jörg Schmid (ed.), *Entrenchment and the psychology of language learning: How we reorganize and adapt linguistic knowledge*, 153–174. Berlin & Boston: De Gruyter Mouton.

Giora, Rachel. 2003. *On our mind: Salience, context, and figurative language*. Oxford: Oxford University Press.

Günther, Franziska, Hermann J. Müller & Thomas Geyer. 2016. Salience, attention, and perception. In Hans-Jörg Schmid (ed.), *Entrenchment and the psychology of language learning: How we reorganize and adapt linguistic knowledge*, 289–312. Berlin & Boston: De Gruyter Mouton.

Haiman, John. 1994. Ritualization and the development of language. In William Pagliuca (ed.), *Perspectives on grammaticalization*, 3–28. Amsterdam & Philadelphia: John Benjamins.

Harder, Peter & Kaspar Boye. 2011. Grammaticalization and functional linguistics. In Heiko Narrog & Bernd Heine (eds.), *The Oxford handbook of grammaticalization*, 56–68. Oxford: Oxford University Press.

Hartmann, Stefan & Tobias Ungerer. 2021. The mother of all constructions: A corpus-based approach to the productivity of 'snowclones.' Paper presented at the *11th International Conference on Construction Grammar*, Antwerp, 18–20 August.

Haspelmath, Martin. 1999. Why is grammaticalization irreversible? *Linguistics* 37(6). 1043–1068.

Haspelmath, Martin. 2000. The relevance of extravagance: A reply to Bart Geurts. *Linguistics* 38(4). 789–798.

Heine, Bernd, Ulrike Claudi & Friederike Hunnemeyer. 1991. *Grammaticalization: A conceptual framework*. Chicago: University of Chicago Press.

Himmelmann, Nikolaus P. 2004. Lexicalization and grammaticization: Opposite or orthogonal? In Walter Bisang, Nikolaus P. Himmelmann & Björn Wiemer (eds.), *What makes grammaticalization?*, 21–42. Berlin & New York: De Gruyter Mouton.

Hopper, Paul J. 1991. On some principles of grammaticization. In Elizabeth Closs Traugott & Bernd Heine (eds.), *Approaches to grammaticalization*, vol. 1, 17–35. Amsterdam & Philadelphia: John Benjamins.

Hopper, Paul J. & Elizabeth Closs Traugott. 2003. *Grammaticalization. 2nd ed*. Cambridge: Cambridge University Press.

Ito, Rika & Sali Tagliamonte. 2003. *Well* weird, *right* dodgy, *very* strange, *really* cool: Layering and recycling in English intensifiers. *Language in Society* 32. 257–279.

Jaeger, T. Florian & Kodi Weatherholtz. 2016. What the heck is salience? How predictive language processing contributes to sociolinguistic perception. *Frontiers in Psychology* 7. 1115.

Jespersen, Otto. 1917. Negation in English and other languages. Copenhagen: Høst.

Keller, Rudi. 1994. *On language change: The invisible hand in language*. Translated by Brigitte Nerlich. London & New York: Routledge.

Kiparsky, Paul & Cleo Condoravdi. 2006. Tracking Jespersen's cycle. In Mark Janse, Brian Joseph & Angela Ralli (eds.), *Proceedings of the 2nd International Conference of Modern Greek Dialects and Linguistic Theory*, 179–197. Mytilene: Doukas.

Lehmann, Christian. 2017. Grammaticalization and automation. In Martin Eberl, Sara Ingrosso, Enkhmaa Narmandakh, Sebastian Ortner, Katharina Scholtz & Aleksander Wiatr (eds.), *Grammatikalisierung in interdisziplinärer Perspektive* (JournaLIPP 5), 33–48. München: LIPP. https://doi.org/10.5282/journalipp/2017H5

Levinson, Stephen C. 2000. *Presumptive meanings: The theory of generalized conversational implicature*. Cambridge: MIT Press.

Meillet, Antoine. 1912. L'evolution des formes grammaticales. *Scientia (Rivista di Scienza)* 12 (26).6). Reprinted in Antoine Meillet. 1958. *Linguistique historique et linguistique générale*, 130–148. Paris: Champion.

Neels, Jakob & Stefan Hartmann. 2018. Reduction or expansion? A bit of both. A case study on the development of German degree modifiers. In Evie Coussé, Joel Olofsson & Peter Andersson (eds.), *Grammaticalization meets construction grammar*, 137–168. Amsterdam & Philadelphia: John Benjamins.

Neels, Jakob & Stefan Hartmann. 2022. Grammaticalisation, schematisation and paradigmaticisation: How they intersect in the development of German degree modifiers. In Gabriele Diewald & Katja Politt (eds.), *Paradigms regained: Theoretical and empirical arguments for the reassessment of the notion of paradigm*, 267–296. (Empirically Oriented Theoretical Morphology and Syntax 10). Berlin: Language Science Press.

Perek, Florent. 2016. Using distributional semantics to study syntactic productivity in diachrony. A case study. *Linguistics* 54(1). 149–188.

Petré, Peter. 2016. Unidirectionality as a cycle of convention and innovation: Micro-changes in the grammaticalization of [be going to INF]. *Belgian Journal of Linguistics* 30. 115–146.

Petré, Peter. 2017. The extravagant progressive: An experimental corpus study on the history of emphatic [be Ving]. *English Language and Linguistics* 21(2). 227–250.

Schäfer, Roland. 2015. Processing and querying large web corpora with the COW14 architecture. In Piotr Bański, Hanno Biber, Evelyn Breiteneder, Marc Kupietz, Harald Lüngen & Andreas Witt (eds.), *Proceedings of the 3rd Workshop on Challenges in the Management of Large Corpora (CMLC-3)*. Mannheim: IDS. https://ids-pub.bsz-bw.de/frontdoor/deliver/index/docId/3826/file/Schaefer_Processing_and_querying_large_web_corpora_2015.pdf (accessed 23/08/2021)

Schäfer, Roland & Felix Bildhauer. 2012. Building large corpora from the web using a new efficient tool chain. In Nicoletta Calzolari, Khalid Choukri, Terry Declerck, Mehmet Uğur Doğan, Bente Maegaard, Joseph Mariani, Asuncion Moreno, Jan Odijk & Stelios Piperidis (eds.), *Proceedings of LREC 2012*, 486–493.

Schmid, Hans-Jörg & Franziska Günther. 2016. Toward a unified socio-cognitive framework for salience in language. *Frontiers in Psychology* 7.

Smith, Kenny, Monica Tamariz & Simon Kirby. 2013. Linguistic structure is an evolutionary trade-off between simplicity and expressivity. In Markus Knauff, Michael Pauen, Natalie Sebanz & Ipke Wachsmuth (eds.), *Proceedings of the 35th Annual Meeting of the Cognitive Science Society*, 1348–1353. Austin, TX: Cognitive Science Society.

Stefanowitsch, Anatol & Stefan Th. Gries. 2003. Collostructions: Investigating the interaction of words and constructions. *International Journal of Corpus Linguistics* 8(2). 209–243.

Traugott, Elizabeth Closs. 1995. Subjectification in grammaticalization. In Dieter Stein & Susan Wright (eds.), *Subjectivity and subjectivisation: Linguistic perspectives*, 37–54. Cambridge: Cambridge University Press.

Traugott, Elizabeth Closs. 2008. The grammaticalization of NP of NP Patterns. In Alexander Bergs & Gabriele Diewald (eds.), *Constructions and language change*, 23–45. (Trends in Linguistics. Studies and Monographs 194). Berlin & New York: Mouton De Gruyter.

Traugott, Elizabeth Closs. 2017. Low salience as an enabling factor in morphosyntactic change. In Marianne Hundt, Sandra Mollin & Simone Pfenninger (eds.), *The changing English language: Psycholinguistic perspectives*, 93–109. Cambridge: Cambridge University Press.

Traugott, Elizabeth Closs & Richard B. Dasher. 2002. *Regularity in semantic change*. Cambridge: Cambridge University Press.

Traugott, Elizabeth Closs & Graeme Trousdale. 2013. *Constructionalization and constructional changes*. Oxford: Oxford University Press.
Trousdale, Graeme. 2012. Grammaticalization, constructions and the grammaticalization of constructions. In Kristin Davidse, Tine Breban, Lieselotte Brems & Tanja Mortelmans (eds.), *Grammaticalization and language change: New reflections*, 167–198. Amsterdam & Philadelphia: John Benjamins.
Ungerer, Tobias & Stefan Hartmann. 2020. Delineating extravagance: Assessing speakers' perceptions of imaginative constructional patterns. *Belgian Journal of Linguistics* 34. 345–356.
Weinreich, Uriel, William Labov & Marvin I. Herzog. 1968. Empirical foundations for a theory of language change. In Winfred P. Lehmann & Yakov Malkiel (eds.), *Directions for historical linguistics*, 95–195. Austin: University of Texas Press.

Lauren Fonteyn and Enrique Manjavacas

4 Maximizing the data-drivenness of grammaticalization research

A case study of 'to death'

Abstract: This paper looks into the grammaticalization of *to death* from a resultative phrase into an intensifying expression, by describing the process in terms of changes in compositionality, productivity and schematicity and subsequently outlining a procedure in which the investigation of changes along these parameters is approached in a 'maximally data-driven' way. By doing so, we show that functional-semantic explorations of grammaticalization need not be at odds with a radically data-driven, 'hands-off', quantitative methodology. Yet, at the same time, we acknowledge that there are still some limitations associated with 'hands-off' functional-semantic analysis, and argue that, to determine its reliability, it will prove valuable to extensively revisit known cases of grammaticalization.

Keywords: Grammaticalization, Intensifiers, Computational Linguistics, Distributional Semantics

1 Introduction

Grammaticalization is one of the most well-studied phenomena in historical linguistics, and even after over three decades of extensive scrutiny, researchers are still compelled to describe, model and explain its dynamics (for a survey, see, e.g., Cuyckens 2018). In doing so, researchers increasingly started to rely on quantitative evidence in historical corpora, ultimately rendering grammaticalization research (much like historical linguistics more generally) into an even more "data-centric" endeavour (Jenset & McGillivray 2017: 2) that considers historical documents as its only "firm knowledge base" (Fischer 2004). This synthesis of corpus methodology and grammaticalization studies has led to a wealth of new insights, in that it enabled researchers "to answer old questions with more precision", and to "begin to ask – and answer – new questions that simply could not have been asked in this way only a few years ago" (Hilpert & Cuyckens 2016: 4; also see Lindquist & Mair 2004). At the same time, as pointed out by Cuyckens (2018), research on grammaticalization has also seen a shift from a more form-oriented treatment, to studies where semantics play a central role (Heine, Claudi & Hünnemeyer 1991; Traugott & König 1991; Traugott 1989; Traugott 2003; Traugott 2010; Traugott & Dasher 2002). Following (and perhaps through)

https://doi.org/10.1515/9783110753059-004

the functional-semantic turn of Grammaticalization studies, where processes such as metaphor, metonymy, subjectivity, and invited inferencing are placed centre-stage, grammaticalization research soon started to be "approached from a more encompassing view, integrating grammaticalization into (Cognitive) Construction Grammar" (Cuyckens 2018; in reference to Traugott & Trousdale 2013).

For a long time, the interest in approaching grammaticalization as a functional-semantic process (accompanying or underlying the formal changes that affect grammaticalizing constructions) was somewhat at odds with an increasing reliance on quantitative corpus methodologies, as focussing on semantics poses a methodological problem. Unlike with formal linguistic properties, gathering semantic features of linguistic constructions traditionally involves often meticulous (and, consequently, labour-intensive) introspective annotation, but such introspection-based approaches run the risk of being ad-hoc, problematically subjective, and notoriously difficult to replicate, quantify, or measure (Gries & Divjak 2009; Sagi, Kaufmann & Clark 2011; Jenset 2013; Perek 2016).

This has, however, started to change in recent years: following the rise of an increasingly powerful body of computational models that aim to approximate the meaning of words over time by numerically encoding their linguistic context (or 'distributional properties'), the path towards a fully data-driven, quantifiable and measurable approach to semantic change appears to have been cleared (Sagi, Kaufmann & Clark 2011; Hamilton, Leskovec & Jurafsky 2016a; Hamilton, Leskovec & Jurafsky 2016b; Rosenfeld & Erk 2018; Kutuzov et al.; Hu, Li & Liang 2019; Dubossarsky et al. 2019; Tahmasebi, Borin & Jatowt 2019; Del Tredici, Fernández & Boleda 2019; Schlechtweg et al. 2017). At present, these models have mainly been applied in rather coarse-grained studies to capture and quantify some aspect of lexical semantic change (and, occasionally, grammaticalization; see Luo, Jurafsky & Levin 2019) at large, with sample sizes ranging from hundreds (e.g., Mitra et al. 2014; Dubossarsky et al. 2019) to thousands of linguistic items (e.g., Hamilton, Leskovec & Jurafsky 2016b).

Yet, distributional semantic models have found their way into specific historical linguistic case studies too. Over the last decade, various forms of diachronic collexeme analysis and behavioural profile analysis, where functional-semantic differences and similarities between contructions over time are examined and quantified through a curated selection of collocational preferences and/or other distributional properties, have become increasingly established methods in historical linguistics (e.g. Hilpert 2006; Coussé 2014; Fonteyn & Hartmann 2016; Jansegers & Gries 2020). A logical continuation of this increased data-drivenness of functional-semantic analysis, then, constituted the adoption of more holistic methods, where a linguistic item's contextual distribution is turned into a numerical vector without an a priori selection of contextual features being made by the analyst. In doing so, recent work on constructional change has not only utilized such computational models to minimize (or even avoid) introspective data annotation (Sagi, Kaufmann & Clark 2011; Jenset 2013), but also to operationalize theoretical concepts in quantifiable terms in order to verify or falsify hypotheses on the nature and causes of constructional change in the case under scrutiny (Hilpert & Correia Saavedra 2017; Perek 2016; Perek 2018; Budts & Petré 2020; Budts 2020).

Following this direction, the aim of the present contribution is to bring models and methods developed in the computational literature on semantic change into the well-established tradition of grammaticalization research. The specific case we address concerns the grammaticalization of the phrasal expression *to death* from a literal, resultative phrase into an 'amplifying' (Quirk et al. 1985) or intensifying expression (as previously described in Hoeksema & Jo Napoli 2008; Claridge 2011; Margerie 2011; Blanco Suárez 2017). In revisiting this case study, we outline a methodological procedure that maximizes the data-centric character of grammaticalization studies, and provide tentative statistical support for the suggestion that the functional-semantic expansion of *to death* does not take foot until after the 18th century. Section 2 will first outline the diachronic development of *to death* and describe it along the grammatical constructionalization parameters (changes in compositionality, productivity and schematicity) set out by Traugott & Trousdale (2013). Subsequently, Section 3 will describe and motivate how vector-based models can be used to study changes in the productivity and schematicity of a construction. The methodological design of the study will be explained in more technical detail in Section 4, followed by a concluding discussion of the results and limitations in Section 5. Through the discussion of the limitations, we hope to show why it will be important for future computational research to revisit prior corpus-based grammaticalization case studies before proceeding to new challenges.

2 The grammaticalization of 'to death'

As explained by Margerie (2011), the development of *to death* into an intensifier can be broken down into three stages. Initially, prior to the 16th century, *to death* functioned as adverbial complement of verbs expressing physical harm, which may literally result in death (e.g. *beat, bleed, wound, murder, starve;* see (1)). A distinction can be made between verbs that are atelic, where the verb itself does not imply a resulting state (e.g. beating, bleeding or wounding need not result in death) and telic verbs, where a resultant state is implied (e.g. verbs such as *murder* or *slay,* as in (2), imply that the patient dies even without the additional resultative phrase). While the verbs in both groups are clearly semantically similar, and while *to death* can still be read as the literal result of all verbs in both groups, Margerie (2011: 121–122) argues that the verbs in the latter group are more likely to trigger a subjective, amplifying rather than a resultative reading of *to death* (also see Luo, Jurafsky & Levin 2019, who suggest that adverbs that collocate with adjectives that partially semantically overlap are more likely to invite re-interpretation as intensifying expressions).

(1)   . . . because she durst compare hirself, with Diana was by the goddesse *wounded* to death with an arrow; (1641, EEBO)

(2)   He *sloh* him wið a stan to deaðe. (a1225, OED s.v. death, n. 12a; Margerie 2011: 122)

Yet, *to death* already started showing traces of "incipient subjectivity" in Old English, being used in combination "with verbs or adjectives of feeling" such as *hate* and *afraid* (3) – for which a literal, death-resulting reading is unlikely or even impossible (Blanco Suárez 2017: 185).[1] Margerie's (2011) study, which examines data from 1500 onwards, also attests such cases sporadically in her 16th and 17th century data, and more frequently in her 18th century data.

(3)   Þa þa cyningas..þæt gehyrdon ['heard'], hig wæron swyðe gedrefede ['very disturbed'] and to deaðe afærede ['afraid to death']. (OE. OED, s.v. death n. phrases P1b; Blanco Suárez 2017: 185)

Usage of *to death* as an intensifier was, at this intermediate stage, still connected to its non-grammaticalized source (Hopper 1991; Lorenz 2002): even when used in a non-literal sense, *to death* still retained strong ties to its original meaning, where it referred to a negative end result, combining with verbs that have negative connotations (Margerie 2011; Blanco Suárez 2017):

(4)   Reflection never agreed with me: I hate it confoundedly. It brings a consumed long string of past transactions, that *bore* me to death. (1779, ECCO; Margerie 2011: 127)

(5)   That look of yours *frightens* me to death. (CLMET3.1, 1750)

---

1 Also see Clardige (2011: 201), who reports a 14th century example of *laugh to death*. Yet, Claridge points out that even with laughing, there is a physical reaction that causes discomfort when extended over a longer period of time. In a footnote, she adds that laughing oneself to death is extremely unlikely, but possible.

(6)   A dale too many of the square-headed haythens. I am *pestered* to death with them. (1920, COHA)

This strong preference of *to death* for negative situations persisted into the 19th and 20th century (Margerie 2011; Claridge 2011: 203; Blanco Suárez 2017: 357, 363). Yet, it seems that the combinatory possibilities of the phrase did start to expand to more positively oriented verbs:

(7)   "It seems to delight you to think that you are to leave Paris, and that we shall not see each other for months, perhaps. Tarzan, you are a most ungrateful beast!" and D'Arnot laughed. "No Paul; I'm a little child. I have a new toy and I'm *tickled* to death." (1913, Gutenberg; Margerie 2011: 130)

(8)   Who ever heard or imagined grandparents not being just *pleased* to death at the coming of their first grandchild! (1930, COHA)

An important part of Margerie's (2011) account of the historical trajectory of *to death* is that its development constitutes an instance of grammaticalization. Resultative phrases are an unusual source for intensifying expressions in English, which more commonly derive from adverbs (e.g. *horribly, terribly, awfully*, etc.). As a case of grammaticalization, the development of *to death* outlined here can be viewed in light of the three parameters of grammaticalization (or 'grammatical constructionalization') outlined by Traugott & Trousdale (2013). First, Traugott & Trousdale (2013: 121) note that grammaticalizing constructions tend to undergo a decrease in compositionality, where their new, grammatical meaning is "not strictly derivable from its parts". Second, grammaticalized constructions tend to undergo an increase in productivity, which Traugott & Trousdale consider as an expansion both of type frequency and of token frequency of the collocates. Finally, grammaticalizing constructions also tend to become more schematic. This development has two facets: constructions may become more schematic "as they participate in and become 'better' members of abstract schemas", and "schemas themselves may expand, i.e. may come to have more members" (Traugott & Trousdale 2013: 116). Because increases in schematicity often result in the collocates of constructions becoming more open or diverse, it is not always easy to separate increases in schematicity from increases in productivity. Yet, the two processes can be distinguished if we understand productivity as "the range of lexical items that may fill the slots of constructions" and schematicity as "the level of detail in the form or the function of constructions, and correspondingly the restrictions that are placed on their instances" (Perek 2018). In such terms, a construction can, in principle, become more productive without becoming more schematic (e.g. the number of its collocates increases, but they are similar to the extent that they are still justified by the original schema). Applied to the development of *to death* we get the following the picture:

1. *Decrease in compositionality.* Perhaps most straightforwardly, the phrase *to death* becomes less compositional, in that its new intensifying meaning is not strictly derivable from its component parts (despite its persistent negativity). Rather than referencing literal death, the phrase is extended to represent an endpoint or extreme. As such, there is a (slight) decrease in "the transparency of the link between meaning and form", but the structure itself is still analysable (Traugott & Trousdale 2013: 113).

2. *Increase in productivity.* With respect to token frequency, an increase of intensifying *to death* has been attested approximately from the 18th century onwards. Compared to the overall use of the resultative phrase *to death*, the intensifying use is, however, a low-frequency phenomenon (Blanco Suárez 2017: 364). Similarly, Margerie (2011) and Blanco Suárez (2017) report that the type frequency of the verbs *to death* collocates with is low. Precise type frequencies and type-token ratios are not reported, but Margerie's (2011) account strongly suggests that the emergence of more neutral or positive verb collocates towards the 19th century would also result in a diversification of *to death*'s verb collocates (yet, Blanco Suárez (2017) finds no evidence for such trends).

3. *Increase in schematicity.* The extension to positive collocate verbs can also be seen as an increase in schematicity, in the sense that it constitutes the loss of a negativity restriction. If the collocates of *to death* indeed become freer, the use of *to death* as an intensifier becomes more schematic, or abstract. By increasing its range of collocates, *to death* also aligns with the regularities we observe with the schemas of other intensifying expressions (Barðdal 2008: 22).

Because of the overall low frequency of *to death* (in intensifying uses), it has proven difficult to support the description of its development as an instance of grammaticalization on the dimensions of its productivity and schematicity with statistical evidence. In terms of chronology, non-literal, grammaticalized uses of *to death* appear to date back to early records pre-dating the Early Modern English period, but there is some disagreement on whether the construction in fact expanded (at least to verbs with positive polarity) in more recent periods. In absence of precise information on collocate diversity, it is difficult to say whether this rise in token frequency can be understood as the growing popularity of an unchanged, lexically restricted schema, or whether *to death* is also the subject of weakening semantic restrictions (increased schematicity) and expanding combinatory behaviour (increased productivity) in (Late) Modern English. To attain a more precise picture of these developments, we will revisit this case study.

3 Data and methodology

Questions regarding changes in productivity and schematicity lend themselves well to computational analysis, as demonstrated by Perek (2016, 2018). With an eye on quantifying the relation between productivity and schematicity in constructional change, Perek relies on semantic vector representations of the verb types occurring in the open verb slot of the *hell*-construction (e.g. [*beat/scare/hug*] *the hell out of someone*) and the *way*-construction (e.g. [*swim/beat/smile*] *one's way to something*). Crucially, Perek brings the notion of semantic diversity into the study of productivity (following, among others, Barðdal 2008), and distinguishes the lexical diversity of the construction's verb collocates (measured by the number of unique lexical items that occur in a construction) from the schematicity or semantic openness of constructional slots (measured by the semantic diversity between those lexical items). To do so, he employs clustering density measures over the vector representations of the verb collocates over time. While neither of the examples considered by Perek are strictly speaking examples of grammaticalization, the research design he employs can still serve as a valuable starting point to further hone in on the development of grammaticalizing constructions in a 'hands-off', data-driven manner.

Such a hands-off approach is indeed appealing, perhaps particularly when focussing on the grammaticalization of intensifiers such as *to death*. While the manual semantic annotation scheme in prior work is commonly meticulously documented, it is still often based on the (potentially wrong) intuitions and often categorical decisions of a single individual. Margerie (2011) and Blanco Suárez (2017: 189) report, for instance, that prior to the analysis of resultative and intensifying *to death*, "irrelevant occurrences" were removed from the data set. Among the cases they deem irrelevant was the combination *put to death*, but no clear motivation is given as to why *putting someone to death* is not included in the data as a resultative (given that someone who is put to death dies as a result of an underspecified action). Different individuals may hence disagree on whether this structure is indeed irrelevant for understanding the development of *to death*. Similarly, when proceeding from filtering to annotation, different annotators may make different decisions when faced with questions such as whether the verb *yawn* constitutes a neutral (Blanco Suárez 2017) or negative collocate. Such issues can be addressed, of course, by relying on a collection of native speaker judgements – or, given that these are not available for historical language varieties, by involving more expert annotators – but this is not always practically feasible (see the discussion in Perek 2016). A reasonable alternative solution, then, is the methodological procedure presented here, in which changes in the behaviour of *to death* are approached with minimal manual intervention, both in terms of filtering as well as semantic annotation.[2]

We will start by outlining the data collection procedure in Section 3.1. Subsequently, in Section 3.2, we explain how we constructed the distributed meaning representations that will serve as the main input for our further analysis. In Section 3.3, we introduce our methodology, which is partially based on the approach presented by Perek (2016, 2018). More specifically, we conduct a diachronic cluster analysis, in which we optimize the number of clusters across time with respect to the clustering quality measure known as "silhouette" in order to trace changes in *to death*'s contextual distribution (Section 3.3.1). Subsequently, we fine-tune the procedure to better suit the diachronic analysis of structures grammaticalizing into intensifiers in two important ways. First, distributed meaning representations are known to fail to distinguish synonymy (e.g. *hate* & *despise*) from antonymy (e.g. *hate* & *love*). Hence, we introduce a way to capture any possible erosion of its original negative (or positive) polarity (which is common for grammaticalizing intensifying expressions, see e.g., Lorenz 2002) by means of a sentiment analysis (Section 3.3.2). Furthermore, we make sure that any expansions in cases such as *to death* (and other death-related intensifiers, see Blanco Suárez 2017), where grammaticalized uses are vastly outnumbered by persistent literal uses, can be captured by means of a statistical model. The statistical model we use is described in Section 3.3.3.

3.1 Corpus pre-processing and data collection

In the present study, we focus on the development of *to death* from Early Modern English into the 20th century. We focus on this time window partially because this is when we expect the most notable changes in collocational behaviour to occur, but also for practical reasons. While there is no shortage of Historical English corpora, corpora that span all the way from the Old English period up to Present-day

---

2 Note that the procedure presented here relies on distributed meaning respresentations of verb collocates at the type level. As such, it does not provide a way to distinguish, for instance, examples where *to death* (possibly) has a clear resultative reading from cases where it functions as an intensifier. In other words, the methodological design aims to capture and robustly quantify changes in the semantic diversity of the collocates of a grammaticalizing structure, but it does not discriminate grammaticalized for non-grammaticalized uses of a construction, nor flag bridging contexts where multiple readings are possible. To pursue such questions by means of computationally, models that generate distributed meaning representations at the token level would be required (for some examples, see Hilpert & Correia Saavedra 2017; Budts 2020; Fonteyn 2020).

English are rare, and when they do exist (e.g. the suite Penn-Helsinki Corpora Kroch 2020), they tend to be too small to be of use for the 'data-hungry' models that generate distributed meaning representations. To maximize sample sizes, this study resorted to combining large diachronic corpora covering different time windows, together spanning the period from 1550 to 1949. These corpora include Early English Books Online (EEBO), the Corpus of Late Modern English Texts (version 3.1; CLMET3.1), the Evans Early American Imprints Collection (EVANS), Eighteenth Century Collections Online (ECCO), the Corpus of Historical American English (COHA), and the Hansard corpus (Hansard). In terms of text types, these corpora are varied, covering an array of literary works, religious and legal text and news reports. The sole exception is Hansard, which offers transcriptions of British parliamentary debates (starting in 1800).

All corpora were submitted to the following pre-processing pipeline. First, we applied a language identification module in order to sort out foreign text. We relied on two language identification modules – Google's Compact Language Identifier (v3)[3] and FastText Language Identification system (Grave 2017) – which we combined to maximize the retrieval precision of the foreign text. For a given fragment of 500 characters, we flagged the text as foreign if both systems indicated a language other than English as the highest probability language. Manual inspection of a random sample indicated a sufficiently low false positive rate in order for the filtering to be effective (while throwing out an insignificant amount of English text). Second, we tokenized and sentence-tokenized the remaining text using the Punkt tokenizers provided by the NLTK package (Bird, Klein & Loper 2009). After tokenization, we enriched all text with part-of-speech tags, using an in-house tagger for historical English.[4] The resulting patchwork corpus consists of a total of 3.9 billion tokens, which we utilized in various ways in subsequent steps of the research process.

The attestations of *to death* were retrieved from the corpus collection (excepting the specialized Hansard corpus) and divided into bins of 50-year periods (8 in total). As not all corpora in the collection are balanced in terms of the amount of text a single author may contribute, we applied an additional filtering step to ensure that no author dominated more than 25% of the instances in a particular bin. The total number of instances retrieved from each corpus per bin is listed in Table 1.

---

3 The code repository is accessible through the following url: https://github.com/google/cld3/releases/tag/3.0.13.

4 The tagger was trained on the PCEEME (Nevalainen et al. 2006) – a corpus of letters from 1410 to 1695 that amounts to about 2.2M labelled tokens. We used the state-of-the-art Conditional Random Field (CRF) tagger implemented by the library PIE (Manjavacas, Kádár & Kestemont 2019). Overall, the tagger obtained 96% accuracy on a held-out dataset.

Table 1: Distribution of *to death* per bin (by corpus) and verb type fre-quency in the sample (last row).

	1550	1600	1650	1700	1750	1800	1850	1900
CLMET3.1				39	45	182	100	26
COHA						488	700	774
ECCO				78	395	12		
EEBO	800	800	794	413		2		
EVANS			6	211	360	116		
Total	*800*	*800*	*800*	*741*	*800*	*800*	*800*	*800*
Type freq	87	101	93	95	97	150	131	135

In the bin covering the period between 1700 and 1749, the total corpus size (and hence, the token frequency of *to death*) was substantially lower than for other bins. To ensure that any observed differences in the number of verb types that collocate with *to death* across bins is not affected by large differences in sample size, we decided to cap the maximum number of instances of *to death* per bin by taking a random sample of 800 tokens from the total number of tokens in a particular bin. The proportion of the sampled number of tokens per corpus per bin is therefore comparable to the proportion of tokens each corpus contributed to total number of tokens per bin.

After removing any duplicates, we identified the verb that collocates with each instance *to death* by relying on part-of-speech tags: each instance of *to death* was assumed to collocate with the verb in closest proximity (using a window of 15 words). In a number of cases, the tagger failed to find *to death*'s collocate verb. These cases included instances where the copula *be* was used in combination with an adjective or past participle (e.g. *be frozen/sick to death*), or cases where the verb form in closest proximity of *to death* was not the verb it modified (e.g. *we could prevent Scipio from* pummelling[actual collocate] *the* dreaded[identified collocate] *wizard to death*, COHA 1840), which were subsequently corrected and included in the dataset. Other absences of collocate verbs (109 in total) included cases where *to death* functioned as a prepositional modifier of a noun (e.g. *on her way to death*), fixed expressions (e.g. *from birth to death, be nigh to death*), and cases where the verb was illegible (e.g. *And when my mother euen before my sighte, Was (-) to death*; 1550, EEBO). In absence of manually retrievable collocate verb or adjective, these examples (1% of the data set) were ultimately discarded. During the manual correction of the sampled tokens, (spelling) variants of the same verb lemma were indentified and normalized, so that each verb is represented by a single type in the collocate sample.

3.2 Word embeddings

In order to capture semantic similarity between *to death's* collocate verbs across time, we rely on distributed meaning representations or 'word embeddings' computed by the *word2vec* algorithm (Mikolov et al. 2013).[5] Word embeddings represent a powerful distributional semantics approach to infer semantic relatedness between words from corpus data. We use the entire corpus collection introduced in Section 3.1 in order to train these representations, with additional pre-processing steps with the goal of improving the quality of the resulting embeddings.[6]

In order to validate the resulting embedding space, we ran a number of semantic similarity benchmarks, seeking to contextualize the quality of our embeddings within the state-of-the-art. The employed benchmark datasets comprise of sets of Present-day English word pairs, each of which have been manually assigned a similarity score. The evaluation proceeds by correlating these human semantic judgments with the cosine similarities between the corresponding vector representations, using the Spearman correlation coefficient.[7] We compared our embedding space with 200 dimensions *Glove* vectors (Pennington, Socher & Manning 2014) trained on 6B Wikipedia tokens,[8] as well as 300 dimensions *word2vec* vectors trained on the Google News dataset (about 100B tokens), restricting the vocabulary of all embedding spaces to the vocabulary defined by our space and using the average word embedding vector for out-of-vocabulary words.

---

5 The training details are as follows. We trained distributed representations with a dimensionality of 200 using the gensim library (Rehurek & Sojka 2010). This means that each word is represented by a vector of 200 dimensions. In the construction of these vectors, we employed the skip-gram objective approximated with negative sampling (i.e., training to predict the context in which a given target word will appear, aiming to maximize the similarity of words in the same context and minimize similarity of word occurring in different contexts). The process was optimized using a learning rate of 0.025 over 5 epochs, discarding words with frequencies lower than 50 and a window size of 20 tokens.

6 First, we lower-cased all tokens. Secondly, unicode composite characters were normalized using the so-called NFKD unicode normalization. Furthermore, we removed all non-alphanumeric tokens and replaced numbers by a code <NUM>. Finally, we ignored all punctuation marks and substituted the long s character < ſ > with modern day < s >. Note that the corpus underlying the embeddings is not normalized with respect to spelling variation. This may reduce the quality of the embeddings of words with a large number of spelling variants – especially if the distribution is not skewed towards one variant. A common approach to tackle this is to use word embedding algorithms that build representations from sequences of characters (see FastText (Bojanowski et al. 2017)).

7 While it is obviously not ideal to evaluate our model with respect to a Present-day English reference point, no such human similarity judgements are available for historical English. In order to conduct at least some sort of sanity check, we used the off-the-shelf Present-day English spaces.

8 The embeddings are available through the following url: https://nlp.stanford.edu/projects/glove/.

Table 2: Word embedding benchmark results for the utilized word embedding space in comparison to off-the-shelf present-day English spaces.

	MEN	WS353	SimLex999	MTurk	RW	RG65	Mean
Glove	0.611	0.372	0.303	0.554	0.242	0.664	0.458
Word2Vec	*0.708*	*0.602*	*0.414*	*0.645*	*0.379*	*0.747*	*0.582*
Our model	0.581	0.451	0.325	0.503	0.278	0.751	0.482

As Table 2 shows, our embedding space generates scores comparable to the *Glove* space, while lying behind those generated by the *word2vec* space. Considering that our embedding space is trained on a smaller dataset and covers a large period of historical English, we take these results to validate the semantic similarity properties of the inferred word representations. For a sanity check, Table 3 shows the 20 nearest neighbours of a selection of verbs from our dataset of *to death* collocates based on cosine distance. The embeddings of the verb types that collocate with *to death* in our data sample serve as the input for further analysis.

Table 3: Top 10 nearest neighbours (cosine) of *burn, stab, whip* (physical actions) and *amuse, scare, vex* (mental verbs) in the verb collocate dataset.

	physical actions			mental verbs		
	burn	stab	whip	amuse	scare	vex
1	beat (0.57)	strangle (0.59)	cudgel (0.69)	delude (0.73)	frighten (0.78)	afflict (0.72)
2	kill (0.57)	knife (0.59)	bludgeon (0.66)	flatter (0.63)	terrify (0.73)	perplex (0.72)
3	consume (0.56)	bleed (0.58)	lash (0.66)	perplex (0.61)	startle (0.67)	harass (0.71)
4	scorch (0.55)	slash (0.58)	kick (0.59)	terrify (0.60)	worry (0.55)	annoy (0.69)
5	shoot (0.55)	bang (0.56)	cuff (0.57)	frighten (0.60)	drive (0.54)	oppress (0.69)
6	spoil (0.53)	kill (0.55)	spur (0.57)	tickle (0.58)	sweep (0.52)	fret (0.67)
7	smother (0.53)	poison (0.55)	flog (0.56)	harass (0.54)	delude (0.51)	grieve (0.64)
8	smoke (0.53)	bite (0.55)	bang (0.55)	tire (0.54)	astonish (0.51)	terrify (0.61)
9	hunt (0.53)	cudgel (0.54)	goad (0.55)	annoy (0.52)	annoy (0.50)	pester (0.60)
10	hang (0.53)	prick (0.54)	scourge (0.54)	vex (0.51)	amuse (0.50)	worry (0.58)

3.3 Method

A basic way of quantifying the expansion of *to death* is by examining whether there has been a quantitative change in diversity in the set of attested collocate verbs over time. One such index of collocate diversity, which is commonly used to designate changes in a construction's productivity, is given by the type frequency of collocate verbs per time bin – listed in the last row of Table 1. However, while the slight increase in type frequency of collocates is potentially indicative of an expansion (in terms of productivity or even schematicity), it need not indicate that *to death* has indeed undergone semantic change. Given that our data was not pre-filtered to exclude literal, resultative uses, changes in lexical diversity alone could potentially be explained in terms of language-external, cultural change. It may be the case, for instance, that different modes of execution have become prevalent or obsolete over time, or that the specificity and lexical diversity with which causes of death are described may increase or decrease as the topic becomes more or less taboo. In these scenarios, the set of lexical items *to death* collocates with may indeed shrink or expand, but the semantics of the phrase remain stable. To probe into the grammaticalization of *to death*, then, we move beyond relying solely on measures of lexical diversity, and operationalizes the process as a change in the structure of the semantic space that the collocate verbs of to death occupy.

3.3.1 Clustering

For a given period, the taken approach first extracts the set of attested verbs and collects the corresponding distributed semantic representations. These representations delineate a semantic space, on which hierarchical clustering algorithms can be run in order to find groupings of verbs relying on semantic similarity. These groupings often align with semantic domains, so that changes in the number and size of clusters over time can be linked to changes in the semantics of *to death.*

However, a known problem with automated cluster analysis of semantic spaces is that the induced clusters are not always easy to interpret. For this reason, its application typically requires manual fine-tuning of hyper-parameters and post-filtering steps (as is the case in Perek 2016, 2018) to ensure that clusters are meaningful before any measures of interest can be computed. When it comes to agglomerative hierarchical clustering, there are several choices that influence the interpretability of the computed clusters, such as the distance measure (cosine, Euclidean), the amalgamation rule (e.g. single, complete or average)[9] and the number of clusters to compute. Because our aim is to minimize the amount of manual interference, we dispense with manual fine-tuning and inspection of the resulting clusters. In particular, we focus on the number of clusters, since this hyper-parameter is perhaps the one that most strongly affects the interpretability of the resulting clusters. Our strategy consists in fixing the distance measure and amalgamation rule (using cosine distance and the complete amalgamation rule) and automating the process of selecting the number of clusters based on a measure of the quality of the induced clusters. More specifically, we first identify a measure of clustering quality that aligns with the process of host-class expansion, find the hyper-parameter value that optimizes this quantity and, finally, treat this optimal value as a statistical correlate of the expansion process that we are ultimately interested in describing.

As *to death* develops new, non-literal meanings, we expect the semantic space defined by the verbs appearing in this construction to expand, with clusters becoming denser and new clusters representing novel semantic fields starting to form. A clustering metric that aligns with this process is the silhouette score (Rousseeuw 1987). The silhouette score combines an estimate of the tightness of the clusters – computed as the average intra-cluster distance between data points in each cluster – with an estimate of the separation between clusters – measuring the distance between each point to the closest point in a different cluster. Theoretically, the collocational expansion commonly observed in grammaticalizing constructions as a result of increased schematicity implies a process in which the number of semantic domains that fill the construction slot increases, as does the semantic separation between these domains. At the same time, with increasing productivity, more verbs may be attested in specific semantic domais, which leads to an increase in the tightness or density of these domains.

In order to monitor the expansion of *to death*, we, thus, target the number of clusters that optimizes the silhouette score (i.e. the 'optimal number of clusters'). Practically, hierarchical clustering algorithms induce a so-called merge tree in which each node represents a full clustering of the dataset. The optimal number of clusters is computed by inspecting the silhouette scores at different nodes in the merge tree until reaching the merge node that maximizes the silhouette score.

---

9 With hierarchical agglomerative clustering, each word embedding is first considered to be a cluster of its own, and is then linked to its closest neighbour. With complete linkage, once multiple embeddings are clustered, finding their next neighbouring element will be done based on the numerical representation of all elements in the cluster (rather than to their average, or to one item in the cluster, as in single linkage). We use the reference implementations provided by the Python library scikit learn (Pedregosa et al. 2011).

One risk that can be linked to the presented methodology is that the optimal number of clusters may increase due to an increase in the size of the pool of available verbs – i.e. regardless of the semantic composition of the space arising from the corresponding period. This effect is even more likely in the case of the long-tail distributions common in linguistic data, since an increase in the number of sampled tokens is typically associated with an even larger increase in the number of sampled types. In order to control for the effect of the size of the sample, we employ the following bootstrap procedure. For each period, we sample 500 verbs with replacement from the observed distribution in the dataset and compute the optimal number of clusters based on silhouette score. Repeating this process a 1,000 times per period yields a dataset with 8,000 observations (i.e. for 8 periods). Crucially, we record the total number of distinct verbs sampled in each bootstrap iteration, which allows us to statistically control for the effect of population size on the obtained optimal number of clusters. Using the bootstrap dataset, we use a statistical model to quantify the effect of time on the optimal number of clusters, while controlling for the size of the underlying pool of verbs (further information on the statistical model is given in Section 3.3.3).

3.3.2 Sentiment analysis

As explained in Section 2, the grammaticalization of *to death* was also suggested to involve increased co-occurrence with verbs with progressively more positive connotations. In order to capture this process, we devise a way to quantify the average polarity (or semantic prosody) of verbs over time using word embeddings, and statistically describe any changes in polarity. As already evident from the data presented in Table 3, differences in sentiment polarity are not straightforwardly captured by means of hierarchical clustering (as antonyms are represented by highly similar vectors): the positive mental verb *amuse*, or instance, is recognized as being similar to more negative mental verbs like *delude* and *terrify*, as well as its antonyms *annoy* and *vex*. To remedy this issue, we leverage the embedding space described in Section 3.2 in order to capture the sentiment polarity of the sampled verbs.

A first approach to induce word-level sentiment scores is to exploit the proximity of a given vector representation of a verb to the vector representations of the words 'good' and 'bad'. The closer to the vector for 'good', the more positive the sentiment of that verb. Yet indeed, because word embedding spaces tend to conflate synonym and antonym relations, the vectors for 'good' and 'bad' also tend to be located in the proximity of each other. As a result, this approach lacks discriminative power for classifying words with respect to their sentiment. Thus, we resort to a second-order approach that induces sentiment scores on the basis of the proximity to a list of nearest neighbors of 'good' and 'bad', from which antonyms and confounding terms that are not clearly indicative of the sentiment polarity were manually filtered (e.g., for 'good': 'bad', 'but', 'done', 'really'; for bad: 'good', 'sound', 'excellent'). This allows us to obtain a reasonable estimate of the overall word polarity with minimal manual work. The filtering process involves sifting through the entire vocabulary in ranked order by cosine similarity to 'good' and 'bad', discarding confounding words until reaching a total of 20 words per polarity. We compute the sentiment score as the average cosine similarity to nearest neighbors of 'good' (list: 'better', 'excellent', 'great', 'well', 'best', 'splendid', 'proper', 'decent', 'strong', 'valuable', 'firstrate', 'probably', 'reasonable', 'fair', 'admirable', 'high', 'wise', 'satisfactory', 'wholesome', 'true') minus the average cosine similarity to nearest neighbors of 'bad' (list: 'dangerous', 'ill', 'inefficient', 'wrong', 'hard', 'unsound', 'unfortunate', 'worse', 'weak', 'unhealthy', 'unfavourable', 'foolish', 'worst', 'rotten', 'low', 'unwholesome', 'badly', 'evil', 'defective', 'disastrous'). This method identifies 'dispirit', 'pester', 'plague', 'stink' and 'aggravate' as verbs with the highest negative polarity in our dataset, whereas 'interest', 'work', 'offer', 'study', and 'give' are assigned the highest positive polarity.

Finally, to test the effect of time on the polarity of *to death*'s collocates, we assign each verb in the dataset to the bin where they are first attested. Grammaticalizing structures often retain their original function (see the notion of 'layering' in, e.g. Hopper & Traugott 1993), and it has been shown that the well-established negative use of *to death* vastly outnumbers and hence overshadows cases where *to death* has expanded to intensify new, more positive verbs (Blanco Suárez 2017: 357). Thus, we suggest that working with the sentiment of collocate verbs that were first attested in a given bin – rather than the distribution of sentiment in each bin – captures more directly and robustly the ongoing changes.

3.3.3 Statistical modelling

In order to quantify the change in the structure of the semantic space of *to death* collocates as well as their polarity over time, we fit a linear regression model using the target quantities as the dependent variable – i.e. the optimal number of clusters and the average polarity of newly attested verbs – and the time period as the independent variable. Importantly, linguistic processes involving diachronic change often result in non-linear patterns for which linear effects – i.e. an effect that is constant in magnitude across the entire diachronic range – can only provide a weak approximation. For example, several diachronic processes in historical linguistics are better described by s-curves (Blythe & Croft 2012; Denison

2003), where the magnitude of the effect varies across time. To account for such possible variability, we incorporate the dependent variable as a monotonic effect, which we implement following the approach by Bürkner & Charpentier (2018). A monotonic effect shares the assumption with a linear effect that the direction of the effect is constant – for example, more recent periods are associated with an increase or a decrease in the target statistic – but, in contrast to linear effects, the magnitude of this effect may differ over adjacent time periods.

The linear regression models deployed in the present study rely on Bayesian inference. Bayesian inference produces posterior probability distributions that can be used to inspect the implications of a given model in probabilistic terms. For example, in a linear regression model, Bayesian inference outputs the (posterior) probability that the model assigns to each possible value of a predictor. As a result, the reported statistics are more interpretable than in frequentist approaches, which rely on notoriously problematic Null-Hypothesis significance testing (Nicenboim & Vasishth 2016). Moreover, thanks to modern inference approaches based on Markov Chain Monte Carlo (MCMC) more complex and expressive models – like, for example, the monotonic effects model used in the present study – can be readily fitted to data. We fit our models using the Hamiltonian Monte-Carlo sampler provided by the *stan* library (Carpenter et al. 2017) through the R language package *brms* (Bürkner 2018).

4 Results

In this section, we report on the results of the statistical modelling. We use a model comparison approach in order to test the relevance of different predictors, including, for example, linear vs. monotonic effects. Having identified a particular model as the most adequate given the data, we proceed to inspect the implications of that model for the relevant research questions.

4.1 Clustering

We are interested in the effect of time on the optimal number of clusters in the space delineated by collocates of *to death*. In order to test the monotonicity of the effect, we compare a model that incorporates the effect of the time period with an ordinary linear predictor – LINEAR(P) – and a model that uses a monotonic effect – MONO(P). Moreover, in order to control for the size of the sampled population on

Table 4: Comparison of statistical models of optimal number of clusters and polarity using the WAIC criterion (lower is better). Besides absolute WAIC, we also show an estimate of the effective number of parameters (P), the difference in WAIC (WAICΔ(SE)) and the model weight (Weight), quantifying the relative value of eachmodel with respect to the remaining models.

Outcome	Model	WAIC (SE)	P	WAICΔ (SE)	Weight
Clusters	MONO(P)+S	50,777 (137)	5.73	*reference*	1.00
	LINEAR(P)+S	50,995 (136)	4.30	−218.42 (25.10)	0.00
	MONO(P)	52,211 (132)	4.86	−1,434.14 (71.02)	0.00
	LINEAR(P)	55,780 (128)	2.75	−5,003.14 (117.48)	0.00
Polarity	MONO(P)	784.82 (25.08)	3.73	*reference*	0.79
	LINEAR(P)	787.52 (25.03)	3.18	−2.7 (1.38)	0.21

the outcome, we fit two additional models including the number of unique verbs in the bootstrap sample (S) as a linear predictor – LINEAR(P)+S and MONO(P)+S.

We compare the four models using the Widely Applicable Information Criterion (WAIC), which estimates the plausibility of the models in terms of both predictive performance and model complexity. The results of the comparison are shown in the top row of Table 4. Including time period as a monotonic effect improves the predictive power of the model over the linear effect. Moreover, controlling for sample size is even more important, as evidenced by the fact that including this predictor results in a larger improvement in WAIC than modeling period as a monotonic effect.

Using the most strongly predictive model – i.e. MONO(P)+S – we can visualize the (monotonic) effect of time period on the optimal number of clusters. We use the posterior predictive distribution, which we summarize using credible intervals containing the estimated number of clusters at 0.99, 0.89 and 0.5 probabilites. Figure 1 depicts the posterior predictive distribution of the optimal number of clusters using a counter-factual triptych plot.

We generate the model's implied posterior predictions fixing the underlying sample size at the 10%, 50% and 90% percentiles (corresponding respectively to 59, 71 and 98 distinct verbs). Overall, we observe a clear monotonic effect, resembling an s-curve, with a leap starting in the 1750 bin. The shape of the effect remains stable across the three sample size percentiles. Because the effect of sample size on number of clusters is positive, the range of the outcome (i.e. the y-axis) increases across plots in the triptych – i.e. the average number of clusters increases with an increase in sample size. Moreover, the distribution of uncertainty varies from plot to plot. At smaller sample sizes, the uncertainty in the predicted number of clusters is larger towards the later time bins, whereas for larger sample sizes the most uncertain

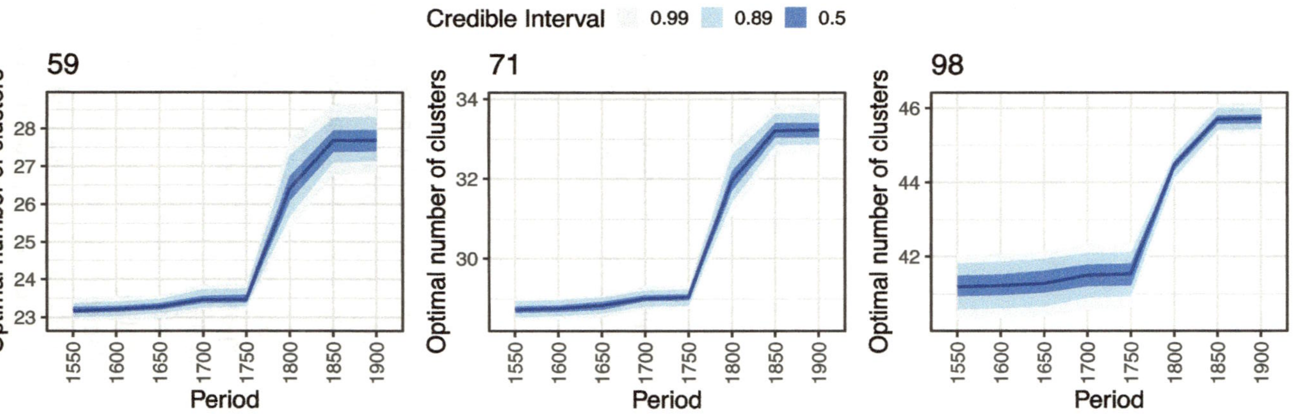

Figure 1: Posterior predictive distribution of the optimal number of clusters by period, showing different credible intervals, while varying the sample size over 59 (left), 71 (middle) and 98 (right) items, corresponding respectively to the 10%, 50% and 90% percentiles. The visualization is based on 200 samples from the MCMC posterior draws.

predictions come from the earlier bins. This is likely due to the fact that the sample size in pre-1800 bins is always smaller than in post-1800 bins (as shown in Figure 2).

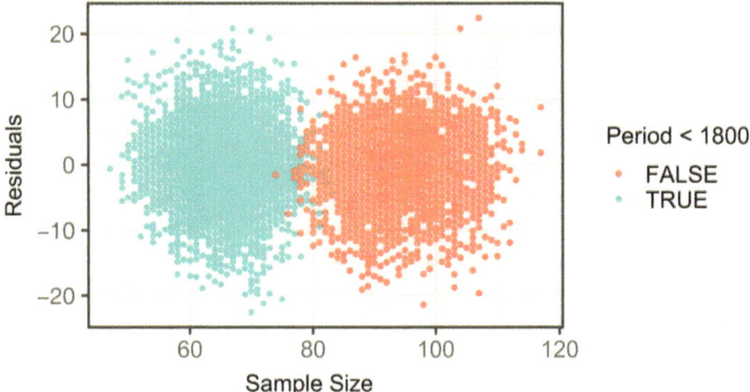

Figure 2: Residuals of the model by sample size. Color highlights are used to distinguish pre-1800 and post-1800 observations. Despite the increase in sample size starting in 1800, residuals do not seem to be correlated with sample size.

However, by counter-factually controlling for sample size, we can observe that the statistical model predicts a constant effect shape regardless of the sample size.

4.2 Sentiment

In line with the experiments from Section 4.1, we now compare the effect of time period on sentiment using a linear predictor – LINEAR(P) – and a monotonic effect – MONO(P). We use the standardized average sentiment polarity of the verbs as the outcome. The results in terms of WAIC are shown in the bottom row of Table 4. Modeling time with a monotonic effect produces an improvement over the linear predictor, although in this case the difference with respect to the linear effect model is smaller than in the clustering experiments. The left plot shown in Figure 3 does indicate a slight jump starting in the 1750 bin. However, the large credible intervals observed do not rule out a merely linear effect.

Moreover, as the plot in the right hand-side of Figure 3 shows, a considerable amount of variance in the dataset is left unexplained by the model. While statistically controlling for other predictors – such as, for example, document topic or genre – could improve the fit, the current model does show a predominantly linear upward effect of moderate size – about 1 standard deviation – of time on average sentiment.

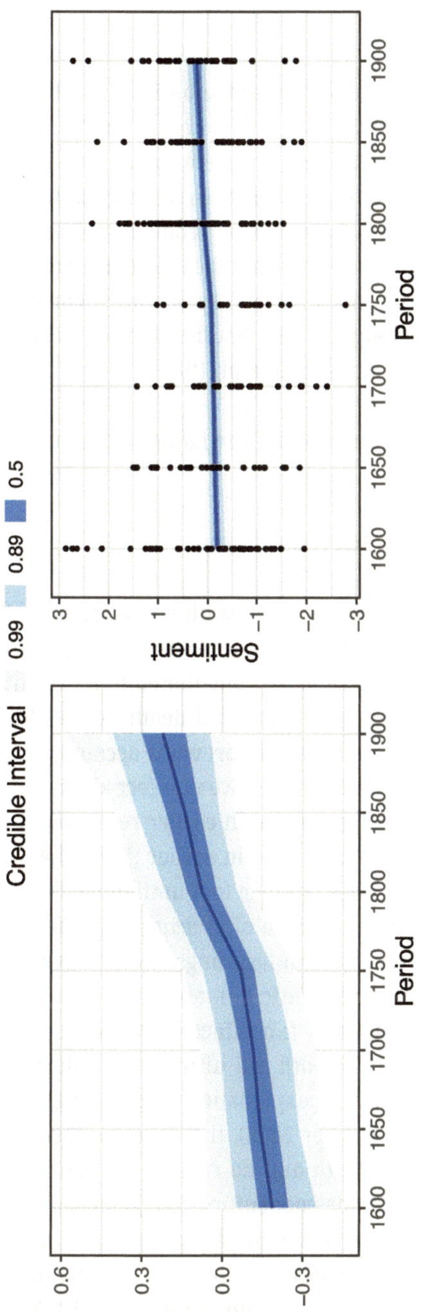

Figure 3: Posterior predictive distribution of the statistical model of sentiment using time period as monotonic effect (left), posterior predictive distribution with overlaid empirical observations (right).

5 Discussion

Overall, the results of the statistical analyses indicate that the optimal number of clusters of verb collocates increases substantially over the course of the 18th century. As such, if we take these results at face value, they seem to align with the suggestion that, despite there being non-literal uses even in early records, the expansion of *to death* to new semantic domains only seems to become more systematic centuries later. Similarly, the statistical analysis also indicates that there is a weak shift away from negative polarity from the 18th century onwards. Partially contributing to the weak effect of polarity change is also that the data set includes examples with positive collocates such as the ones in (9) and (10):

(9) it would please him to entertaine them, they would bee *faithfull* to him even to death (EEBO, 1600)

(10) He swore he wou'd *love* me to death (EEBO, 1700)

Here, *to death* likely functions as a time adverbial ('until death') and not as a resultative ('being faithful/loving resulting in death') or an intensifier ('very faithful', 'love a lot'). These structures could, of course, have contributed to *to* death's acquisition of intensifying meaning (e.g. loving someone until death implies loving them a lot) – and they may have been overlooked in previous accounts as a potential bridging context. Be that as it may, the attested weak effect aligns well with the strong persistence of negative meaning attested in earlier research, and again indicates that even if there were positive collocates in earlier times, the use of *to death* with non-negative verb collocates does not take foot until much later.

A possible way of explaining the delayed expansion of *to death* could be that the sporadic first coinages of *to death* with non-literal meanings and positive collocates did not constitute densely populated semantic domains, and thus they lack the lexical coverage that drives productivity (an effect witnessed by e.g. Perek 2016). Yet, this does not explain why *to death* did ultimately undergo a more systematic expansion when it did. If such an explanation is to be sought in the realm of analogical attraction (see, e.g., Fischer 2008), the data employed in the present case study (which cover only *to death* and no related constructions that may have served as an analogical model) does not suffice. Yet, given that the exploratory, descriptive results are intuitive, the procedure adopted here is promising for future 'hands-off' investigations of grammaticalization, and given its minimal reliance on manual annotation, those follow-up studies could take a more encompassing, holistic scope on death-related intensifiers, or intensifiers more generally. Such studies could potentially help address the question whether such delayed expansions are common, and incorporate questions exploring the cause of such delayed expansions.

Note however, that due to the relatively low frequency of *to death*, which also presented an issue in prior, non-computational analyses, caused us to resort to a 'patchwork corpus' solution. An issue with these patchwork solutions is that individual time bins are likely not represented by a comparable number of texts and text types, and because of the inconsistency with which text types are labelled across different corpora, it is very difficult if not impossible to smoothly ensure register and genre consistency across bins. In the present case, such text type inconsistency is indeed very unfortunate: the time bin in which *to death* seems to expand more systematically also appears to be the time bin in which the COHA corpus starts, which introduces newspaper and magazine texts into the sample. As only 10.25% of the tokens in the 1800 bin are attested in these text types (out of 800 tokens: 0 from newspaper texts; 82 from magazine texts), the issue may not be substantial, but it still draws the attested late expansion into question. A possible solution in future work could be to refrain from working with corpus patchworks, and turn to the Google Books Corpus (1500–2008) or other large library dumps. Yet, even then issues of overrepresentation (and mislabelling) of text types may remain (Younes & Reips; Pechenick, Danforth & Dodds 2015). Additionally, even diachronic trends in balanced diachronic corpora may in a strict sense also be artefacts, as genres and registers are also subject to change. With respect to newspaper and magazine text, for instance, it has been shown that the changing "readerships and purposes of magazines versus newspapers result in different historical-linguistic patterns of use" (Biber & Gray 2013). As such, a limitation of the present case study (and of some related studies) is that it devotes relatively limited attention to balancing data and/or controlling for text type variation across time bins. We wish to stress that such variation should be controlled for as much as possible in future work, but acknowledge that this may limit the extent to which the approach we present can be applied to low-frequency phenomena.

Finally, it is worth bringing up the fact that the procedure presented here aimed to minimize manual filtering and annotation, but it did not refrain from manual filtering entirely (as indicated in Section 3.1), and there are various points where further manual corrections could be considered. In some instances that were retained in the dataset, *to death* occurs with collocates with verbs of motion, as in (11) and (12):

(11) ſeeing it confirms the Courage, makes men run to death as to a Feaſt (EEBO, 1650)

(12)   How unreasonable is the belief that we are wearing out life and hastening
to death (COHA, 1850)

In these cases, the connection between the query hit and the semantic development described is unclear at best, and given their limited relevance and potential
effects on the output of the statistical analyses, it may be worth flagging or even
excluding them from the dataset prior to analysis. One reason why such examples
of limited relevance may be problematic is that, due to the bootstrapping procedure set out in Section 3.3.1, it is virtually impossible to 'peer into' the collocate
clusters the model generates. This means we have little insight into whether such
non-relevant cases end up in a distinct, coherent cluster – and, more generally,
we have little insight into whether and at what level of functional-semantic granularity the verb clusters that were fed into the statistical analysis correspond
with the semantic verb classes proposed in earlier research (e.g. actions of physical harm vs. mental verbs; telic and atelic verbs of physical harm; etc.). Thus,
while the bootstrapping procedure renders the procedure more robust, it also
makes it less transparent, as it becomes more difficult to examine which verbs
constitute what cluster at which points in time.

6 Conclusion

By revisiting the case of the grammaticalization of *to death* from a resultative
phrase into an intensifying expression, we showed that by expanding our corpus-
linguistic toolkit with quantitative and computational models, we can statistically
verify and come to a more precise understanding of known cases of grammaticalization. By means of this new toolkit, it is indeed no longer the case that functional-semantic explorations of grammaticalization are at odds with a fully data-
driven, quantitative methodology – which opens up many possibilities to explore
questions that we were not able to (quantitatively) explore or verify before. Yet,
there are still some challenges to overcome. What we consider to be one of the
most important challenges in automating exploratory and/or explanatory analyses
of grammaticalization (and constructional change more generally) is finding a way
to strike the right balance between robustness and transparency, and between automation and manual/introspective correction. Before turning to new questions,
then, it will be crucial to determine the reliability of new computational tools and
methods by revisiting the vast and valuable body of case studies corpus-based
grammaticalization research has produced.

References

Barðdal, Johanna. 2008. *Productivity: Evidence from Case and Argument Structure in Icelandic*. Amsterdam: John Benjamins.

Biber, Douglas & Bethany Gray. 2013. Being Specific about Historical Change: The Influence of Sub-Register. *Journal of English Linguistics* 41(2). 104–134. https://doi.org/10.1177/0075424212472509.

Bird, Steven, Ewan Klein & Edward Loper. 2009. *Natural language processing with Python: analyzing text with the natural language toolkit*. O'Reilly Media, Inc.

Blanco Suárez, Zeltia. 2017. *Death-related intensifiers in the history of the English language: Grammaticalisation and other processes of language change*. Spain: Universidade de Santiago De Compostela PhD dissertation.

Blythe, Richard A. & William Croft. 2012. S-curves and the mechanisms of propagation in language change. *Language* 88(2). 269–304. https://doi.org/10.1353/lan.2012.0027.

Bojanowski, Piotr, Edouard Grave, Armand Joulin & Tomas Mikolov. 2017. Enriching Word Vectors with Subword Information. *Transactions of the Association for Computational Linguistics* 5. 135–146. https://doi.org/10.1162/tacl_a_00051.

Budts, Sara. 2020. *On periphrastic do and the modal auxiliaries : a connectionist approach to language change*. Antwerp: Universiteit Antwerpen PhD dissertation.

Budts, Sara & Peter Petré. 2020. Putting connections centre stage in diachronic construction grammar. In Lotte Sommerer & Elena Smirnova (eds.), *Nodes and Networks in Diachronic Construction Grammar*, 317–352. Amsterdam: John Benjamins.

Bürkner, Paul – Christian & Emmanuel Charpentier. 2018. Modeling Monotonic Effects of Ordinal Predictors in Bayesian Regression Models. PsyArXiv. https://doi.org/10.31234/osf.io/9qkhj. psyarxiv.com/9qkhj.

Bürkner, Paul Christian. 2018. Advanced Bayesian Multilevel Modeling with the R Package Brms. *R Journal*. https://doi.org/10.32614/rj-2018-017.

Carpenter, Bob, Andrew Gelman, Matthew D. Hoffman, Daniel Lee, Ben Goodrich, Michael Betancourt, Marcus A Brubaker, Jiqiang Guo, Peter Li & Allen Riddell. 2017. Stan: A Probabilistic Programming Language. *Grantee Submission*. ERIC 76 (1).1–32.

Claridge, Claudia. 2011. *Hyperbole in English: A Corpus-based Study of Exaggeration*. Cambridge: Cambridge University Press.

Coussé, Evie. 2014. Lexical expansion in the HAVE and BE perfect in Dutch: A constructionist prototype account. *Diachronica* 31(2). 159–191. https://doi.org/10.1075/dia.31.2.01cou.

Cuyckens, Hubert. 2018. Reconciling older and newer approaches to grammaticalization. *Yearbook of the German Cognitive Linguistics Association* 6(1). 183–196. https://doi.org/10.1515/gcla-2018-0009.

Del Tredici, Marco, Raquel Fernández & Gemma Boleda. 2019. Short-term meaning shift: A distributional exploration. In *Proceedings of the 2019 conference of the north American chapter of the association for computational linguistics: Human language technologies, volume 1 (long and short papers)*, 2069–2075. Minneapolis, Minnesota: Association for Computational Linguistics. https://doi.org/10.18653/v1/N19-1210. https://www.aclweb.org/anthology/N19-1210.

Denison, David. 2003. Log(ist)ic and simplistic S-curves. In Raymond Hickey (ed.), *Motives for Language Change*, 54–70. 1st edn. Cambridge: Cambridge University Press. https://doi.org/10.1017/CBO9780511486937.005. https://www.cambridge.org/core/product/identifier/CBO9780511486937A013/type/book_part (26 January, 2020).

Dubossarsky, Haim, Simon Hengchen, Nina Tahmasebi & Dominik Schlechtweg. 2019. Time-Out: Temporal Referencing for Robust Modeling of Lexical Semantic Change. In *Proceedings of the

57th Annual Meeting of the Association for Computational Linguistics, 457–470. Florence, Italy: Association for Computational Linguistics. https://doi.org/10.18653/v1/P19-1044. https://www.aclweb.org/anthology/P19-1044 (28 June, 2020).

Fischer, Olga. 2004. What counts as evidence in historical linguistics? *Studies in Language* 28. 710–740. https://doi.org/10.1075/sl.28.3.21fis.

Fischer, Olga. 2008. On analogy as the motivation for grammaticalization. *Studies in Language* 32(2). 336–382. https://doi.org/10.1075/sl.32.2.04fis.

Fonteyn, Lauren. 2020. What about grammar? Using BERT embeddings to explore functional-semantic shifts of semi-lexical and grammatical constructions. In Folgert Karsdorp, Barbara McGillivray, Adina Nerghes & Melvin Wevers (eds.), Proceedings of the Workshop on Computational Humanities Research: http://ceur-ws.org/Vol-2723/short15.pdf (accessed 30/ 09/2022)

Fonteyn, Lauren & Stefan Hartmann. 2016. Usage-based perspectives on diachronic morphology: a mixed-methods approach towards English ing-nominals. *Linguistics Vanguard* 2(1). 1–12.

Grave, Edouard. 2017. Language Identification $\cdot$ fastText. https://fasttext.cc/blog/2017/10/02/blog-post.html (21 June, 2021).

Gries, Stefan Th. & Dagmar Divjak. 2009. Behavioral profiles: A corpus-based approach to cognitive semantic analysis. In Vyvyan Evans & Stéphanie Pourcel (eds.), *Human Cognitive Processing*, Vol. 24, 57–75. Amsterdam: John Benjamins Publishing Company. https://doi.org/10.1075/hcp.24.07gri. https://benjamins.com/catalog/hcp.24.07gri (26 January, 2020).

Hamilton, William L., Jure Leskovec & Dan Jurafsky. 2016a. Diachronic Word Embeddings Reveal Statistical Laws of Semantic Change. In *Proceedings of the 54th Annual Meeting of the Association for Computational Linguistics (Volume 1: Long Papers)*, 1489–1501. Berlin, Germany: Association for Computational Linguistics. https://doi.org/10.18653/v1/P16-1141. http://aclweb.org/anthology/P16-1141 (26 January, 2020).

Hamilton, William L., Jure Leskovec & Dan Jurafsky. 2016b. Cultural shift or linguistic drift? Comparing two computational measures of semantic change. In *Proceedings of the 2016 conference on empirical methods in natural language processing*, 2116–2121. Austin, Texas: Association for Computational Linguistics. https://doi.org/10.18653/v1/D16-1229. https://www.aclweb.org/anthology/D16-1229.

Heine, Bernd, Ulrike Claudi & Frederike Hünnemeyer. 1991. *Grammaticalization: A Conceptual Framework*. Chicago: University of Chicago Press.

Hilpert, Martin. 2006. Distinctive collexeme analysis and diachrony. *Corpus Linguistics and Linguistic Theory* 2(2). 243–256. https://doi.org/10.1515/CLLT.2006.012.

Hilpert, Martin & David Correia Saavedra. 2017. Why are grammatical elements more evenly dispersed than lexical elements? Assessing the roles of text frequency and semantic generality. *Corpora* 12(3). 369–392.

Hilpert, Martin & David Correia Saavedra. 2020. Using token-based semantic vector spaces for corpus-linguistic analyses: From practical applications to tests of theoretical claims. *Corpus Linguistics and Linguistic Theory* 16. 393–424.

Hilpert, Martin & Hubert Cuyckens. 2016. How do corpus-based techniques advance description and theory in English historical linguistics? An introduction to the special issue. *Corpus Linguistics and Linguistic Theory* 12(1). 1–5. https://doi.org/10.1515/cllt-2015-0065.

Hoeksema, Jack & Donna Jo Napoli. 2008. Just for the hell of it: A comparison of two taboo-term constructions. *Journal of Linguistics* 44(2). 347–378. https://doi.org/10.1017/S002222670800515X.

Hopper, Paul. 1991. On some principles of grammaticalisation. In Elizabeth Closs Traugott & Bernd Heine (eds.), *Approaches to grammaticalization*, Vol. 1, 17–35. Amsterdam: John Benjamins.

Hopper, Paul & Elizabeth Closs Traugott. 1993. *Grammaticalization*. Cambridge: Cambridge University Press.

Hu, Renfen, Shen Li & Shichen Liang. 2019. Diachronic sense modeling with deep contextualized word embeddings: An ecological view. In *Proceedings of the 57th annual meeting of the association for computational linguistics*, 3899–3908. Florence, Italy: Association for Computational Linguistics. https://doi.org/10.18653/v1/P19-1379. https://www.aclweb.org/anthology/P19-1379.

Jansegers, Marlies & Stefan Th. Gries. 2020. Towards a dynamic behavioral profile: A diachronic study of polysemous sentir in Spanish. *Corpus Linguistics and Linguistic Theory* 16(1). 145–187. https://doi.org/10.1515/cllt-2016-0080.

Jenset, Gard B. 2013. Mapping meaning with distributional methods: A diachronic corpus-based study of existential *there. Journal of Historical Linguistics* 3(2). 272–306. https://doi.org/10.1075/jhl.3.2.04jen.

Jenset, Gard B. & Barbara McGillivray. 2017. *Quantitative Historical Linguistics: A Corpus Framework*. Oxford: Oxford Univeristy Press.

Kroch, Anthony. 2020. *Penn Parsed Corpora of Historical English*. Philadelphia: Linguistic Data Consortium. https://www.ling.upenn.edu/hist-corpora/.

Kutuzov, Andrey, Lilja Øvrelid, Terrence Szymanski & Erik Velldal. 2018. Diachronic word embeddings and semantic shifts: a survey. In Emily M. Bender, Leon Derczynski, Pierre Isabelle (eds.), *Proceedings of the 27th International Conference on Computational Linguistics*, 1384–139714. Santa Fe, New Mexico: Association for Computational Linguistics.

Lindquist, Hans & Christian Mair (eds.). 2004. *Corpus Approaches to Grammaticalization in English*. Amsterdam: John Benjamins.

Lorenz, Gunter. 2002. Really worthwhile or not really significant ?: A corpus-based approach to the delexicalization and grammaticalization of intensifiers in Modern English. In Ilse Wischer & Gabriele Diewald (eds.), *Typological Studies in Language*, vol. 49, 143–161. Amsterdam: John Benjamins Publishing Company. https://doi.org/10.1075/tsl.49.11lor. https://benjamins.com/catalog/tsl.49.11lor (30 June, 2021).

Luo, Yiwei, Dan Jurafsky & Beth Levin. 2019. From Insanely Jealous to Insanely Delicious: Computational Models for the Semantic Bleaching of English Intensifiers. In *Proceedings of the 1st International Workshop on Computational Approaches to Historical Language Change*, 1–13. Florence, Italy: Association for Computational Linguistics. https://doi.org/10.18653/v1/W19-4701. https://www.aclweb.org/anthology/W19-4701 (30 July, 2021).

Manjavacas, Enrique, Ákos Kádár & Mike Kestemont. 2019. Improving Lemmatization of Non-Standard Languages with Joint Learning. In *Proceedings of the 2019 Conference of the North American Chapter of the Association for Computational Linguistics: Human Language Technologies, Volume 1*, 1493–1503. Association for Computational Linguistics. https://www.aclweb.org/anthology/N19-1153.

Margerie, Hélène. 2011. Grammaticalising constructions: to death as a peripheral degree modifier. *Folia Linguistica Historica* 45(Historica vol. 32). https://doi.org/10.1515/flih.2011.005. https://www.degruyter.com/view/j/flih.2011.32.issue-1/flih.2011.005/flih.2011.005.xml (26 January, 2020).

Mikolov, Tomás, Kai Chen, Greg Corrado & Jeffrey Dean. 2013. Efficient Estimation of Word Representations in Vector Space. In Yoshua Bengio & Yann LeCun (eds.), *1st International Conference on Learning Representations, ICLR 2013, Scottsdale, Arizona, USA, May 2- 4, 2013, Workshop Track Proceedings*. http://arxiv.org/abs/1301.3781.

Mitra, Sunny, Ritwik Mitra, Martin Riedl, Chris Biemann, Animesh Mukherjee & Pawan Goyal. 2014. That's sick dude!: Automatic identification of word sense change across different timescales. In

Proceedings of the 52nd Annual Meeting of the Association for Computational Linguistics, Volume 1: Long Papers, 1020–1029. Baltimore, Maryland: Association for Computational Linguistics. https://doi.org/10.3115/v1/P14-1096. https://www.aclweb.org/anthology/P14-1096 (22 May, 2020).

Nevalainen, Terttu, Helena Raumolin-Brunberg, Jukka Keränen, Minna Nevala, Arja Nurmi, Minna Palander-Collin, Ann Taylor, Susan Pintzuk, Anthony Warner, & others. 2006. Parsed Corpus of Early English Correspondence (PCEEC). *Oxford Text Archive Core Collection*. University of Oxford.

Nicenboim, Bruno & Shravan Vasishth. 2016. Statistical methods for linguistic research: Foundational Ideas-Part II: Statistical methods for linguistics–Part II. *Language and Linguistics Compass* 10(11). 591–613. https://doi.org/10.1111/lnc3.12207.

Pechenick, Eitan Adam, Christopher M. Danforth & Peter Sheridan Dodds. 2015. Characterizing the Google Books Corpus: Strong Limits to Inferences of Socio-Cultural and Linguistic Evolution. *PLOS ONE* 24.

Pedregosa, Fabian, Gaël Varoquaux, Alexandre Gramfort, Vincent Michel, Bertrand Thirion, Olivier Grisel, Mathieu Blondel, et al. 2011. Scikit-learn: Machine learning in Python. *the Journal of machine Learning research*. JMLR. org 12. 2825–2830.

Pennington, Jeffrey, Richard Socher & Christopher Manning. 2014. GloVe: Global Vectors for Word Representation. In *Proceedings of the 2014 Conference on Empirical Methods in Natural Language Processing (EMNLP)*, 1532–1543. Doha, Qatar: Association for Computational Linguistics. https://doi.org/10.3115/v1/D14-1162. https://www.aclweb.org/anthology/D14-1162.

Perek, Florent. 2016. Using distributional semantics to study syntactic productivity in diachrony: A case study. *Linguistics* 54 (1). https://doi.org/10.1515/ling-2015-0043. https://www.degruyter.com/view/j/ling.2016.54.issue-1/ling-2015-0043/ling-2015-0043.xml (26 January, 2020).

Perek, Florent. 2018. Recent change in the productivity and schematicity of the way-construction: A distributional semantic analysis. *Corpus Linguistics and Linguistic Theory* 14(1). 65–97. https://doi.org/10.1515/cllt-2016-0014.

Quirk, Randalph, Sidney Greenbaum, Geoffrey Leech & Jan Svartvik. 1985. *A Comprehensive Grammar of the English Language*. London: Longman.

Rehurek, Radim & Petr Sojka. 2010. Software Framework for Topic Modelling with Large Corpora. *Proceedings of the LREC 2010 Workshop on New Challenges for NLP Frameworks* 45–50.

Rosenfeld, Alex & Katrin Erk. 2018. Deep Neural Models of Semantic Shift. In *Proceedings of the 2018 Conference of the North American Chapter of the Association for Computational Linguistics: Human Language Technologies, Volume 1 (Long Papers)*, 474–484. New Orleans, Louisiana: Association for Computational Linguistics. https://doi.org/10.18653/v1/N18-1044. http://aclweb.org/anthology/N18-1044 (26 January, 2020).

Rousseeuw, Peter J. 1987. Silhouettes: a graphical aid to the interpretation and validation of cluster analysis. *Journal of computational and applied mathematics*. Elsevier 20. 53–65.

Sagi, Eyal, Stefan Kaufmann & Brady Clark. 2011. Tracing semantic change with Latent Semantic Analysis. In Kathryn Allan & Justyna A. Robinson (eds.), *Current Methods in Historical Semantics*. Berlin/Boston: Mouton De Gruyter. https://doi.org/10.1515/9783110252903.161. https://www.degruyter.com/view/books/9783110252903/9783110252903.161/9783110252903.161.xml (26 January, 2020).

Schlechtweg, Dominik, Stefanie Eckmann, Enrico Santus, Sabine Schulte im Walde & Daniel Hole. 2017. German in Flux: Detecting Metaphoric Change via Word Entropy. In *Proceedings of the 21st Conference on Computational Natural Language Learning (CoNLL 2017)*, 354–367. Vancouver, Canada: Association for Computational Linguistics. https://doi.org/10.18653/v1/K17-1036. https://www.aclweb.org/anthology/K17-1036 (15 November, 2020).

Tahmasebi, Nina, Lars Borin & Adam Jatowt. 2019. Survey of Computational Approaches to Lexical Semantic Change. *arXiv:1811.06278 [cs]*. http://arxiv.org/abs/1811.06278 (30 June, 2021).

Traugott, Elisabeth C. & Graeme Trousdale. 2013. *Constructionalization and Constructional Changes*. Oxford: Oxford University Press.

Traugott, Elizabeth Closs. 1989. On the rise of epistemic meanings in English: An example of subjectification in semantic change. *Language* 57. 33–65.

Traugott, Elizabeth Closs. 2003. From subjectification to intersubjectification. In Raymond Hickey (ed.), *Motives for language change*, 124–139. Cambridge: Cambridge University Press.

Traugott, Elizabeth Closs. 2010. (Inter)subjectivity and (inter)subjectification: A reassessment. In Kristin Davidse, Lieven Vandelanotte & Hubert Cuyckens (eds.), *Subjectification, intersubjectification and grammaticalization*, 29–71. Berlin: De Gruyter Mouton.

Traugott, Elizabeth Closs & Richard Dasher. 2002. *Regularity in semantic change*. Cambridge: Cambridge University Press.

Traugott, Elizabeth Closs & Ekkehard König. 1991. The semantics-pragmatics of grammaticalization revisited. In Elizabeth Closs Traugott & Bernd Heine (eds.), *Approaches to grammaticalization*, Vol. 1, 189–218. Amsterdam: John Benjamins.

Younes, Nadja & Ulf-Dietrich Reips. 2019. Guideline for improving the reliability of Google Ngram studies: Evidence from religious terms. *PLOS ONE* 14. e0213554.

María José López-Couso and Belén Méndez-Naya

5 From chance to epistemic possibility

On the grammaticalization of happenstance expressions in English

Abstract: This chapter draws attention to the notion of happenstance, i.e. something that happens (by chance), a common cross-linguistic source for expressions of possibility, among them the core English epistemic adverbs *perhaps* and *maybe*. We show here that these adverbs are just two members of a wider set of happenstance adverbial formations available in earlier English, which also included low-frequency expressions such as *peraventure, by hap, may fall, may fortune*, and *chance*. Based on data from the Historical Thesaurus of the Oxford English Dictionary and from the standard historical dictionaries and their quotation databases, we examine the two major pathways followed by these happenstance expressions in their adverbialization process: (i) from phrase to adverb (e.g. *perhaps* < *per* 'for, by' + *hap* 'occurrence, chance'); and (ii) from clause to adverb (e.g. *maybe* < *(it) may be that* . . .). We argue that the development of these happenstance epistemic adverbs shows defining features of grammaticalization, including bleaching, decategorialization, fusion, layering, and cross-linguistic generality, alongside the acquisition of subjective and intersubjective functions.

Keywords: epistemic adverbs, happenstance, adverbialization, grammaticalization, (inter)subjectification

1 Introduction

Modality is a very broad area of meaning that comprises the notions of speaker's attitudes and commitment towards the truth of a given proposition (epistemic modality), obligations and permissions (deontic modality), as well as abilities and dispositions (dynamic modality). The manifestations of modality across languages are very diverse, ranging from grammatical devices, like synthetic and analytic mood systems (e.g. subjunctive mood, modal verbs), to those which are closer to

Acknowledgements: This research is funded by the Spanish Ministry of Science, Innovation, and Universities (National Programme for Excellence in Scientific and Technical Research; grants FFI2017-86884-P and PID2020-114604GB-I00) and the Regional Government of Galicia (Consellería de Cultura, Educación e Universidade; grant ED431B 2020/01). We also thank two anonymous reviewers and the editors of this volume for their insightful comments. The usual disclaimers apply. The chapter is dedicated to Hubert Cuyckens, an excellent scholar and an even better friend.

https://doi.org/10.1515/9783110753059-005

the lexical pole, such as modal adverbs (e.g. *probably, perhaps*). The present study is a further step in our current research project, which focuses on the origin, development, and present-day use of a number of epistemic adverbs and epistemic parentheticals, in particular those conveying some degree of doubt towards the truth of the speaker's proposition.

Weak possibility or doubt is a central modal notion across languages. Ramat and Ricca's (1998) study of sentence adverbs in European languages shows that weak possibility is typically lexicalized in dedicated adverbs, which tend to be diachronically unstable and are therefore often affected by processes of competition, loss, and renewal (Ramat and Ricca 1998: 235). In this chapter we draw attention precisely to the notion of weak possibility by exploring a common cross-linguistic source for expressions of epistemic possibility, namely happenstance or chance, i.e. something that happens (by chance). Examples of epistemic happenstance adverbs and adverbial expressions from a wide range of languages are provided in Section 2. While in Present-day English the source meaning of happenstance is mostly represented by the core epistemic adverbs *perhaps* and *maybe*, in earlier stages the inventory of happenstance forms was much larger than it is today. Thus, the Middle and Early Modern English periods witnessed the emergence of a group of adverbs similar in form, function, and meaning to *perhaps* and *maybe*, including low-frequency formations such as *perchance, peradventure, mayfall,* and *mayhap*, among others. Section 3 is devoted to the description of the catalogue of such forms in the history of the language, with data from the Historical Thesaurus of the Oxford English Dictionary (HTOED), as well as the standard historical dictionaries and their quotation databases. In turn, Section 4, which is based on both corpora and dictionary evidence, shows that these epistemic happenstance adverbs follow two different adverbialization pathways: on the one hand, from phrase to adverb (e.g. *perhaps* < Latin preposition *per* 'for, by' + Scandinavian noun *hap* 'occurrence, chance' + adverbial –*s*; cf. Section 4.1); and, on the other, from clause to adverb (e.g. *maybe* < *(it) may be that . . .*; cf. Section 4.2). Finally, in Section 5 we show that these two adverbialization pathways illustrate both structural and semantico-pragmatic features characteristic of grammaticalization processes.

2 From chance to possibility

The long research tradition on modality has shown that epistemic meanings tend to grammaticalize relatively late across languages. One of the most prominent sources of epistemic meanings is to be found in agent-oriented (i.e. deontic or dynamic) modality meanings, which are in turn derived from lexical sources conveying notions such as ability, power, and the like (Traugott 1989; Bybee, Perkins, and Pagliuca 1994: 194, 199, 240; Kuteva et al. 2019: 343, 346). Well-known examples of this common developmental pathway are the English modals *can* and *may*, which originally conveyed mental ability (i.e. 'know how to') and physical ability (i.e. 'have strength'), respectively. From this ability meaning, *can* and *may* became markers of root possibility and eventually came to express epistemic possibility (Bybee, Perkins, and Pagliuca 1994: 191–202).

An additional lexical source for epistemic possibility is happenstance, that is, "something that happens by chance, an event or circumstance considered to be influenced by chance; chance, luck" (OED s.v. *happenstance* n. and adj.). The notion of chance can easily be linked to the modal domain of epistemic possibility by means of a relatively straightforward conceptual jump: chance implies that there is likelihood for something either to happen or not to happen. Such a close relationship explains the productivity of the meaning 'chance' as a source for epistemic possibility across languages. Examples of this lexical source from a wide range of languages include the following: Sanskrit *sam-bhavá* 'occurrence' > 'capacity, ability, possibility' (Monier-Williams 1899: 1179); the Latin adverbs *forte* (ablative of *fors* 'fortune, chance'), *fortasse* (<*forte an sit* 'chance be that'), *forsit* (< *fors sit* 'chance be'), *forsitan* (< *fors sit an* 'chance be that'; Ramat and Ricca 1998: 232–233), and its reduced form *forsan*, all of them meaning 'perhaps' (OLD s. vv. *forte* adv. 4, *fortasse* adv., *forsit* adv., *forsitan* adv., and *forsan* adv.); French *par aventure* (DMF s.v. *aventure* D.1.a); the Spanish adverb *acaso* (< Latin *casus* 'chance'; DRAE s.v. *acaso* 1 'chance'; 3 'perhaps'; see also Ramat and Ricca 1998: 232, 235–236); Irish (*tá*) *seans* (literally 'there is chance'; Ramat and Ricca 1998: 234–235); and Hungarian *esetleg* (< *eset* 'case, chance'; Ramat and Ricca 1998: 236).

Moreover, the epistemic auxiliaries of two languages as distant as Abkhaz (a Northern Caucasian language) and Maidu (a Penutian language of California) derive directly from happenstance verbs meaning 'happen, befall' (Bybee, Perkins, and Pagliuca 1994: 206). Clauses containing a verb meaning 'happen' may also evolve into epistemic expressions. This is the case of various formations deriving from conditional clauses, such as Galician *se cadra* 'perhaps' (DRAG s.v. *se cadra*; Rodríguez Espiñeira 2019; Míguez Rego 2021) and its Portuguese counterpart *se calhar* (Pinto da Lima 2008), of Old Piedmontese *salacàd* (< *s'al acàd*) and Calabrian *sambatti* (< *s'ambatti*), all of them originally meaning 'if it happens (by chance)', and of Breton *marteze* (literally 'if-comes-this') (Ramat and Ricca 1998: 232). Additional examples of the clause-to-adverb pathway include the Scandinavian adverbs *kanhända, måhända, törhända, kanske,* and *måske* (Ramat and Ricca 1998: 232–233, 235), all of which go back to complementation structures in which a matrix clause containing a modal auxiliary is combined with a verb meaning 'happen' (< (*det*) *kan* / *må* / *tör hända* (*att*) 'it can / may / must happen that'). The Dutch adverb *misschien* (< *tmachschien* 'it may happen') has a similar origin (see Ramat and Ricca 1998: 235; Boye and Harder 2007: 591; Beijering 2010: 5).

3 Inventory of epistemic expressions deriving from the notion of happenstance in the history of English

In addition to the various expressions mentioned in Section 2, happenstance is also the source of a number of epistemic markers in English, among them, the two major present-day adverbs of doubt *perhaps* and *maybe*. In order to make an inventory of epistemic happenstance adverbs in the history of English, we first resorted to the HTOED and searched for adverbs expressing the epistemic meaning of possibility. The search yielded a total of 37 items, out of which 25 (67.6%) go back to a lexical source from the domain of happenstance or chance. In this respect, English follows the cross-linguistic tendency identified by Ramat and Ricca (1998: 235) according to which the concept of chance is one of the most widespread sources for epistemic adverbs conveying the meaning of weak possibility, i.e. 'perhaps'.

The evidence offered by the Oxford English Dictionary (OED) and the Middle English Dictionary (MED) suggests the existence of two major lexical sources for epistemic adverbs and adverbial expressions deriving from the notion of happenstance in English: on the one hand, those which contain a noun meaning 'chance' and, on the other, adverbs which go back to clauses featuring a verb meaning 'happen (by chance)'. Table 1 provides the happenstance etyma, together with the individual epistemic adverbial expressions deriving from them and the corresponding dates of their first attestations in the OED and/or the MED. As shown here, the list of lexical sources contains both native forms (e.g. *fall, tide, happen*) alongside borrowings from French (e.g. *adventure, chance, fortune*) and from Scandinavian (e.g. the noun *hap*). Moreover, most of the happenstance epistemic adverbs included in Table 1 are attested for the first time in the Late Middle and Early Modern English periods, two particularly productive stages in the history of English as far as lexical expansion is concerned. The coexistence in Early Modern English of synonymous forms such as those in Table 1 is likely to be related to the lexical experimentation characteristic of the period, when it was frequent to find "formally related words . . . without any clear difference in meaning" (Nevalainen 1999: 334).

Table 1: Epistemic happenstance expressions in the history of English: Lexical sources, inventory, and dates of first OED/MED attestations.

Lexical source		Epistemic happenstance expression	Earliest OED/MED attestation
Noun	*adventure*	peradventure	1300
		aunters	1663
		aunterens	1825
	case	by case	1300
		percase	1377
		upon case	1387
		on case	1387
		in case	1398
	chance	perchance	1350
		by chance	1526
		chance	1595
		chances are	1926
	fortune	fortune	1600
	hap	through hap	1375
		up hap	1375
		by hap	1382
		haply	1390
		in hap	1425
		of hap	1425
		on hap	1450
		upon hap	1450
		perhap	1450
		in haps	1499
		perhaps	1520
		haps	1570
		p'raps	1745
Verb	*be*	maybe	1400
		mebbe	1825
	chance	may chance	1556
	fall	may-fall	1400
	fortune	may-fortune	1548
	hap	mayhap	1533

Table 1 (continued)

Lexical source		Epistemic happenstance expression	Earliest OED/MED attestation
	happen	*happen*	1487
		mayhappen	1577
	tide	*may-tide*	1500
Unclear source		*perhappen*	1578
		mayhaps	1696

The sections that follow describe the three groups of forms included in Table 1 in some detail.

3.1 Epistemic happenstance expressions deriving from nouns meaning 'chance'

The first group of epistemic adverbs and adverbial expressions included in Table 1 above contains the happenstance nouns *adventure, case, chance, fortune*, and *hap*. Interestingly, none of these forms is of native origin: *hap* is a Scandinavian borrowing (first OED record: 1225), while *adventure* (1200), *case* (1250), *chance* (1297), and *fortune* (1300) are loanwords from French. A look at Table 1 also shows that the group of epistemic expressions deriving from nouns meaning 'chance' is attested earlier and shows greater structural variability than the set of forms originating from happenstance verbs, allowing for three different patterns. The first one corresponds to those adverbs which derive from the relevant source nouns by means of a process of derivation. These include the Middle English formation *haply* (1390), as well as the Modern English adverbs *haps* (1570), the Northern *aunters* (1663), and its variant *aunterens* (1825).[1] *Haply* is the result of the combination of the noun *hap* and the adverb-forming suffix *-ly* (OED s.v. *-ly* suffix[2]), while the three remaining forms feature the adverbial *-s* suffix (OED s.v. *-s* suffix[1]).[2] Examples of these derivative epistemic adverbs are given in (1)-(3) below.

---

1 Molencki (2021: 419) also refers to the adverb *happily* (see OED s.v. *happily* adv. 1). This adverb has not been considered here as it is not listed in the HTOED.

2 The OED also mentions an alternative source for *haps*: the plural of the noun *hap* (OED s.v. *hap* n[1]). See below the discussion on the variant forms *perhap* and *perhaps*.

(1) Þe dore I-closet..to [kepe] þe þer-oute; **Hapliche** [c1400 Trin. Cambr. R.3.14 *happily*], an Hundred ȝer er þou eft entre. (c1390 (a1376) Langland *Piers Plowman* (Vernon) (1867) A. vi. l. 104; OED s.v. *haply* adv.)

(2) They, **haps**, would vs preserue, our wilfull owne. (1584 T. Hudson tr. G. de S. Du Bartas *Hist. Judith* iii. 43; OED s.v. *haps* adv.)

(3) **Aunters**, Peradventure. (1673 J. Ray *N. Countrey Words in Coll. Eng. Words*; OED s.v. *aunters* adv. and conj.)

The second pattern comprises those adverbs formed by conversion, such as Early Modern English *chance* (1595) and *fortune* (1600), illustrated in (4) and (5).

(4) It may **chaunce** cost some of vs our liues (1600 W. Shakespeare *Henry IV, Pt. 2* II.i.12; OED s.v. *chance* n., adj., and adv. C)

(5) ȝour feet are not so sicker sett Bot **fortun** ȝe may fall. (a1600 A. Montgomerie *Misc. Poems* v. 56; OED s.v. *fortune* adv.)

However, by far the most productive pattern of epistemic expressions deriving from a noun meaning 'chance' involves the combination of the corresponding happenstance noun with a preposition, written either as two separate words (e.g. *up hap, on hap, by case*, etc.) or spelt solid (e.g. *perchance, percase, perhap(s)*, etc.).

The earliest OED occurrences of epistemic happenstance adverbs and adverbial expressions originating in a noun correspond to the French borrowings *peradventure* and *perchance*, which are already attested in the early 14th century (1300 and 1350, respectively). Another French loan, *percase*, occurs for the first time in English in the late 14th century (1377). These three adverbs have their origin in French prepositional phrases featuring the preposition *par/per* 'through, for, by' (see AND s.v. *par* 1) followed by a noun meaning 'chance' (*par aventure, par cas, par chance*).[3] According to Molencki (2021: 415), the increasing popularity of argumentative texts in the Late Middle English period required the coinage of new possibility adverbs, and French, "the major lexifier of English", was the most

---

3 In Anglo-Norman and Medieval French *par aventure* could be used both with a happenstance and with an epistemic meaning (see AND s.v. *aventure*; DMF s.v. *aventure* subst. fém. D.b). The same holds for *par case*, which in Anglo-Norman can be glossed as both 'by chance' and 'possibly' (AND s.v. *cas* 1). *Par chance*, by contrast, is only rendered in the historical French dictionaries as 'by chance, by accident' (AND s.v. *chance*; DMF s.v. *chance* subst. fém. A), that is, with the happenstance meaning.

straightforward source. Examples (6)-(8) illustrate these three borrowed adverbial formations with the meaning of epistemic possibility 'perhaps, maybe'.

(6)   Þei heo bidde hire beden at churche, hire þouȝht is athom more; **perauenture** heo schal it bete þare. (c1300 *All Souls* (Laud) 122 in C. Horstmann *Early S.-Eng. Legendary* (1887) 424 (MED); OED s.v. *peradventure* adv. 1)

(7)   Thou schalt mowe senden hire a lettre, And, **per cas**, wryte more plein Than thou be Mowthe durstest sein (1393 J. Gower *Confessio Amantis* (Fairf.) iv. 39 (MED); OED s.v. *percase* adv. 2)

(8)   It mai **par chance** faile. (*a*1393 J. Gower *Confessio Amantis* (Fairf.) i. 2225 (MED); OED s.v. *perchance* adv., n., and adj. A.1)

In the course of the Late Middle English period, these French adverbs served as a model for a number of native formations where the French happenstance nouns *case* and *chance* and the Scandinavian *hap* combined with different native prepositions, among them *by, in, through, up, upon, on, of*, and, in the case of *hap*, also with Latin or Anglo-Norman *per*.[4] Some of these combinations are illustrated in (9)-(11). Note that in (9b-d) *on caas, vppon caas*, and *in case* are used to render the Latin epistemic adverbs *forte* and *forsan* (cf. Section 2 above); moreover, in (9b-c) the adverb *peradventure* is used in a different version of the same text. In (11a), in turn, the expression *by hap* is coordinated with the earlier adverb *peradventure*. This is an example of the widespread Middle and Early Modern English practice to combine a borrowed word or expression with a native synonym. Note also that in (11c) *perhap* and *up hap* are found in variant manuscripts.

(9) a. He the wole bere anhonde, And bynyme thi stat **bicas** and bringe the of thi londe. (c1300 *Life & Martyrdom Thomas Becket* (Harl. 2277) (1845) l. 912; MED s.v. *cas* n. 3 (d))
     b. Men..worshipped hym instead of God and, **on caas** [L *forte*; Higd. (2): *perauenture*], took occasioun of his sawe. (a1387) Trev. *Higd.* (StJ-C H.1) 3.197; MED s.v. *cas* n. 3 (d))
     c. **Vppon caas** [L *forsan*; Higd.(2): *perauenture*] William..wroot so by tellynge of oþere men. ((a1387) Trev. *Higd.* (StJ-C H.1) 2.59; MED s.v. *cas* n. 3 (d))

---

4 In this respect, *hap* behaves in a similar way to French *aventure*, which expressed epistemic meaning ('perhaps') not only in the combination *par aventure* (which seems to have been borrowed as a set phrase into English), but also with other prepositions such as *à* and *en* in the phrases *à l'aventure* and *en l'aventure* (DMF s.v. *aventure* subst. fém. I.D.b).

    d. Þe vertu of worchinge **in case** [L *forte*] worchiþ no þing perfitliche or at þe fulle. ((a1398) *Trev. Barth. (Add 27944) 38a/a; MED s.v. *cas* n. 3 (d))

(10)   Thou mayst lese thy goodes..and also **by chaunce** the helth of thy body. (1526 W. Bonde *Pylgrimage of Perfection* i. sig. Bvii; OED s.v. *chance* n., adj., and adv. P1.b)

(11) a. Perauenture eyther **by happe** it shall be euyll serued or elles suffre moche dysease of enmyes. (EEBO, 1497, Alcock, *The abbaye of the Holy Ghost*)

    b. **In hap** the drede of God is not in this place. (a1425 (c1395) WBible (2) (Roy 1.C.8) Gen. 20.11; MED s.v. *hap* n. 2c)

    c. Othir men write that on Johannes Patricius schul a mad this Cherch in tyme of Liberi the Pope; **Perhap** [*v.r. Up hap*] this Pope mored it, or arayed it, as he ded many othir. (a1464 J. Capgrave *Chron. Eng.* (Cambr.) 85; OED s. v. *perhap* adv.; MED s.v. *per-hap* adv.)

    d. So brod was þe see þat sayle hem bihoued holliche al a niȝt &, **vp happe**, wel more. (a 1375 *WPal.* (KC 13) 2722; MED s.v. *hap* n. 2c)

    e. Wilen ȝe..In this vessel forth gone, and **vppon hap** neuere Comen Ageyn? (a1450 (c1410) Lovel. *Grail* (Corp-C 80) 51.361); MED s.v. *hap* n. 2c)

    f. Þat was ordaynd of goddis gudnes, **On hap** for his desert was les, þarfore **on hap**, god walde Þat lange seknes herbert suld halde. (?c1450 St. Cuth. (Eg 3309) 3030-1; MED s.v. *hap* n. 2c)

In the course of time, however, the range of prepositions combining with the happenstance nouns gradually narrowed down, so that most of the Middle English prepositional combinations discussed above became obsolete (OED s.v. *hap* n^1. Phrases P1.b; OED s.v. *case* n. P1), with a few exceptions: *by hap* and *by haps*, which have not entirely disappeared in Present-day English (OED s.v. *hap* n^1 Phrases P1.a, today mostly in the form *by lucky hap*), though only with the meaning 'by chance', and, most importantly, the epistemic adverbs *perhaps, perchance, percase*, and *peradventure*.

As regards *perhap(s)*,[5] both the OED and the MED provide earlier attestations of *perhap* (the form without the final *-s*) than of *perhaps*. Examples of the former adverb are given in (11c) above, dated 1464, and in (12) below, dated 1450.

(12)   Pan clewfyf vy an tan tyn, **parhap** y wrussen fye. (?a1450 (?1350-75) *Origo Mundi* in Norris Anc.Corn.Drama (Bod 791) 1352; MED s.v. *per-hap* adv.)

---

5 On *perhaps*, see also Molencki (2021).

The earliest OED occurrence of the form *perhaps* goes back to 1520, as shown in (13), while its (reduced) variant form *p'raps* is first attested in 1745 (see (14) below).

(13)   He shall here those thingis **perhappis** that he nold. (c1520 tr. Terence *Andria* v. iv, in *Terens in Eng.* sig. D.iiiv; OED s.v. *perhaps* adv. and n. A.1)

(14)   Ay' b't then, **p'rhaps**, says you, t's a m'rry Whim. (a1745 J. Swift *Poems* (1937) III. 1020; OED s.v. *p'raps* adv.)

However, the MED entry for *per-happes* provides a couple of earlier occurrences of the variant form *perhappous*, dated c1475. One of them is (15), which shows the occurrence of the forms *per case* and *perhaps* in parallel structures.

(15)   Par case thi men in mynde she kepethe hem alle, **Perhappous** [?read: *Perhappans*] one is loved that wol not fade. (c1475 *A philosophre* (Hrl 372) p. 35; MED s.v. *per-happes* adv. Also *-happous*, ?*-happons*, ?*-happans*)

Although the OED accounts for the form *perhaps* as the combination of the preposition *per* and the plural noun *haps*, an alternative explanation is also possible here. In our view, the final *-s* present in *perhaps* is not the plural *-s* suffix, but rather the adverbial *-s* suffix (OED s.v. *-s* suffix[1]), added to the earlier formation *perhap* (see *haps* and *aunters* discussed above).[6] A similar explanation could be given for other adverbial happenstance expressions which also show variation between forms with and without final *-s*, such as *peradventures*, a variant which is not included in the historical dictionaries, and *in haps*. By way of illustration, see (16), which is the only example of *peradventures* in the whole EEBO, and (17), which features *in happes*.

(16)   This **peraduentures** is the roote of your euil. (EEBO, 1632, Camus, *A spirituall combat a tryall of a faithfull soule or consolation in temptation*)

(17)   A merueylous thyng and **in happes** not seyn to fore thre daies of fastynge and prayers. (?1499 (?a1440) S. Winter tr. *St. Ierom* (de Worde) sig. Biii; OED s.v. *hap* n.[1] P2)

------

6 Parallel adverbial formations are found in the Middle English period, including *ammides* 'in the middle' and *aȝeines* 'again', which co-existed with the corresponding adverbs lacking the final *-s*: *amid, again*. According to the OED, "the frequent coexistence of the two forms of the same adv., one with and the other without *s*, led to the addition of *s* to many advs. as a sign of their function".

Along with the forms discussed so far, which appear for the first time in the Middle and Early Modern English periods, the early 20th century saw the emergence of a new epistemic marker which also contains the noun *chance*, namely the parenthetical *chances are* (see López-Couso and Méndez-Naya 2021a). This is illustrated in (18a-b) below, the only two occurrences of this more recent epistemic pattern in the OED quotation database.

(18) a. She'll give you a sit-down for yourself, **chances are**, but bring back a 'lump' for us. (1926 J. Black *You can't Win* vi. 67; OED s.vv. *lump* n.[1] 1.g; *sit-down* adj. and n. B.1.b)

    b. **Chances are**, he's having a go-round with some editor out there who's just shit-canned one of his articles. (1973 T. Crouse *Boys on Bus* I. v. 100; OED s.vv. *go-round* n. 3; *shitcan* v. 1.b)

3.2 Epistemic happenstance adverbs deriving from verbs meaning 'happen (by chance)'

In addition to the formations examined in Section 3.1, which go back to a noun, Table 1 above contains a second group of epistemic happenstance adverbs which derive from clauses containing a verb meaning 'happen (by chance)'. The list of relevant source verbs features native forms going back to Old English, such as *be* (OED s.v. *be* v. I.2), *fall* (OED s.v. *fall* v. VIII), and *tide* (OED s.v. *tide* v.[1]), together with the Middle English verbs *hap* (OED s.v. *hap* v.[1] 1), *happen* (OED s.v. *happen* v.), and *chance* (OED s.v. *chance* v.), all three derived from borrowed nouns (the Scandinavian noun *hap* 'chance' and the French noun *chance*), as well as the verb *fortune* (OED s.v. *fortune* v. 3), borrowed from French at the end of the 14th century. With these verbs the idea of possibility becomes most prominent when they are inflected for the subjunctive or appear in combination with the epistemic modal *may*.

A present subjunctive form is precisely the source of the adverb *happen* (OED s.v. *happen* adv.), illustrated in (19):

(19) **Happin** [1489 Adv. *hap*] to vencus ['achieve military victory'] the gret battale. (1487 (a1380) J. Barbour *Bruce* (St. John's Cambr.) xii. 273; OED s.v. *happen* adv.)

In turn, adverbs such as *maybe* (and its weakened, colloquial, and regional variant *mebbe*), *may chance, may-fall, may-fortune, mayhap, mayhappen*, and *may-tide* correspond to a pattern attested in other Germanic languages, illustrated in the

Scandinavian formations *kanhända*, *måhända*, *törhända*, *kanske*, and *måske* and in the Dutch adverb *misschien* (cf. Section 2 above). The examples in (20) below are the earliest attestations of these *may*-formations in the OED.

(20) a. **May be** [*a*1400 Vesp. *Mai fall*] sum goost awey him ledde. (a1400 (a1325) *Cursor Mundi* (Trin. Cambr.) 17553; OED s.v. *maybe* adv., n., and adj. A. 1)

    b. **Mebby, mebbys**.., perhaps, probably. It may be. (1825 J. T. Brockett *Gloss. North Country Words* 136; OED s.v. *mebbe* adv.)

    c. If þou þar findes..Fifty or fourte o þi lele men – Tuenti **mai falle**, or tuis fiue – Ne sal þai alle haue þar for liue? (a1400 (a1325) *Cursor Mundi* (Vesp.) 2759 (MED); OED s.v. *may* v.^{1} P2)

    d. **May tyde** he will oure giftis take. (a1500 (a1460) *Towneley Plays* (1897–1973) 54; OED s.v. *may* v.^{1} P2)

    e. **May happe** I wyll thynke on you when you be gone. (1533 J. Heywood *Play of Wether* sig. Ciiii^v; OED s.v. *mayhap* adv.)

    f. **Mafortune** as then ye tyme did not suffer so inexplycable a misterie to be put in wryting to all mens knowledge. (1548 N. Udall tr. Erasmus *Paraphr. John* 7; OED s.v. *may* v.^{1} P2)

    g. Many yong gentlemen, which haue **may chaunce** an opinion that to be in me, that is not in deed (1561 T. Hoby in tr. B. Castiglione *Courtyer* Ep. Translatour sig. B.i; OED s.v. *may* v.^{1} P2)

    h. Another tyme **may happen** he, may doe as much for thee. (1577 H. Rhodes *Bk. Nurture* (new ed.) sig. D.viii; OED s.v. *mayhappen* adv.)

Although all these *may*-adverbs are listed in the HTOED, only *maybe/mebbe*, *mayhap*, and *mayhappen* have dedicated entries in the OED, and are the only *may*-forms surviving to the present day. *Maybe* is used both in the standard and in dialects and has become one of the most common epistemic adverbs of doubt in Present-day English together with *perhaps* (cf. Biber et al. 1999: 868–870). In turn, *mayhap* and *mayhappen* are restricted to archaic and dialectal use in British English (OED s.vv. *mayhap* adv., *mayhappen* adv.; Visser 1963–1973, 1: 20).[7] *Mayhap* and *mayhappen* are also attested in Contemporary American English, as shown in the Merriam-Webster Dictionary (s.vv. *mayhap*, *mayhappen*), where the former is regarded as rare and the latter as a dialectal variant of *mayhap*. The remaining *may*-forms given in Table 1 do not have individual entries in the OED, but appear in the entry for the verb *may* (OED s.v. *may* v.^{1} P2), where they are labelled as

---

7 The OED locates these two adverbs in the frequency bands 4 (0.01–0.99 pmw) and 2 (<0.0099 pmw), respectively, testifying to their low frequency.

'obsolete'; no examples of these adverbs are provided in the dictionary later than the end of the 16th century. Corpus evidence for *may*-adverbs is also very scanty. A rough search in EEBO (775 million words, covering the period 1470–1700), including only cases in which the adverbs are spelt hyphenated or solid, yielded about 400 examples of *maybe* (ca. 0.51 pmw), 20 occurrences of *mayhap* (0.02 pmw), and just a few sporadic instances of the other *may*-formations. Examples of *mayhap* also occur in COHA (558 instances, 1.39 pmw), especially from the 19th century), COCA (127 exx., 0.12 pmw), and BNC (10 exx., 0.1 pmw).

3.3 Unclear source

As shown in Table 1, most of the adverbial forms included in the inventory of epistemic happenstance expressions go back either to a noun or to a verb meaning 'chance'. We find, however, a couple of adverbs whose origin is not straightforward. These are the Early Modern English formations *perhappen*,[8] shown in (21), and *mayhaps*, illustrated in (22).

(21) Gif I ane Ill taill tell..It may perchance siclyke cum to my sell **Perhappin** war (1578 J. Rolland *Seuin Seages* 237; OED s.v. *perhappen* adv.)

(22) **Mayhaps** I can, **mayhaps** I won't; what then? (EEBO, 1696, Motteux, *Love's a jest a comedy*)

Perhappen seems to result from a blending process involving features of the two sources discussed in Sections 3.1 and 3.2, nominal and verbal: it is the combination of the preposition *per* and a form of the verb *happen*. As to *mayhaps*, two alternative paths of development are possible: on the one hand, it may derive from the adverb *haps* when occurring after the modal verb *may*, as in (23); on the other, *mayhaps* may result from the combination of the adverb *mayhap* plus the adverbial suffix -*s* (OED s.v. -*s* suffix[1]) found in other formations such as *peradventures*, *in haps*, and *perhaps* (cf. Section 3.1 above).

(23) but we may **haps** be both dead and rotten before the lawyers would end it. (EEBO, 1604, Dekker, *The honest whore*)

---

8 This adverb is characterized in the OED as Scottish and English regional, obsolete, and rare.

4 On the adverbialization of *per*-adverbs and *may*-adverbs

Ramat and Ricca (1998: 201) identify four different processes in the formation of sentence adverbs in European languages: (i) derivation (e.g. *possibly*); (ii) conversion (e.g. adjective > adverb, as in German *angeblich* 'alleged, allegedly'); (iii) non-derivational processes giving rise to idiosyncratic adverbial formations, typically resulting from univerbation, i.e. "the union of two (or, rarely, more) syntagmatically adjacent word forms into one" (Lehmann 2020: 208); and, finally, (iv) borrowings from other languages. A look at the formations in Table 1 above reveals that all these four processes are relevant for English epistemic adverbs derived from the notion of happenstance or chance. However, as shown in Section 3, the most recurrent adverbial patterns and those which are most stable over time and survive into the present day correspond to *per*-adverbs and to *may*-adverbs, with *perhaps* and *maybe* as the most representative formations of each set. The development of these two patterns is discussed in the following sections.

4.1 *Per*-adverbs

From a structural point of view, the *per*-adverbs discussed in Section 3.1 correspond to Ramat and Ricca's (1998) idiosyncratic adverbial formations. However, some of the relevant adverbs also illustrate the process of borrowing: as seen above, the first adverbial expressions with a noun meaning 'chance' are precisely the French phrases *par aventure, par chance*, and *par cas*, which later served as the model for native formations with a noun meaning 'chance' combined with various prepositions (e.g. *by case, in haps*, etc.). Over time, these prepositional phrases came to be univerbated, thus becoming adverbs proper. This pathway is relatively straightforward, since prepositional phrases "need not change any syntactic/distributional property to become full-fledged adverbs" (Ramat and Ricca 1998: 203). Interestingly, the prepositional phrase-to-adverb pathway is a very common source for sentence adverbs in European languages (Ramat and Ricca 1998: 231–232). Consider, for instance, the Spanish epistemic adverb *acaso* 'perhaps' (literally 'at chance') mentioned in Section 2 above.

Illustrative examples of the univerbated forms *perauenture, bicas*, and *perhap* are given in (6), (9a), and (11c) above, while (24) below shows the univerbated form *uphap*:

(24) **Vphap** it semeth a bischop for to were swech on, þouȝ it semeth not..a pore
man. (c1450 J. Capgrave *Life St. Augustine* (1910) 46; OED s.v. *uphap* adv.)

After a period of coexistence, the adverbs originating in a prepositional phrase
were restricted to *perhaps, perchance, percase,* and *peradventure,* all of them featuring the preposition *per.* These *per*-adverbs entered in competition in the Early
Modern English period, as shown in Figure 1, based on data from EEBOCorp 1.0
(1470–1700).

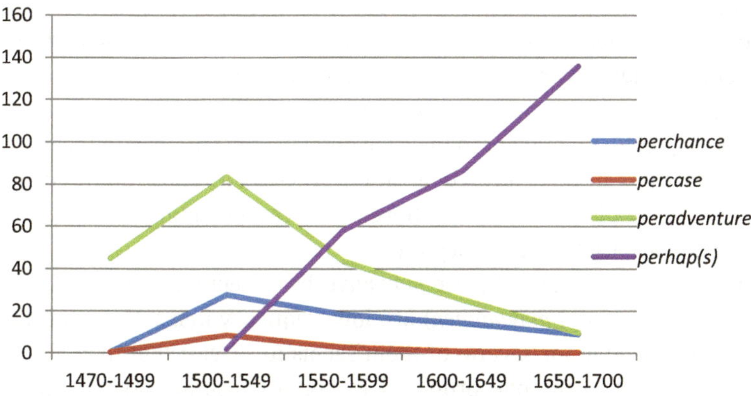

Figure 1: Competition of *per*-adverbs in EEBOCorp 1.0 (normalized frequencies pmw). Data from
López-Couso and Méndez-Naya (2017).

As shown here, the data from EEBOCorp 1.0 corroborate the information drawn
from historical dictionaries: *peradventure* and *perchance* are the earliest forms to
appear in the data (1470s) and remain the most frequent *per*-adverbs until the
first half of the 16th century, with *peradventure* taking the lead in terms of frequency. *Percase* is recorded slightly later (1480s) and remains a minor variant,
reaching only some currency in the first half of the 16th century, precisely when
the other two Romance adverbs experience their heyday. The native formation
perhaps is first attested in the EEBOCorp 1.0 material in the early 16th century,
but its frequency grows exponentially from the second half of the 17th century at
the expense of the three Romance formations, whose use becomes extremely restricted after the end of the 17th century.[9] The decreasing use over time of all *per*-
adverbs but *perhaps* is confirmed by the information provided in the OED on

---

9 See also Suzuki (2018a) for similar results based on the OED quotation database and the Corpus
of English Dialogues.

frequency in current use. Thus, *percase* is band 2 (<0.0099 pmw), *peradventure* and *perchance* are band 4 (0.01–0.99 pmw), whereas *perhaps* is band 7 (100–1000 pmw).

4.2 *May*-adverbs

Like the *per*-formations discussed in Section 4.1, *may*-adverbs also qualify as idiosyncratic formations in Ramat and Ricca's structural typology, more specifically as univerbations of former main clauses (1998: 231–232). In line with their Germanic counterparts *kanske*, *måske*, *törhända*, *kanhända*, *måhända*, and *misschien* (see Section 2), English *may*-adverbs derive from matrix clauses in complementation structures in what seems to be a common cross-linguistic grammaticalization pattern (Beijering 2010: 6). In what follows we describe the pathway followed by these *may*-formations in their adverbialization process and illustrate their development with examples taken from different sources, including the historical dictionaries and various historical corpora.

As seen in Section 3.1, most of these *may*-adverbs (except for *maybe* and, to a certain extent, *mayhap* and *mayhappen*) are low-frequency items. However, the scanty evidence available for several of them seems to suggest that they all followed a similar route to the one proposed in López-Couso and Méndez-Naya (2016) for *maybe*, the most prominent member of the set and the only one which has survived into Present-day standard English. The historical development of these *may*-adverbs can be summarized in five different stages.

Stage 1: The starting point in the emergence of these forms is to be found in examples such as those in (25).[10] In such instances, the happenstance predicates (*be, chance, fall, fortune, hap, happen, tide*) occur in an impersonal matrix clause followed by an extraposed complement clause. In the examples in (25) the complement clauses are introduced by the conjunction *that*, which was the dominant complementizer in English until the Late Middle English period (López-Couso 1996: 271). Examples can be found in which the matrix clause also features a *per*-formation, as *peradventure* in (25a), thus reinforcing the epistemic reading of the sequence.

---

10 López-Couso and Méndez-Naya (2016: 172–173) maintain that the pattern *it may be* + phrasal constituent, as in (i) below, may have played a subsidiary role in the development of *maybe*, especially in those cases in which the adverb is used in a modifying function (e.g. *maybe two years ago*).

(i) I see I cannot stir hence till next terme be over, **it may be a good while after**. (CEECS2, QBAS_1666_IBASEIREJR; quoted from López-Couso and Méndez-Naya (2016: 162)).

(25) a. Charmes for woundes or maladie of men or of beestes, if they taken any effect, **it may be** peraventure **that** God suffreth it, (PPCME2; CMCTPARS, 308.C1.819)

b. because **it might chance that** he should neuer see him againe. (EEBO, 1603, Knolles, *The general historie of the Turkes*)

c. For **it may fall** sumtyme þat þe trubylyere þat þou hase bene owtwarde with actyfe werkes, (PPCME2; CMROLLTR, 32.678)

d. **it may fortune** somtyme **that** thou shalt haue so many thynges to do? (EEBO, 1530, Fitzherbert, *A newe tracte or treatyse moost p[ro]fytable for all husba[n]de men*)

e. **It might hap that** for the good suppose and credite I haue with hym, he would doe much in a cause for me, (EEBO, 1586, Day, *The English secretorie*)

f. **hit may happen þat** þou schalt anoþyr tyme have þe wors, (PPCME2; CMMIRK, 116.3176)

Stage 2: The frequency of the complementizer *that* started to decline from the Late Middle English period onwards, counterbalanced by a dramatic rise of the complementizer zero, an increase which continued during Early Modern English (López-Couso 1996). The examples in (26) illustrate the matrices *it may be/fall/fortune/happen* followed by a zero complement clause.

(26) a. Syr, **it may be** Ø Thai tary to thay bryng. (HC, QM4_XX_MYST_TOWN)

b. **it maie fall**, Ø I wil eate no browesse sops This daie. (EEBO, 1543, Heywood, *A dialogue conteinyng the nomber in effect of all the prouerbes in the englishe tongue*)

c. **it may fortune** Ø the pryst would like wyce say / (EEBO, 1549, Hooper, *A declaration of the ten holy co[m]maundementes*)

d. **It may happen** Ø he shalle repente that they toke their lodgyng here. (EEBO, 1485, Malory, *La mort darthur*)

Stage 3: The increase in frequency of the zero complementizer triggered a process of reanalysis of the whole complementation structure, in accordance with Thompson and Mulac's (1991) 'matrix clause hypothesis'. Thus, the original matrix clause acquired some syntactic freedom which enabled it to occur parenthetically, while the former complement clause became the primary focus of the message (Boye and Harder 2007: 581–585) and acquired main-clause status. The examples in (27a-b) illustrate clear cases of the parenthetical use. Note that *it may be* and *it may chance* appear in medial position and are also marked typographically by means of brackets. As seen here, parenthetical clauses of this kind no longer have a complete syntactic structure, since they lack the arguments realized by the subordinate clauses in their complementation counterparts (examples in (25) and (26) above).

(27) a. If French-men doe amisse therein, we neglect (**it may be**) manye other good customes w=c= [^SUPERSCRIPT LETTER UNCLEAR^] they do obserue. (CED, 1605, D2HFERON)

   b. For this cause hathe he deliuered new rules to the world, new trades of lyuyng, ordinaunces, and commaundementes, suche (**it may chance**) as he dremed, when he was in some frensy, vtterlye pugnant, (EEBO, 1549, Ochino, *A tragoedie or dialoge of the vniuste vsurped primacie of the Bishop of Rome*)

Stage 4: In a more advanced stage, some instances of *it may V* are further downgraded to approach adverbial status. This shift is evinced in the gradual disappearance of the dummy subject *it* (see Visser 1963–1973, 1: 20),[11] as shown in the 16th century examples in (28). This is certainly relevant, since in Early Modern English the occurrence of the anticipatory pronoun became mandatory in cases of extraposition (Rissanen 1999: 249–252). Moreover, in contrast with the complementation structures illustrated in (25) and (26), the verb *may* is restricted to its present form (cf. the past form *might* in (25b) and (25e) above) and no intervening elements between the modal and the happenstance verb are allowed.

(28) a. **May be** he tels you true. (PPCEME, SHAKESP-E2-P2, 51.C2.330) (1599, printed 1600)

   b. **May chaunce** some man wyll thinke and say, That great pittie it was, That suche a treatise fas thys is, Shoulde thus so rudely passe. (EEBO, 1555, Huggarde, *A mirrour of loue*)

   c. **may fortune** he wyll often tymes be soner werye than he can fynde hym. (EEBO, 1532, Xenophon, *Xenophons treatise of housholde*)

   d. **may hap** ye stumble, (EEBO, 1525, Rastell, *A new co[m]modye in englysh*)

   e. **May tyde** he will oure giftis take. (a1500 (a1460) *Towneley Plays* (1897–1973) 54; OED s.v. *may* v.[1] P.2)

---

11 In their discussion of the historical development of Swedish *kanske* from *det kan ske att* 'it can happen that', Beijering and Norde (2019) prove that the loss of the formal subject *det* preceded the loss of the complementizer in the adverbialization process of the Swedish form: while *det* can be omitted as early as the Old Swedish period (ca. 1225–1525), the loss of the complementizer *att* was rare until Early Modern Swedish (ca. 1526–1732). As discussed above, the sequence of events in the case of the English formations seems to be slightly different.

Stage 5: Finally, the adverbialization process of *may*-formations can be said to have reached completion in cases such as those under (29).[12] Here the *may*-forms occur in unequivocal adverbial positions: clause-medially (29a, b, f, g) and clause-finally (29e). They can have scope over the whole clause (as in (29a, d, e, f, g) below) or can also modify noun phrases (29b), non-finite clauses, and adverbial clauses (29c). Moreover, the modal and the happenstance verb may appear uni-verbated, either hyphenated (29f, g) or spelt solid (29c, d).

(29) a. This, **may be**, was the reason some imagin'd Hell there. (1661 J. Glanvill *Vanity of Dogmatizing* 175; OED s.v. *maybe* adv., n., and adj. A.1.a)

 b. that euery Paysant or Husbandman shall sow no more then he can (**may chance**) ten pounds, another sixe, another more, or lesse, according to the number of people hee sets aworke, (EEBO, 1618, Sala, *Opiologia*)

 c. **machance** being corrupted by the kinde of Musick, as the olde complaint was: **machance** bycause it is vsed but for pleasure and delite onely, (EEBO, 1581, Mulcaster, *Positions*)

 d. **Mafortune** as then ye tyme did not suffer so inexplycable a misterie to be put in wryting to all mens knowledge. (1548 N. Udall tr. Erasmus *Paraphr. John* 7; OED s.v. *may* v.^{1} P.2)

 e. *Bon.* Going to London, **may hap**? *Arch.* No. (PPCEME, 1707, FARQUHAR-E3-H, 4.151)

 f. it will **may-hap** seem more kindly further on, (EEBO, 1674, Fairfax, *A treatise of the bulk and selvedge of the world*)

 g. the rule that **may-tide** lords of Mis-rule finde, such lord, such Lawes let be to rome assign'd: (EEBO, 1624, *Babels balm: or The honey . . .*)

As evinced by these examples, adverbialization of *may*-forms was already under way in the Early Modern English period. However, evidence suggests that not all *may*-adverbs developed simultaneously. The adverbialization process seems to have taken place at a very early stage in the case of *mayfall*, for which indisputable adverbial uses (without univerbation) are already attested in the 14th century. A couple of examples from the OED are given in (30a-b), which show *may fall* as a

---

12 Interestingly, in Kaltenböck et al.'s (2011) terms (see also Heine 2013), the expressions at issue start in canonical 'Sentence Grammar', as matrix clauses in complementation structures (stage 1), move into 'Thetical Grammar' (concerned with discourse organization), when they become par-entheticals (stage 3), and then move back to 'Sentence Grammar', once they become adverbs (stage 5). The development 'Sentence Grammar' > 'Thetical Grammar' > 'Sentence Grammar' un-dergone by these expressions underscores the fluidity between these two systems. We are grate-ful to Hendrik de Smet for this observation.

post-modifier of the numeral *tuenti* and in clause-medial position (intervening between the subject and the verb), respectively.

(30) a. If þou þar findes..Fifty or fourte o þi lele men – Tuenti **mai falle**, or tuis fiue – Ne sal þai alle haue þar for liue? (a1400 (a1325) *Cursor Mundi* (Vesp.) 2759 (MED); OED s.v. *may* v.[1] P2)

    b. Thai that war vithin, **ma fall**, slepit all. (1487 (1380) J. Barbour *Bruce* (St. John's Cambr.) ix. 376; OED s.v. *may* v.[1] P2)

Figure 2 summarizes the adverbialization process of *may*-adverbs: an originally impersonal matrix in a complementation structure of the type *it* + *may* + happenstance verb + complement clause becomes over time an adverb, via an intermediate parenthetical stage. This intermediate stage, where the sequence lacks its complete syntactic structure, seems to be key in the development of *may*-adverbs.[13]

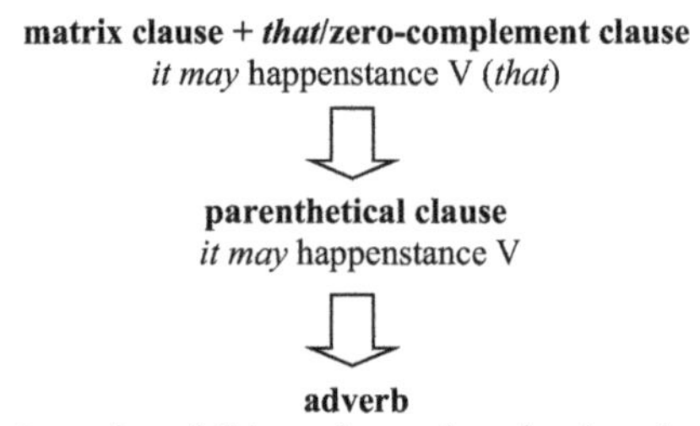

Figure 2: The adverbialization of *may*-forms.

5 Closing remarks: *Per*-adverbs and *may*-adverbs as cases of grammaticalization

The foregoing discussion has shown that a wide range of formations deriving from the notion of happenstance were used to express weak probability ('perhaps') in the Late Middle and Early Modern English periods. As shown by Ramat and Ricca (1998), the meaning of weak probability is central in European languages, which typically possess dedicated lexical items to convey such a notion.

---

13 A similar developmental pathway has been suggested by Lorenz (2019) for the incipient grammaticalization of *could be* towards an adverbial in contemporary English.

Moreover, this area of modality is prone to processes of competition, loss, and renewal across languages (Ramat and Ricca 1998: 235), as evinced by the history of the English epistemic happenstance adverbs discussed in this article. These adverbs have been shown to follow two major developmental pathways: on the one hand, from prepositional phrase to adverb (*per*-adverbs; Sections 3.1 and 4.1) and, on the other, from (impersonal) matrix clause to adverb (*may*-adverbs; Sections 3.2 and 4.2).

Processes of lexical competition commonly result in the establishment of one of the various competing forms at the expense of its rivals (Samuels 1972: 65). In the case of our English epistemic happenstance adverbs, two forms eventually triumphed, one per pathway: *perhaps* and *maybe*. Interestingly, these two adverbs have started to compete among themselves from the 20th century, with *perhaps* leading in frequency (Suzuki 2014, 2018b), though *maybe* is rapidly gaining ground across time, dialect, and register (López-Couso and Méndez-Naya 2021b).

The two pathways identified in the development of epistemic happenstance adverbs are already attested in the Late Middle English period. However, the prepositional phrase-to-adverb pathway is the first one to appear in the historical record, as proved by the occurrence around 1300 of the formation *peradventure*. On the other hand, the earliest OED attestations of *may*-adverbs are traced back to the early 15th century (*maybe, may-fall*). Moreover, the phrase-to-adverb pathway is found in French borrowings (e.g. *peradventure*) as well as in native formations modelled on French (e.g. *perhaps*). By contrast, the clause-to-adverb pathway has Germanic roots (cf. the Scandinavian and Dutch adverbs mentioned in Section 2) and is first attested with native verbs (e.g. *fall, hap, tide*) before it occurs with French borrowings (e.g. *chance, fortune*). A further difference between the two pathways concerns formal variability: while the phrase-to-verb path allows for different prepositions in combination with the happenstance etymon, the adverbs resulting from the clause-to-adverb pathway invariably show the modal *may* combined with a happenstance verb.

Despite these differences, however, *per*-adverbs and *may*-adverbs also share some features which characterize their historical development as an instance of grammaticalization. To begin with, from the point of view of semantics, the original lexical meaning 'chance' or 'happen (by chance)' evolves into a more abstract meaning, that of epistemic possibility. As we have seen in Section 2, this development, which involves semantic bleaching, is attested across languages which are not necessarily genetically related with English. Cross-linguistic generality is precisely one of the features of grammaticalization as defined by Brinton and Traugott (2005: 28).

Alongside semantic bleaching, the development of epistemic happenstance adverbs illustrates a number of structural traits which also point at grammaticalization.

The two pathways involve decategorialization (Hopper 1991: 22): a prepositional phrase becomes an adverb (with the same syntactic and distributional properties) and an originally complement-taking-predicate clause is downgraded to a parenthetical clause, which lacks a complete syntactic structure. This parenthetical clause then moves even further in this categorial shift, with the loss of the anticipatory subject *it*, eventually becoming an adverb. In this respect, *may*-adverbs have followed in their evolution similar steps to other epistemic adverbial expressions, such as *looks like* (López-Couso and Méndez-Naya 2014), as in (31a), which derives from the impersonal matrix clause *it looks like* in a complementation structure (31b).

(31) a. "They're buildin' a bar trap, **looks like**. They'll be sartin to ketch one too, . . . (COHA, 1878, FIC, *BoyTrapper*)

  b. **It looks like** we were going to lose some of our own territory, don't it? (COHA, 1867, FIC, *WearingGrayBeing*)

In the case of *may*-formations, the co-existence of the adverbial forms (stage 5) with examples corresponding to the other four stages in the developmental pathway points at another concomitant feature of grammaticalization, namely layering (Hopper 1991: 22).

In their development both *per-* and *may*-adverbs also lose morphological variability: in the case of the former pattern, the range of prepositions available in the prepositional phrase is drastically reduced over time to the preposition *per*, thus illustrating Hopper's (1991: 22) parameter of specialization. *May*-formations, in turn, show a restriction to the present tense form of the modal verb.

Moreover, both *per*-adverbs and *may*-adverbs show fusion (Brinton and Traugott 2005: 27) and eventually univerbation, not allowing any intervening material between their constituent parts. Such insertions, however, are possible in the case of the original prepositional phrases and clauses, as seen in examples (32a-b). In (32a) a pronoun intervenes between the preposition *by* and the noun *hap*, which is used here in its happenstance sense. In turn, (32b), an example of a complementation structure, features the adverb *well* between *may* and *be*.

(32) a. ʒif sche [the goshawk] failleþ **by any happe** of þe pray þat sche resiþ to þat day, vnneþe sche comeþ to þe lordes honde. (a1398) * Trv. Barth. (Add 27944) 143a/b; MED s.v. *hap* n. 2a)

  b. **It may well be**, I have received from them that naturall dispathie vnto Phisicke. (1603 J. Florio tr. Montaigne *Ess.* ii. xxxvii. 438; OED s.v. *dyspathy* n.)

Finally, from the semantico-pragmatic point of view, the epistemic happenstance adverbs under discussion acquire over time subjective and intersubjective functions (López-Couso 2010). The adverbs are used to express the speaker's stance, as hedges to tone down the speaker's commitment to the truth of the proposition. Moreover, they can also be used to pay attention to the addressee's needs, thus serving an intersubjective function.[14] For example, they can be found in confirmation tags, as in our earlier example (29e), with *may hap*, or in (33) below, with *perhaps*. They can also be used in responses, as in (34), which features the adverb *maybe* forming an utterance on its own, serving as a response.

(33) *bertr.* thought of the queen, **perhaps**? [.] [.] *torr.* why, if it were, Heav'n may be thought on, though too high to climbe: (EEBO, 1681, *The Spanish Fryer*)

(34) Bond smiled. 'How many zeros have they got on the Roulette?' 'Two, I guess.' 'There's your answer. At least we play against the right percentage in Europe. You can have your neon lighting. The other zero keeps it alight.' '**Maybe**. But the craps only pay just over one per cent to the House. And that's our national game.' (ARCHER, 1956_flem. f8b)

All in all, the morphosyntactic and semantico-pragmatic features discussed in the preceding paragraphs show that the changes undergone by epistemic happenstance adverbs belonging to the phrase-to-adverb and the clause-to-adverb pathways provide a clear example of movement down the cline of grammaticality.

References

AND = *Anglo-Norman Dictionary*. https://anglo-norman.net/ (accessed 15 July 2021).
ARCHER-3.2 = *A Representative Corpus of Historical English Registers* version 3.2.
1990–1993/2002/2007/2010/2013/2016. Originally compiled under the supervision of Douglas Biber and Edward Finegan at Northern Arizona University and University of Southern California; modified and expanded by subsequent members of a consortium of universities. Current member universities are Bamberg, Freiburg, Heidelberg, Helsinki, Lancaster, Leicester, Manchester, Michigan, Northern Arizona, Santiago de Compostela, Southern California, Trier, Uppsala, and Zurich.

---

14 On the subjective and intersubjective functions of *perhaps*, see also Suzuki (2018a, 2018b). In addition, Rozumko (2022) discusses what she calls the textual functions of *perhaps* in Present-day English (e.g. reformulation, exemplification, etc.), i.e. the text organization function associated with theticals by Kaltenböck, Heine, and Kuteva (2011).

Beijering, Karin. 2010. The grammaticalization of Mainland Scandinavian MAYBE. *Bergen Language and Linguistics Studies* 1 (1). https://doi.org/10.15845/bells.v1i1.39 (accessed 24 June 2021).

Beijering, Karin & Muriel Norde. 2019. Adverbial semi-insubordination constructions in Swedish: Synchrony and diachrony. In Karin Beijering, Gunther Kaltenböck & María Sol Sansiñena (eds.), *Insubordination*, 79–106. Berlin: De Gruyter Mouton.

Biber, Douglas, Stig Johansson, Geoffrey Leech, Susan Conrad & Edward Finegan. 1999. *Longman Grammar of Spoken and Written English*. Harlow: Pearson Education.

BNC = Davies, Mark. 2004. *British National Corpus* (from Oxford University Press). https://www.english-corpora.org/bnc/

Boye, Kasper & Peter Harder. 2007. Complement-taking predicates: Usage and linguistic structure. *Studies in Language* 31 (3). 569–606. https://doi.org/10.1075/sl.31.3.03boy (accessed 28 June 2021)

Brinton, Laurel J. & Elizabeth C. Traugott. 2005. *Lexicalization and Language Change*. Cambridge: Cambridge University Press.

Bybee, Joan, Revere Perkins & William Pagliuca. 1994. *The Evolution of Grammar: Tense, Aspect, and Modality in the Languages of the World*. Chicago: University of Chicago Press.

CED = *A Corpus of English Dialogues 1560–1760*. 2006. Compiled under the supervision of Merja Kytö (Uppsala University) & Jonathan Culpeper (Lancaster University).

CEECS = *Corpus of English Correspondence Sampler*. 1998. Compiled by Terttu Nevalainen, Helena Raumolin-Brunberg, Jukka Keränen, Minna Nevala, Arja Nurmi & Minna Palander-Collin at the Department of Modern Languages, University of Helsinki.

COCA = Davies, Mark. 2008– *The Corpus of Contemporary American English (COCA)*. https://www.english-corpora.org/coca/ (accessed 15 February 2022).

COHA = Davies, Mark. 2010– *The Corpus of Historical American English (COHA): 400 million words, 1810–2009*. https://www.english-corpora.org/coha/ (accessed 15 February 2022).

DMF = *Dictionnaire du Moyen Français (1330–1500)*. http://zeus.atilf.fr/dmf/ (accessed 17 July 2021).

DRAE = REAL ACADEMIA ESPAÑOLA: *Diccionario de la Lengua Española*, 23rd edn. [online version 23.4] https://dle.rae.es/ (accessed 20 July 2021).

DRAG = González González, Manuel (dir.): *Dicionario da Real Academia Galega*. A Coruña: Real Academia Galega. https://academia.gal/dicionario (accessed 20 July 2021).

EEBO = Davies, Mark. 2017. *Early English Books Online Corpus*. https://www.english-corpora.org/eebo/ (accessed 12 November 2021).

EEBOCorp 1.0 = *Early English Books Online Corpus 1.0*. 2013. Compiled by Peter Petré. Leuven: KU Leuven.

HC = *The Helsinki Corpus of English Texts*. 1991. Department of Modern Languages, University of Helsinki. Compiled by Matti Rissanen (Project leader), Merja Kytö (Project secretary), Leena Kahlas-Tarkka, Matti Kilpiö (Old English), Saara Nevanlinna, Irma Taavitsainen (Middle English), Terttu Nevalainen, Helena Raumolin-Brunberg (Early Modern English).

Heine, Bernd. 2013. On discourse markers: Grammaticalization, pragmaticalization, or something else? *Linguistics* 51 (6). 1205–1247.

Hopper, Paul J. 1991. On some principles of grammaticization. In Elizabeth C. Traugott & Bernd Heine (eds.), *Approaches to Grammaticalization*, vol. I, 17–35. Amsterdam: John Benjamins.

HTOED = *Historical Thesaurus of the Oxford English Dictionary*. https://www.oed.com/public/htoed/loginpage (accessed 20 July 2021).

Kaltenböck, Gunther, Bernd Heine & Tania Kuteva. 2011. On thetical grammar. *Studies in Language* 35 (4). 848–893. https://doi.org/10.1075/sl.35.4.03kal (accessed 3 March 2021).

Kuteva, Tania, Bernd Heine, Bo Hong, Haiping Long, Heiko Narrog & Seongha Rhee. 2019. *World Lexicon of Grammaticalization*. 2nd. edn. Cambridge: Cambridge University Press.

Lehmann, Christian. 2020. Univerbation. *Folia Linguistica Historica* 41. 205–252. https://doi.org/10.1515/flih-2020-0007 (accessed 20 July 2021).

López-Couso, María José. 1996. *That*/zero variation in Restoration English. In Derek Britton (ed.), *English Historical Linguistics 1994*, 271–286. Amsterdam: John Benjamins.

López-Couso, María José. 2010. Subjectification and intersubjectification. In Andreas H. Jucker & Irma Taavitsainen (eds.), *Historical Pragmatics*, 127–163. Berlin & New York: De Gruyter Mouton.

López-Couso, María José & Belén Méndez-Naya. 2014. From clause to pragmatic marker: A study of the development of *like* parentheticals in American English. *Journal of Historical Pragmatics* 15 (1). 66–91. https://doi.org/10.1075/jhp.15.1 (accessed 12 January 2021).

López-Couso, María José & Belén Méndez-Naya. 2016. From clause to adverb: On the history of *maybe*. In Gunther Kaltenböck, Evelien Keizer & Arne Lohmann (eds.), *Outside the Clause*, 157–176. Amsterdam: John Benjamins.

López-Couso, María José & Belén Méndez-Naya. 2017. From happenstance to epistemic possibility: Corpus evidence for the adverbialization of happenstance expressions. Paper presented at the ICAME 38 Conference, Charles University in Prague, 24–28 May 2017.

López-Couso, María José & Belén Méndez-Naya. 2021a. From complementizing to modifying status: On the grammaticalization of the complement-taking-predicate-clauses *chances are* and *odds are*. *Language Sciences* 88. https://doi.org/10.1016/j.langsci.2021.101422 (accessed 11 January 2022).

López-Couso, María José & Belén Méndez-Naya. 2021b. Converging and/or differential patterns of change across the Atlantic? A look into epistemic adverbs of doubt in the recent history of British and American English. Paper presented at the ICEHL 21 Conference, University of Leiden, 7–11 June 2021.

Lorenz, David. 2019. Could be it's grammaticalization. Paper presented at the 8th Biennial International Conference on the Linguistics of Contemporary English (BICLCE 8), University of Bamberg, 26-28 September 2019.

MED = *Middle English Dictionary*. https://quod.lib.umich.edu/m/middle-english-dictionary/dictionary (accessed 20 July 2021).

Merriam-Webster Dictionary. https://www.merriam-webster.com/ (accessed 21 July 2021).

Míguez Rego, Vítor. 2021. *Aproximación á Modalidade Epistémica en Galego: O Dominio Adverbial*. Santiago de Compostela: University of Santiago de Compostela PhD dissertation.

Molencki, Rafal. 2021. The grammaticalization of the epistemic adverb *perhaps* in Late Middle and Early Modern English. *Studia Anglica Posnaniensia* 56. 411–424. https://doi.org/10.2478/stap-2021-0005 (accessed 3 March 2022).

Monier-Williams, Monier. 1899. *Sanskrit-English Dictionary*. https://www.sanskrit-lexicon.uni-koeln.de/scans/MWScan/2020/web/webtc/indexcaller.php (accessed 5 May 2021).

Nevalainen, Terttu. 1999. Early Modern English lexis and semantics. In Roger Lass (ed.), *The Cambridge History of the English Language*, vol. III, 1476-1776, 332–458. Cambridge: Cambridge University Press.

OED = *The Oxford English Dictionary*. http://www.oed.com (accessed 20 July 2021).

OLD = *Oxford Latin Dictionary*. 1982. Edited by P.G.W. Glare. Oxford: Clarendon Press.

Pinto de Lima, José. 2008. Ongoing lexicalization and grammaticalization: A case from European Portuguese. In Maria Clotilde Almeida, Bernd Sieberg & Ana Maria Bernardo (eds.), *Questions on Language Change*, 49–67. Lisboa: Colibri.

PPCEME = Kroch, Anthony, Beatrice Santorini & Lauren Delfs. 2004. *The Penn-Helsinki Parsed Corpus of Early Modern English (PPCEME)*. Department of Linguistics, University of Pennsylvania. CD-ROM, first edition, release 3.

PPCME2 = Kroch, Anthony & Ann Taylor. 2000. *The Penn-Helsinki Parsed Corpus of Middle English (PPCME2)*. Department of Linguistics, University of Pennsylvania. CD-ROM, second edition, release 4.

Ramat, Paolo & Davide Ricca. 1998. Sentence adverbs in the languages of Europe. In Johan van der Auwera & Dónall P. Ó Baoill (eds.), *Adverbial Constructions in the Languages of Europe*, 187–273. Berlin: De Gruyter Mouton.

Rissanen, Matti. 1999. Syntax. In Roger Lass (ed.), *The Cambridge History of the English Language, vol. III, 1476–1776*, 187–331. Cambridge: Cambridge University Press.

Rodríguez Espiñeira, María José. 2019. La expresión epistémica *si cuadra* en español de Galicia. *Estudos de Lingüística Galega* 11. 197–231. https://doi.org/10.15304/elg.11.5343 (accessed 10 May 2021).

Rozumko, Agata. 2022. Textual functions of low confidence adverbs: The case of *perhaps. Lingua* 268. https://doi.org/10.1016/j.lingua.2021.103191 (accessed 3 March 2022).

Samuels, Michael L. 1972. *Linguistic Evolution with Special Reference to English*. London & New York: Cambridge University Press.

Suzuki, Daisuke. 2014. A historical study of English modal adverbs: Evidence from a combination of diachronic corpora. *Token: A Journal of English Linguistics* 3. 187–210.

Suzuki, Daisuke. 2018a. The semantics and pragmatics of modal adverbs: Grammaticalization and (inter)subjectification of *perhaps. Lingua* 205. 40–53. https://doi.org/10.1016/j.lingua.2017.12.014 (accessed 3 March 2021).

Suzuki, Daisuke. 2018b. Variation between modal adverbs in British English. The cases of *maybe* and *perhaps. Functions of Language* 25 (3). 392–412. https://doi.org/10.1075/fol.16009.suz (accessed 3 March 2021).

Thompson, Sandra & Anthony Mulac. 1991. A quantitative perspective on the grammaticization of epistemic parentheticals in English. In Elizabeth C. Traugott & Bernd Heine (eds.), *Approaches to Grammaticalization, vol. II*, 313–339. Amsterdam: John Benjamins.

Traugott, Elizabeth C. 1989. On the rise of epistemic meanings in English: An example of subjectification in semantic change. *Language* 65. 31–55. http://dx.doi.org/10.2307/414841 (accessed 5 May 2021).

Visser, Frederikus Theodorus. 1963–1973. *An Historical Syntax of the English Language*. Leiden: Brill.

Dirk Geeraerts

6 The structured nature of prepositional meaning

Abstract: Drawing on an analysis of the Dutch preposition *over*, the paper discusses an alternative to the popular description of prepositional meaning as a radial network of image schemas and image schema transformations. As a nuance w.r.t. the radial network model, the paper highlights the multidimensional nature of semasiological structure. As a nuance w.r.t. the emphasis on image schemas, the paper shows how any region in the semasiological range of a multidimensionally structured word may be the source for further meaning extensions.

Keywords: image schema, lexical meaning, 'over', preposition, radial network

1 A dedication

The semantics of prepositions constituted Hubert Cuyckens' first area of scholarly activity. It is the topic of his dissertation of 1991 and a number of publications growing out of that thesis (including Cuyckens 1994, 1995, 2002, Cuyckens & Radden 2002), all of which contributed to putting Cognitive Semantics on the map as an original and inspirational framework for the description of word meaning. Hubert has long shifted his attention to other matters – not least the study of grammaticalization that forms the focus of the present volume – but I feel that in a tribute to his career, it is fitting and necessary to also look back at his original field of activity. In this paper, then, I will present an alternative to the description of prepositional meaning as a radial network of image schemas, a model that also informed Hubert's approach in his PhD. Two aspects of the model will be addressed: the radial structure of the network, and the mechanism of semantic extension. With regard to the first aspect, as a refinement of the radial network model, the paper highlights the multidimensional nature of semasiological structure. With regard to the second aspect, as an alternative to the emphasis on image schemas as the individual sources of semantic extension, the paper shows how any region in the semasiological range of a multidimensionally structured word may be the source of further meaning extensions. In line with its retrospective topic, the paper employs a traditional methodology of conceptual analysis, without quantitative corpus data, and with a preference for visualization rather than formalization.

https://doi.org/10.1515/9783110753059-006

2 Prepositions, radial networks and image schemas

The emergence of innovative models of semasiological structure in the context of Cognitive Semantics owes a lot to the analysis of prepositional meaning. Specifically, the pioneering prepositional studies of Lindner (1981) and Brugman (1981, 1988) introduced two features that would prove very productive in the following years. First, they showed that the semantic range of application of prepositions can be insightfully described as a network of applications woven around a central meaning. Simultaneously to the work of Lindner and Brugman, such a prototype-theoretical model of the organization of linguistic categories, which had originally been developed in psycholinguistic research by Rosch (a.o. 1978), was introduced into diachronic lexicological research by Geeraerts (1983). Second, the prepositional studies of Lindner and Brugman illustrate the idea of an image schema, i.e. a sensory (predominantly spatial) pattern that not only captures the literal meanings of the prepositions, but that may also underlie some of their figurative, metaphorical extensions. Both of these features[1] were developed enthusiastically in the context of Cognitive Semantics: see Geeraerts (2010) for a general overview. Specifically, for image schemas as embodied experiential gestalts, see Johnson (1987) and Hampe (2005), and for prototypicality, see Taylor (1989). For the popularity of spatial preposition research in the first decades of Cognitive Semantics, see a.o. Radden (1981), Herskovits (1986), Vandeloise (1986), Dewell (1994, 1996), Bellavia (1996), Meex (2002), Evans & Tyler (2001), Tyler & Evans (2004), Deane (2005) – and, of course, Cuyckens (1991).

In spite of the inspirational force of papers like Lindner's and Brugman's, some features of their approach need to be nuanced. In particular, the relationship between the various applications of the prepositions is represented by a so-called radial network (a model of description popularized by Lakoff 1987) in which the various readings are represented by separate points that are interconnected with each other and that are specifically also connected to the central, prototypical reading of the word. As I intend to illustrate in the following pages, such a representation paints a more atomistic picture of the semantic structure of prepositions than

---

1 The two features are not necessarily linked. The radial network model is a general model of the relationship between the various senses of an expression, with each node in the network representing a specific sense, but those senses are not necessarily associated with image schemas as is the case in many analyses of prepositional meanings. In the general context of Cognitive Linguistics, the link with image schemas illustrates an important theoretical point, i.e. that linguistic meaning may rely on extralinguistic experience like the sensorimotoric experience of space.

is descriptively adequate, i.e. there is very often more interconnectedness than the radial set representation with its relatively autonomous, clearly distinguishable nodes suggests. In this paper, then, I will focus on two features of the semantic structure of prepositions that illustrate the high degree of interwovenness and internal cohesion of the prepositional categories.

The first point, corresponding with the prototype-theoretical dimension of the description, is the same that I made earlier (1992, reprinted in Geeraerts 2006) in an analysis of the spatial readings of the Dutch preposition *over*: semantically, words like *over* have a multidimensional structure that is not optimally represented by radial networks.[2]

The second point, corresponding with the image-schematic dimension of the description, focuses on the way further readings – specifically, figurative ones – are derived from the core spatial applications. Elaborating on the analysis of *over*, and linking up with a theoretical point made in Geeraerts (1997), I will show that meaning extensions do not necessarily stem directly from the individual image schemata that typically feature as nodes in a prepositional radial network, but may basically take their starting-point in any subarea of the multidimensional structure of the core.

Overall, the purpose of the paper is not to present a full-fledged analysis of the uses of Dutch *over*. That would require, among other things, a confrontation with corpus data, which is beyond the scope of the present text. Rather, the aim is theoretical with a methodological corollary: to emphasize the multidimensional, non-atomistic nature of semasiological structure, and to warn against an exclusive focus on individual image schemata.[3] In the context of cognitive linguistic approaches to prepositional meaning, the paper offers an alternative not just for the original radial network model but also for later research such as the 'principled polysemy' approach of Evans & Tyler (2001), Tyler & Evans (2004). Like the latter, the present paper moves from a model in which the various readings of the prepositions are listed as separate senses in the network towards one in which the information provided by context and co-text contributes structurally to the polysemy of the preposition. By contrast with the 'principled polysemy' approach, however, the meaning of *over* will not be reduced to a single primary sense that is modulated into contextualized readings, but it will be described as a

---

2 For this part of the paper, I will reuse some of the materials from the 1992 publication, but add a graphical representation that brings out the multidimensionality more clearly.

3 Terminologically speaking, I will not make a distinction between *image schema* and *image schema complex*. From an analytic point of view, an image schema like for instance the one associated with [b] in Figure 1 is itself a complex entity, composed by a number of more basic image schemata like, path, motion or contact. Accordingly, when I talk about 'individual image schemata' it is these complexes that are meant.

multidimensional semantic architecture in which the various dimensions interact to produce spatial and non-spatial modulations of meaning.

3 Beyond radial networks: The multidimensional nature of semasiological structure

The multidimensional type of representation that is particularly appropriate for prepositional meaning may be introduced abstractly. At the core of a prototype-theoretical view of semasiological structure is the idea that core meanings or applications may be employed flexibly by modulating the feature set representing the central case. Thus, if ABCD is the central application, characterized by a high frequency, less frequent cases could be BCDE, ACDE, ABDE, ABC, ABD etcetera. The family resemblance structure emerging from these modulations may be represented graphically in the form of a radial network with ABCD as the central node. In many cases, however, features that play a role in the family resemblance structure are themselves interconnected. In the study of clothing terms presented in Geeraerts, Grondelaers & Bakema (1994), the central exemplar of the concept *legging* is a pair of trousers for women, tightfitting, as long as the ankles, made of elastic material, and worn as a final layer of clothing. Less frequent examples will then be, for instance, less tightfitting or slightly shorter: the variation is structured along dimensions like 'length' and 'width'. In the abstract example, this means that rather than for instance BCDE, a derived case would be A'BCD where A' is a shifted value on the same dimension as A. In the case of prepositions such a dimensional structure is particularly relevant because prepositions have relational meaning: they specify a relationship (very often spatial, and very often of an image-schematic kind) between what is commonly referred to in Cognitive Semantics as a *trajector* and a *landmark* (Langacker 1987), with the trajector as the entity that is in focus and that is being situated, and the landmark as the reference point with regard to which it is situated. The activity or state referred to by the verb that characterizes the relationship between trajector and landmark may constitute an additional dimension in the structure. If the core reading of the preposition is characterized by a specific spatial relationship between a certain type of trajector, a certain type of landmark, and a certain type of verbal meaning, other usages may take the form of modulations on these dimensions: not just different spatial relations but also, for instance, different kinds of landmark. These shifts on the constitutive dimensions interact and as such define a multidimensionally structured semantic space.

The Dutch preposition *over* as analyzed in Geeraerts (1992) provides an example of such a multidimensional structure. Taking its inspiration from the radial network analysis suggested by Cuyckens (1991), reprinted here as Figure 1, the 1992 paper reduces the number of image schemas to three, as represented in Figure 2, and describes the other spatial usages of the preposition through modulations of the kind just mentioned. The description takes its starting-point in the observation that (1) can be understood in three different ways.

(1)   Emmelien fietst over de lijn
        "Emmelien bicycles over the line"

First, Emmelien may be riding *across* the line (as when she moves from one lane to the other). Second, she may be riding *on and along* the line, staying roughly within its boundaries as she follows it. (She might be doing this as a game, or as a kind of test to enable the police to ascertain whether she is riding under the influence of alcohol). And third, Emmelien may be riding *at the other side* of the line (seen through the eyes of an implicit observer). For instance, imagine a group of children riding their bikes at a schoolyard, but being forbidden to cross a particular line. Sentence (1) could then be used to point out that Emmelien ignores the prohibition. The three situations that fall within the scope of (1) may then be associated with the image schemas in Figure 2. In terms of definitions, the meaning of the three readings can be described by specifying the spatial characteristics of the activity referred to by the verb: it is an activity that extends from one point to another (either within the spatial area defined by the prepositional object x, or by crossing that area), or an activity that is situated in a region construed as being to the other side of x. This yields the following definitions:

[a] extending from a point or region at one side of x to a point or region at the other side of x, while crossing x
[b] extending from one point or region within the space defined by x, to another point or region within that space (without going outside of it)
[c] situated at the other side of x, relative to the position of an observer.

Now, it is crucial for the semantic structure of *over* that the three spatial relations as just defined can also occur in other syntagmatic contexts than the one represented by (1). First, the prepositional phrase can indicate the spatial extension of a fictive rather than a real motion. In (2), for instance, there is no real motion of the line; still, the line extends from a point on one side of the prepositional object x to a point to the other side of that object (which motivates the use of *over*), and further, this extension is construed, through the use of *lopen*, as a process of fictive motion. Second, if *over* can be used to express stative spatial relations, it can also be combined with

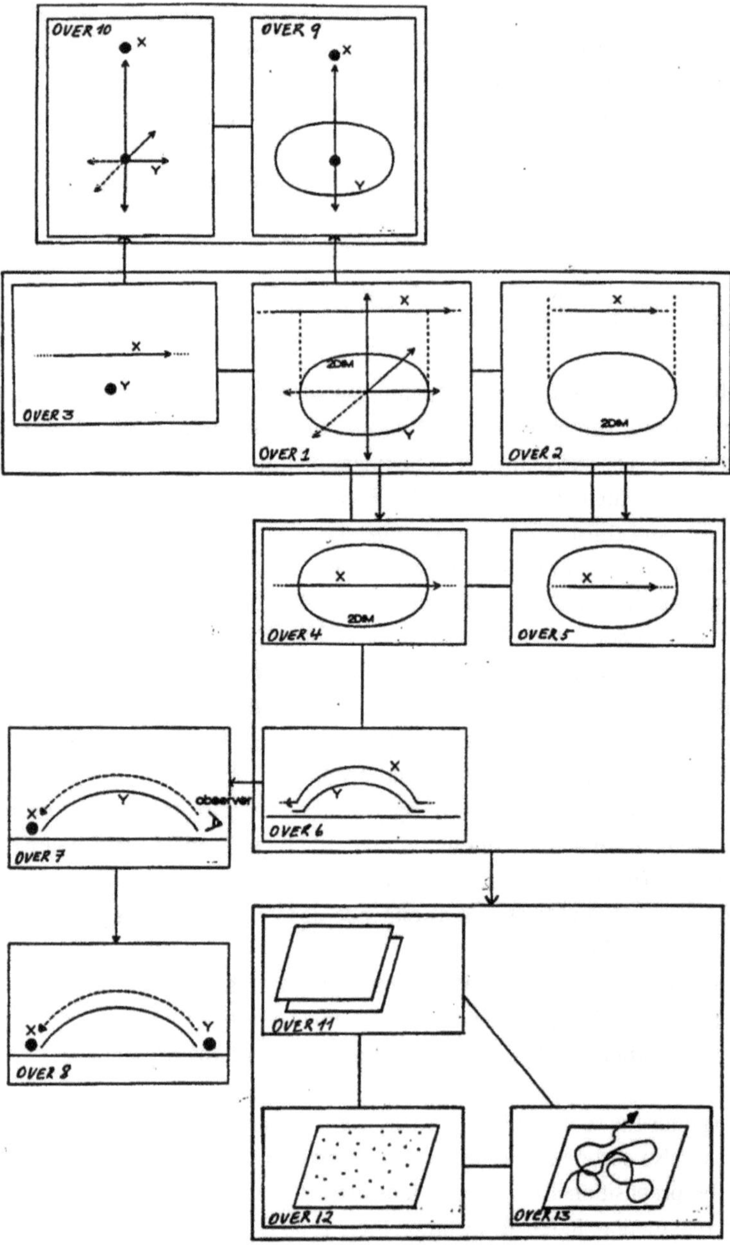

Figure 1: The network of Dutch *over*, reprinted from Cuyckens (1991).

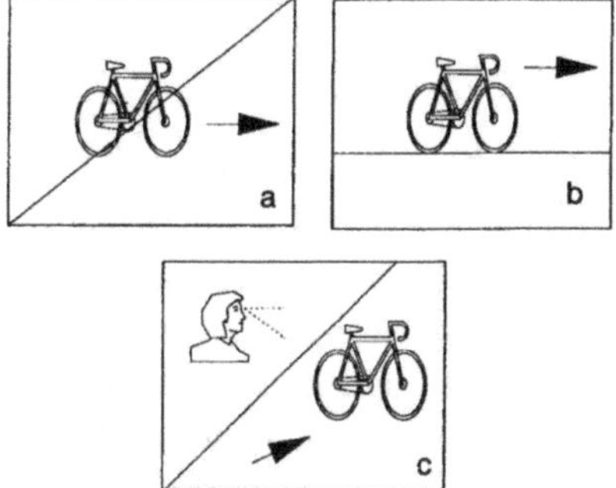

Figure 2: Three basic image schemas for *over*, reprinted from Geeraerts (1992).

stative verbs that do not express motion. An example is (3), where it is said that the blanket extends from one side of the fence to the other; it thus covers the fence, if one likes. Example (4) presents another syntagmatic context in which the 'zero motion' option is realized. If the prepositional phrase modifies a noun rather than a verb (and if the noun does not refer to a process or an action), the interpretation is automatically stative.

(2)   Er liep een rode streep over het woord *verantwoort*
       "A red line ran across the word *verantwoort* (which contains a spelling mistake)"

(3)   De deken hangt over de schutting
       "The blanket hangs over the fence"

(4)   De deken over de schutting is van de buren
       "The blanket across the fence belongs to the neighbours"

It will be clear by now that the semantic structure of *over* involves at least two dimensions: on the one hand, the spatially relational dimension in the strict sense (with regard to which three distinct spatial configurations have to be distinguished), and on the other, the 'motional' dimension, with regard to which we have to distinguish between cases of real motion, fictive motion, and zero motion. A third dimension to be added involves the existence of actual contact between the prepositional object and the other entity involved in the spatial relation. As (5) exemplifies, the reading defined in [a] can also occur when there is no physical contact between trajector and landmark. In fact, (5) could be ambiguous along the three readings [a]-[c] mentioned above (even though [c] is less likely).

(5)   Het vliegtuig vliegt over de stad
        "The airplane flies over the town"

On the basis of these three dimensions, the referential range of application of the spatial meaning of *over* can be charted systematically. As Figure 3 and the examples (6)-(22) show, almost all possible combinations of all values on the three dimensions actually occur. (The distinction between <-contact> and <+contact> cases is irrelevant for the examples (19), (20) and (21) of [c], because the position of the trajector x to the other side of the prepositional object that is the landmark automatically implies that there is no contact between them. When we add (22) as a further example of [c], it could be remarked that the distinction between (21) and (22) does involve a <-contact> versus <+contact> situation. But because the contact in question does not involve the landmark, i.e. the bridge, the distinction does not affect the structure of *over*. In this sense, then, the gaps in the structure represented in Figure 3 are systematic, not incidental ones.)

(6)   De bal rolt over de lijn
        "The ball rolls over the line (to the other side of it)"

(7)   De ballon zweeft over de stad
        "The balloon floats over the town (to the other side of it)"

(8)   Er loopt een rode verticale lijn over de blauwe horizontale
        "A red vertical line rans across the blue horizontal one"

(9)   De spoorlijn loopt over de rivier
        "The railway line runs across the river"

(10)   Over de trapleuning hangt een handdoek
        "A towel hangs over the banister"

(11)   Er hangen donkere wolken over de stad
        "Dark clouds hang over the town"

(12)   Een toerist kuiert over de markt
        "A tourist strolls over the market-place"

(13)   De jongen rijdt over de lijn
        "The boy rides over (on and along) the line"

(14) Het vliegtuig cirkelt over de stad
  "The airplane circles above the town"

(15) Condensatiestrepen lopen kriskras over de blauwe lucht
  "Condensation trails run haphazardly over the blue sky"

(16) Haar blik dwaalde over het blad
  "Her eye wandered over the sheet of paper"

(17) Er ligt een armoedig kleedje over de vloer
  "A shabby rug lies on the floor"

(18) Een dunne streep mist hangt over de rivier
  "A small trail of fog hangs over (above and along) the river"

(19) Over de rivier exerceerde de vijandelijke militie
  "Across the river, the enemy militia was exercising"

(20) Over de rivier loopt een rij bomen langs de beek
  "Across the river, a row of trees runs along the brook"

(21) Dordrecht ligt over de Moerdijkbrug
  "Dordrecht lies across the Moerdijk bridge"

(22) Over de brug hangt een ballon
  "Across the bridge, a balloon hangs in the air"

A further structural element may be added on the basis of (12) and (13). These two examples are different only to the extent that in one case the landmark is one-dimensional (a line) and in the other two-dimensional (a surface). This distinction can be generalized: if we restrict the attention to cases of actual motion, Figure 4 together with examples (23)-(26)[4] shows how the dimensionality of the landmark adds to the dimensionality of the semasiological structure. As can be seen in Figure 1, an eminently spatial feature like the distinction between lines and surfaces is readily incorporated into an analysis based on image schemas. We could in fact go even further and include the dimensionality of the trajector, but since this is not directly

---

4 Some of the examples lend themselves to various readings. Example (24) for instance could in principle be read in an 'along' sense – except that highways don't normally lead to cornfields.

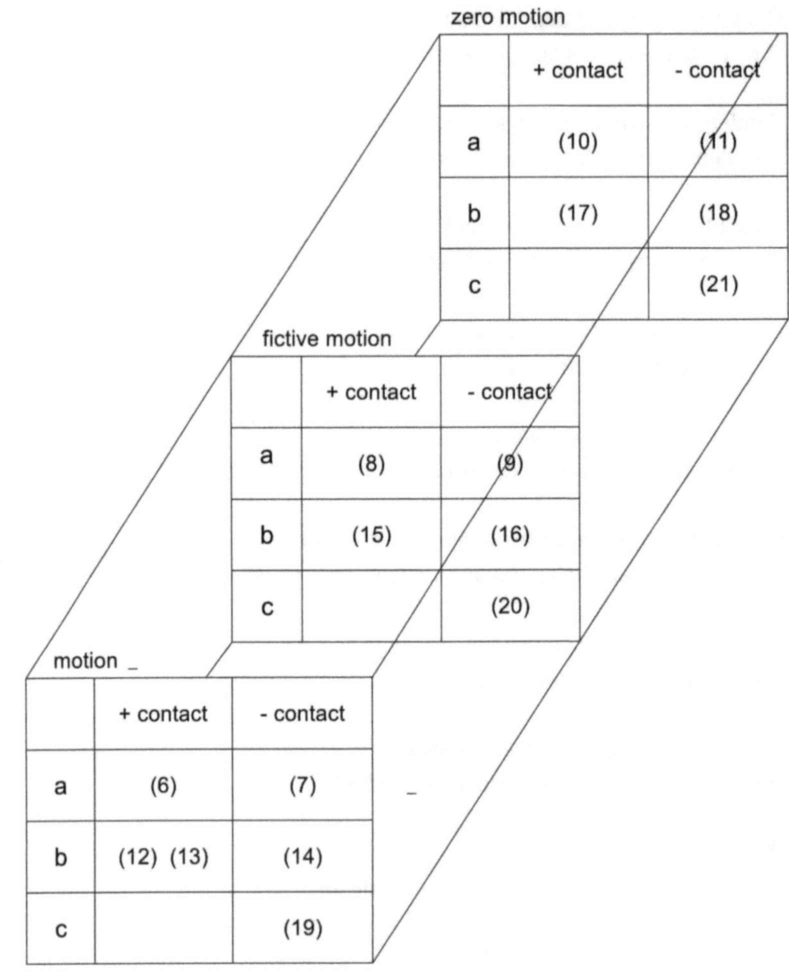

Figure 3: The multidimensional nature of the core readings of *over*.

relevant for the further steps to be taken in this paper, I refer to the 1992 publication for an exploration of the combinations of trajector and landmark dimensions.

(23) De bal rolt over het gazon tot op de straat
      "The ball rolls across the lawn till the street"

(24) De ballon zweeft over de snelweg naar het korenveld
      "The balloon floats over the highway to the cornfield"

	+contact		-contact	
	1D	2D	1D	2D
a	(6)	(23)	(24)	(7)
b	(13)	(12)	(25)	(14)
c			(19)	(26)

Figure 4: The core readings of *over* with the addition of dimensionality.

(25) Eenden vliegen over de rivier en landen plonsend
"Ducks fly over the river, landing with a splash"

(26) Over het moeras exerceerde de vijandelijke militie
"Across the swamp, the enemy militia was exercising"

If we compare Figure 1 with Figures 3 and 4, the relevance of a multidimensional perspective will be clearer. More so than a radial network analysis, the analyses embodied in the latter figures make explicit the semantic dimensions that through their interaction shape the semasiological scope of the preposition. From a theoretical perspective, recognizing the multidimensionality of that semasiological structure takes an important step away from a traditional view of lexical meaning as consisting of distinct senses. Even a radial network representation, in spite of highlighting the closely knit interconnectedness of the various usages, still seems to evoke the traditional view of word meaning in terms of separate senses – a view that is sometimes referred to as the 'dictionary model' because it is reminiscent of the numbered lists of senses that one finds in dictionaries. In multidimensional representations, by contrast, it is not immediately clear what such dictionary-like senses would be. If we combine Figures 3 and 4, we arrive at a total of thirty different usage configurations for *over*, even without taking into account figurative readings. But thinking of each of the separate cells in those figures as individual meanings leads to an unappealing model in which the level of granularity at which we define 'sense' is too high, so to speak. It makes more intuitive sense to think of the basic schemas [a]-[c] as senses in a more or less traditional sense, but then – do they also function as such? If [a]-[c] are meanings according to a 'dictionary model', the more detailed configurations, like the more than twenty different usage types that we distinguished in the examples, would be mere contextual specifications, belonging to usage rather than to the stable, stored lexicon. But that would also mean that further meaning extensions, like metaphorical usages, would have to be related directly to [a], [b], or [c]. If [a]-[c]

are the semantics of *over* and the rest is pragmatics,[5] then further semantic phenomena (like figurative meaning extensions), should be explainable in terms of [a], [b], or [c]. When we turn to the description of a number of *over* usages that we have not dealt with yet, we shall see that such is not the case. To explain the derived readings of *over*, we need a multidimensional view of the word, and not just a list of three separate senses.

4 Beyond image schemas: The multiperspectival nature of semasiological structure

Systematically speaking, there are two basic respects in which readings that we have not mentioned yet could depart from a model in which only [a], [b], or [c] would be the anchoring points for those senses. In one direction, additional usages may be derived from a subset of the readings associated with the three central image schemas, or in other words, the relevant area of Figure 3 can be smaller than that corresponding to [a], [b], or [c]. In the other direction, additional readings may be based on areas of Figure 3 that are bigger, i.e. that cross the boundaries of the territory occupied by [a], [b], or [c]. Scrutinizing some actual cases, we will come across both types.

A first set of additional readings can be considered image schema transformations, staying within the spatial domain. (As such, these meanings were already discussed in the 1992 paper.) The reading illustrated by (27)-(29) can be explained as an extension from [c], with a meaning defined as 'situated at the end of a virtual path that extends from x in a straight line across an open space'. Examples (21) and (27) are superficially similar, but note that in (21) the bridge is a landmark that needs to be virtually crossed, whereas in (27) the trajector is not found at the other side of the court. In both cases, a paraphrase with *across* is possible, but in (27), *on the other side of* does not apply. In more general terms, in (27)-(29) the prepositional object is the starting-point of a virtual path rather than an obstacle or other entity that defines the virtual path to the extent that starting-point and end-point of the path are situated at other sides of the obstacle. In contrast with [c], the path in (27)-(29) is necessarily an open area such as a street or a square or a corridor rather than just any obstacle that can be crossed. As such, this reading of *over* is not just a metonymic transformation of [c], but it is subject

---

5 I am using *pragmatics* in a broad sense here, including the cotextual and contextual specification of meaning, and not restricted to inferencing in the sense of logical pragmatics.

to additional restrictions on the landmark that are absent in the case of [c]. The image transformation can be seen as a reinterpretation of the landmark in [c] as the locus of an observer: whereas [c] distinguishes between the implicit observer and the path-defining obstacle expressed by the landmark, in the present case the observer's position coincides with the landmark.

(27) Het museum bevindt zich over de rechtbank
      "The museum is situated across the court "

(28) Hij woont schuin over het stadhuis
      "He lives at an angle across the town hall"

(29) Neem de deur recht over de trap
      "Take the door right across the stairs"

(30) De lamp hangt over de tafel
      "The lamp hangs over the table"

(31) Het ongeluk gebeurde over de zee
      "The accident happened over the sea"

(32) De ketel hangt over het vuur
      "The kettle hangs over the fire"

Crucially for our line of thought, the transformation illustrated by (27)-(29) has its origin in a single image schema, [c]. In that sense, it fits into a traditional view in which the meanings [a]-[c] are so to speak all the semantics you need. That is not the case for the reading in (30)-(32), which can be defined as 'situated above x, within the spatial boundaries of x'. This type of usage links up with the <-contact> cases of [a] and [b]. As in the latter, the trajector is situated spatially above x, but in contrast with the <-contact> cases of [a] and [b], the trajector in (30)-(32) is typically point-like ànd stable. If the trajector were a line or surface, we would not talk of a separate reading, because the 'crossing' or 'covering' senses that we identified as [a] and [b] would straightforwardly apply. And similarly, if the trajector were point-like but moving (*the kettle is swinging over the fire*), [a] or [b] would also unambiguously apply. We conclude that (30)-(32) generalizes the 'above' feature that is present in (11) and (18), i.e. in the <zero motion, -contact> cases of [a] and [b]. As such, the starting-point for the reading 'situated above x, within the spatial boundaries of x' is not a single image schema, but a subset of the combination of two image schemas.

A second set of additional readings finally brings us to some of the figurative, metaphorical usages of *over*. The examples (33)-(35) are fairly straightforward instances of a TIME IS SPACE metaphor. Examples (33)-(34) illustrate an 'after' reading that links up with [a], to the extent that they imply the crossing of a temporal boundary. Example (35) illustrates a 'during' reading that links up with [b], in the sense that the trajector stays within the temporal boundaries expressed by the landmark. Although the 'during' reading is subject to more restrictions than the 'after' reading (an example like (35) only occurs in some varieties of Dutch), it is also present in the high-frequency compound *overdag* "during the day".

(33) Het is nu kwart over vijf
      "It is now quarter past five"

(34) Hij gaat over drie jaar met pensioen
      "He retires in three years"

(35) We kunnen dat over de middag bespreken
      "We can discuss that during noontime"

(36) Zij is over de negentig
      "She is over ninety"

(37) De wijnkelder bevat over de duizend flessen
      "The wine cellar contains over a thousand bottles"

(38) Zulk gedrag gaat over de limiet van het fatsoen
      "Such behavior goes beyond the limits of decency"

(39) Dat gaat er ver over
      "That is way over the top"

Examples (36)-(39) rely on a metaphorization of spatial boundaries: crossing a line equals exceeding a quantitative or normative limit. As such, these cases link up with [a], but specifically with that subset of [a] in which the landmark is one-dimensional, given the importance of the boundary line in the motivating image. But whereas the distinction between one-dimensional and two-dimensional landmarks is important for the metaphorical image, the distinction between configurations with or without contact does not seem particularly relevant for the derived reading. This illustrates a general phenomenon: distinctions that play a constitutive role with regard to the spatial senses of *over* may be neutralized in the figurative senses. To mention another example, it is not immediately clear how the distinction between fictive motion and zero motion could be meaningfully applied to the temporal senses represented by (36)-(39).

(40) Hun heerschappij over de zeeën bleef niet duren
      "Their rule over the seas did not last"

(41) Zij is de baas over het marketingbeleid
      "She is the boss of the marketing strategy"

(42) Ik ga niet over die zaak
      "I have no say on that matter"

Next, (40)-(42) show how *over* can express relations of dominance, authority, control. This usage is motivated by the conceptual metaphor CONTROL IS UP, i.e. the metaphorical construal of a position of power as a higher one.[6] Within the semasiological context of *over*, this usage is a figurative interpretation of the 'above' aspect of spatial *over*, as represented by the <-contact> cases, and in a derived way, by (30)-(32).

(43) Daar moet ik nog even over nadenken
      "I will have to think about that"

(44) Maak je maar geen zorgen over de terugreis
      "Don't worry about the return journey"

(45) Het is moeilijk te oordelen over zijn gedrag
      "It's difficult to judge about his behaviour"

(46) Ik geef een college over semantiek
      "I teach a class on semantics"

(47) Mag ik uw mening over deze kleur?
      "Can I have your opinion about this colour?"

(48) Dit is een artikel over voorzetsels
      "This is an article on prepositions"

---

6 As is well known, this metaphor relies on an image schema of its own: the up-down schema of verticality is metaphorized in terms of control, with the upper position for the controller and the lower position for the controlled; see Lakoff and Johnson (1980: 15).

Finally, examples (43)-(48) exhibit a reading that is very frequent in Dutch, and that is largely absent in English, where *about* or *on* would typically be used as the equivalent expression. Here, the preposition introduces the intentional object of a cognitive and more broadly psychological activity like thinking, reflecting, pondering, rejoicing, worrying, panicking etc., or a communicative activity like writing, talking, complaining, teaching etc. The nouns referring to the product of those activities may then also typically be specified by means of an *over*-phrase. (This is not to say that verbs of these classes invariably take *over*. Numerous alternative prepositions occur, sometimes alternating with *over*, and the subtleties of their distinctions have not yet been entirely unraveled.) How then can this usage of *over* be related to the spatial readings at the core of the item? The image ties in with [b]: if the topic of concern or the focus of attention is thought of as a surface (like a 'field' of investigation), then paying attention to it is, in a <+contact> configuration, a matter of exploring it, of mapping it out, of covering it, of going over it – all spatial metaphors – to get a grip on it. In a <-contact> configuration, focusing on a topic is overseeing it: surveying, observing, inspecting, scanning from a higher position (with the additional suggestion of the control feature that we encountered earlier, as an aim to be achieved). The distinction between the <-contact> and the <+contact> basis of the imagery should not be seen as a source of polysemy, though. Rather, the 'about' reading seems to be derived from two imagistic sources at the same time.

So, if we bring together the various extensions we have considered – for the sake of conciseness, we can refer to them in the order of introduction as 'across', 'above$_1$', 'after', 'during', 'beyond', 'above$_2$', and 'about' – we find that only a minority are straightforward extensions of an image schema, and only one image schema. This applies to 'across', 'after', and 'during'. In other cases, the semantic extensions have their origin in a subset of the semasiological area covered by a given image schema. This applies to 'beyond' and 'about'. In the most extreme cases, the derived readings are based on a subset of the combination of two image schemas. This applies to 'above$_1$' and 'above$_2$'.

Figures 5–11 make the various effects visible by indicating the various areas in a simplified version of Figure 3. (The simplification consists of the removal of the 'fictive motion' layer. It is left out because it does not play a specific role in any of the derived readings that we introduced.) To avoid misunderstanding, it should be kept in mind that the shaded areas in Figures 5–11 only indicate those regions of the original semasiological structure that constitute the source of the additional readings – but obviously not those readings themselves. So for instance, to come back to the extension discussed last, it was suggested that the 'about' reading derives from two sources at the same time: covering or going over a surface as a way of exploring it, or being situated above it (in motion or in a stationary position) as a way of surveying it. In Figure 11, this double source domain is represented by singling out the 2D areas of the [b] section. The relevant features of this representation are the following. First, the motivating image of 'about' is taken to be [b] because the cognitive or communicative aboutness does not evoke an image of going beyond the subject, i.e. there is no sense of crossing as would be signaled by [a]: if you think or talk about a subject matter, you stay with and within it. Second, the subject matter is thought of as having an extension (an area, a field), so the source of 'about' involves the 2D subcases of [b]. And third, both the <-contact> and <+contact> instantiations of the 2D cases of [b] turn out to be relevant, depending on whether the cognitive or communicative attention paid to the subject matter carries an overtone of control and domination or rather one of exploring, finding one's way, mapping out the surface. Accordingly, the shaded part of Figure 11 consists of two beams, one carving out the <-contact> area of 2D sub [b], and the other marking the corresponding <+contact> area.

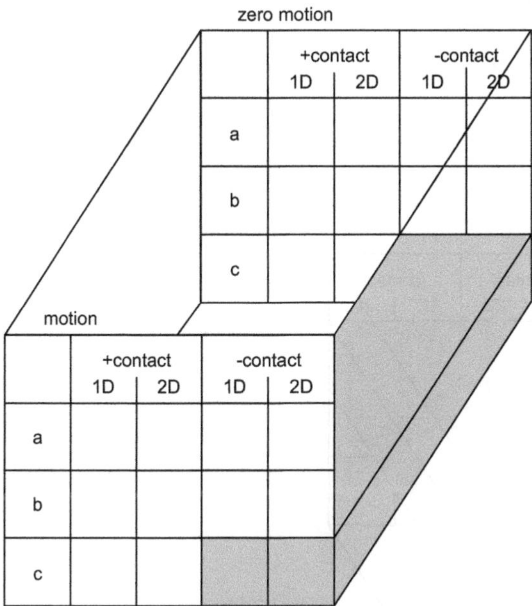

Figure 5: The source region of 'across'.

Taken together, the graphical representations in Figures 5 to 11 show how basically any area in the multidimensional structure of spatial *over* can be the basis of non-spatial readings. In the theoretical terms mentioned at the outset of this section, we see that both types of departure from a 'dictionary model' occur: derived usages may have an origin in a subset of the readings associated with the three central image

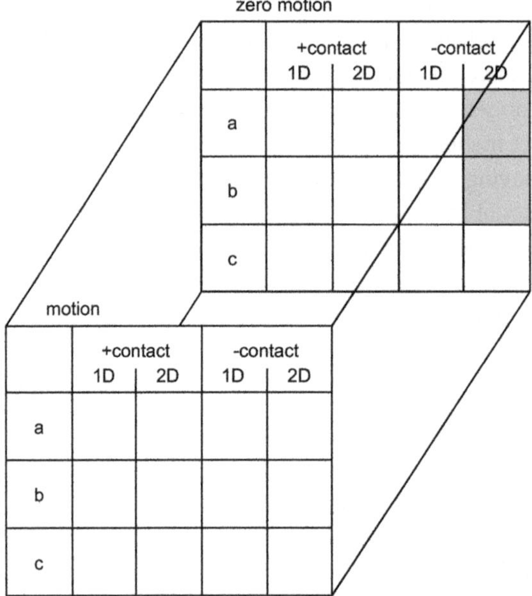

Figure 6: The source region of 'above₁'.

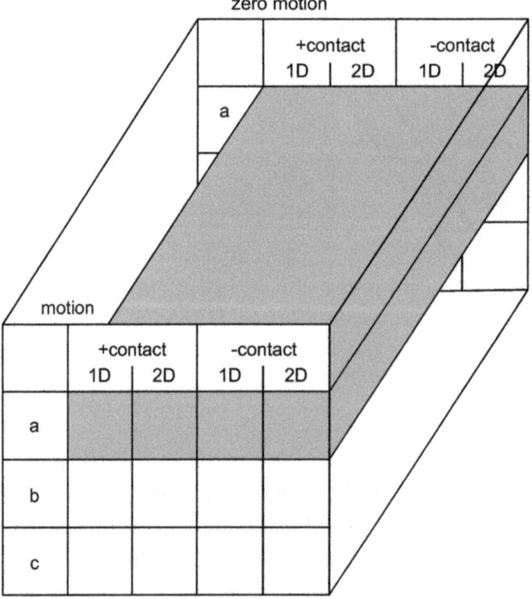

Figure 7: The source region of 'after'.

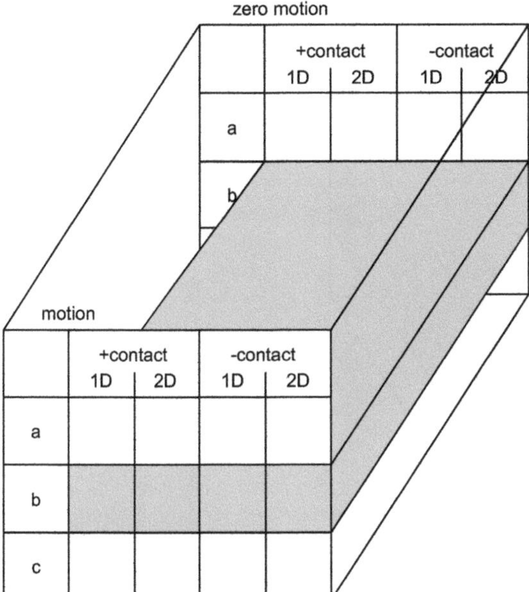

Figure 8: The source region of 'during'.

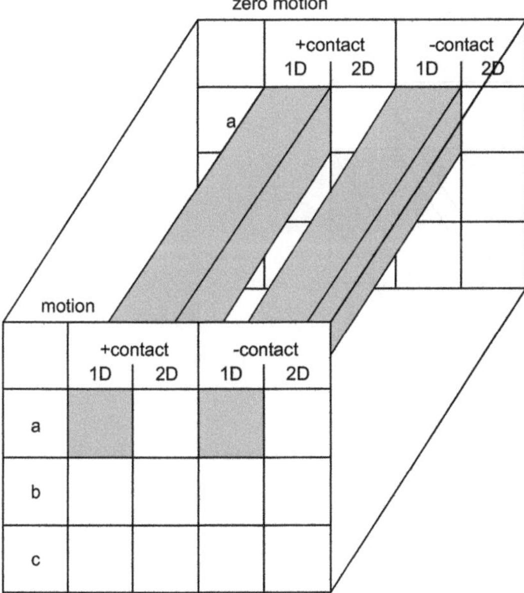

Figure 9: The source region of 'beyond'.

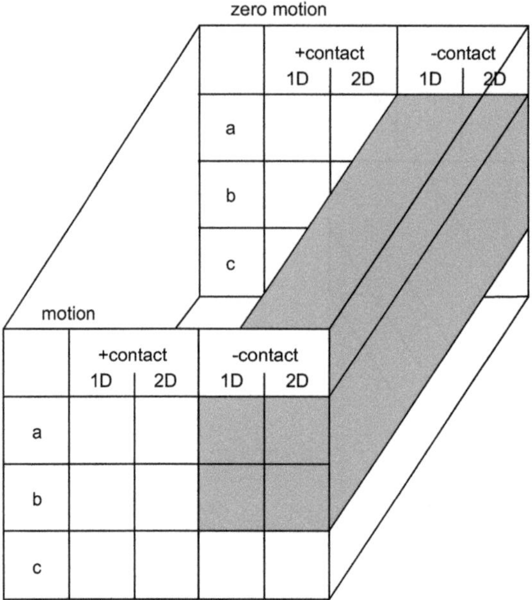

Figure 10: The source region of 'above$_2$'.

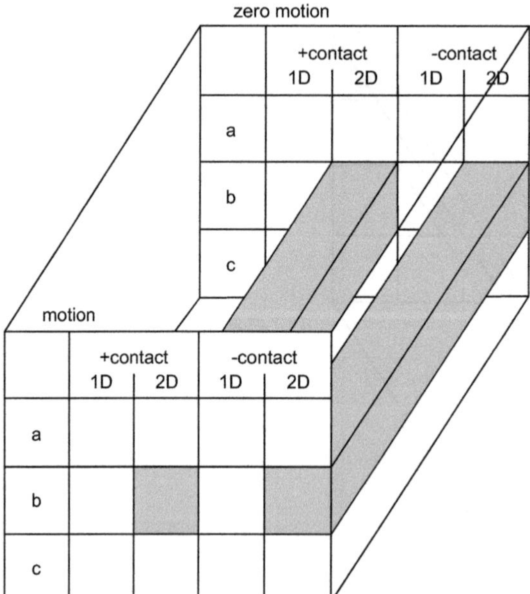

Figure 11: The source region of 'about'.

schemas, but also, they may be anchored in a region that crosses the boundaries of the territory occupied by the three image schemas. Simplistically put, it seems as if any region in the semasosiological range of a multidimensionally structured word may be the source for further meaning extensions. One way of identifying this phenomenon is to say that the semantics of a lexical item is 'multiperspectival': it's not only an integrated structure of interlocking and interacting dimensions, but language users are able to look at that structure from different angles, and take those angles as the source for a flexible use of the word.

5 The complexities of lexical meaning

For this paper, I have taken my starting-point in the analysis of the Dutch preposition *over* that I first discussed in Geeraerts (1992) in response to the description included in Hubert Cuyckens' dissertation of 1991. Elaborating and extending the earlier analysis, I have highlighted two nuances that need to be applied to the popular description of prepositional meaning as a radial network of image schemas and image schema transformations. As a nuance with regard to the radial network model, I have emphasized the multidimensional nature of semasiological structure. As a nuance with regard to the emphasis on image schemas, I have shown how any region in the semasiological range of a multidimensionally structured word may be the source for further meaning extensions.

These observations may now be put in the wider context of the contributions coming from Cognitive Semantics to the study of word meaning. The initial major impetus that Cognitive Semantics gave to lexical semantics was the recognition – the rediscovery, one may say – of the structured nature of polysemy: the insight that the semasiology of a word can only be fruitfully described if we take into account the diversity of its meanings and the way those meanings are interconnected through metaphor or metonymy, or other modulations of a core meaning. The structured nature of polysemy implies flexibility in the use of a word, but it was soon recognized (Taylor 1992, Geeraerts 1993, Tuggy 1993) that that flexibility also complicates the structural description. Rather than a neat network of clearly distinct readings connected by specific semantic mechanisms, the semantic architecture of a word may take the form of multiply interacting dimensions. And further, it may not even always be easy to identify what is a separate meaning, because mostly any region of the complex architecture may be activated in actual usage. Prepositional meaning, as we have seen, is no different.

And that may have consequences for grammaticalization research too. Prepositions grammaticalize into prefixes or grammatical markers, as with the *to*-infinitive or the prepositional dative, i.e. prepositions regularly undergo processes of semantic depletion in which referential meaning gives way to grammatical function. Even if subtle semantic differences can be detected between the prepositional dative and the bare dative, the denotational meaning of *to* has receded far into the background in comparison to the grammatical, dative function as such. Such shifts were not highlighted in the previous pages, but they are not absent from the development of *over*: examples like (42)-(45) for instance see *over* move into the domain of prepositional complement marking. Given such cases, the comparison of models presented in this paper raises a question beyond the field of lexical analysis: what role does the multidimensionality of spatial, referential prepositional meanings play in their grammaticalization? Hubert will have the answer, surely.

References

Bellavia, Elena. 1996. The German 'über'. In Martin Pütz & René Dirven (eds.), *The Construal of Space in Language and Thought*. 73–107. Berlin & New York: Mouton de Gruyter.

Brugman, Claudia. 1981. *The story of 'over'*. M.A. Thesis, Department of Linguistics, University of California at Berkeley.

Brugman, Claudia. 1988. *The Story of 'Over': Polysemy, Semantics and the Structure of the Lexicon*. New York: Garland.

Cuyckens, Hubert. 1991. *The semantics of spatial prepositions in Dutch: A cognitive linguistics exercise*. Ph.D. dissertation, Department of Linguistics, University of Antwerp.

Cuyckens, Hubert. 1994. Family resemblance in the Dutch spatial preposition 'op'. In Monika Schwarze (ed.), *Kognitive Semantik/Cognitive Semantics*. 180–195. Tübingen, Germany: Gunter Narr.

Cuyckens, Hubert. 1995. Family resemblance in the Dutch spatial prepositions 'door' and 'langs'. *Cognitive Linguistics* 6: 183–207.

Cuyckens, Hubert. 2002. Metonymy in prepositions. In Hubert Cuyckens & Günter Radden (eds.), *Perspectives on Prepositions*. 257–266. Tübingen, Germany: Max Niemeyer.

Cuyckens, Hubert & Günter Radden (eds.). 2002. *Perspectives on Prepositions*. Tübingen, Germany: Max Niemeyer.

Deane, Paul. 2005. Multimodal spatial representation: On the semantic unity of 'over'. In Beate Hampe (ed.), *From Perception to Meaning: Image Schemas in Cognitive Linguistics*. 235–282. Berlin & New York: Mouton de Gruyter.

Dewell, Robert B. 1994. 'Over' again: On the role of image-schemas in semantic analysis. *Cognitive Linguistics* 5. 351–380.

Dewell, Robert B. 1996. The separability of German 'über': A cognitive approach. In Martin Pütz & René Dirven (eds.), *The Construal of Space in Language and Thought*. 109–133. Berlin & New York: Mouton de Gruyter.

Evans, Vyvyan & Andrea Tyler. 2001. Reconsidering prepositional polysemy networks: The case of 'over'. *Language* 77. 724–765.

Geeraerts, Dirk. 1983. Prototype theory and diachronic semantics. A case study. *Indogermanische Forschungen* 88. 1–32.

Geeraerts, Dirk. 1992. The semantic structure of Dutch over. *Leuvense Bijdragen* 81. 205–230.

Geeraerts, Dirk. 1993. Vagueness's puzzles, polysemy's vagaries. *Cognitive Linguistics* 4. 223–272.

Geeraerts, Dirk, Stefan Grondelaers & Peter Bakema. 1994. *The Structure of Lexical Variation. Meaning, Naming, and Context*. Berlin & New York: Mouton de Gruyter.

Geeraerts, Dirk. 1997. *Diachronic Prototype Semantics. A Contribution to Historical Lexicology*. Oxford: Clarendon Press.

Geeraerts, Dirk. 2006. *Words and Other Wonders. Papers on Lexical and Semantic Topics*. Berlin; New York: Mouton de Gruyter.

Geeraerts, Dirk. 2010. *Theories of Lexical Semantics*. Oxford: Oxford University Press.

Hampe, Beate (ed.). 2005. *From Perception to Meaning: Image Schemas in Cognitive Linguistics*. Berlin & New York: Mouton de Gruyter.

Herskovits, Annette H. 1986. *Language and Spatial Cognition: An Interdisciplinary Study of Prepositions in English*. Cambridge: Cambridge University Press.

Johnson, Mark. 1987. *The Body in the Mind: The Bodily Basis of Meaning, Imagination, and Reason*. Chicago: University of Chicago Press.

Lakoff, George. 1987. *Women, Fire and Dangerous Things: What Categories Reveal about the Mind*. Chicago: University of Chicago Press.

Lakoff, George & Mark Johnson. 1980. *Metaphors We Live by*. Chicago: University of Chicago Press.

Langacker, Ronald W. 1987. *Foundations of Cognitive Grammar 1. Theoretical Prerequisites*. Stanford: Stanford University Press.

Lindner, Susan J. 1981. *A lexico-semantic analysis of English verb-particle constructions with 'out' and 'up'*. Ph.D. dissertation, University of California, San Diego.

Meex, Birgitta. 2002. Die Wegpräposition 'über'. In Hubert Cuyckens & Günter Radden (eds.), *Perspectives on Prepositions*. 157–176. Tübingen: Max Niemeyer.

Radden, Günter. 1981. Die übertragenen Bedeutungen der englischen Raumpräpositionen. In Günter Radden & René Dirven (eds.), *Kasusgrammatik und Fremdsprachendidaktik*. 133–179. Trier, Germany: Wissenschaftlicher Verlag Trier.

Rosch, Eleanor. 1978. Principles of categorization. In Eleanor Rosch & Barbara B. Lloyd (eds.), *Cognition and Categorization*. 27–48. Hillsdale, N.J.: Lawrence Erlbaum.

Taylor, John R. 1989. *Linguistic Categorization: Prototypes in Linguistic Theory*. Oxford: Clarendon Press. 3rd ed. 2003.

Taylor, John R. 1992. How many meanings does a word have? *Stellenbosch Papers in Linguistics* 25. 133–168.

Tuggy, David. 1993. Ambiguity, polysemy, and vagueness. *Cognitive Linguistics* 4. 273–290.

Tyler, Andrea & Vyvyan Evans. 2004. Applying cognitive linguistics to pedagogical grammar: The case of 'over'. In Michael Achard & Susanne Niemeier (eds.), *Cognitive Linguistics, Second Language Acquisition, and Foreign Language Teaching*. 257–280. Berlin & New York: Mouton de Gruyter.

Vandeloise, Claude. 1986. *L'Espace en Français: Sémantique des Prépositions Spatiales*. Paris: Seuil. Translated as *Spatial Prepositions: A Case Study from French*. 1991. University of Chicago Press.

Marianne Hundt

7 Competition in antagonistic verb complementation

A diachronic, corpus-based study of *fight, oppose* and *protest*
in (Late) Modern British and American English

Abstract: Verbal complementation is a popular topic for language historians and World Englishes scholars alike, not least because it provides a rich playing field for the study of variation and (ongoing) language change. The present paper adds to previous research a case study on three antagonistic verbs with a focus on phrasal complementation. Corpus evidence from the Late Modern period shows that antagonistic *fight, oppose* and *protest* do not unanimously drift towards a unified Argument Structure Construction. The study also provides preliminary evidence from a corpus of very recent news writing; these data indicate that the one case of twentieth-century divergence between British and American English is likely to disappear again, with popular newspapers in the UK adopting the 'American' preference for bare NP complementation. Probabilistic modelling of the AmE data suggests that PP complements are likely to survive on both sides of the Atlantic in a language-internally conditioned niche context.

Keywords: antagonistic verbs, phrasal complements, competition, regional variation and change, Americanization, constructional loss

1 Introduction

Previous research indicates that there is regional variation among national standard varieties of English in the complementation patterns of some antagonistic verbs: for *protest*, for instance, current American English (AmE) shows a clear

Acknowledgements: Carlos Hartmann retrieved the data from the parsed CLMET for me and Bethany Dallas helped with annotating the COHA data for *protest* and semantically analyzing the set of verbs to which *against* attaches in the PPMBE. The datasets for *against* come from a larger project on prepositions in English argument structure constructions (SNF grant 100015_175987) and were extracted by Eva Zehentner. Thanks to all three of them! I am also grateful for the constructive feedback from two anonymous reviewers on an earlier draft.

https://doi.org/10.1515/9783110753059-007

preference for NP complements (see (1)) whereas British English (BrE) prefers a PP complement (as illustrated in (2)).

(1)　Initially, I wore a camouflaged vest and helmet given to me by George Kennedy, the first of the US officials to resign from the State Department to *protest* _ the government's Bosnia policy. (Samantha Power, 2019. *The Education of an Idealist*. London: William Collins, 85)

(2)　He told the CBI conference in Glasgow that Britain could protect its own interests within the European Community without having to *protest* **about** threats to national sovereignty (ICE-GB, S2B-007)

For other verbs (e.g., *fight* and *oppose*), the results of previous studies suggest that the regional contrasts are likely to be less marked, but there seems to be a clear preference for the bare NP-complements in certain registers such as journalese in BrE (see Rohdenburg, 2009: 199).

Even though there is a vast body of research on change and regional variation in verb complementation, generally, variation in complementation of antagonistic verbs has received relatively little attention so far. Callies (2018: 151–153) provides a useful summary of the studies that have commented on differences in this respect between BrE and AmE. With the exception of Hundt (1998) and Rohdenburg (2009), previous studies rely on anecdotal evidence and do not provide corpus data on regional variation. Even less is known about the particulars of the diachrony in this area of grammar, as Rohdenburg (2009: 200) points out: "As yet, very few details are known about the evolution of the contrasting options over the last few centuries. With at least some verbs it is clear, however, that the direct object has only become the American majority variant in the course of the twentieth century." The question is whether this development has led to divergent language use in the two varieties of English or whether BrE may recently have started to follow suit in this development (see Leech et al., 2009: 253).

The current study uses diachronic corpus data from the *Corpus of Historical American English* (COHA) and a collection of diachronic corpora for BrE to investigate the trajectory for the competition between a bare NP-complement and a PP-complement in the two varieties for all three verbs. Additionally, diachronic data for BrE is provided to verify whether *against* – arguably the most prototypical antagonistic preposition – has been 'losing' verbs in the course of the Early (EModE) and Late Modern (LModE) periods, which would provide indirect evidence of a trend towards direct complementation of antagonistic verbs. To complement this bird's eye view, a more detailed analysis of the verb with the clearest regional and diachronic divergence is provided, including the modelling of both language-internal and contextual predictor variables, and additional evidence from twenty-first century newspapers on recent change in BrE. The results are discussed against the background of long-term changes in Argument Structure Constructions (ASC) in English.

2 Background

2.1 Previous research into direct transitivization and antagonistic verbs

Rohdenburg (2009) investigates antagonistic verbs as part of a larger study on nominal complementation. He defines them as verbs that denote an activity which is directed against a person or thing. Rohdenburg (2009: 198) observes that a diachronic development from PP-complementation towards direct NP complementation with antagonistic verbs would fit in with a long-term tendency towards 'direct transitivization' in English postulated in earlier research by Jespersen (1927), Kirchner (1955), Hawkins (1986) and Legenhausen and Rohdenburg (1995). Callies (2018: 153) points out that the origins of this trend towards direct transitivization go back to Early Modern English (EModE). However, matters are complicated by differences between individual verbs.

Rohdenburg (2009: 199) provides quantitative evidence for the verbs *fight, battle, protest, appeal, race, play* and *offend* from 1990s newspaper databases for BrE and AmE. While there is some regional variation (notably for *protest* and *appeal*), not all verbs in his study equally tend towards bare complementation in AmE (notably *race*) and some have a sizeable amount of bare NP complements even in BrE (particularly *fight* and *play*). Similarly, as a result of his largely qualitative observations, Algeo (1988, 2006) finds that tendencies towards direct complementation with individual verbs can be found on both sides of the Atlantic; he concludes that, while the overall trend is shared, it results in regional differences on the lexical level. In other words, variation in ASCs may lead to regional lexico-grammatical divergence or nativization.

However, the hypothesis that there has been a long-term trend away from prepositional complements towards direct transitivization is not uncontroversial. Fischer and van der Wurff (2006: 165), for instance, postulate that, beginning in early Middle English, there has been a long-term increase in the use of prepositional complements at the expense of bare NPs. With respect to Modern English, they claim that "... this development has continued to the point where there are systematic pairs like *hit/stab/poke* versus *hit at/stab at/poke at* or *live/feed/subsist* versus *live on/feed on/subsist on*" (Fischer and van der Wurff 2006: 165). It is likely that both trends exist, but the question is at which level of granularity we will find them. At the highest level of schematicity, i.e., competition between PP and NP complements with verbs taking one non-subject complement, a general trend towards PP complementation cannot be corroborated (see e.g. Zehentner and Hundt, 2022). For Romance loanwords, on the other hand, Hundt and Van Driessche (accepted) have found a systematic decrease in PP complements from the beginning of the Early to the end of the Late Modern period. At the same time, there is substantial variation at the level of individual verbs. This has partly to do with the fact that at the highest level of abstraction, transitive constructions (whether with a direct NP or a PP complement) are not unified by a single constructional meaning. Even at a lower level of granularity, however, constructional meaning may be polysemous. Perek (2014) for instance has not been able to isolate a semantic core for the conative construction, i.e., to V *at* NP. Similarly, verb meaning also tends to be polysemous and is not necessarily stable across time.

Finally, the whole question of diachronic change in complementation patterns is further complicated by aspects that go beyond constructional and lexical meaning, e.g., the balancing between cognitive factors that favor a more explicit/transparent encoding of meaning and the need to be economical. The verb *enter*, for instance, is not only construed with a preposition in contact varieties of English – as in *He entered into the room* – but has a history of acquiring (and losing) prepositional complements already in Latin (see Hundt and Van Driessche, accepted). Likewise, analogical levelling is a factor that is occasionally at work, e.g., when speakers extend the use of the preposition *about* from the nominal pattern (*to have a discussion about*) to its verbal use (*to discuss about*), as e.g. Nesselhauf (2009) has pointed out. With respect to the need for economy, certain text types (i.e., newspapers and academic texts) have been found to foster a trend towards densification in the recent history of English; this holds not only for changes within the NP but for shorter expressions, more generally (see e.g. Leech et al., 2009). The question is whether antagonistic *fight, oppose* and *protest* are (all) part of a trend towards bare or prepositional complementation and whether any (recent) changes in ASC have resulted in (lasting) regional divergence.

2.2 Verb meaning and complementation

To speakers of English in the US and Britain today, the antagonistic meaning of *fight, oppose* and *protest* as well as *against* are probably the most prominent ones. However, a closer look shows that they all have either more neutral or even positive uses. Of the three verbs, *oppose* is the most antagonistic one; but even this verb has been used with a more neutral sense of 'to contrast' or 'to compare' since the late sixteenth century, according to the *Oxford English Dictionary* (OED online, viz. *compare*, v., sense 5):

(3)   Belonging to a Problem, which is opposed to a Theoreme. (1696, E. Phillips *New World of Words* (new ed.) at *Problematical*; OED online)

Similarly, *fight* in its earliest attested uses from the Anglo-Saxon chronicle, is clearly an antagonistic verb, but there is also a non-antagonistic sense when it is construed with the preposition *for* (since the 1330s). When it is used with a bare NP complement in a semi-fixed expression *fight the good fight*, which is attested since the sixteenth century (OED online, viz. *fight*, v.), the meaning of the verb is also non-antagonistic. In terms of its diachrony, *protest* is the least antagonist verb of the three, as early meanings cover aspects such as 'to assert', 'to vow', 'to declare' or 'to proclaim' (OED online, viz. *protest*, v.).[1] These senses are all attested in the *Corpus of Late Modern English Texts* (CLMET), with (6) providing the clearest indication of its non-antagonistic use.

(4)   . . . I *protest*, and assert, and avow, that this person is as pig [sic!] a necromancer as you would desire to behold; (CLMET_FICT, 1751)

(5)   I *protest* you kill me with confusion ELIZA. (CLMET_MISC, 1841)

(6)   I *protest* I love you. (CLMET_FICT, 1807)

Historically, antagonistic meanings emerge with the transitive use of *protest* meaning 'non-acceptance' or 'non-payment' of a bill, which is attested from the Late Middles Ages (1479). Most antagonistic uses of *protest* quoted in OED are either without a complement or with a PP headed by *against, about* or *at*. In the meaning of 'public demonstration', the transitive use is considered to be typical of US English and attested since the late nineteenth century (see (7)), according to OED online (viz *protest*, v., sense 4. and 6., respectively).

(7)   Mr. Rendle *protested* the decision, but his protest was not sustained. (OED, 1887)

---

1 In the non-antagonistic sense, the related noun in Present Day English is *protestation* rather than *protest*, even though the affirmative speech act sense for the noun *protest* is also attested (until 1876, see OED visz *protest*, n., sense 1.)

With respect to constructional variation, *protest* can take either clausal (see examples (4) to (6)) or phrasal complements (see (8) and (9)). Phrasal complementation can give rise to semantic ambiguity, as in (10), which – without further context – could have either an antagonistic or a non-antagonistic interpretation. In (11), the potential ambiguity can be contextually resolved towards the non-antagonistic meaning 'to assert'.

(8)   . . . I die *protesting* my innocence! (CLMET_FICT, 1760/1)

(9)   I *protest* the loveliest couple that ever eye beheld. (CLMET_FICT, 1749)

(10)   I *protest* it in the face of the world! (CLMET_MISC, 1841)

(11)   And when the court granted a small supply, *protesting* their poverty, he believed their protestations . . . (CLMET_BIO, 1813)

Polysemy of different antagonistic and non-antagonistic senses extends to the preposition *against* too, which has been used with spatial meanings to express 'motion towards' since the Old English period (for a recent attestation of this sense, see (12)); *against* is also used from early on in constructions that express active hostility or opposition to a person or thing (viz. OED online, *against*, prep.). In relation to time, *against* can be used in positive context, too, to mean 'in anticipation of' or 'preparation for'. This sense is illustrated in (13) from the *Penn-Parsed Corpus of Early Modern English* (PPCEME).

(12)   She is already undressed, and she comes *against* him bare and loose when he touches her. (COHA, FIC, 1979)

(13)   the xii day of september the citizens began to adorn the city *against* the queens coronation to hang the streets and prepare pageants . . . (PPCEME, 1556, MA-CHYN-E1-H,43.103).

The more fine-grained analyses in this paper will take semantic context and the different meanings of both the verbs and the preposition into account.

Diachronic corpus data will be used here to test (a) whether there is an overall trend towards bare complementation for the verbs *fight, oppose* and *protest*, (b) whether there are divergent trends in AmE and BrE in the complementation patterns for the three verbs, (c) whether, if a clear diachronic and regional trend can be observed, this is driven by particular language-internal or contextual variables. Section 3 provides detail on the corpora used to study potential divergent trends in complementation, the approach taken in data extraction, and the predictor variables used for the close-up on *protest*. The results of the quantitative analyses presented in section 4 will be discussed against general developments in English ASCs in the final section of this paper.

3 Methodology

3.1 Corpora

An exploratory study of *protest* in CLMET showed that, out of the 908 occurrences of the verb, only 127 were instances of the antagonistic sense. The majority of these (i.e., 123 or 97%) took a PP complement with *against.* Three of the four instances of bare NP complementation combined the passive voice with a specific NP complement, i.e., the noun *bill,* a use that, according to OED online (viz *protest* v., sense 4. B.) is now obsolete. There is only one instance with a bare NP complement following antagonistic *protest,* which is from a late nineteenth-century non-fictional text:

(14)   . . . in Germany the reformers called themselves Protestants, because they *protested* some of the teachings of the Church of Rome. (CLMET_HIST, 1870)[2]

With data for bare NP complements in earlier stages of English for the verb with – reportedly – the clearest trend towards regional divergence and change towards bare complementation being rather sparce in CLMET, the focus of the present study is therefore on corpus data that includes the twentieth century. For BrE, the evidence comes from the diachronic *Hansard Corpus* of parliamentary speeches, which contains about 1.6 billion words from the years 1803–2005. For AmE, data were extracted from COHA, a more stratified corpus with respect to text types but providing comparable diachronic coverage, i.e., from the 1810s to the 2010s.

---

2 The etymology given in this extract from CLMET is a late nineteenth-century folk etymology with respect to the antagonistic reading, i.e. it projects contemporary complementation and semantics onto the historical use of the verb. The OED (online, viz. *Protestant,* n. and adj.) quotes the contemporary use of German *protestieren* as part of its entry on the word's etymology: " . . . (in the wording of the protest at Speyer): *so protestieren und bezeugen wir hiermit öffentlich vor Gott,* literally 'thus we protest and testify publicly before God'," where the parallel use of Latinate *protestieren* and Germanic *bezeugen* serves not only to make the use of the verb *protestieren* transparent but also to simultaneously emphasize the declarative speech act.

3.2 Data retrieval and manual post-editing

As pointed out in section 2, a study on complementation patterns of antagonistic verbs is made complicated by the fact that verbs which, at first sight, have antagonistic meaning may turn out to be polysemous, including non-antagonistic senses. Rohdenburg (2009) works around issues related to polysemy of the antagonistic verbs he studies by employing a narrow approach at retrieval, i.e. he limits the different forms of the verbs (e.g. includes only past tense *fought*) and the semantics of the set of NPs that follow the verbs, i.e. only nouns such as *law, rule, legislation* that typically combine with the antagonistic sense of the verbs. He further restricts retrieval to those instances where the NP or PP directly follow the verb on the assumption that intervening material ". . . almost invariably prompts the choice of the prepositional variant in accordance with the Complexity Principle" (2009: 200). However, (15) shows that there may be elements occurring between the verb and the complement even with a bare nominal complement. Moreover, allowing for a single word to occur between the verb and its complement does not necessarily provide perfect recall, either: in (16) a PP consisting of three words occurs between the verb and its NP complement. Limiting the retrieval to instances that are directly followed by the preposition *against* further reduces recall by missing any instances of coordinated verb phrases where one of the antagonistic verbs targeted in this study is followed by another (non-targeted) verb, as is the case in (17).

(15)   Shortsightedly, Costa Rica *protested* **vigorously** the proposed destruction of its entire territory, . . . (COHA, FIC, 1947)

(16)   I ask the North American people that, just as with the Honduran people, you *protest* **to your government** the injustices that it commits. (COHA, FIC, 1994)

(17)   The old company *protested* **and petitioned** against a grant . . . (COHA, NEWS, 1875)

The present study, therefore, uses a step-wise approach, starting with more restricted retrieval to obtain information on the general trajectories of change and moving towards an approach that improves recall at the cost of precision but that at the same time allows to take contextual factors into account and to model the extent to which intervening material may have an impact on the choice between a bare NP or PP complement.

In a first step, all forms of the verbs (including potential non-antagonistic uses) were retrieved from the corpora, followed directly by either a definite or indefinite article (as a proxy for bare NP complementation) or the preposition *against* (as a proxy for PP complementation).[3] These data provide a rough indication on the global variance of NP vs. PP complements with *fight, oppose* and *protest*. The latter turns out to, indeed, show the clearest trajectory with respect to diachronic change and regional divergence (see section 4.1). The follow-up study on predictor variables therefore focuses on *protest* in AmE, where the bare NP comes to dominate in the course of the twentieth century.

In a second step, a random set of a hundred instances per decade of antagonistic *protest* with either bare nominal or prepositional complement were retrieved from COHA for the years 1900–2010. The search window for the retrieval of this dataset was not restricted, i.e. the instances were taken from a randomized lists of all instances of the verb, which were manually post-edited to exclude e.g. tagging errors (instances where the noun *protest* had wrongly been tagged as a verb) or potentially non-antagonistic uses such as (18), where the verb could also mean 'proclaim'.

(18)   He *protested* some of Ozinga's criticisms as unfair . . . (COHA, NEWS, 1972)

The prepositional complements in this dataset include instances with other prepositions than *against,* such as *about, over* or *at*:

(19)   . . . we who should have *protested* to Britain **about** her anti-Soviet propaganda. (COHA, MAG, 1927)

(20)   . . . Argentina, which *protested* to the United Nations **over** a violation of its sovereignty, . . . (COHA, NEWS, 1961)

(21)   the general checked Marteau, . . . who had sprung forward to *protest* to the Emperor **at** the words of the woman he loved. (COHA, FIC, 1915)

However, only instances with phrasal complements were included in the dataset, i.e. complement clauses such as (22) were not selected from the concordance lists. Similarly, the data were restricted to complements that followed the verb rather than those that preceded it; this meant that instances like (23) to (27) were not included in the random sample of 100 instances. The reasons for excluding

---

3 The search strings in the Hansard and COHA corpora thus took the following form (illustrated for *fight*: [fight]_v the|a (for the bare NP complement) and [fight]_v against (for the PP complement). For *oppose,* an additional preposition (*to*) was included in the search algorithm. For *protest,* additional prepositions were also included but returned only few hits and are therefore not reported in section 4.1 below and are omitted from the tables in the Appendix.

instances where the complement precedes the verb are that they are difficult to annotate with respect to the predictor variable 'distance' (see below) and that they added further complications, such as the potential for pied-piping.

(22) I want to rally, hit back, *protest* **how self-centred Father is** . . . (COHA, FIC, 2009)

(23) . . . **what** they were *protesting* when they were in college . . . (COHA, NEWS, 2004)

(24) Against **barbarism of this sort** we urgently *protest*. (COHA, MAG, 1922)

(25) . . . **the kind of police abuse** they *protest* against in the streets. (COHA, MAG, 2000)

(26) They provoke **a return to the heresies** against which they *protest* . . . (COHA, MAG, 1903)

(27) **More games** likely will be *protested* if the umpires have discretion . . . (COHA, NEWS, 1943)

The resulting set of 1100 hits was then annotated for a set of predictor variables. The two contextual variables are the DECADE (for the diachronic dimension) and the REGISTER (or text type). Language internal predictors include the VERBFORM (base form, present tense, past tense, non-finite forms in *-ing* and *-ed*), the DEFINITENESS of the NP (whether as bare NP or part of the PP complement) and the DISTANCE between the verb/preposition and the complement, measured in number of words. The predictor variables and their levels are summarized in Table 1.

Table 1: Overview of predictor variables.

Variable label	Variable levels
Decade	1900, 1910, 1920, . . . 2000
Register	'FIC' (fiction), 'MAG' (magazine), 'NEWS', 'NF/ACAD' (non-fiction/academic), 'TV/MOV' (TV and movie scripts)
VerbForm	base, present, past, -ing, -ed
Definiteness	def, indef
Distance	0, 1, 2, . . .

4 Results

4.1 Diachronic trajectories: Regional variation

The corpus searches for the broad diachronic trends were not manually post-edited as the amount of data retrieved (a total of 22,594 contexts from COHA and 165,390 from *Hansard*) made this unfeasible. This means that false positives – non-antagonistic senses as in (28), tagging errors such as (29), but also instances where e.g. the indefinite and definite articles did not introduce NP complements, as in examples (30) and (31) or those where a clause boundary separated the verb and the following phrase, as in (32) are still included in the data presented in Figures 1a and Figure 1b (for raw frequencies, see Table A in the Appendix).

(28)   The Prime Minister has *protested* the importance that the Government place on carers' needs: . . . (Hansard, House of Commons, 2000)

(29)   I, personally, would like to know what *protest* the Government intend to make to the United States Government . . . (Hansard, House of Commons, 1964)

(30)   Gentleman the Secretary of State for India will not deny that we *protested* the moment we were consulted . . . (Hansard, House of Commons, 1929)

(31)   . . . I *protested* **a good many years ago** against British lives being placed in jeopardy by attempting to deal with the Slave Trade in so ineffectual a manner . . . (Hansard, House of Commons, 1890)

(32)   . . . when I ventured to *protest* the Parliamentary Secretary with his usual suavity told me that I need not worry . . . (Hansard, House of Commons, 1933)

Instances with *against*, on the other hand, include those where the following NP is headed by a demonstrative pronoun (see (33)); since the search string serving as a proxy for bare NPs did not include those introduced by a demonstrative, the proportion of bare complementation reported in Figures 1a and Figure 1b data-sets is therefore a little conservative.

(33)   I *protest* against **this** blatant discrimination against public enterprise

Thus, for a subset of the COHA data (1920–2010), all 1,610 instances for the verb *protest* were manually post-edited to gauge the extent to which the inclusion of false positives and poorer recall for bare NPs may have impacted diachronic developments. The results of the comparison with the unedited data are discussed below; they indicate that the unedited frequencies provide a good indication of the general direction of change. The initial trajectory for *oppose* included instances of the semi fixed phrase *(be) opposed to*, which amounted to 99.4% and 97.7% in the *Hansard* and COHA corpora, respectively. Since these would unduly skew the trajectories for this verb, they were excluded from the counts in Figures 1a and Figure 1b below.

Across the two hundred years covered by the British *Hansard* corpus, the three antagonistic verbs do not change substantially in their complementation patterns (see Figure 1a). For *fight* and *oppose*, the bare NP complement is the dominant ASC, and despite an increase in PP complements with *fight* in the second half of the nineteenth century, the trendline does not show any long-term diachronic change in the ASC for this verb, either. For *oppose* (without *opposed* (*to*)), bare complementation is almost categorical by the end of the twentieth century. Examples (34) and (35) illustrate this rare pattern.

(34) . . . the more people hear the arguments against change, the more they rally to *oppose* to change . . . (Hansard, House of Commons, 1996)

(35) It is guesswork about the right size and type of force to *oppose* against that threat: . . . (Hansard, House of Commons, 1976)

The verb *protest*, on the other hand, is categorically used with a PP complement at the beginning of the nineteenth century and, despite an apparent decline in PP complements towards the end of the twentieth century, this is the case throughout the decades covered by the British *Hansard* corpus. On closer inspection, moreover, only 7 of the 145 hits of *protest* followed by *the|a* in the *Hansard* corpus turn out to be unambiguous instances of the antagonistic use with a bare NP complement. The earliest of these, example (36), is from 1900 and the most recent example ((39)) is from 1995; there is only one instance (namely (37)) from the House of Lords.

(36) . . . he should take every opportunity of *protesting* a loan for the purposes of prolonging a war which the Irish regarded as unjust and inhuman . . . (Hansard, House of Commons, 1900)

(37) The right reverend Prelate might also like to consider what will happen if someone *protests* a decision that he or she . . . was not accepted as a child . . . (Hansard, House of Lords, 1981)

(38) They are all *protesting* the regulations and are making it clear that they are
completely opposed to them (Hansard, House of Commons, 1986)

(39) However much Conservative Members *protest* the valid points made from
this side of the House, they seem reluctant to address the fundamental
issue . . . (Hansard, House of Commons, 1995)

Overall, there is thus clearly no general trend towards bare complementation
with the three antagonistic verbs in BrE, least of all with *protest*. This cannot be
attributed to a potentially conservative style in parliamentary speeches as both
Hundt (1998: 110) and Rohdenburg (2009: 199) report similarly low proportions of
bare NP complements from their BrE newspaper evidence (at 2% and 5.9%,
respectively).

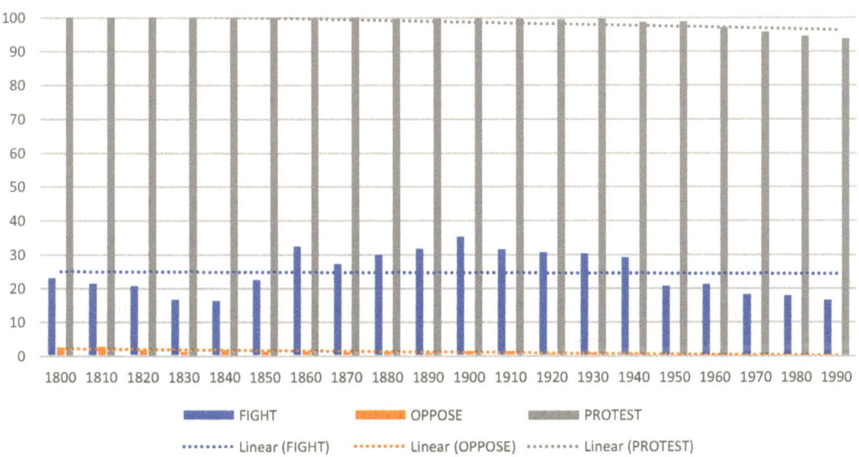

Figure 1a: Proportion of PP complements with antagonistic verbs in the British *Hansard* corpus.

Figure 1b, by contrast, shows that PP complements with antagonistic verbs decline in
COHA, but the trajectories are different for the three verbs. Bare NP complements
are the preferred argument type for *fight* and *oppose* already at the beginning of the
nineteenth century, and both show further decline of the PP variant towards the beginning of the twenty-first century. The most extreme change occurs with *protest*,
which – as in BrE – has a categorical rule of using PP complements at the beginning

of the nineteenth century. The proportion of PP arguments drops below 50% by the 1950s and declines to under 20% by the 1970s. At the beginning of the twenty-first century, *protest* is the verb that shows the most marked preference for bare NP complements. The focus in the variationist part of this study therefore looks more closely at the changing predictors with *protest* in the twentieth century COHA data.

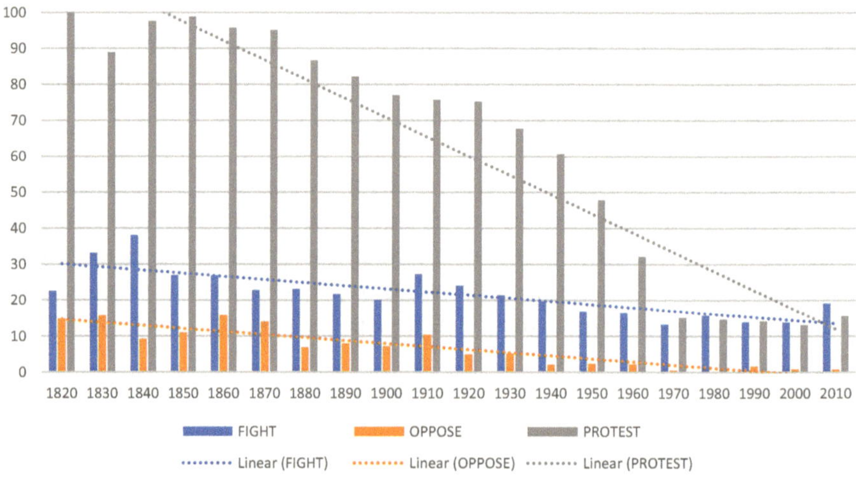

Figure 1b: Proportion of PP complements with antagonistic verbs in the *Corpus of Historical American* English.

In order to gauge the reliability of the general trends indicated in Figures 1a and Figure 1b, all instances of *protest* from the 1920s-2010s from COHA were manually post-edited. Of the original 1,610 instances, 474 false positives were removed, and the remaining instances coded for the type of complementation. Figure 1c shows the proportion of PP complements for the unedited and post-edited data sets: for the first data point, the unedited dataset over-reports bare NPs, but the remaining data points show that the trajectories provided in Figures 1a and Figure 1b are likely to be conservative with respect to the proportion of bare complementation. It is thus likely that the trends that emerge from Figures 1a and Figure 1b are fairly reliable with respect to the potential developments towards bare complementation.

Even if there is a marked trend towards bare complementation with *protest* in twentieth-century AmE, and the proportion of PP complements with *oppose* also decline in this variety, this does not support a more general development towards direct transitivization with antagonistic verbs in English. In fact, if PP complementation of antagonistic verbs were in decline, we should see a decrease in the number of verb-attached *against* across time. This does not seem to be the

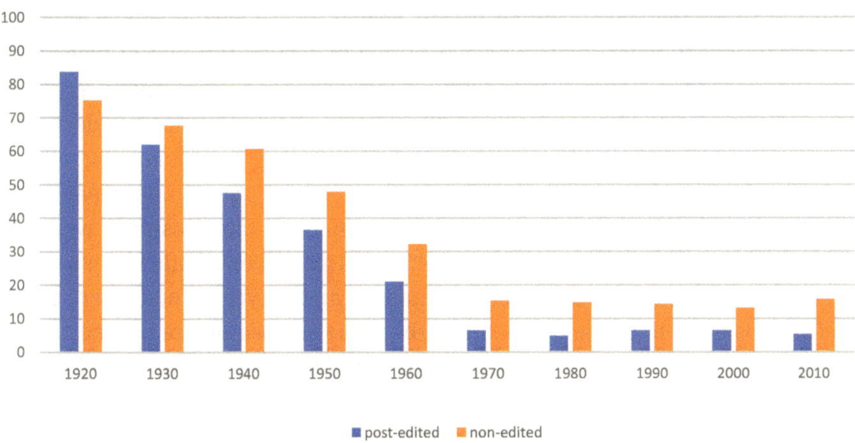

Figure 1c: Proportion of PP complements: comparing unedited (N=1,610) and post-edited (N=1,136) results from COHA for *protest*.

case, though. In COHA, the relative frequency (per million words) of *against* (preceded by any verb) does not reveal a marked decline across the nineteenth and twentieth centuries (see Figure 2a).

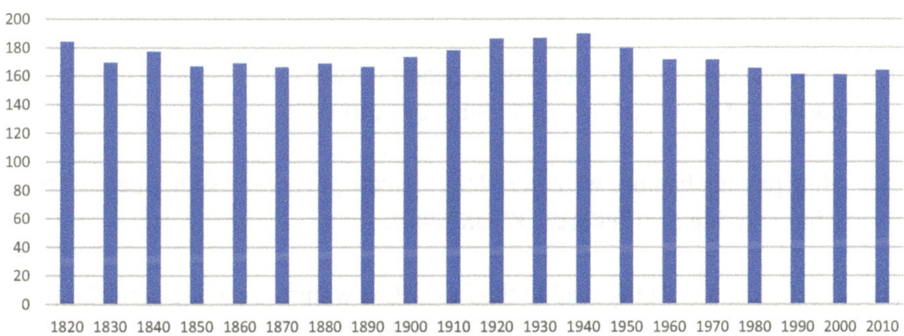

Figur 2a: Normalized frequency (per million) of **_v against* in COHA.

Similarly, verb-attached instances of *against* do not appear to decline in Late Modern BrE. The analysis undertaken for the data from the *Penn-Parsed Corpus of Modern British English* (PPCMBE) was somewhat more fine-grained than that for the occurrences of **_v against* in COHA. First of all, while the total number of instances of verb-attached occurrences of *against* decreases from 317 in the first subperiod of the corpus to 247 in the last subperiod, the number of different types of verbs that take a PP argument headed by *against* does not undergo change (from 140 types to 137 types), resulting in a slight increase of type-token ratios from 0.44 to 0.55, which would indicate increased productivity constructions with (potentially) antagonistic PP complements rather than a decrease. However, as polysemy is also a potential problem with respect to *against*, all 808 occurrences of verb-attached PPs were analyzed with respect to the meaning of the construction. In manual post-editing a number of false positives were excluded. Apart from tagging errors (as in (40)), PPs that followed other prepositions (as in (41)) or that could also be seen to attach to an intervening noun were coded as false positives. In (42) and (43), the verbs *frame* and *season* are not the carrier of the antagonistic meaning but the nouns *complaint* and *discourse*; and in (44) and (45), finally, the preposition is used not in an antagonistic but rather in a directional and comparative sense, respectively.

(40)   . . . for we can understand the gradation only as a *prolonged* struggle against unfavourable conditions (PPCMBE, DARWIN-1842-2,109.300)

(41)   . . . he had been thereby enabled to *stand out* against the most powerful confederacy 0 that ever was formd in Europe (PPCMBE, GIBSON-1729-2,42.40)

(42)   . . . no one has ever been able to *frame* a complaint *against* the boys into the definite shape of a demand for damages. (PPCMBE, THRING-187X-1)

(43)   . . . [they] *seasoned* their discourses *against* the doctrines with invectives against the vices of the churchmen (PPCMBE, LINGARD-1823-2)

(44)   after passing lismore we *entered* the narrow part of the sound *against* both wind and tide . . . (PPCMBE, KNOX-1786-2)

(45)   didst thou entrust thy seed to the fields thou wouldst *set off* the fruitful years *against* the barren (PPCMBE, BOETHJA-1897-2)

The results in Figure 2b show that, once false positives and clearly non-antagonistic uses of the preposition have been removed, the number of instances (text frequency) of antagonistic *against* declines in the course of the Late Modern period. However, there is no significant decrease in type frequency, which indicates that antagonistic *against* has not been 'losing' verbs.

In other words, with respect to more global changes, complementation of antagonistic verbs in Late Modern English presents a case of stable variation rather

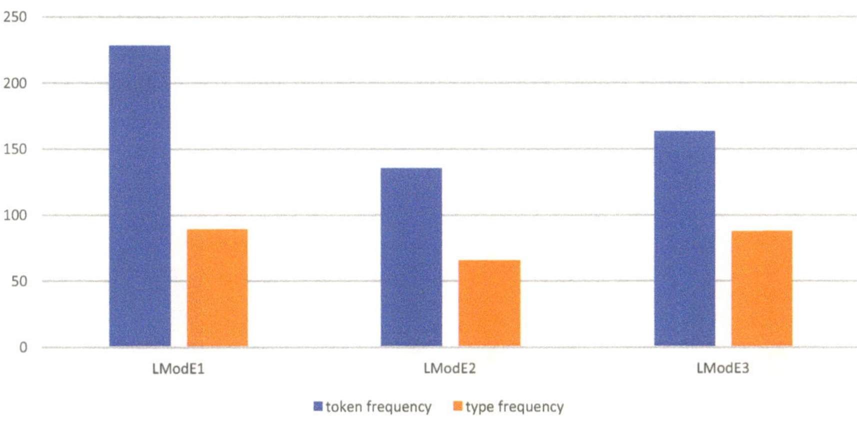

Figure 2b: Diachronic development of verb-attached instances of *against* in the PPCMBE.

than shift in ASCs. This occurs much more 'locally', i.e. with individual verbs, as is the case with *protest.* We will look at this verb in some more detail in the next two sections.

4.2 Close-up on *protest* in American English

The analysis of the 100 randomly sampled relevant instances per decade for *protest* from COHA provide further proof of a development towards near-categorical complementation with a bare NP (see Figure 3). The majority of PP complements were headed by *against* (482), with *at* (a total of 26) coming second and *about* (totaling 15 hits) third; *over* was used in only six instances and *on* in only one. Examples of the lower frequency prepositions are given in (46) to (49):

(46)   I suppose the good citizens have screamed and *protested* <u>at</u> the improvements, as good citizens always do. (COHA, FIC, 2013)

(47)   It is not Britain who should have *protested* to us **about** anti-British propaganda . . . (COHA, MAG, 1927)

(48)   The strange thing was, he hadn't *protested* **over** his advertising job. (COHA, FIC, 1939)

(49)   All the opposition is *protesting* **on** this issue. (COHA, NEWS, 2006)

Moreover, *against* is the dominant preposition throughout the course of the twentieth century, with alternatives being available as low-frequency options throughout. In other words, the prepositional option does not undergo paradigmatic attrition (a common concomitant of constructional loss) as the ASC is focused on a main variant, to start with.

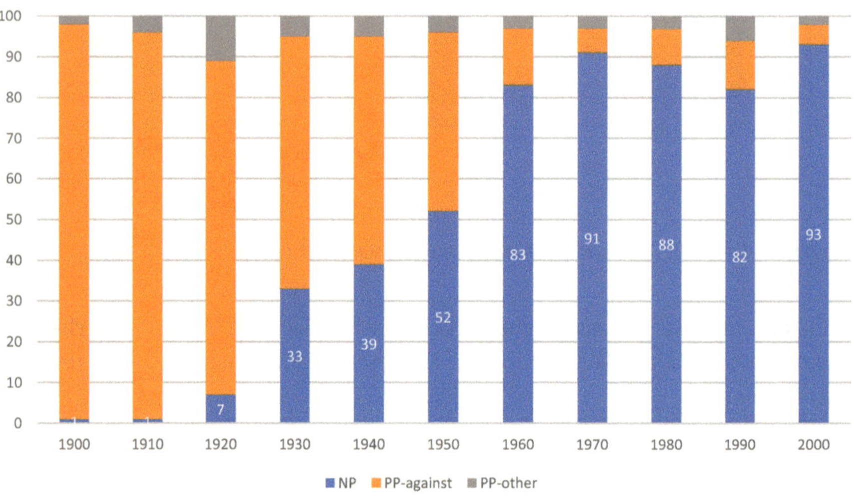

Figure 3: Complementation of *protest* in COHA (set of 100 random relevant hits per decade).

In a next step, the post-edited data were coded for the predictor variables listed in Table 1 and then subjected to multi-variate modelling. A random forest (RF) was fitted to the data for overall predictor ranking, and a single conditional inference tree (ctree) to investigate interaction between the predictor variables (see Tagliamonte & Baayen 2012). For the RF, ntree was set to '500' and mtry to '4'. For the single tree, the settings were maxdepth = 4 and mincriterion = 0.95.

The RF analysis returns DECADE as the most important predictor variable (see Figure 4), with GENRE and DISTANCE paling by comparison, and VERBFORM and DEFINITENESS turning out not to be significant as predictors. Model fit was tested with Somers2, which returned a C index of 0.9316 (dxy = 0.8632), i.e. well above the level recommended by Tagliamonte & Baayen (2012).

The single ctree also returns DECADE as the most important predictor variable and VERBFORM and DEFINITENESS as insignificant (model fit with Somers2 turned out to be satisfactory at C=0.836 and dxy = 0.672). Figure 5 shows that the PP complement dominates in the period before the 1950s, with bare complementation taking over as the dominant argument type in the second half of the twentieth

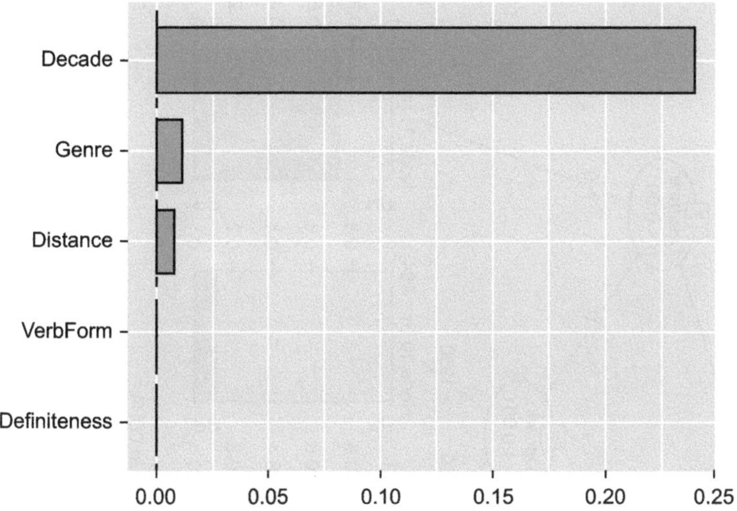

Figure 4: Variable importance (RF analysis) for choice of NP vs. PP complement following *protest* in COHA.

century (nodes 2 and 7). That the trend towards a bare NP complement is led by informal text genres (MAG and NEWS), as well as scripted spoken texts from the 1920s, is evidenced by the split in node 4. This is not surprising, as direct complementation with a bare NP fits well with the trend towards densification in these text types (see e.g. Leech et al., 2009 for examples of densification on the phrasal and word level).

With words intervening between the verb and the complement, the PP complement remains the preferred option (node 11), thus corroborating the effect of the Complexity Principle (Rohdenburg, 2009: 200) to some extent. Without intervening material, the change towards bare complementation accelerates significantly from the 1960s onwards (node 8). The single ctree thus nicely illustrates the factors driving the change-over from PP complement to bare NP complement in the course of the twentieth century.

Node 11 in the ctree clearly shows that intervening elements between the verb and the complement greatly increase the likelihood of a PP complement with *protest* in the second half of the twentieth century. The longest distance (11 words) is between the verb and a PP complement (see (50)). However, intervening material is also (marginally) attested with bare NPs. The longest distance for a bare NP complement is six words (see (51)); note that the latter is from a coordinated verb phrase where the first verb (*question*) could not be used with a preposition. There are two instances of bare complementation with three words between verb and NP, one of

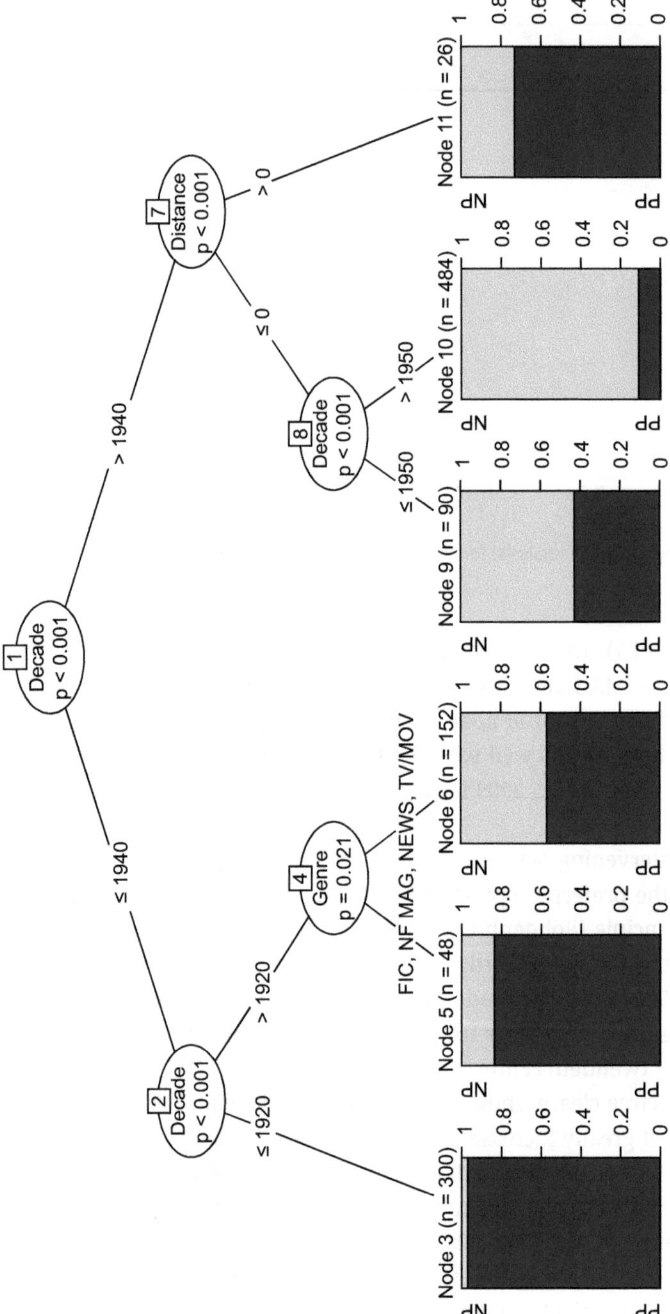

Figure 5: Variable interaction (ctree analysis) for choice of NP vs. PP complement following *protest* in COHA.

them with comma separation of the insert (see (52)). The most common distance between verb and complement for bare NPs is a single adverbial, as in (53) (a total of five instances).

(50) Some of the most vehement orators . . . who *protested* in Trafalgar Square on the first Sunday of war – August 2 – *against* our entry into the conflict in association with Russia, were addressing recruiting meetings themselves a few weeks later, or volunteering for the front. (COHA, MAG, 2017)

(51) Without Yalta the United States would have no legal basis *to question*, let alone to *protest* **on behalf of the satellite populations**, the Soviet violation of its pledge to let them choose their own form of government . . . (COHA, MAG, 1953)

(52) They were *protesting*, **among other things**, the continued imprisonment of 40 students . . . (COHA, MAG, 1971)

(53) Environmentalists have *protested* **strongly** such possible "options" as making the Environmental Protection Agency a subordinate part of a new Natural Resources Department . . . (COHA, NEWS, 1978)

4.3 Constructional Americanization?

The two previous studies that looked at complementation patterns of *protest* in BrE and AmE (Hundt 1998, Rohdenburg 2009) both used evidence from 1990s newspaper databases. These data indicated a clear regional difference between the two varieties, with AmE clearly favouring bare NP complementation, which is attested at very low frequencies in 1990s newswriting from the UK. The question is whether with an increase in international communication on the world wide web, such regional difference may turn out to be only temporal effects. Leech et al. (2009) review a number of grammatical changes in twentieth century BrE and AmE. They find that " . . . the evidence is cumulatively persuasive in indicating AmE 'leadership' being one of the major moving forces on BrE" (Leech at al. 2009: 253–54). Thus, the question is whether the divergence in the ASC for AmE *protest* has continued into the twenty-first century or whether BrE has started to follow suit.

Data for very recent constructional change come from the *News On the Web* (NOW) corpus, a web-based monitor corpus of newswriting with texts from the

2010s onwards, which is regularly updated. It includes texts from online newspapers but also other types of news outlets (e.g. uk.news.yahoo.com or politico.eu). All instances of the verb *protest* were included in the search and a total of 1'000 relevant instances sampled from a randomized list of all hits, including all possible prepositions but excluding false positives (see examples (18) to (27) and the related discussion in section 3.2). An additional type of false positive included uses of PPs headed by *at* which introduced an adverbial of place (see (54)) rather than a prepositional complement.

(54) CodePink demonstrators *protest* at an anti-Donald Trump rally in Cleveland. (NOW-GB, *The Independent*, 2022-07-16)

For the final analysis, only instances from national news outlets (BBC news), regional and national newspapers were included, resulting in a total of 757 hits (see Table B in the Appendix for raw frequencies). National newspapers were further subdivided into broadsheets and tabloids (i.e. quality vs. popular). Hundt's (1998) findings for the distribution of ASC in the early 1990s *Guardian* are set next to the findings from NOW in Figure 6. The graph shows that there has, indeed, been an increase in bare NP complements following *protest* at the beginning of the twenty-first century. Moreover, there has been a shift towards *against* at the expense of alternatives (notably *at* and *about*). This reduction in paradigmatic variability, or

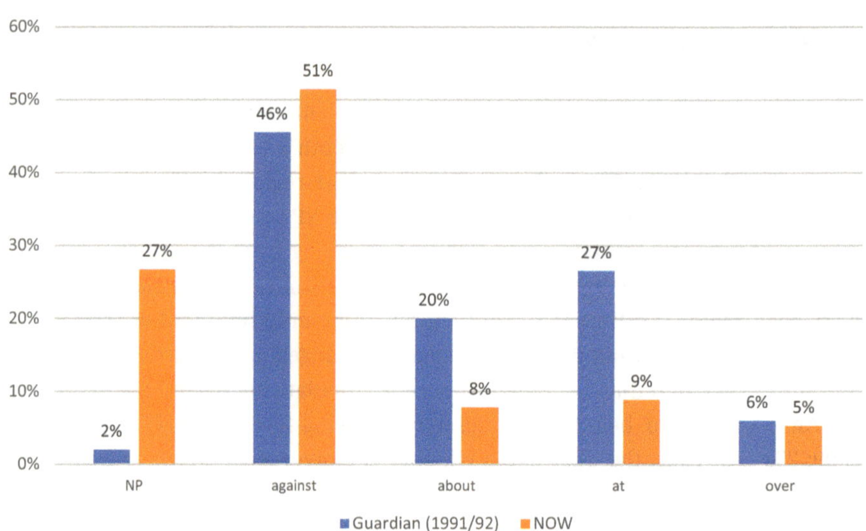

Figure 6: Complementation of *protest* in BrE: 1990s *Guardian* (N=400) vs. 2010+ NOW (N=757) data.

'paradigmatic attrition', of the ASC is a parameter typical of processes of syntactic loss (see e.g. Hundt and Leech, 2012, Hundt 2014).

A single conditional inference tree for the NOW dataset is provided in Figure 7. The ctree shows that the rise in bare NP complements in BrE news writing is a relatively recent phenomenon, dating from the years 2014 onwards. The proportion of PPs in the data drops from above 80% in the years 2010–2013 to 65.5% in 2014. Moreover, as the split in node 3 shows, the trend away from PP complement towards bare NP arguments is spearheaded by the tabloids (below 40% PP complements), with broadsheet newspapers at around 60% PP complements being much more conservative; the national news outlets and regional papers still show a marked preference for the original BrE ASC with *protest*. In other words, while the former American ASC is being adopted in the UK, there is clear stylistic stratification in this ongoing trend.

5 Discussion and concluding remarks

The diachronic bird's eye view on ASC used with *fight, oppose* and *protest* in BrE and AmE has not provided convincing evidence of a unified trend towards bare NP complements. That all antagonistic verbs are unlikely to have shifted away from PP complements finds support from the analysis of *against*, arguably the most antagonistic preposition in Present Day English, which does not show a loss in the type of different antagonistic verbs that combine with it in the course of the Late Modern period. Thus, a shift towards direct transitivization was only found with a single verb, namely *protest*, and in one regional variety (AmE) in the second half of the twentieth century. Curiously enough, out of the three verbs investigated here, it is the one that is the least antagonistic which shifts towards bare NP complementation in AmE in the latter half of the twentieth century. The change affects the verb and not the related nominal construction, where the antagonistic meaning still requires the use of a preposition (see (55)) unless the entity against which the protest is directed is not mentioned, of course (see (56)).

(55)   For God's sake, Mom, this was a *protest* **against** the way they treat immigrants. (COHA, FIC, 2010)

(56)   Our methods of *protest* were different, absolutely. (COHA, FIC, 2010)

Overall discourse frequency cannot explain the shift towards bare NP complementation for *protest* among the group of verbs investigated here, either: a search

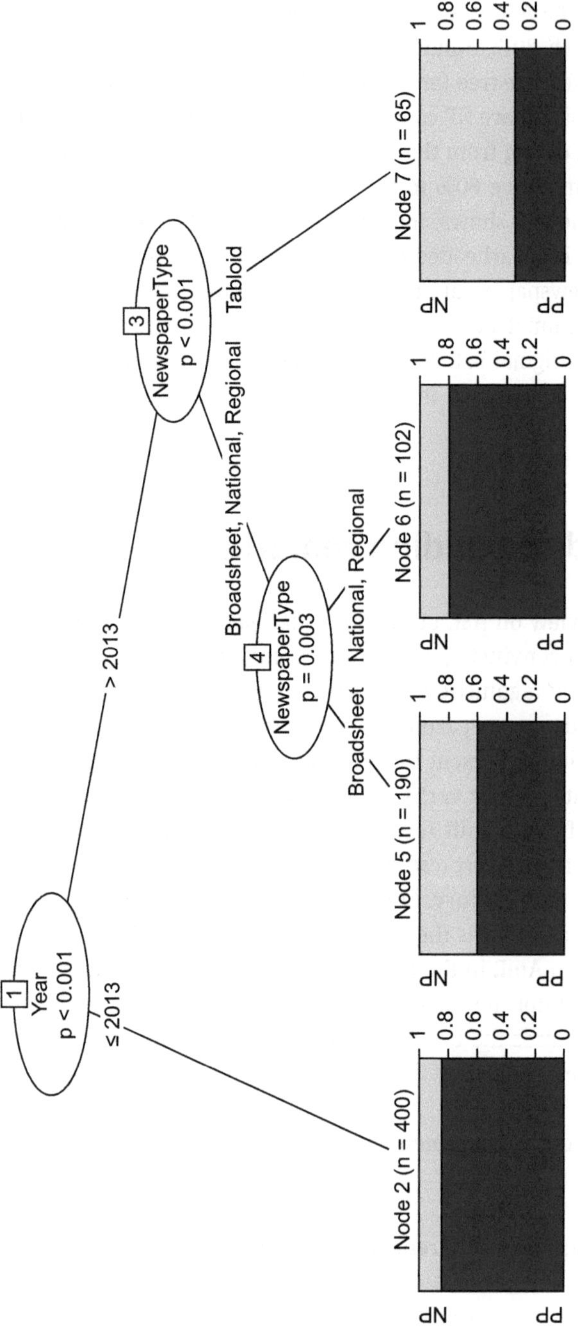

Figure 7: Complementation of *protest* in BrE: 1990s *Guardian* (N=400) vs. 2010+ NOW (N=757) data (Somers2 C = 0.583).

for all verb forms of *protest* in COHA yields a total of 13,711 hits (as opposed to 21,730 for *oppose* and 71,104 for *fight*). The fact that a general trend towards NP complementation with antagonistic verbs does not find support in the present study should therefore caution us against drawing such sweeping conclusions with respect to a (semantic) group of verbs on the basis of a few single items. As is often the case, lexical variation is an important determinant in constructional change.

The change in ASC found with *protest* in the second half of the twentieth century is clearly regional in origin but unlikely to remain a grammatical Americanism in the long run: The NOW data provide suggestive evidence of ongoing change in British newswriting. Moreover, this is characterized by the most prominent hallmark of (grammatical) Americanization, namely stylistic stratification: The competitor first spreads in popular (tabloid) publications with so-called quality newspapers (the former broadsheets) lagging considerably behind in this trend. The change in ASC for *protest* thus resembles patterns observed for the spread of noun-phrase name appositions from AmE to BrE, where the spread of pseudo-title construction like *Suffolk teenager Jenny Jenkins* (at the expense of older from older constructions like *the teenager from Suffolk, Jenny Jenkins*) was, likewise, first found attested in tabloids and only later in broadsheet papers (see Jucker 1992, Meyer 2002). Unlike pseudo-titles, however, which were associated with the style of writing characteristic of *Time Magazine* (e.g. Quirk et al., 1985: 276), direct transitivization of *protest* is not, to the best of my knowledge, a grammatical shibboleth of AmE. In an online discussion from 2010 about the 'correct' preposition to use with *protest* in BrE vs. AmE,[4] a native speaker of BrE is apparently unaware of the possibility to use a bare NP complement with this verb in the US: he uses the COCA and BNC corpora and starts wondering about the apparent differences in frequency between the different options of *in protest*_preposition on both sides of the Atlantic, but it is in a comment to the original blog entry that somebody points out the reason for this discrepancy, i.e. the fact that the complementation pattern without a preposition is the default pattern in AmE today. With most speakers being unaware of the cross-Atlantic differences, the driving force behind the change towards direct complementation in BrE news writing could therefore also be a language-internal factor, such as the trend towards densification in informational prose. This interpretation is also compatible with the spread from popular to quality papers that is indicated in the most recent NOW data. The important lesson to be learnt from the present case study is

---

4 See https://separatedbyacommonlanguage.blogspot.com/2010/03/protesting-prepositions.html (last visited 17.08.2021).

that the quest for grammatical regionalisms in World Englishes research will ultimately return transitory phenomena.[5] Even though AmE had diverged in its use of *protest* by the end of the twentieth century, BrE is in the process of following suit (with New Zealand English having started down the road of the same change in the mid 1990s, see Hundt 1998: 110).

That we are likely, ultimately, to deal with an instance of constructional loss in BrE is evidenced by the fact that the range of available prepositions has reduced between the 1990s and the early decades of the twenty first century. There is a clear trend towards just one option, and change in complementation of *protest* in BrE newswriting is thus characterized by 'paradigmatic attrition'. As in AmE, the prepositional variant is likely to retreat to a niche context, i.e. patterns with more than a single word intervening between the verb and its argument.

Appendix

Table A: Overview of complementation in the COHA and Hansard corpora for antagonistic verbs (raw frequencies).

COHA	FIGHT PP	NP	OPPOSE PP	NP	PROTEST PP	NP	Total
1820	14	48	9	52	28	0	151
1830	44	89	17	91	48	6	295
1840	65	106	10	99	82	2	364
1850	43	116	9	73	88	1	330
1860	67	182	18	96	111	5	479
1870	61	207	13	80	132	7	500
1880	80	266	9	122	128	20	625
1890	75	270	9	103	135	28	620
1900	74	294	9	118	141	42	678
1910	119	318	13	112	168	54	784
1920	129	409	7	135	182	60	922
1930	115	426	9	163	134	64	911
1940	163	664	3	139	99	64	1132
1950	132	656	4	164	66	72	1094
1960	109	556	5	219	53	112	1054
1970	82	536	1	190	28	156	993
1980	110	587	0	170	26	151	1044

---

5 See Hansen (2018) for a similar finding on modal verbs across different types of Englishes.

Table A (continued)

COHA	FIGHT PP	NP	OPPOSE PP	NP	PROTEST PP	NP	Total
1990	92	572	2	115	15	91	887
2000	107	666	1	112	16	106	1008
2010	148	632	1	119	18	97	1015
Total	**1829**	**7600**	**149**	**2472**	**1698**	**1138**	**14886**

Hansard	FIGHT PP	NP	OPPOSE PP	NP	PROTEST PP	NP	Total
1800	8	27	11	431	128	0	605
1810	17	63	19	691	280	0	1070
1820	9	35	16	964	483	0	1507
1830	26	131	33	2621	1620	0	4431
1840	35	181	35	2213	1241	2	3707
1850	56	195	28	2306	1512	0	4097
1860	59	124	22	1831	1568	3	3607
1870	86	231	20	1992	2275	1	4605
1880	170	402	35	3035	3551	10	7203
1890	135	294	15	2088	2878	5	5415
1900	254	472	24	1785	3003	5	5543
1910	360	792	19	1494	2223	8	4896
1920	284	648	8	1657	1855	9	4461
1930	311	721	16	2393	1645	6	5092
1940	536	1380	6	1110	834	11	3877
1950	293	1126	4	1846	770	9	4048
1960	331	1241	9	2841	607	19	5048
1970	370	1679	7	3442	354	16	5868
1980	393	1827	10	5298	256	15	7799
1990	344	1771	5	5495	209	14	7838
Total	**4077**	**13340**	**342**	**45533**	**27292**	**133**	**90717**

Table B: Complementation of *protest* in the NOW corpus for BrE (random sample).

	NP	PP
2010	47	218
2011	9	59
2012	6	46
2013	2	13
2014	10	19

Table B (continued)

	NP	PP
2015	18	18
2016	18	38
2017	39	48
2018	17	32
2019	20	24
2020	9	23
2021	7	17
Total	202	555

References

Corpora

CLMET = The *Corpus of Late Modern English Texts,* version 3.0 (https://perswww.kuleuven.be/~u0044428/clmet3_0.htm)

COHA = The *Corpus of Contemporary American English* (https://corpus.byu.edu/coha/)

OED online = *Oxford English Dictionary* online (http://www.oed.com;lastaccessed11.08.2021)

Hansard = The *Hansard Corpus* of British Parliamentary Speeches (https://www.english-corpora.org/hansard/)

ICE = *International Corpus of English* (https://www.ice-corpora.uzh.ch/en.html)

PPCEME = The *Penn-Parsed Corpus of Early Modern* English (http://www.ling.upenn.edu/ppche-release-2016/PPCEME-RELEASE-3)

PPCMBE = The *Penn-Parsed Corpus of Modern British English* (https://www.ling.upenn.edu/hist-corpora/PPCMBE2-RELEASE-1/index.html)

NOW = *News On the Web* Corpus (https://www.english-corpora.org/now)

References

Algeo, John. 1988. British and American grammatical differences. *International Journal of Lexicography* 1(1). 1–31.

Algeo, Joh. 2006. *British or American English? A handbook of word and grammar patterns.* Cambridge: University Press.

Callies, Marcus. 2018. Patterns of direct transitivization and differences between British and American English. In Mark Kaunisto, Mikko Höglund & Paul Rickmann (eds.), *Changing structures: Studies in constructions and complementation*, 151–167. Amsterdam: Benjamins.

Fischer, Olga & Wim van der Wurff. 2006. Syntax. In Richard Hogg & David Denison (eds.), *A history of the English language*, 109–198. Cambridge: Cambridge University Press.

Hansen, Beke. 2018. *Corpus linguistics and sociolinguistics: A study of variation and change in the modal systems of World Englishes*. Leiden: Brill.

Hawkins, John A. 1986. *A comparative typology of English and German: Unifying the contrasts*. London: Croom Helm.

Hundt, Marianne. 1998. *New Zealand English grammar – Fact or fiction? A corpus-based study in morphosyntactic variation*. Amsterdam: John Benjamins.

Hundt, Marianne. 2014. The demise of the *being to V* construction. In *Transactions of the Philological Society* 112(2). 167–187.

Hundt, Marianne & Geoffrey Leech. 2012. Small is beautiful: On the value of standard reference corpora for observing recent grammatical change. In Terttu Nevalainen & Elizabeth Traugott (eds.), *The Oxford handbook of the history of English*, 175–88. New York: Oxford University Press.

Hundt, Marianne & Laetitia van Driessche. *Forthcoming*. Prepositions in English Argument Structure constructions: Gauging the importance of language contact for diachronic and regional constructional variation. To appear in Hans C. Boas & Steffen Höder (eds.), *Constructions in contact 3*. Amsterdam: John Benjamins.

Jespersen, Otto. 1927. *A modern English grammar on historical principles*, Part III: *Syntax (Second Volume)*. London: George Allen & Unwin.

Jucker, Andreas. 1992. *Social stylistics: Syntactic variation in British newspapers*. Berlin: Mouton de Gruyter.

Kirchner, Gustav. 1955. Direct transitivisation. *English Studies* 36: 15–23.

Leech, Geoffrey, Marianne Hundt, Christian Mair & Nicholas Smith. 2009. *Change in contemporary English. A grammatical study*. Cambridge: Cambridge University Press.

Legenhausen, Lienhard & Günter Rohdenburg. 1995. Konstrastivierung ausgewählter Strukturen im Englischen und Deutschen. In Rüdiger Ahrens, Wolf-Dietrich Bald & Werner Hüllen (eds.), *Handbuch English als Fremdsprache*, 133–139. Berlin: Schmidt.

Meyer, Charles F. 2002. Pseudo-titles in the press genre of various components of the International Corpus of English. In Randi Reppen, Susan M. Fitzmaurice & Douglas Biber (eds.), *Using corpora to explore linguistic variation*, 147–166. Amsterdam: Benjamins,

Nesselhauf, Nadja. 2009. Co-selection phenomena across New Englishes. Parallels (and differences) to foreign learner varieties. *English World-Wide* 30(1). 1–26.

Perek, Florent. 2014. Rethinking constructional polysemy. The case of the English conative construction. In Dylan Glynn & Justyna A. Robinson (eds.), *Corpus methods for semantics: Quantitative studies in polysemy and synonymy*, 61–85. Amsterdam: John Benjamins.

Quirk, Randolph, Sidney Greenbaum, Geoffrey Leech & Jan Svartvik. 1985. *A comprehensive grammar of the English language*. London: Longman.

Rohdenburg, Günter. 2009. Nominal complements. In Günter Rohdenburg & Julia Schlüter (eds.), *One language, two grammars? Differences between British and American English*, 194–211. Cambridge: Cambridge University Press.

Tagliamonte, Sali & Harald Baayen. 2012. Models, forests, and trees of York English: *Was/were* variation as a case study for statistical practice. *Language Variation and Change* 24(2). 135–178.

Zehentner, Eva & Marianne Hundt. 2022. Prepositions in Early Modern English argument structure. In Bettelou Los, Claire Cowie, Patrick Honeybone & Graeme Trousdale (eds.), *English historical linguistics: Change in structure and Meaning*, 202–224. Amsterdam: John Benjamins.

María José López-Couso and Javier Pérez-Guerra

8 Promoting and inhibiting forces at work

A corpus-based analysis of negative contraction in the recent history of English

Abstract: The first clear orthographic signs of negative contraction in English (e.g. *is not > isn't*) go back to the late sixteenth or early seventeenth century. In the following centuries, such reduced forms were openly criticized in grammars and spelling books as being improper, vulgar, colloquial, inelegant, barbarous, harsh and even ungrammatical, especially in writing, except for poetic use. In spite of this "war upon contractions" (Leonard 1929: 170), however, the Late Modern English period witnessed a considerable increase in the use of contracted forms in published material, an expansion which has continued to the present day. The aim of this chapter is to examine the role that different factors played in the selection of negative contractions and their uncontracted counterparts in eighteenth, nineteenth and twentieth-century written English. For our purposes, data have been drawn from A Representative Corpus of Historical English Registers (ARCHER). The selection of contracted and uncontracted negatives in Late Modern English and twentieth-century English is taken here to be the result of the interplay of promoting and inhibiting forces of various kinds, involving both intralinguistic (structural and semantic) determinants of variation together with extralinguistic factors, such as register and dialect. In an attempt to corroborate or refute the null hypothesis 'negative contraction is not conditioned by the variables considered in this investigation', a multivariate analysis will identify the list of variables with greater explanatory power within the model.

Keywords: contraction, negation, Late Modern English, twentieth-century English, multivariate analysis

Acknowledgements: We are grateful to the Spanish State Research Agency and the European Regional Development Fund (grants no. PID2020-114604GB-I00 and PID2020-117541GB-I00), and the Xunta de Galicia (grants no. ED431B 2020/01 and ED431C 2021/52) for generous financial support. We also thank two anonymous reviewers for their insightful comments on an earlier version of this chapter.

https://doi.org/10.1515/9783110753059-008

1 Introduction

It is generally agreed that the first clear orthographic signs of negative cliticization, negative contraction or *not* contraction (e.g. *is not* > *isn't*; *have not* > *haven't*) go back to the late sixteenth or early seventeenth century (cf., among others, Strang 1970: 151; Barber 1976: 254; Brainerd 1989[1993]; Denison 1993: 309; 1998: 195; Warner 1993: 207–208; Lass 1999: 179–180; Mazzon 2004: 62; 104–105; Tagliamonte and Smith 2002: 273; Huber 2007), somewhat later than the first occurrences of auxiliary cliticization or verb contraction (e.g. *he is* > *he's*; *I will* > *I'll*), which is attested by around 1600 (cf. Jespersen 1917: 117; Lass 1999: 179). However, negative and auxiliary cliticized forms were probably employed in the spoken language much earlier than they were represented with clitic forms in print, as proved by the scanning as monosyllables of sequences with full-form spellings such as *I am, he is* or *cannot* in Shakespeare's works (cf. Jespersen 1909–1949, vol. V: 429–430; Jespersen 1917: 117; Lass 1999: 179–180).

In the following centuries, negative contractions were the object of a fierce campaign against all kinds of reduced forms which was initiated in the early eighteenth century by Jonathan Swift and Joseph Addison. Addison, for instance, maintained that the English have a "natural taciturnity" and a "natural aversion to loquacity", which leads them to express themselves as concisely and succinctly as possible. As regards negative contractions, "this humour of speaking no more than we need" explains why "we have drawn two words into one, which has likewise very much untun'd our language, and clogged it with consonants, as 'mayn't, can't, sha'n't, wo'n't,' and the like, for 'may not, can not, shall not, will not,' &c." (*Spectator* nº 135, Saturday August 4, 1711). Normative grammarians of the time openly objected to and disapproved contracted forms of all kinds, but more strongly criticized contractions across word boundaries such as those resulting from negative cliticization. Except for poetic use, such forms were characterized as barbarous, improper, inelegant, harsh and vulgar throughout the eighteenth (cf. Sundby et al. 1991: 159–165; Haugland 1995) and the nineteenth centuries (cf. Philipps 1984: 68–70). Despite this "war upon contractions" (Leonard 1929: 170), however, the use of negative contracted forms in printed material increased considerably in the Late Modern English period, an expansion which has continued to the present day.

In this context, this chapter aims at examining the role played by different factors on the selection of negative contractions and their uncontracted counterparts in eighteenth, nineteenth and twentieth-century written English, based on data from ARCHER: A Representative Corpus of Historical English Registers. Along the lines suggested by Kjellmer (1998) for Present-day English, we believe that the selection of contracted and uncontracted negatives in the ARCHER material is conditioned by the interplay of a number of potential determinants of variation, promoting and inhibiting forces of various kinds, involving both intralinguistic (structural and semantic) determinants of variation together with extralinguistic factors, such as register and dialect.

The outline of the chapter is as follows. Section 2 provides an overview of the corpus material used for the study, while Section 3 introduces the different (dependent and independent) variables which have been selected for the analysis. Section 4, in turn, is devoted to the statistical treatment of the data, with a view to identifying the list of variables with greater explanatory power within the model. Finally, in Section 5 we offer a summary of the major findings and some concluding remarks.

2 The corpus

As mentioned in Section 1, the data for our study have been drawn from ARCHER 3.2: A Representative Corpus of Historical English Registers.[1] The texts we have selected for the analysis total some one million words in all (see Table 1). These texts, which represent a wide range of register types (see Section 3 below), belong to the six subperiods in the corpus which correspond to the second half of the eighteenth, nineteenth and twentieth centuries of both British and American English.

Table 1: The corpus.

Dialect	Period	Word total
British English	1750–1799	173,306
	1850–1899	189,721
	1950–1990	199,270
American English	1750–1799	159,564
	1850–1899	185,296
	1950–1990	160,680
Total words		1,067,837

Since our aim is to identify the determinants of the variation between full verb operators and full/reduced negators (e.g. *is not/isn't*), negative verbal groups featuring so-called auxiliary cliticization or verb contraction (e.g. *he's not*) have been

---

1 For a description of ARCHER, see, among others, Biber et al. (1994) and Yáñez-Bouza (2011).

disregarded here. Our analysis focuses on those cases where the verb form and the negative particle *not* are adjacent, as in (1) below. By contrast, instances where the verbal form and the negator are separated by intervening material, as in (2), have not been included in the count.

(1)   'This **is not** the place to preach the theory of direct inspiration,' said the Nalghai, returning Torpenhow's large and workmanlike bellows to their neail on the wall. (1899, Rudyard Kipling, *The Light That Failed*)

(2)   Then followed the flower of the Norwegian nobility, who have much intrinsic merit, but **are** certainly **not** made for show; (1827, Marchioness of Westminster, *Diary of a Tour in Sweden, Norway and Russia*)

Moreover, we had to sift out the relevant data from those examples of the sequence 'verb + *not*' which did not constitute an example of clausal negation and, therefore, could not be contracted. Example (3) below illustrates this pattern.

(3)   Oh what a comfort it is not to be oppressed with fear every moment. (1876, Reverend Edward Roe, *Near to Nature's Heart*)

3 The variables

Starting from the premise, already mentioned in the introduction, that several forces may have had a bearing on the choice between contracted and uncontracted negatives in our Late Modern English and Present-day English material from ARCHER, a somewhat wide range of variables has been considered here as potential determinants of variation. Thus, together with the binary dependent or response variable 'presence/absence of contraction', we have considered a total of 12 independent variables: period, dialect, register, verbal operator, tense of the operator, person and number of the operator, subject type, clause type, clause depth, position, category of the constituent immediately occurring after *not/n't* and frequency of the lexical verb under the scope of negation. This list of variables is by no means exhaustive. Other determinants, such as degree of emphasis, social class, gender, age, string frequency or phonological factors of various kinds,[2] among others, have been disregarded in

---

2 We are grateful to an anonymous reviewer for drawing our attention to the potential influence on the variation of factors of a phonological nature, including the fact that some contractions reduce the syllable count in comparison to their uncontracted counterparts (e.g. *don't*), while

our analysis. Some of these variables are not easily measured in written texts (e.g. degree of emphasis), while for some others we lack sufficient data (e.g. age factor or social factor). The 12 selected variables are described individually in some detail in the paragraphs that follow.

(i) Period: As already mentioned, *not*-contractions have steadily gained ground in the written mode of expression from their first occurrences in the late sixteenth or early seventeenth century to the present day. Different corpus-based studies on the topic testify to this gradual increase of negative contractions in written English. For example, although uncontracted negatives of the present tense forms of the verbs *be* and *have* have been shown to represent the unmarked variant in the Late Modern British English data examined by López-Couso (2007a), the evidence also shows a growing acceptance of negative cliticization in writing throughout the period, most noticeably during the second half of the nineteenth century. The increase of contacted forms is also observable in the course of shorter time spans in the more recent history of the language. Consider, among others, the studies by Castillo-González (2007), who finds an increase in the proportion of contracted forms in her comparison of written material from the 1960s to the 1990s as represented in the Brown family of corpora, and Krug (1994), who detects the same tendency in his study of contractions in *The Guardian* in the period 1990–1993. Biber (1988) also reports that older texts use uncontracted forms to a greater extent than recent texts in the same register (see (iii) below).

In order to measure the importance of the chronological variable, the texts selected for our analysis belong to those periods in ARCHER which correspond to the second half of the eighteenth, nineteenth and twentieth centuries, i.e. 1750–1799, 1850–1899 and 1950–1990.

(ii) Dialect: Dialect distinctions have also proved relevant to the variation between contracted and uncontracted negatives in Present-day English. In his comparative analysis of British and American English writings, Biber (1987) concludes that American English shows a higher incidence of contraction than British English, "apparently because of greater attention to grammatical prescriptions by British writers" (Biber 1988: 243). The divergent behaviour of the two reference varieties as regards the frequency of *not*-contractions is also reported in Bell (1984), Hiller (1987), Yaeger-Dror et al. (2002) and Castillo-González (2007), among others. For instance, Bell (1984) shows that the uncontracted variant is more

---

others do not (e.g. *doesn't*), or that not all contracted forms are equally well represented by uncontracted graphic representations (e.g. <does not> represents /dʌznt/ better than <will not> represents /wəʊnt/).

common in British English than in American English in declarative clauses both in news reporting and in conversation (see (iii) and (viii) below). Hiller (1987), in turn, finds that *not* contractions with the verb *be* are more numerous in American than in British English; for the present forms of the verb *have*, by contrast, negative cliticization is more frequent in the British variety.

Since, as mentioned in Section 2, ARCHER comprises data from the two reference varieties of English, our analysis also pays attention to the potential relevance of the geographical variable. Among other things, the comparison between British and American English texts will allow us to check whether the stronger preference for contraction of the American variety identified in the present day also holds true for earlier stages of the language.

(iii) Register: The register factor also plays a crucial role in the variation between contracted and uncontracted negatives. In this respect, assertions such as the following are commonplace in Present-day English grammars:

> contractions such as *didn't* are appropriate in both informal and neutral English; they are excluded from formal English. (Quirk et al. 1985: 26)

> The synthetic [contracted] forms are a mark of informal style. While they are the default form in ordinary conversation and informal writing, they are not used in very formal and solemn contexts or in some kinds of written (especially published) language. (Huddleston and Pullum et al. 2002: 800)

A number of corpus-based studies corroborate the existence of this close connection of contracted forms with the spoken language and with written text types showing a high degree of speechlikeness, both in contemporary English (cf. Biber 1987; Tottie 1991; Krug 1994: 19; Yaeger-Dror 1997; Kjellmer 1998: 170–171; Biber et al. 1999: 166; 1129–1132; Greenbaum and Nelson 2002: 211; Yaeger-Dror et al. 2002) and in earlier stages of the language (cf. López-Couso 2007a: 312–315; Huber 2007; cf. also Brainerd 1989[1993]: 184–191; Sundby et al. 1991: 161–165). Various scholars (cf., among others, Biber 1988; Yaeger-Dror 1997; Westergren 1998; Yaeger-Dror et al. 2002) have expressed this dichotomy in terms of informative registers (e.g. news, written descriptive texts) vs. interactive registers (e.g. conversation, written dialogue), with uncontracted negatives being more common in the former type of settings. Yaeger-Dror (1997) explains such a difference in the following way: full *not* is favoured in informative registers because it has focal import, i.e. it carries important semantic information; by contrast, in interactive settings *not*-contractions are preferred in order to aid social agreement (cf. also Tagliamonte and Smith 2002: 261–262; Yaeger-Dror et al. 2002: 80–81).

ARCHER turns out to be a suitable source of data in order to measure the importance of the register variable, since it is a multi-genre corpus. It includes nine different text types: drama, fiction, journals-diaries, legal opinion, letters, medicine, news, science and sermons-homilies. As seen here (see also Section 4), the registers in ARCHER range from speech-based categories (e.g. drama or sermons) to written registers, both formal (e.g. scientific prose or medical research articles) and informal (e.g. personal letters or journal-diaries).

(iv) Form and function of the verbal operator: A number of intralinguistic factors have also been shown in the literature to play a major role in the selection of contracted and uncontracted negative variants. Among the potential determinants of variation included in our analysis, we find the form of the operator. It is a proven fact that not all contractible 'verb + *not*' sequences undergo contraction to the same extent. For example, Kjellmer's (1998: 169–170) data from the LOB corpus show that the degree of contraction with different verb forms varies from 0% for *am not, shall not* and *may not*[3] to 50% for *will not* and 64% for *do not*. His data also show that the verb *be* in all its forms ranks very low in its degree of negative contraction (below 16% for all forms except *was not* = 30%). This is probably related to the tendency for this verb to select auxiliary cliticization, both in Late Modern English (cf. López-Couso 2007a) and in Contemporary English (cf. Selkirk 1981: 114; Quirk et al. 1985: 1597; Biber et al. 1999: 166, 1129–1132; Kortmann 2003: 70–71; Tagliamonte and Smith 2002: 258, 277), in clear contrast to all the other verbs susceptible to undergoing contraction, which prefer *not* cliticization instead (cf. Selkirk 1981: 114; Quirk et al. 1985: 123).

Our analysis includes the three primary auxiliaries *be, have* and *do*, together with the modals *can, may, will, shall, must, need, ought, dare* and *be to* in all their possible forms as regards person, number and tense, as well as different orthographic (e.g. *shan't / sha'nt / sha'n't; aren't / arent / arnt*) and dialectal variants (e.g. *wasna / wuzn't < was not, dassn't < does not*). Other possible contracted forms, such as those involving the verbs *care* (e.g. *carent*), *know* (e.g. *known't*), *mun* (e.g. *munn't*), *use* (e.g. *usen't*), etc. (cf. Brainerd 1989[1993]) have been disregarded.

Whether *be* and *have* function as main verbs or as auxiliaries has also proved to be a relevant factor in the selection of contracted and uncontracted negatives in Present-day English. In grammars of contemporary English, contraction is said to be favoured with *have* as auxiliary rather than as main verb and with *be* as a copulative verb or an auxiliary in progressive constructions rather than as a passive auxiliary (cf., among others, Biber et al. 1999: 1129; cf. also Quirk et al. 1985: 123). As regards corpus-based studies, Kjellmer (1998: 172–173), for example, finds

---

3 This finding is in line with the characterization of the contracted forms of these verbs (*ain't, mayn't* and *shan't*) in the standard grammars as becoming rare or obsolete (cf. Quirk et al. 1985: 122; Biber et al. 1999: 166).

that *not*-contraction in the LOB corpus is "about twice as frequent with main verbs and auxiliaries as with copulas (41% and 37% vs. 20%)". By contrast, in Westergren's (1998) data from the Uppsala Press Corpus the verb *be* shows a higher incidence of contraction when it is used as a copula than when it functions as an auxiliary (1998: 148–150). The distinction between passive *be* and progressive *be* also plays a part in the variation: in Kjellmer's data, the proportion of contracted forms with *be* as a passive auxiliary is as low as 9%, while *be* as a progressive auxiliary contracts with the negator in 34% of the cases (1998: 175).

In our analysis, following Kjellmer (1998: 165), main verb *be* includes both its use as a copula (in (4)) and as an existential verb in so-called existential-*there* sentences (in (5)). For *be* as an auxiliary verb, a threefold distinction has been established: progressive auxiliary, passive auxiliary and perfect auxiliary (e.g. *he is gone*). As regards *have*, we have classified the examples into main *have* and perfective *have*.

(4)   The patient **was** a strongly built, pale-looking man. (1905, Karl Furth and F. Parkes Weber, *A case of malignant Endarteritis after Gonorrhoea . . .*)

(5)   There **is** a very common tendency in our minds to classify actions according to their outward form, rather than according to the spirit or motive which pervades them. (1857, John Caird, *Religion in the Common Life*)

(v) Tense of the operator and (vi) Person/number of the operator: In addition to verb form and function, the corpus examples have also been coded for the grammatical categories of tense (present – e.g. *will, shall, can, do, have* – vs. past – e.g. *would, should, could, did, had*), person (first vs. second vs. third) and number (singular vs. plural), in order to check whether such variables play a role in the selection between contracted and uncontracted variants.

(vii) Subject type: Hiller (1988: 96), Westergren (1998: 132ff; 173ff) and Biber et al. (1999: 1129–1132) for Present-day English, and López-Couso (2007a) for Late Modern English have shown that increased complexity of subject correlates with a higher proportion of uncontracted forms. More specifically, pronominal subjects are said to favor the occurrence of contractions to a greater extent than noun phrase subjects.[4] The strong connection between pronominal subjects and cliticized forms is definitely related to a further potential factor, namely string

---

4 Though relevant to both negative cliticization and auxiliary cliticization, the so-called 'pronoun effect' seems to be particularly pertinent to cases of the latter type of contraction (cf. Zwicky 1970: 331; Labov 1972: 106; Quirk et al. 1985: 123; Rickford and Blake 1990; López-Couso 2007a: 316–317).

frequency (Krug 1998, 2003), i.e. the frequency with which two (or more) adjacent linguistic units occur in the language. Given that "[f]orms which frequently co-occur tend to be treated as single units in speech processing" (Biber et al. 1999: 166–167; cf. also Bybee 2003: 617; 2006), string frequency no doubt plays a major role in the variation between contracted and uncontracted variants.[5]

Therefore, in our analysis, we have distinguished between pronominal subjects (also including dummy *it* and existential *there*) and non-pronominal ones (including noun-phrase and clausal subjects).

(viii) Clause type: Clause type has also been recognized as a conditioning factor in the selection of *not*-contraction by various scholars, among them Yaeger-Dror 1996, 1997; Kjellmer (1998: 175–177), Westergren (1998: 135ff; 177–178), Biber et al. (1999: 1131, Table A.7), Tagliamonte and Smith (2002) and Yaeger-Dror et al. (2002: 82). These studies show that contracted negatives are more frequent in questions (especially, but not exclusively, question tags) than in statements, and that imperatives show the highest proportion of contracted forms, so that the following cline can be established:

– contracted negatives				+ contracted negatives
declarative clauses	>	interrogative clauses	>	imperative clauses

In view of this, our data from ARCHER were initially classified according to this threefold distinction: declarative, interrogative (also including verb-subject exclamative clauses) and imperative. Figure 1 displays the frequencies of contracted and uncontracted tokens in each of the three levels of the variable. In keeping with the literature, higher proportions of contracted forms were attested in the interrogative and imperative examples.

However, since this chapter focuses on the variation between (complete) verbal forms followed by either *not* or *n't* and does not consider cases of so-called auxiliary cliticization or verb contraction (cf. Section 1 above), i.e. contraction between subjects and reduced forms of the verbs in negative verbal groups, as in *you're not*, we have decided to remove all the interrogative tokens from the database. In interrogative sentences like *don't you agree . . . ?*, *don't* and *do not* do not constitute a natural pair of contraction choices since *do not you agree* is not a straightforward alternative to *don't you agree*. Therefore, our study is based on a database of non-interrogative sentences, that is, declarative and (subjectless)

---

5 On the effects of frequency on negative proclisis in the Middle English period (e.g. *nis* < negative particle *ne* + *is*), see López-Couso (2007b).

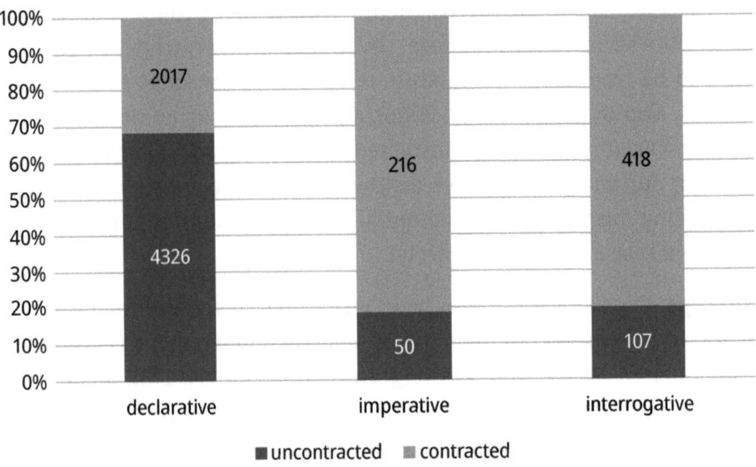

Figure 1: Contraction and clause type.

imperative examples, where variation is at work in pairs such as, respectively, *you do not agree/you don't agree* and *don't agree/do not agree*.

(ix) Clause depth: Although no information has been found in the literature on the topic as regards the potential influence of clause depth on the selection of contracted and uncontracted negatives, we have considered it worth investigating whether the dichotomy main clause vs. subordinate clause plays a part in the variation between the competing forms in the ARCHER data.

(x) Position: Only sporadic mention is made in the specialized literature of another factor included in our survey: the position occupied by the contractible verb + *not* sequence in the clause. Biber et al. (1999: 166) state that the contracted forms *isn't* and *aren't* tend to occur clause-initially (yes/no questions), whereas Kjellmer (1998: 173) points out that the incidence of *not*-contractions before a break or a punctuation mark in the LOB data he analyzed is higher (42%) than the average rate of these contracted forms (34%).

Given the potential influence of position on the variation between contracted and uncontracted negatives, our examples have been classified according to whether the verb + *not* sequence is placed in (absolute) clause-initial position (e.g. **Don't** *be asking that*), in (absolute) clause-final position (e.g. *What makes you think it **isn't**?*) or occupies any other position (e.g. *this house **isn't** mine to sell*).

(xi) Category of the constituent following *not/n't*: Although in the literature the significance of this variable has not been associated with negative contraction but with auxiliary contraction in potential contexts of negative polarity, we have tentatively decided to add this predictor to our statistical model. Hiller (1987: 544) reports that adjectival and nominal categories promote contraction of subjects and auxiliaries to a greater extent than complement clauses or progressive predicates. Tagliamonte and Smith (2002: 261) claim that the category of the constituent following the subject and the operator interacts with the auxiliary vs. main status of the verb (see (iv) above) since auxiliaries tend to be followed by participial constituents, whereas main verbs select adjectival, nominal and clausal complements instead. For this reason, they argue that the variable at work should not be the category of the postverbal constituent but rather the status of the verbal group.

Our instances from ARCHER have been classified according to the category of the constituent immediately following the sequence 'verb + *not*', i.e. noun phrase (in (6)), pronoun (7), adjective phrase (8), adverb phrase (9), prepositional phrase (10), *-ed* (11), *-ing* (12) and infinitive verbal forms (13), tag question (14), clause (15) and none (in (16)).

(6)   The error in GOODSIR'S observations was not **a very radical one** (1874, Charles Tomes, *On the development of the teeth of the Newt, Frog, Slowworm and Green Lizard*)

(7)   There aren't **any** (1957, Philip Larkin, *A Girl in Winter*)

(8)   it isn't **very warm** in the stokehold (1899, Rudyard Kipling, *The Light That Failed*)

(9)   . . . which, however, was not **now** very strong, (1775, William Heath, *Heath's Memoirs of the American War*)

(10)   I am not **on the trail of any elephants** (1852, F.B. Sanborn ed., *The Writings of Henry David Thoreau*)

(11)   If the bulb is not **heated** during the exhaustion, (1875, William Crookes, *On repulsion resulting from radiation*)

(12)   I have to pinch myself to be sure I am not **dreaming** (1880, Edward Bellamy, *Dr. Heidenhoff's Process*)

(13)   his purpose was not **to sign it** (1892, James Monaghan, *Pennsylvania State Reports*)

(14)   She did not, **did she**! (1753, Samuel Foote, *The Englishman in Paris*)

(15)   the Perpetration of this Murder was not **as the Wretch desired** (1752, *The London Evening Post*)

(16)   If they are not, I will wait Ø (1877, Henry James, *The American*)

(xii) Frequency of the main (lexical) verb under the scope of negation: Inspired by seminal studies such as Ellis (2002) and Bybee (2003, 2006), which highlight the positive significant role played by frequency in phenomena involving phonological reduction, in this chapter we have also considered the overall frequency of the lexical verbs in the predicates affected by negative contraction. Specifically, this potential predictor uses the normalized frequency per 1,000,000 words of the lemmas of our 894 lexical verb types in the enTenTen20 corpus (Jakubíček et al. 2013). Aware of the impossibility of obtaining frequencies from massive Late Modern English corpora, we have decided to use Present-day English frequencies. EnTenTen20, available through Sketch Engine (Kilgarriff et al. 2014; www.sketchengine.eu), is a massive corpus of Present-day English which comprises 44,968,996,152 word tokens, with texts downloaded from the Internet between 2019 and 2021.

Table 2 summarizes the variables and levels described in this section:

Table 2: Variables and levels.

Variable type	Variable	Levels
Dependent	contraction	contracted uncontracted
Independent	period	18(th-)c(entury) 19c 20c
Independent	dialect	Br(itish)E(nglish) Am(erican)E(nglish)
Independent	register	drama medicine fiction news journals-diaries science legal opinion sermons-homilies letters

Table 2 (continued)

Variable type	Variable	Levels
Independent	operator	*be*_main *be*_pass(ive) *be*_progr(essive) *be_to* *can* *dare* *do* *have*_main *have*_perf(ect) *may* *must* *need* *ought* *shall* *will*
Independent	tense	present past
Independent	person_no	1s(ingular) 1p(lural) 2s 2p 3s 3p
Independent	subject (type)	pro(nominal) (inc. dummy *it* and existential *there*) full (non-pronominal)
Independent	clause_type	declarative imperative
Independent	clause_depth	main subordinate
Independent	position	initial final other (medial)

Table 2 (continued)

Variable type	Variable	Levels
Independent	(category) post_*not*	n(noun)p(hrase)
		pro(noun)
		a(djective)p
		adv(erb)p
		p(repositional)p(hrase)
		v(erb)_*ed*
		v_*ing*
		v_inf(initive)
		clause (finite verb)
		tag (question)
		none
Independent	(normalized) freq(uency) of verb types	(numeric)

4 Analysis of the data

This section is devoted to the statistical treatment of the data. Regression models were used to identify the predictors described in Section 3 that have a significant determining effect on negative contraction.

Some adjustments to the dataset were made early on to facilitate the implementation of the model owing to the scarcity of examples in some of the subcategories. In this regard, the number of levels had to be simplified for the following variables. First, the nine levels of the variable 'register' were reduced to four, the new levels being 'written_formal' (including journals, legal, medicine, news and science), 'written_informal' (letters), 'speech' (drama, sermons) and 'mixed' (fiction). Given the size of the database, it has not been possible to discriminate between narrative and dialogistic passages in the fiction texts, and we therefore opted for categorizing the fiction examples as 'mixed'. Second, the variable 'person_no' had to be rearranged, given the few examples of, in particular, second-person plural subjects. The definitive levels entering the model are: first-singular, second-singular, third-singular and plural subjects. Third, the variable 'position' has been simplified as a dichotomous predictor, the levels 'final' and 'other (medial)' being comprised within the level 'non_initial'. Finally, the 11 levels of the predictor 'post_not', accounting for the category of the constituent immediately following the negator *not/n't*, had to undergo simplification on two occasions: on the one hand, 'vp' has been used to label all the verb-governed categories, namely 'cl' (initially used for clauses containing finite predicates), 'v_ed' (past-participle verb phrases), 'v_ing' (*ing* verb phrases) and 'v_inf' (infinitival predicates); on the other hand, 'tag', which was used for appended tag questions, was eventually added to the level 'none', thus recognizing that tags lead intonationally and syntactically to new independent structures. Consequently, the definitive list of levels of the predictor 'post_not' consists of the following levels: 'np', 'pro', 'ap', 'advp', 'pp', 'vp' and 'none'.

Also, to avoid severe collinearity among variable levels, some variables needed to undergo recoding. Firstly, since the main-*be* and the main-*have* levels of the variable 'operator' were already identified by the normalized frequencies of, respectively, lexical *be* and lexical *have*, such levels were grouped together into the single value 'main'. Besides, given that *do* was the only level of the predictor 'operator' when 'clause_type' was imperative and that the number of instances resulting from combinations of the *be*-passive, the *be*-progressive and the *have*-perfect levels of 'operator' with other variables was very low, we decided to recognize only two levels of 'operator', namely 'main' and 'aux(iliary)', the latter comprising *do*, *be*-passive, *be*-progressive, *have*-perfect and modal.[6] Secondly, collinearity between, on the one hand, the 'imperative' clause type and, on the other hand, the level 'main' of the variable 'operator' and the value 'initial' of the predictor 'position' led to the removal of the variable 'clause type' from the model. Put differently, the imperative force of our database examples is somehow encoded by the interaction of other options such as 'initial' position and 'main' operator.

The final revised list of variables of negative contraction, their levels and the number of instances per alternative are presented in Table 3, where frequency is the criterion used in most cases to establish the reference levels for each predictor.

In an attempt to determine the relative weights of the predictors within a multivariate model, we implemented a fixed-effects binomial regression model using the functions 'glm'[7] in the 'stats' package (R Core Team 2021) and 'lrm' in the 'rms' package (Harrell 2019) in R. The lack of significant mutual collinearity of the data was corroborated using the functions 'alias' ('MASS' package, Venables and Ripley 2002) and 'vif' (Variance Inflation Factor; 'car' package, Fox and Weisberg 2018), the latter with overall values ranging from 1.054 and 3.074. Backward stepwise (step (emode_glm, direction="backward"; 'MASS' package) operationalized the reduction of the number of variables in the initial model with no statistically significant loss of explanatory power, as denoted by the models' AIC (Akaike Information Criterion)

---

6 The initial 'modal' level of the predictor 'operator' grouped the options 'be_to', 'can', 'dare', 'may', 'must', 'need', 'ought', 'shall' and 'will'.

7 glm(contraction ~ period + dialect + register + operator + tense + person_no + subject + position + clause_type + clause_depth + post_not + frequency, data = data, family=binomial).

Table 3: Summary of the database.

Contraction		period		dialect		register		operator		tense	
Uncontracted	4,375	18c	1,825	BrE	3,386	speech	2,141	main	1,240	present	4,109
Contracted	2,233	19c	2,276	AmE	3,222	mixed	1,683	aux	5,368	past	2,499
		20c	2,507			written_formal	2,191				
						written_informal	593				

person_no		subject		position		clause_depth		post_not		frequency
1s	1,644	pro	4,283	initial	390	main	4,471	vp	4,799	(numeric)
2s	790	full	2,325	non_initial	6,218	subordinate	2,137	advp	408	
3s	3,107							ap	514	
P	1,067							np	410	
								pp	182	
								pro	88	
								none	207	

values (5420.6 vs. 5418.02). This implied dropping only the variables 'frequency' and 'dialect', and recognizing that neither dialectal information nor the frequency of the main lexical verbs in the negative verbal groups was strongly explanatory in the variation. That the final model's residual deviance is in all cases lower than the degrees of freedom indicates lack of overdispersion of the data (see Appendix). Both the C(oncordance) (0.879) and Nagelkerke R^2 (0.516) discrimination indices provided by 'lrm' reveal that the model is very good at explaining the variation (C≈0.9 indicates the model's outstanding fit and predictive power, and $R^2>4$ its plausibility) and, consequently, adequate to the research question.

In order to obtain a more detailed picture of the influence exerted by specifically the significant predictors on the variation, Figures 2 to 5 show the corresponding effects plots (function 'predictorEffects', 'effects' package, Fox and Weisberg 2018; 95% error-bar confidence), where the *y*-axes evince the predicted probabilities for each level's outcome, ranging from better chances of the uncontracted variant (low on the scale) to higher probability of contraction. In what follows we

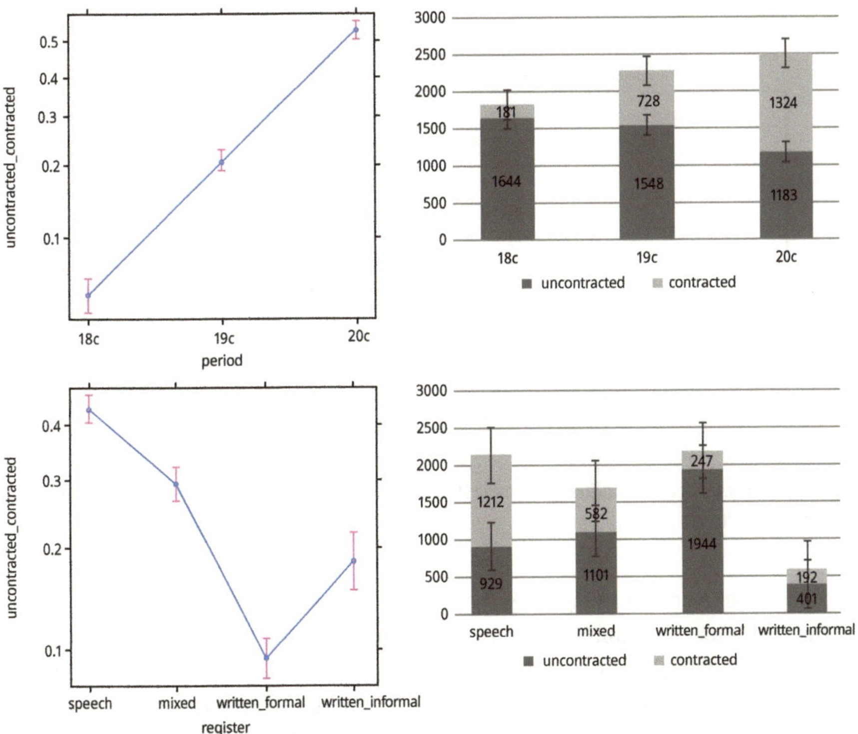

Figure 2: Effects plots and stacked barplots (95% confidence interval) of extralinguistic variables 'period' and 'register'.

discuss the results by commenting on the effects plots of extralinguistic, verb-related, subject-related and clausal predictors.

First, as regards the variable 'period', Figure 2 shows the highly significant progressive increase in the probability of contracted forms from the eighteenth to the twentieth century. In turn, the plot for 'register' reveals that the chances of contraction decrease significantly along the continuum 'speech' > 'mixed' > 'written_informal' > 'written_formal' text types.

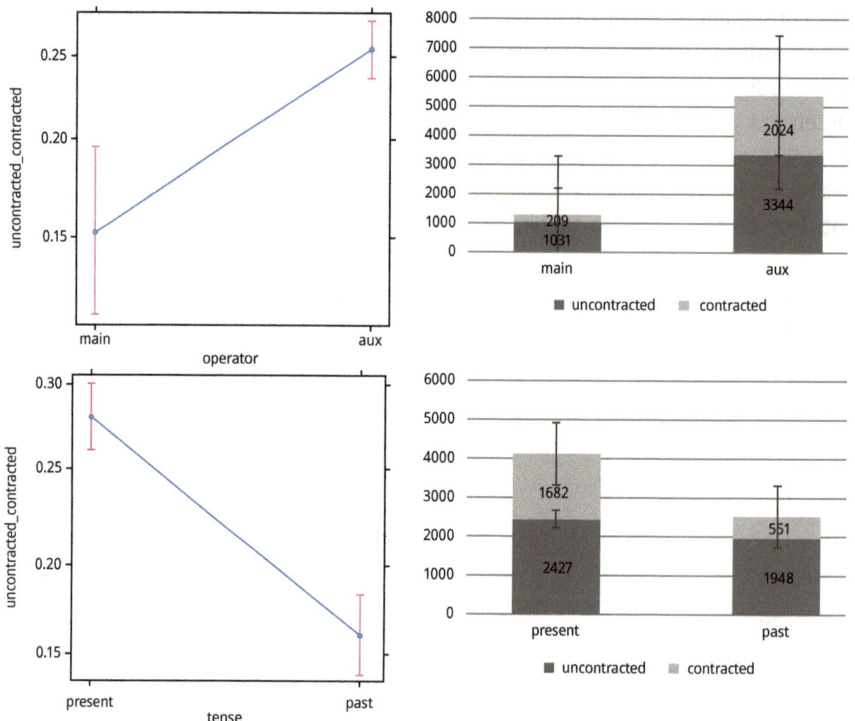

Figure 3: Effects plots and stacked bar plots (95% confidence interval) of verb-related variables 'operator' and 'tense'.

Second, as represented in Figure 3, the significant trends corroborated by the effects of the predictor 'operator' are the high probability of contraction with auxiliaries. As far as the variable 'tense' is concerned, the probability of opting for the contracted solution decreases when the tense of the finite verb is past and not present.

Third, as regards the variables that feature subject-related variation, the plots in Figure 4 indicate that contraction is significantly more likely when the subject is first- or second-person singular (the difference between these two

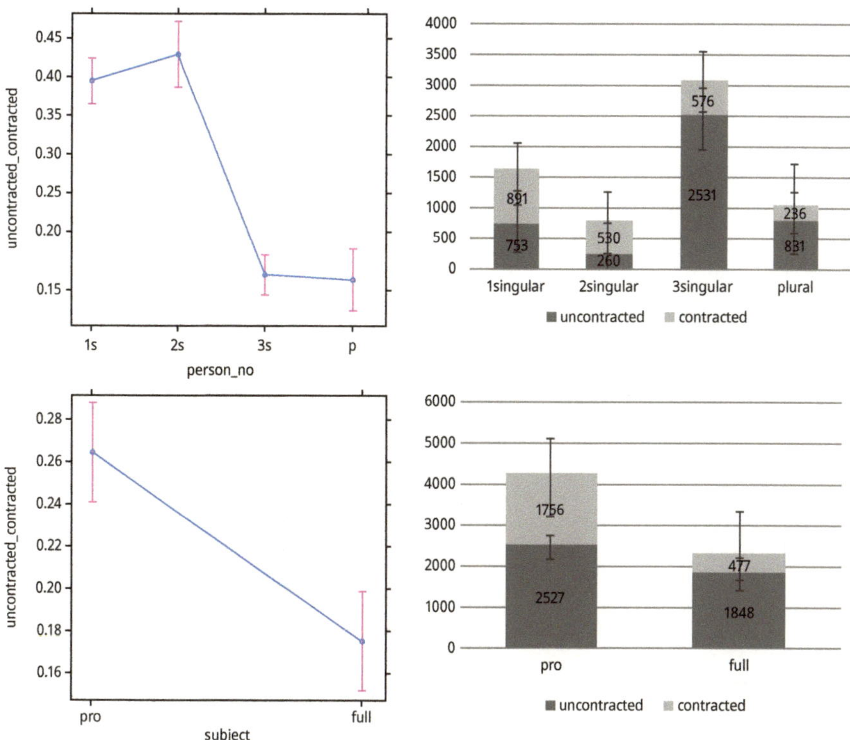

Figure 4: Effects plots and stacked barplots (95% confidence interval) of subject-related variables 'person_no' and 'subject'.

options not being significant), whilst plural and third-person singular subjects disfavor the contracted alternative. Also, pronominal subjects have greater chances of being followed by contracted negative forms than non-pronominal (phrasal and clausal) subjects.

Finally, the plots in Figure 5 show the probability trends of the intralinguistic clausal variables in the model. Contraction has more chances when the verbal group occurs in sentence-initial position. With respect to the variable 'clause_depth', the plot shows that the occurrence of the sequence 'verb + *not*' in a main clause also favours the probability of contraction. As far as the effects of 'post_not' are concerned, the only phrasal category associated with highly significant probability of contraction when following the negator is the pronominal one.

The regression model described in the preceding paragraphs was used to assess the significance of the contribution of the predictors to the overall variation. Random Forests (function 'cforest', 'party' package, Hothorn et al. 2006), first applied to linguistic analysis by Tagliamonte and Baayen (2012), have been used to

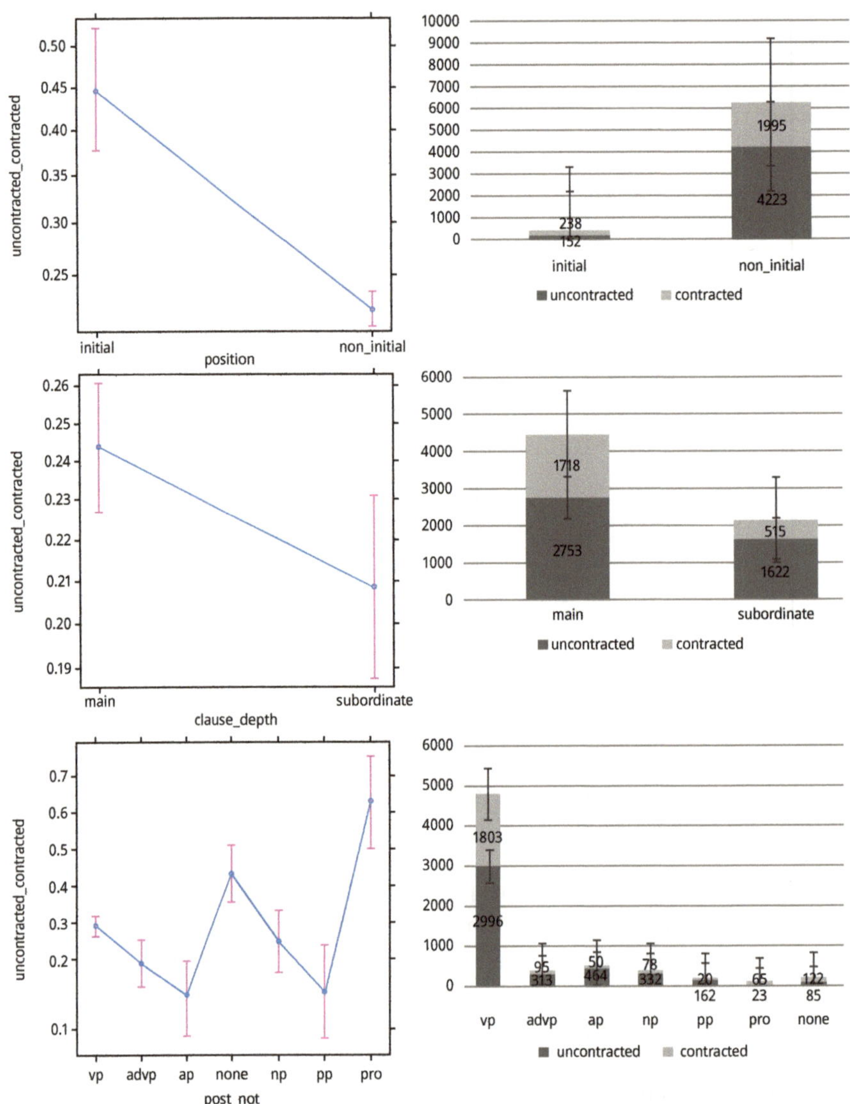

Figure 5: Effects plots and stacked barplots (95% confidence interval) of clausal variables 'position', 'clause_depth' and post_not'.

rank the fixed predictors according to their impact on the explanation of the variation. Figure 6 below presents the Random Forests corresponding to the model's predictors (importance values calculated by growing a large forest with 1,000 trees – 'ntree' – and two randomly preselected predictors at each split –'mtry');

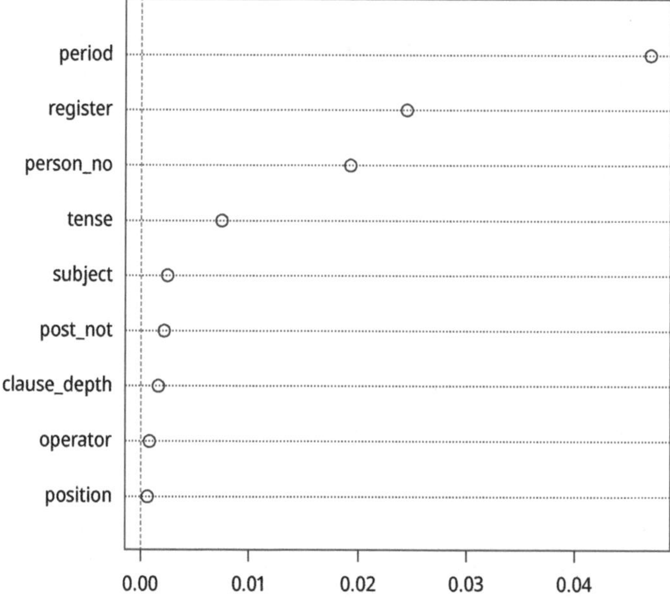

Figure 6: Dot chart of conditional variable importance.

the C-index of the Random Forests (0.8982) is, as expected, slightly better than that of the regression model. Figure 6 reflects the impact of the fixed predictors 'period', 'register', 'person_no' and 'tense', and the less important contribution of 'operator', 'position', 'clause-depth', 'post_not' and 'subject' to the model.

5 Interpretation of the results and concluding remarks

This chapter has explored the alternation between uncontracted negatives (e.g. *is not*) and contracted 'verb + *not*' sequences (e.g. *isn't*) in Late Modern and Present-day English on the basis of evidence from the ARCHER corpus (cf. Section 2). The statistical modelling of a database of 6,608 examples of contracted and uncontracted forms has been based on a set of predictors compiled from the relevant literature (cf. Section 3), which included a total of 12 independent variables, namely period, dialect, register, verbal operator, tense of the operator, person and number of the operator, subject type, clause type, clause depth, position, category of the constituent immediately occurring after *not/n't* and frequency of the lexical verb under the scope of negation, each of them containing two or more levels. However, collinearity effects among several variable levels implied the re-coding of some of these 12 variables and even the removal of the predictor 'clause type' from the model. The data have been analyzed through two multi-variable statistical techniques (regression and Random Forests) that determine which predictors contribute significantly to the explanation of the linguistic phenomenon under investigation and rank the variables according to their explanatory importance within the statistical model (cf. Section 4).

This study has revealed, first, that dialect – British vs. American – and the frequency of the lexical verb in the construction were not strong predictors of negative contraction and, in consequence, these two variables were also removed from the statistical model. Second, the variables with higher importance indices in our ARCHER material were those reporting extralinguistic information, such as period and register. Concerning the variable 'period', the data showed a highly significant progressive increase in the probability of the contracted variant from the eighteenth to the twentieth century, thus confirming the growing acceptance of negative cliticization in Late Modern and Present-day written English observed in the literature (cf. Section 3). As expected, the analysis of the variable 'register' confirmed the close connection of negative contracted forms with text types exhibiting a high degree of speechlikeness; our results showed that the chances of contraction diminish significantly along the continuum 'speech' > 'mixed' > 'written_informal' > 'written_formal' text types. On the other hand, the statistical analysis determined the weight of the levels of the intralinguistic variables associated with vivid (author-/addressee-centred) involved/interpersonal style (as in Biber 1988). Specifically, contraction has been determined to be most probable in the following linguistic contexts: with first- and second-person singular subjects, with present-tensed verbs (featuring, in Biber's 1988: 224 words, "unplanned speech styles [in] immediate, as opposed to removed, situations"), with pronominal subjects, with pronominal elements occurring after *not/n't*, in main clauses (corresponding to immediate, rather than reported, style) and in sentence-initial position. Other linguistic predictors such as 'operator' turned out to have a much less significant impact on the variation between uncontracted and contracted negative forms, though the probability of contractions seems to be higher with auxiliaries than with main verbs.

These findings suggest that, as compared to intralinguistic factors, extralinguistic factors rank much higher among the determinants that explain the variation between uncontracted and contracted negatives and therefore seem to exert a stronger influence on the variation, at least in Late Modern English. Since period can be seen as a factor only in the statistical sense (i.e. as a control variable), but not actually a factor in the psychological sense (i.e. one that speakers would take into account when deciding between a contracted and an uncontracted variant), this leaves register as the major determinant of variation in our ARCHER material. Specifically, negative contraction has been shown to be more probable in text types with a high degree of speechlikeness than in formal registers, as well as in linguistic environments associated with an involved, interpersonal style, a trend that proved to be statistically more salient across time.

The multivariate analysis of the ARCHER data presented in this chapter has shed interesting new light on the interplay of the intralinguistic and extralinguistic variables with greater explanatory power in the variation between uncontracted negatives and negative contracted forms in Late Modern English and Present-day English. Nevertheless, the picture is still far from complete. Much can certainly be gained from incorporating into the model further potential determinants of variation, including the phonological and the sociolinguistic factors mentioned in Section 3, from adding to the picture auxiliary cliticization or verb contraction (e.g. *he's not*) as a third possible alternative or by expanding the analysis to sets of data representing earlier stages of the language, such as the Enhanced Shakespearean Corpus (http://corpora.lancs.ac.uk/esc-user-service) or A Corpus of English Dialogues 1560–1760 (https://www.engelska.uu.se/research/english-language/electronic-resour ces/english-dialogues). Such welcome additions, which must be left for follow-up research, would be helpful to check the validity of the findings in this chapter concerning the variation between contracted and uncontracted negatives in the history of English.

Appendix

Fixed-effects binomial regression coefficients (backward stepwise):

	Estimate	Std. Error	z value	Pr(>|z|)	
(Intercept)	-0.12371	0.26086	-0.474	0.635318	
period19c	1.49853	0.10496	14.277	< 2e-16	∗∗∗
period20c	2.95190	0.10830	27.256	< 2e-16	∗∗∗
registermixed	-0.59548	0.08417	-7.075	1.50e-12	∗∗∗
registerwritten_formal	-1.98896	0.09829	-20.236	< 2e-16	∗∗∗
registerwritten_informal	-1.21819	0.12284	-9.917	< 2e-16	∗∗∗
operatoraux	0.66435	0.17385	3.822	0.000133	∗∗∗
tensepast	-0.69748	0.07684	-9.077	< 2e-16	∗∗∗
person_no2s	0.16097	0.11388	1.413	0.157516	
person_no3s	-1.16420	0.09226	-12.618	< 2e-16	∗∗∗
person_nop	-1.19483	0.11316	- 10.559	< 2e-16	∗∗∗

```
subjectfull                  -0.59444   0.08895   -6.683   2.35e-11   ***
positionnon_initial          -1.04951   0.16398   -6.400   1.55e-10   ***
clause_depthsubordinate      -0.20117   0.07723   -2.605   0.009191   **
post_notadvp                 -0.46141   0.15639   -2.950   0.003174   **
post_notap                   -0.83637   0.23483   -3.562   0.000369   ***
post_notnone                  0.63097   0.17980    3.509   0.000449   ***
post_notnp                   -0.19063   0.21774   -0.876   0.381293
post_notpp                   -0.80172   0.29589   -2.710   0.006738   **
post_notpro                   1.66086   0.33033    5.028   4.96e-07   ***
```

Signif. codes: 0 '***' 0.001 '**' 0.01 '*' 0.05 '.' 0.1 ' ' 1

References

ARCHER 3.2 = *A Representative Corpus of Historical English Registers version 3.2*.1990–1993/2002/2007/2010/2013/2016. Originally compiled under the supervision of Douglas Biber and Edward Finegan at Northern Arizona University and University of Southern California; modified and expanded by subsequent members of a consortium of universities. Current member universities are Bamberg, Freiburg, Heidelberg, Helsinki, Lancaster, Leicester, Manchester, Michigan, Northern Arizona, Santiago de Compostela, Southern California, Trier, Uppsala, Zurich.

Barber, Charles. 1976. *Early Modern English*. London: André Deutsch.

Bell, Allen. 1984. Language styles as audience design. *Language in Society* 13. 145–204.

Biber, Douglas. 1987. A textual comparison of British and American writing. *American Speech* 62. 99–119.

Biber, Douglas. 1988. *Variation across Speech and Writing*. Cambridge: Cambridge University Press.

Biber, Douglas, Edward Finegan & Dwight Atkinson. 1994. ARCHER and its challenges: Compiling and exploring *A Representative Corpus of Historical English Registers*. In Udo Fries, Gunnel Tottie & Peter Schneider (eds.), *Creating and Using English Language Corpora*, 1–14. Amsterdam: Rodopi.

Biber, Douglas, Stig Johansson, Geoffrey Leech, Susan Conrad & Edward Finegan. 1999. *Longman Grammar of Spoken and Written English*. London: Longman.

Brainerd, Barron. 1989 [1993]. The contractions of *not*: A historical note. *Journal of English Linguistics* 22(2). 176–196.

Bybee, Joan L. 2003. Mechanisms of change in grammaticization: The role of frequency. In Brian D. Joseph & Richard D. Janda (eds.), *The Handbook of Historical Linguistics*, 602–623. Oxford: Blackwell.

Bybee, Joan L. 2006. From usage to grammar: The mind's response to repetition. *Language* 82(4). 711–733.

Castillo-González, María Pilar. 2007. *Uncontracted Negatives and Negative Contractions in Contemporary English: A Corpus-based Study*. Santiago de Compostela: University of Santiago de Compostela PhD dissertation.

Denison, David. 1993. *English Historical Syntax: Verbal Constructions*. London: Longman.

Denison, David. 1998. Syntax. In Suzanne Romaine (ed.), *The Cambridge History of the English Language, vol. IV, 1776–1997*, 92–329. Cambridge: Cambridge University Press.

Ellis, Nick C. 2002. Frequency effects in language processing. *Studies in Second Language Acquisition* 24(2). 143–188.

Fox, John & Sanford Weisberg. 2018. Visualizing fit and lack of fit in complex regression models with predictor effect plots and partial residuals. *Journal of Statistical Software* 87(9). 1–27.

Greenbaum, Sidney & Gerald Nelson. 2002. *An Introduction to English Grammar*. 2nd edn. London: Pearson.

Harrell, Frank E. Jr. 2019. rms: Regression modeling strategies. http://biostat.mc.vanderbilt.edu/rms (accessed 30 of July of 2022).

Haugland, Kari E. 1995. Is't allowed or ain't it? On contraction in early grammars and spelling books. *Studia Neophilologica* 67. 165–184.

Hiller, Ulrich. 1987. She isn't studying vs. she's not studying. *Die Neueren Sprachen* 86. 531–553.

Hiller, Ulrich. 1988. *Contracted forms* im Englischen. In Wolf-Dietrich Bald (ed.), *Kernprobleme der englischen Grammatik*, 91–105. München: Langenscheidt-Longman.

Hothorn, Torsten, Peter Buehlmann, Sandrine Dudoit, Annette Molinaro & Mark Van Der Laan. 2006. Survival ensembles. *Biostatistics* 7(3). 355–373.

Huber, Magnus. 2007. The Old Bailey Proceedings, 1674–1834. Evaluating and annotating a corpus of 18th- and 19th-century spoken English. In Anneli Meurman-Solin & Arja Nurmi (eds.), *Studies in Variation, Contacts and Change in English. Volume 1. Annotating Variation and Change*. Helsinki: Research Unit for Variation, Contacts and Change in English (VARIENG), University of Helsinki. https://varieng.helsinki.fi/series/volumes/01/huber/.

Huddleston, Rodney & Geoffrey K. Pullum et al. 2002. *The Cambridge Grammar of the English Language*. Cambridge: Cambridge University Press.

Jakubíček, Miloš, Adam Kilgarriff, Vojtěch Kovář, Pavel Rychlý & Vít Suchomel. 2013. The TenTen corpus family. In Andrew Hardie & Robbie Love (eds.), *7th International Corpus Linguistics Conference*, 125–127. Lancaster: Lancaster University (UCREL).

Jespersen, Otto. 1909–1949. *A Modern English Grammar on Historical Principles*. 7 vols. Copenhagen: Ejnar Munskgaard.

Jespersen, Otto. 1917. Negation in English and other Languages. Det Kgl. Danske Videnskabernes Selskab. *Historisk-filologiske Meddelelser* 1. 1–151. [Reprinted in *Selected Writings of Otto Jespersen* (1962). London: George Allen and Unwin].

Kilgarriff, Adam, Vít Baisa, Jan Bušta, Miloš Jakubíček, Vojtěch Kovář, Jan Michelfeit, Pavel Rychlý & Vít Suchomel. 2014. The Sketch Engine: Ten years on. *Lexicography* 1. 7–36.

Kjellmer, Göran. 1998. On contraction in Modern English. *Studia Neophilologica* 69. 155–186.

Kortmann, Bernd. 2003. Comparative English dialect grammar: A typological approach. In Ignacio M. Palacios-Martínez, María José López-Couso, Patricia Fra-López & Elena Seoane-Posse (eds.), *Fifty Years of English Studies in Spain 1952–2002. A Commemorative Volume*, 63–81. Santiago de Compostela: Servicio de Publicacións da Universidade de Santiago de Compostela.

Krug, Manfred. 1994. *Contractions in Spoken and Written English: A Corpus-based Study of Brachychronic Language Change*. Exeter: University of Exeter MA thesis.

Krug, Manfred. 1998. String frequency. A cognitive motivating factor in coalescence, language processing, and linguistic change. *Journal of English Linguistics* 26(4). 286–320.

Krug, Manfred. 2003. Frequency as a determinant in grammatical variation and change. In Günter Rohdenburg & Britta Mondorf (eds.), *Determinants of Grammatical Variation in English*, 7–67. Berlin & New York: Mouton De Gruyter.

Labov, William. 1972. *Language in the Inner City*. Philadelphia: University of Philadelphia Press.

Lass, Roger. 1999. Phonology and Morphology. In Roger Lass (ed.), *The Cambridge History of the English Language, vol. III, 1476–1776*, 56–186. Cambridge: Cambridge University Press.

Leonard, Sterling Andrus. 1929. *The Doctrine of Correctness in English* Usage *1700–1800*. (University of Wisconsin Studies in Language and Literature 25.) Madison: University of Wisconsin.

López-Couso, María José. 2007a. Auxiliary and negative cliticisation in Late Modern English. In Javier Pérez-Guerra, Dolores González-Álvarez, Jorge L. Bueno-Alonso and Esperanza Rama-Martínez (eds.), *Of Varying Language and Opposing Creed: New Insights into Late Modern English*, 301–323. Bern: Peter Lang.

López-Couso, María José. 2007b. Frequency effects: Middle English *nis* as a case in point. In Gabriella Mazzon (ed.), *Studies in Middle English Forms and Meanings*, 165–178. Peter Lang: Frankfurt am Main.

Mazzon, Gabriella. 2004. *A History of English Negation*. London: Longman.

Phillipps, K. C. 1984. *Language and Class in Victorian England*. Oxford: Blackwell.

Quirk, Randolph, Sidney Greenbaum, Geoffrey Leech & Jan Svartvik. 1985. *A Comprehensive Grammar of the English Language*. London: Longman.

R Core Team. 2021. R: A language and environment for statistical computing. Vienna: R Foundation for Statistical Computing. https://www.R-project.org.

Rickford, John R. & Renée Blake. 1990. Copula contraction and absence in Barbadian English, Samana English and Vernacular Black English. *Berkeley Linguistics Society* 16. 257–268.

Selkirk, Elisabeth O. 1981. *The Phrase Phonology of English and French*. Bloomington, IN: Indiana University Linguistics Club.

Strang, Barbara M. H. 1970. *A History of English*. London: Methuen.

Sundby, Bertil, Anne Kari Bjørge & Kari E. Haugland. 1991. *A Dictionary of English Normative Grammar 1700–1800*. Amsterdam: John Benjamins.

Tagliamonte, Sali & R. Harald Baayen. 2012. Models, forests, and trees of York English: *Was/were* variation as a case study for statistical practice. *Language Variation and Change* 24(2). 135–178.

Tagliamonte, Sali & Jennifer Smith. 2002. Either it isn't or it's not. Neg/aux contraction in British dialects. *English World-Wide* 23(2). 251–281.

Tottie, Gunnel. 1991. *Negation in English Speech and Writing*. San Diego: Academic.

Venables, William N. & Brian D. Ripley. 2002. *Modern Applied Statistics with S*. New York: Springer.

Warner, Anthony. 1993. *English Auxiliaries. Structure and History*. Cambridge: Cambridge University Press.

Westergren Axelsson, Margareta. 1998. *Contraction in British Newspapers in the Late 20th Century*. Uppsala: Acta Universitatis Uppsaliensis.

Yaeger-Dror, Malcah. 1996. Register as a variable in prosodic analysis. *Speech Communication* 19. 39–60.

Yaeger-Dror, Malcah. 1997. Contraction of negatives as evidence of variation in register specific interactive rules. *Language Variation and Change* 9. 1–36.

Yaeger-Dror, Malcah, Lauren Hall-Lew & Sharon Deckert. 2002. *It's not* or *isn't it*? Using large corpora to determine the influences on contraction strategies. *Language Variation and Change* 14. 79–118.

Yáñez-Bouza, Nuria. 2011. ARCHER past and present (1990–2010). *ICAME Journal* 35. 205–236.

Zwicky, Arnold M. 1970. Auxiliary reduction in English. *Linguistic Inquiry* 1. 323–336.

Günter Rohdenburg and Julia Schlüter

9 Making interpretation redundant

The grammaticalization of *that*-clauses after verbs of deception

Abstract: This paper explores the changing relationship between two types of construction shared by several verbs of deceiving (e.g. *delude, deceive, fool*), as in (a) *He deceived the public into the belief/into thinking that he would step down* versus (b) *He deceived the public that he would step down*. In the course of the last few centuries, 1) nominal "interpretators" like *into the belief* have largely been replaced by verbal types like *into thinking*, and 2) the interpretive phrases have increasingly been omitted in favor of type (b): directly linked content clauses functioning as arguments of the main clause verbs. We argue that this ongoing replacement process exhibits characteristics of a reductive kind of grammaticalization. As to Present-Day English, our findings indicate that the structural simplification of *deceive*-type sentences is more advanced in British than in American English, in particular in informal registers (spoken language and fiction). Moreover, the contexts facilitating the appearance of the incoming directly linked content clause include the use of negation and reflexive objects. Not unexpectedly, these represent a mirror-image of those conditions that have been shown to mitigate the decline of directly-linked content clauses with other verb types (e.g. *congratulate* and *reproach*).

Keywords: grammaticalization, evolutionary pathways, verb complementation, verbs of deceiving, *deceive, delude, fool*, varieties, register, interpretators, shell nouns, negation, transitivity degrees, reflexivity, individuation, complexity, complementizer *that*

1 Introduction

Inspired by work on so-called "shell nouns" (e.g. Schmid 2012) and "Interpretatoren" ('interpretators'; Lüdtke 1984), this paper explores the changing relationship between two types of construction shared by several transitive verbs of deception (*bamboozle, beguile, con, delude, deceive, dupe, fool, hoodwink, lull, lure, mislead* etc.), as illustrated in (1) to (3).[1]

---

[1] A big "thank you" is in place to Lukas Sönning (University of Bamberg) for statistical counselling, the implementation of the logistic regression models and the plot design used to visualize model estimates. We would also like to thank two anonymous reviewers for their insightful comments. Yet, all remaining errors and inadequacies are our own.

https://doi.org/10.1515/9783110753059-009

(1) a. He **deceived** the public **into the belief/into thinking** that he would step down.

   b. He **deceived** the public Ø that he would step down

(2) a. They are **deluded by the idea/to think** that a copy will convey the same sensation as the original.

   b. They are **deluded** Ø that a copy will convey the same sensation as the original.

(3) a. Don't **fool** yourself **into the notion/by believing** that this goal has been met.

   b. Don't **fool** yourself Ø that this goal has been met.

The two constructions are closely related, with the more explicit type (a) entailing type (b). In the (a)-examples, the content clauses introduced by *that* function as complements of a variety of prepositional phrases containing abstract nouns or verbs specifying (or "interpreting") the mental phenomena in question. Thus, we will henceforth employ the convenient, if novel, term "interpretator" to designate such interpretive phrases. Denoting cognitive processes or states of the experiencers referred to by the object expressions, interpretators represent arguments or adjuncts of the verbs of deception.

In this paper, our analyses are confined to *deceive*, *delude* and *fool*. In the current online version of the OED (s.v. *deceive*, v.; *delude*, v.; *fool*, v.), their senses relevant to our concerns are defined as follows:

deceive 2. a. To cause to believe what is false; to mislead as to a matter of fact, lead into error, impose upon, delude, 'take in'.

delude 3. a. To befool the mind or judgement of, so as to cause what is false to be accepted as true; to bring by deceit into a false opinion or belief; to cheat, deceive, beguile; to impose upon with false impressions or notions.

   3. b. with complement (*on*, *to*, *into*).

fool 3. a. *transitive*. . . . (in later use usually) *spec.* to trick or deceive (someone). See also sense 3d.

   3. d. *transitive*. . . . to dupe or lure (a person) into something unpleasant or undesirable (with the result or aim of the deception indicated by a prepositional phrase following the verb). Now usually with *into* See also sense 3a.

This means that, basically, the object referents are made to undergo a change of their beliefs. Drawing on these definitions, we will be able, in later sections, to adequately circumscribe and select the nominal and verbal interpretators involved. Thus, it is important that the choice of the interpretator should normally be limited by two considerations: The lexical item in question should be compatible with the semantic range of *belief* itself and the relevant state of mind must unambiguously relate to the experiencer rather than the agent.

Discounting their basic transitive uses (S-V-O), both *deceive* and *delude* were for several centuries found only in the construction type illustrated in the (a)-examples above. Data collected from various historical corpora and databases spanning the Modern English period suggest that the relevant interpretators have increasingly been omitted in favor of the (b)-type: directly linked content clauses functioning as arguments of the main clause verbs. Incidentally, we will find that – in the course of the last two centuries – nominal interpretators (like *idea, belief* or *notion*) have been increasingly replaced by verbal ones (like *think, believe* or *imagine*). The analysis of Present-Day English corpora indicates that the proportion of "uninterpreted" (i.e. directly linked) *that*-clauses has currently reached the mid-point of the S-curve, other factors being kept constant. Compared to *deceive* and *delude*, the verb *fool* – although well-established since Early Modern English as a denominal transitive or reflexive verb followed by a prepositional phrase (cf. OED s.v. *fool*, v., senses 2.b. and 3.a.) – was only recently integrated into the group of verbs taking an additional content clause. As will be shown, the variable use of interpretators after *fool* is subject to the same constraints as with the more longstanding exponents of this semantic and syntactic type, though the omission is somewhat delayed.

Regarding Present-Day English, stratified large-scale corpora permit deeper insights into factors impinging on the choice of the competing construction types as well as a number of constructional variants. The findings to be reported in the following sections will make reference to relevant language-external (variety- and situation-dependent) and language-internal (context-dependent) factors. Comparisons between (sub)corpora representing the two major standard varieties indicate that the structural simplification of *deceive*-type sentences is more advanced in British English, while American English follows with a delay, thus providing a counter-example to the more ample cases of American leadership (cf. Rohdenburg and Schlüter 2009: 420–423). In addition, it will be suggested that – in line with other kinds of simplification of complementation patterns – the directly linked *that*-clause is promoted in informal registers (such as spoken language and narrative text types). Parallel reductions have been described by Denison (2018) in terms of the omission of shell nouns like *fact* heading content clauses with monotransitive verbs (*contradict, depict, highlight* etc.). As to language-internal factors, contexts facilitating the appearance of the incoming directly linked content clause will be isolated (reflexive objects and negation). Not unexpectedly, these present a mirror-image of those conditions that have been shown to mitigate the decline of directly-linked content clauses with other verb types (e.g. *congratulate* and *reproach*; Rohdenburg 2014).

We will argue that this ongoing replacement process exhibits characteristics of a reductive kind of grammaticalization, endowing the superordinate verbs with a novel "ditransitive" argument structure and integrating them into the more general pattern of factual and suasive communication verbs (e.g. *advise* in its factual use, *convince, inform, let X know, notify, promise, remind, reassure, tell, warn* in its factual use). A concept that will take center stage in this analysis is that of transitivity, which was analyzed most prominently by Hopper and Thompson (1980) as a continuum determined by an interrelated set of parameters. Our line of argument holds that transitivity exerts an influence on the permeability of a construction to reductive grammaticalization. More specifically, reduced transitivity of the superordinate clause will be suggested as a facilitator of the omission of interpretators after verbs of deception.

2 Transitivity and the grammaticalization of clausal complementation patterns

The analysis of the competition between interpreted and directly linked *that*-clauses leans heavily on the semantic concept of transitivity developed by Hopper and Thompson (1980; see also Givón 2001: 91–95). Adopting this framework, Rohdenburg (2014: 57; 2020: 562) describes the prototypical transitive clause as an asserted, punctual event, in which a human agent willfully and forcefully impinges on a patient other than himself. However, transitivity is a matter of degree, and detransitivization results from contextual factors such as the following (see also Givón 2001: 93; Mondorf and Schneider 2016).

a)   reflexive uses
b)   negation
c)   passivization
d)   inanimate subjects
e)   non-individuated objects
f)   non-finite constructions (e.g. *-ing* clauses) lacking an explicit subject
g)   modality

Previous research has shown that in the case of unstable and weakly entrenched verb-dependent constructions – typically outgoing and incoming ones – low transitivity contexts are likely to enhance acceptability. Following Hopper and Thompson (1980: 280–284), this may be accounted for by the different degrees of prominence in discourse typically expressed by clauses at different transitivity levels:

> In languages like English, foregrounding is not marked absolutely, but is instead indicated and interpreted on a probabilistic basis; and the likelihood that a clause will receive a foregrounded interpretation is proportional to the height of that clause on the scale of Transitivity. (Hopper and Thompson 1980: 284)

High transitivity is thus associated with discourse prominence, and low transitivity with pragmatic backgrounding. We propose that, by the same token, the backgrounding that a clause receives through transitivity reduction safeguards its constituent structures from the forces that impinge on more exposed discourse positions, thereby providing a niche in which marginal constructions can persist or emerge.

Several examples can be adduced to support this assumption: Mondorf and Schneider (2016; see also Schneider 2021) demonstrate that, in addition to several other features, reflexive objects and negation are capable of supporting the recessive causative construction of the verb *bring*, as in (4). In the case of so-called expressive verbs like *blame, reproach* and *congratulate* as in (5), Rohdenburg (2014) has shown that it is in particular the use of reflexive objects that has for a long time delayed the demise of *that*-clauses. By contrast, the ongoing advance of prepositional objects at the expense of the direct ones after *shirk* and *lack* has been found to be promoted by negated clauses as in (6) (Rohdenburg 2020).

(4) I just <u>can't</u> **bring** <u>myself</u> to do it. (COCA, quoted from Mondorf and Schneider 2016: 441)

(5) But I **blame** <u>myself</u> that my openness to another person was reckless. (*The Guardian*, 1996)

(6) "We do <u>not</u> **lack** for laws. We **lack** enforcement of laws," . . . President Charlton Heston said when told of the study. (*Los Angeles Times*, 1999)

(7) "You <u>cannot</u> **rule out** that she could have inhaled or ingested this material," . . . (*Los Angeles Times*, 1999)

(8)   . . . any Person who might endeavour to employ all the good Offices in their Power <u>to</u> **incline** <u>him</u> to forgive his Lady, . . . (ECF, 1759)

(9)   'You have **demonstrated** <u>yourself</u> in the court to be thoroughly arrogant, and . . .' (*Daily Telegraph*, 1992)

Moreover, with the verb *rule out*, we have found in preliminary analyses[2] that negated contexts as in (7) attract a clearly higher share of (presumably more recent) directly linked *that*-clauses than of (presumably older) variants containing shell nouns like *possibility*. In other words, the omission of shell nouns correlates with the use of negation. The supportive effect of non-finite constructions has been observed with the verb *incline* governing object + infinitive or prepositional phrases. In such uses, the verb has typically been confined for centuries to inanimate subject expressions. Crucially, however, we have – in rare cases – also come across non-finite uses such as (8) referring implicitly to animate subjects. A final observation in this context concerns so-called subject-to-object raising constructions. As stated by e.g. Bolinger (1967), in the active – in particular with the basic word order S-V-O – this type of raising represents a receding phenomenon. However, with many verbs including *demonstrate*, the construction survives to this day in specific detransitivizing environments. Among them is the use of reflexive objects as in (9). At this point it should also be mentioned that, with most of such cases, passivization constitutes a further detransitivizing device rescuing the use of outgoing or otherwise less well established constructions.

Given these and related findings on low-transitivity environments supporting individual unstable constructions, our expectation is that the incoming *that*-clause after *deceive, delude* and *fool* should also be supported by manifestations of reduced transitivity. As to the transitivity features (a)-(g), the central regression analyses in Section 4 will focus on the effects of reflexivization, negation and passivization. Beyond that, Section 5 will provide preliminary observations on the rise of reflexive objects (5.1), the role of objects referring to non-individuated entities (5.2), effects of argument complexity (5.3), and the role of direct speech further illustrating an informal aspect of contemporary journalistic style (5.4).

---

2 In an analysis of four years of the *Los Angeles Times*, 76% of 111 hits containing interpretator shell nouns (*possibility* and others) were found to be negated, but as much as 95% of 39 hits that occurred without an interpretator.

3 Data and methods

Given our focus on low-frequency constructions, the verbs *deceive*, *delude* and *fool* were chosen as representatives of verbs of deception due to their relatively high occurrence rate in British and American English, in both interpreted and uninterpreted uses.[3]

3.1 Databases, varieties and genres

Relevant instances of *deceive*, *delude* and *fool* were gleaned from various British and American corpora and text collections spanning the entire Modern English period. Details of the texts and numbers of examples are given in Table 1; full bibliographic details are given in the online appendix at https://osf.io/h8325.

Depending on the format of the respective database, some searches targeting forms of the three verbs had to be carried out manually, others were supported by Part-of-Speech tagging and search expressions restricting hits to cases followed by a verb within the same sentence. All in all, we are reasonably certain of having caught all instances of the verbs followed by complement clauses with an expressed or deleted *that*-complementizer and with or without an intervening interpretator.

For COCA and COHA, the downloadable raw data editions were used, not including texts from Blogs, the Web, or the TV/Movie collection; the overlap between both corpora was cleared. Since a fine-grained distinction of genres would have produced many empty cells in the subsequent analysis, only two macro-genres were distinguished: 'fiction' (more informal, including narrative fiction, drama and a few spoken examples), and 'non-fiction' (more formal, including newspapers, magazines, academic writing and other kinds of non-fictional prose). For the MNC, LNC and ETC collections, the genre distinction was coded manually upon inspection of the text.

---

3 Regarding the two contrasting uses under investigation, the verb *con* is clearly found less frequently in American newspapers of the 1990s and early 2000s than in their British counterparts. In a selection of British newspapers dating from 1993–2004 (totalling 196,416,964 words) we find 29 relevant examples whereas a comparable selection of American newspapers dating from 1993–2001 (totalling 173,606,202 words) yields only 3 relevant examples.

Table 1: Composition of the database and counts of relevant hits.

database	date range	size (mill-ion)	macro-genres (specific genres)	*deceive*		*delude*		*fool*		total
				hits	pmw	hits	pmw	hits	pmw	pmw
British										
EPD	1540–1940	26.4	fiction (drama)	8	0.30	1	0.04	1	0.04	0.38
ECF	1705–1780	9.7	fiction	14	1.44	1	0.10	0	0.00	1.55
NCF	1782–1903	37.6	fiction	39	1.04	23	0.61	0	0.00	1.65
MNC.B	1834–1897	10.1	fiction, non-fiction	4	0.40	8	0.79	0	0.00	1.19
LNC.B	1866–1935	20.8	fiction, non-fiction	10	0.48	6	0.29	0	0.00	0.77
ETC.B	1896–1924	4.8	fiction, non-fiction	5	1.04	7	1.46	0	0.00	2.50
BNC	1960–1993	98.3	fiction (incl. spoken), non-fiction	33	0.34	37	0.38	39	0.40	1.11
BNC2014	2012–2016	11.4	fiction (spoken)	0	0.00	0	0.00	3	0.26	0.26
ChT	1785–1992	11.7	non-fiction (news)	7	0.60	16	1.37	0	0.00	1.97
Br News*	1990–2005	657.8	non-fiction (news)	172	0.26	334	0.51	559	0.85	1.62
American										
AD	1722–1936	17.2	fiction (drama)	7	0.41	3	0.17	0	0.00	0.58
EAF	1789–1850	34.6	fiction	37	1.07	17	0.49	1	0.03	1.59
MNC.A	1812–1905	7.2	fiction, non-fiction	6	0.83	0	0.00	0	0.00	0.83
LNC.A	1854–1922	26.9	fiction, non-fiction	14	0.52	11	0.41	1	0.04	0.97
ETC.A	1895–1927	11.6	fiction, non-fiction	8	0.69	5	0.43	1	0.09	1.21
COHA	1810–2009	444.7	fiction, non-fiction	172	0.39	174	0.39	92	0.21	0.98
COCA	1990–2019	557.1	fiction (incl. spoken), non-fiction	114	0.20	125	0.22	277	0.50	0.93
TAL	1989–1994	12.1	non-fiction (magazine)	1	0.08	12	0.99	6	0.50	1.57
Am News**	1990–2001	844.5	non-fiction (news)	142	0.17	187	0.22	392	0.46	0.85
total				793		967		1372		

The Daily Telegraph 1991, 1992, 2004, 2005; *The Guardian* 1990, 1991, 2004, 2005; *The Independent* 1993, 1994, 2004, 2005, *The Times* 1990, 1991, 2003, 2004.

**Detroit Free Press* 1992, 1993, 1994, 1995; *Los Angeles Times* 1992, 1993, 1994, 1995, 1996, 1997, 1998, 1999; *New York Times* 2001; *Washington Times* 1990, 1991, 1992.

3.2 Manual annotation

Besides the extralinguistic factors 'variety' and 'genre', two intralinguistic variables ('transitivity' and 'negation') and the dependent variables ('interpretator' and 'complementizer') had to be coded manually. To exemplify these categories, consider the following set of examples.

(10) It seemed to him at times that the most delightful thing in the world to do would be to shut his eyes to her defects and to let her **deceive** <u>him</u> **into the belief** <u>that</u> she was good, as she had deceived her husband. (COHA, fiction, 1875)

(11) <u>Nobody</u>, apparently, thinks they can **fool** <u>anybody</u> **into believing** <u>that</u> a photograph of Mr Pitt in armour is an authentic portrait of Achilles – . . . (*The Independent*, 2004)

(12) Such schemes, so far from "elevating the masses," only estrange and offend them with no end of unfair conditions, and **delude** <u>the benevolent</u> **with the notion** <u>that</u> they are doing their best to effect what they are really doing their best to prevent. (COHA, magazine/non-fiction, 1888)

(13) That is one of the merits of the Trinity, that it does <u>not</u> **fool** <u>us</u> **in the confidence** <u>that</u> we can perfectly know and comprehend God by our first thought. (COHA, magazine/non-fiction, 1854)

(14) . . . in words of kindness which I can never forget, and recall with a kind of pride that so great and noble a heart should **deceive** <u>himself</u> **into imagining** <u>that</u> I possessed those great qualities which he ascribed to me. (NCF, fiction, 1884)

(15) Obsessed with dreams of city life, impressed with Gabriel's fame, naïve while **deluding** <u>herself</u> Ø Ø she was experienced, Michelle would have leapt at the excitement of it. (BNC, fiction, 1989)

(16) I could <u>stop</u> **deluding** <u>myself</u> Ø <u>that</u> by sheer accident I had acquired a vast number of raffish friends. (*The Independent*, 1993)

(17) So these people are actually . . . They're <u>being</u> **deceived** by very stupid thinking **to think** <u>that</u> they can make this leap into outerspace. (COCA, spoken/fiction, 1997)

(18) But men, always less aware of prayers than of blows, recognize him chiefly when he is in arms, and so <u>are</u> **deluded into thinking** <u>that</u> love depends on fear to prove his force. (ETC.B, fiction, 1921)

(19) I wasn't completely heart-free during those years; sometimes I allowed my-self <u>to be</u> **fooled Ø** <u>that</u> I loved someone, but when it came to the point of saying yes to anything final . . . (BNC, fiction, 1987)

The factor 'transitivity' was coded with three levels: The label 'transitive' was applied to cases where a direct object expression was not co-referential with the subject, i.e. not reflexive, thus all of examples (10) to (13). The two other levels represent exponents of the "de-transitive voice" (in the sense of Givón 2001: 94). Examples such as (14) to (16) were coded as 'reflexive', examples such as (17) to (19) were coded as 'passive'. While reflexivity and passivization can also be considered as degrees of transitivity, the label 'transitive' is for present purposes reserved for instances that come closest to 'cardinal transitivity' in the sense of Hopper and Thompson (1980: 253). On the semantic side, however, several degrees of transitivity can be distinguished within this level, based on a gradient of individuation of the object referent (see our supplementary observations in Section 5.2). With reference to the OED definitions quoted above, occasional intransitive uses (e.g. ". . . the focus of that for the next five weeks should not delude into thinking that there is not something beyond that for the next five years . . .", COCA, spoken/fiction, 1991) were excluded from the study.

The factor 'negation' was applied in a rather broad sense, covering *never*- and *not*-negation as in (13) and *no*-negation as in *have no intention of* Ving or *can no longer* V. In addition, to capture other types of semantic negation, more distant negative items that have scope over the relevant clause as in (11) were included, as were sentences with negative approximators like *almost* and *hardly* or negative implicative verbs like *stop* in (16). Negation was not extended to other non-assertive contexts, such as questions, sentences with modal verbs, sentences with *any* etc.

The outcome variable 'interpretator' was coded with three different levels: 'nominal', as in (10), (12) and (13), 'verbal', as in (11), (14), (17) and (18), and absent ('none'), as in (15), (16) and (19). For the analyses in Sections 4.2 to 4.4, the levels were conflated to code just the presence or absence of an interpretator. Finally, for the analysis in Section 4.5, the use or omission of *that* introducing the directly linked complement clause was coded as an additional outcome variable ('complementizer'). The absence of *that* is illustrated by (15).

During the process of data preparation, various exclusions were made of related or borderline constructions that did not qualify for the analysis as the full range of interpreted and uninterpreted variants was not available. Details on such cases as well as a subset of corpus hits with manual annotations can be found in the online appendix at https://osf.io/h8325.

3.3 Statistical modelling

Since the outcomes of interest are binary (verbal vs. nominal interpretator, interpretator present vs. absent, complementizer present vs. absent) we use logistic regression models to uncover the sensitivity of these choices to external and internal factors. Analyses were done in R (R Development Core Team 2021) with the help of the following packages: *car* (Fox and Weisberg 2019) for model diagnostics, *effects* (Fox and Weisberg 2018) for extracting predictor effects and *lattice* (Sarkar 2008) for data visualization. We ran separate regressions for verbs (Sections 4.1–4.4) and interpretator types (Section 4.5). Please refer to the (print) Appendix for the selection of data (Table 5), model specifications (Table 6), coding of predictors (Table 7) and model coefficients (Tables 8–12). For the presentation and interpretation of the results, we rely on visual means, i.e. partial effects plots. The R code can be accessed in the online appendix at https://osf.io/h8325.

4 Results

We now turn to the main part of our study. To begin with, Section 4.1 introduces the different types of interpreting expressions heading the complement clauses against the backdrop of a set of seemingly unrelated constructions discussed in the literature. Subsequently, we delineate the change undergone by the complementation patterns. Due to the low frequency of the target structures and the limited amount of data for earlier subperiods, we proceed in three steps, from a long-term, through a mid-term, and on to a short-term perspective, at the same time zooming into an increasingly detailed analysis of extra- and intralinguistic factors. We focus in turn on the long-term change involving *deceive* and *delude* and their associated constructions in British and American English, then on the mid-term development for the same two verbs since 1810 including the factors 'genre', 'negation' and 'transitivity', and finally on a short-term perspective also including the verb *fool* since the year 1990, isolating the effects of 'year', 'variety', 'genre', 'negation' and 'transitivity' (Sections 4.2, 4.3 and 4.4, respectively). Finally, Section 4.5 points to a further reduction process affecting the complementizer *that*.

4.1 A first look at interpretators: Nominal and verbal types

Our study brings together a set of co-existing constructional types that – we argue – enter into a competition since they can fulfil the same communicative function: They all connect a content clause expressing a deceptive, counterfactual assumption with a basically transitive act of deception described by the superordinate clause. The link between these clauses can be made explicit by a nominal or verbal interpreting expression, or it can be left implicit and the interpretators made redundant. In this section, we start out by providing some background on the two types of interpretators.

The defining characteristic of interpretators (our translation of Lüdtke's *Interpretatoren*, a term used in his 1984 book-length study of a range of syntactico-semantic phenomena in French) consists in their not only mentioning a proposition, but perspectivizing it,[4] i.e. speakers or writers put a distance between themselves and the propositional content, which is marked by the classificatory semantics of the interpretator (cf. Lüdtke 1984: 162). Interpreting expressions can be realized as nouns or verbs; they may be optional or obligatory, depending on the matrix verb, and importantly, one of their functions is to allow for an additional subordinate content clause to be integrated into a matrix clause (Lüdtke 1984: 67, 131–132, 157).

The nominal interpreting expressions function as "shell nouns" in the sense of Schmid (2012: 4): They are "an open-ended, functionally defined class of abstract nouns that have, to varying degrees, the potential for being used as conceptual shells for complex, proposition-like pieces of information". According to Schmid's (2012: 187–208) classification of mental shell nouns, the interpretators we found following *delude, deceive* and *fool* include types with conceptual uses from the "Idea" family (*idea, thought, notion* etc.), which serve to highlight the propositional content of ideas, and nouns designating psychological states of their experiencers in "Creditive" uses (*belief, hope, feeling, impression, conviction, view, opinion, thinking, realization, discovery, illusion, fantasy, delusion* etc.).

The verbal constructions considered as interpretators in the present study can be seen as a prototypical subcategory of causative *into* V*ing* constructions. These constructions have been described as following the pattern NP$_{Subj}$ V NP$_{Obj}$ *into* V*ing*, where a causer (the subject) acts upon a patient (the object) so that the patient performs a resulting event, which often has an adverse effect on the patient-performer (cf. Stempel 2019: 147–148). The origins of the construction, its semantics, rapid spread across various main varieties of English since the mid-nineteenth century,

---

4 The original wording is: ". . . es macht einen Unterschied aus, ob ich einen Sachverhalt nenne . . . oder ob ich einen Sachverhalt dadurch anführe, daß ich ihn in Perspektive setze . . ." (Lüdtke 1984: 221).

productivity and versatility and its negative semantic prosody have been amply discussed in recent corpus-based literature (see, e.g., Rudanko 2000, 2015; Duffley 2018; Rickman and Kaunisto 2018; Davies and Kim 2018; Stempel 2019; Flach 2021 and references in these sources). Davies and Kim (2018), for instance, list the verbs *fool*, *deceive* and *delude* in fifth, sixth and tenth place, respectively, among the top frequency instantiations of the construction in COHA. Furthermore, Stempel's (2019: 150–152) collexeme analysis based on COCA identifies a strongly entrenched sub-construction consisting of the three verbs of deception under discussion here (plus the verb *mislead*) and following "psych verbs", most prominently *think* and *believe*. Semantically, this sub-construction differs from others in that the second verb refers to a change in the convictions held by the patient (who is therefore better referred to as an 'experiencer') and that reflexive uses describing acts of self-delusion are possible, while other actions triggered by the causer typically happen against the patient-performer's will (Stempel 2019: 153–154). Syntactically, the sub-construction stands out by virtue of taking finite complement clauses, which form a part of the syntactic pattern that has so far escaped linguists' attention.

Interestingly, the syntactic need for a verb of cognition as an intervening interpretator not infrequently crosses the animate-inanimate divide: Even inanimate 'experiencers' can be connected with a complement clause by gerundial expressions like *into thinking*, as in (20) and (21), thus violating the expectation that the experiencer should be a sentient being capable of cognizance and volition.

(20) So we dug ditches to **fool** the plants **into thinking** they were at high altitude," . . . (*The Guardian*, 1990)

(21) An official admission that tin foil can be used illegally to **fool** vending machines **into thinking** a 10p piece is worth 50p seems likely to hasten changes in Britain's coinage. (*Daily Telegraph*, 1991)

Cases like these provide clear evidence of the desemanticization or bleaching of gerundial interpretators.[5] If we had access to more examples of this type, it would be instructive to see whether the semantic mismatch between inanimate 'experiencers' and verbs of cognition can promote the loss of interpretators, or whether interpretators are less dispensable with inanimate objects because the personification inherent in the construction is more acceptable in their presence.

---

5 Similar cases may also be found with other verbs of deception. For instance:
(i) . . ., where the bacterial chemicals are trying to **con** the human cells **into thinking** they're hormones, . . ., (*The Times* 2004)

Tables 2, 3 and 4 list the three most frequent interpretator types (grouped by nominal and verbal types) found to co-occur with each verb, broken down by verb and (major) period. In addition, they indicate the number of different types and tokens per category.[6] Based on these tables, a number of descriptive observations can be made. Thus, we notice that the verb *deceive* was the earliest of the three to be established in the construction with complement clauses. In the mid-twentieth century, *delude* overtakes its forerunner in terms of frequency. The construction with *fool* is a latecomer to this construction and starts out with a much more limited range of interpretator options than *deceive* and *delude* boasted in their early days.

Table 2: The three most frequent nominal and verbal interpretators combining with *deceive*, type and token counts per time period.

	deceive					
	<1850		**1850–1950**		**1950–2020**	
nominal	*into the belief*	15	*into the belief*	27	*by the idea*	1
	into a belief	11	*with the idea*	8	*by the impression*	1
	into an opinion	6	*into a belief*	4	*into the belief*	1
	types	27	types	23	types	4
	tokens	71	tokens	61	tokens	5
verbal	*in supposing*	8	*into thinking*	45	*into thinking*	202
	in thinking	5	*into believing*	24	*into believing*	131
	in believing	5	*in thinking*	9	*to think*	5
	types	10	types	21	types	11
	tokens	29	tokens	115	tokens	350
total	tokens	100	tokens	176	tokens	355

In addition, over the last few centuries, the interpretators introducing *that*-clauses have undergone a number of reductions and standardizations. These include the following:

a) The use of the indefinite article with shell nouns like *belief* or *opinion*, still common in the period before 1850, has been increasingly abandoned.

b) The incidence and variety of shell nouns and their associated prepositions has experienced a sharp decline, both in terms of types and tokens.

---

6 A full list of interpreting expressions for each timeframe is provided in the online appendix at https://osf.io/h8325.

Table 3: The three most frequent nominal and verbal interpretators combining with *delude*, type and token counts per time period.

	delude					
	<1850		**1850–1950**		**1950–2020**	
nominal	*into the belief*	10	*into the belief*	32	*into the belief*	5
	with the idea	6	*with the idea*	18	*by the idea*	1
	into a belief	6	*with the notion*	11	*with the hope*	1
	types	16	types	21	types	14
	tokens	43	tokens	95	tokens	18
verbal	*into believing*	2	*into believing*	25	*into thinking*	243
	to believe	1	*into thinking*	16	*into believing*	123
	by imagining	1	*into supposing*	3	*to think*	8
	types	3	types	13	types	14
	tokens	4	tokens	56	tokens	400
total	tokens	47	tokens	151	tokens	418

Table 4: The three most frequent nominal and verbal interpretators combining with *fool*, type and token counts per time period.

	fool					
	<1850		**1850–1950**		**1950–2020**	
nominal	*to the fancy*	1	*into the belief*	2	*into the belief*	1
	–		*by the belief*	1	*with the idea*	1
			in the confidence	1	*by the notion*	1
	types	1	types	3	types	7
	tokens	1	tokens	4	tokens	7
verbal	–		*into thinking*	15	*into thinking*	792
			into believing	10	*into believing*	304
			with thinking	3	*to think*	9
	types	0	types	5	types	14
	tokens	0	tokens	30	tokens	1131
total	tokens	1	tokens	34	tokens	1138

c) The option of premodified shell nouns (e.g. *into the sincere belief, with the pleasant idea, into the unfortunate opinion, into the fond hope, by a common male-fantasy*) has become more and more restricted.

d)   A similar reduction has affected the class of verbal interpretators. Gerundial *thinking* and *believing* have virtually ousted other verbs of cognition. Associated prepositions have by and large become limited to *into*. Infinitival *to think* is a minority variant of rather recent origin.

e)   As the frequencies of verbal interpretators rise, the corresponding type-token-ratios drop markedly as their numerical increase does not coincide with an increase in variability.

f)   Moreover, in a separate analysis (Section 4.5), we will follow up on our hunch that the complementizer of the *that*-clause is increasingly omitted in the course of time.

Most prominently, we observe that the nominal interpretator types, dominant in the first major corpus period, have given way to the verbal types. This development appears to have affected *deceive* earlier than *delude*, while *fool* largely skipped the nominal interpretator phase as it came up too late in this construction to partake in the major changeover.

To analyze the momentum of this replacement process and isolate potential differences between the British and American varieties, we ran two binomial logistic regression models, one for *deceive* and one for *delude*. To be able to include as much of the early data as possible while at the same time avoiding a distorting influence of the factor 'genre', the data were restricted to the macro-genre we labelled 'fiction' (as 'non-fiction' is heavily underrepresented among the older data). Figure 1 visualizes the partial effects of 'verb', 'year' and 'variety' on the outcome variable 'interpretator type'. The y-axis shows the estimated percentage of verbal interpretators as compared to nominal ones.

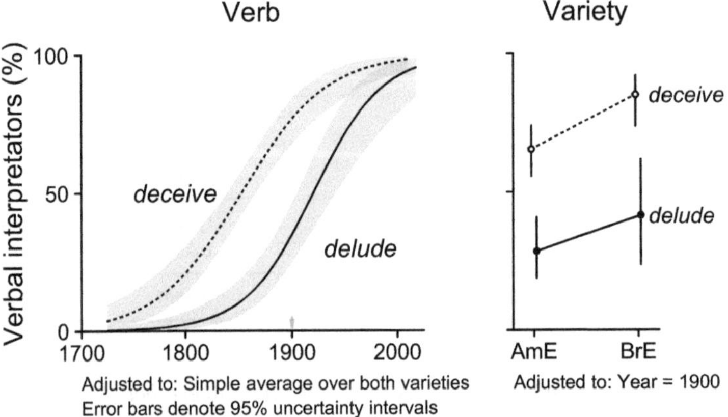

Figure 1: Partial effects of the factors 'verb', 'year' and 'variety' on the choice of verbal interpretators in the genre 'fiction'. Model specifications and coefficients can be found in the Appendix (Table 7).

Both models show that the eighteenth to twentieth centuries frame the almost complete changeover from nominal interpretator types to verbal ones after *deceive* and *delude* in the less formal genres subsumed here under 'fiction'. The development begins earlier for *deceive*, quite possibly on account of its earlier entrenchment with the construction. Thus, Figure 1 suggests that *deceive* crosses the 50% mark (with half the tokens having verbal interpretators) around 1850, while *delude* still hovers at 10 to 20%. There is some indication that the changeover to verbal forms proceeds at a slightly quicker pace for *delude*, which exhibits a somewhat steeper trend line. Moreover, we can establish a variety difference that consistently shows British English in the lead for both verbs, with a larger American delay for the verb *deceive*.

The results confirm the assumed replacement of nominal by verbal interpretators; they pinpoint informal British English as the likely source of the innovation and suggest different rates of change dependent on the verb in question and the point in time when it joined the trend. However, this is only the first shift in the use of interpreting expressions. The decline of the nominal types and the expansion of the verbal ones is followed by the onset of directly linked (uninterpreted) *that*-clauses. It remains unclear if and to what extent the first change can be taken to forebode the second, and postulating causal connections would remain purely speculative here: While the transition from nominal to verbal interpretators is moderated by extralinguistic factors such as time and variety, we have found no indications as to a functional difference between the two.

In the absence of such evidence, the next analyses will conflate nominal and verbal interpretators into the superordinate category of interpreted uses and dig deeper into the language-internal and external factors affecting the use or omission of interpreting expressions in general.

4.2 Long-term diachronic perspective: Loss of interpretators

As a first step in our diachronic analysis of the demise of interpreting expressions, we exploit the entire date range for which the constructions are attested. In our dataset, the first instances of both *deceive* and *delude* connected with complement clauses date from the year 1725, from two different novels by Eliza F. Haywood, whereas *fool* is first used in this construction in a novel by Henry W. Herbert dating from 1843. On account of the distribution of available hits, this long-term perspective is once more restricted to the fictional macro-genre and to the two historically better-established verbs *deceive* and *delude*. In addition, it includes 'variety' as a further predictor. Figure 2 shows the partial effects of these predictors on the estimates for the presence of interpretators (both nominal and verbal totted up).

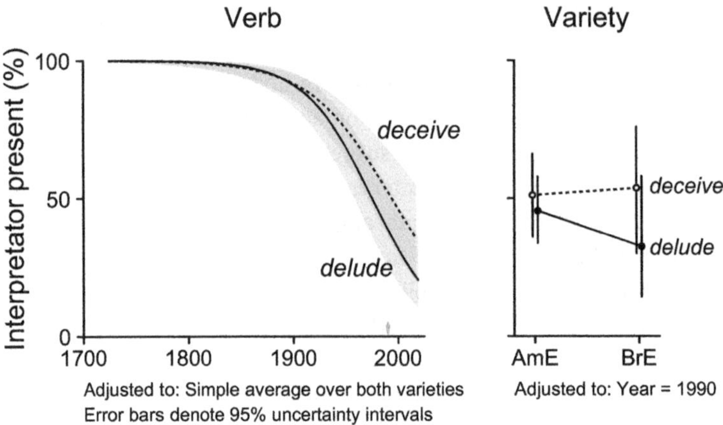

Figure 2: Partial effects of the factors 'verb', 'year' and 'variety' on the presence of interpretators in the genre 'fiction'. Model specifications and coefficients can be found in the Appendix (Table 8).

For fiction, we observe a virtually parallel demise of interpretators after *deceive* and *delude*. Indeed, the first uninterpreted uses of complement clauses after *deceive* and *delude* occur in an American novel and an American play both dating from the year 1833. By the year 1990, the loss has affected over half of the occurrences of the structure. At a closer look (afforded by the right-hand panel, which takes a snapshot of the situation around 1990), the estimates suggest that differences between the varieties only emerge for *delude*, where the change has gained ground a little earlier than for *deceive*, though these comparisons are subject to considerable uncertainty. These minimal divergences will be checked against the larger dataset including other genres in Section 4.4.

Thus, regarding this aspect of the syntactic development of verbs of deception, it once more seems to be British English that is spearheading the change, this time towards more economic linguistic means. Interestingly, in British English, the verb *delude*, which was shown in Section 4.1 to adopt complement clauses later than *deceive* and to lag behind in the replacement of nominal by verbal interpretators, tends to accommodate uninterpreted clauses earlier than the longer-established verb in this construction. Note that the British data in Table 1 indicate that in the twentieth century *delude* has also overtaken *deceive* in terms of its total incidence in the relevant construction: In the newspapers (1990–2005) it ends up being twice as frequent (0.51 pmw) as *deceive* (0.26 pmw) in combination with complement clauses. Even at these extremely low levels of incidence, there may thus be a connection between the frequency and the formal reduction of a construction, as is known from grammaticalization phenomena. It will be instructive to compare the integration of the latecomer *fool* into this pattern (see Section 4.4).

4.3 Mid-term diachronic perspective: Factors driving the loss of interpretators

Narrowing down the scope of our analysis to a mid-term perspective (from 1810 onwards) and focusing on the more ample American English data allows us to gauge the effects of additional language-internal factors. As already mentioned, the reductive nature of the change, resembling the loss of shell nouns noted by Denison (2018), leads us to surmise that the loss of interpretators has taken its impetus from informal registers. Furthermore, previous corpus findings adduced in Section 2 suggest that the negation of a clause and the reduction in transitivity that comes with reflexivization and passivization can support poorly established syntactic constructions. The effects of these predictors on the use or omission of interpreting expressions (both nominal and verbal) are visualized, for each verb, in Figure 3.

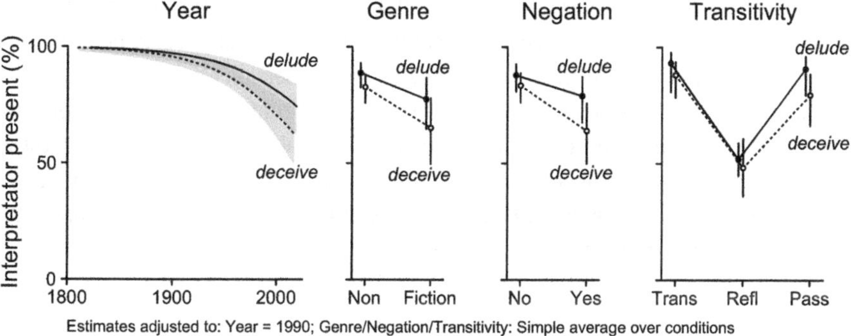

Figure 3: Partial effects of the factors 'verb', 'year', 'genre', 'negation' and 'transitivity' on the presence of interpretators in American English from 1810 onwards. Error bars denote 95% uncertainty intervals. Model specifications and coefficients can be found in the Appendix (Table 9).

The model estimates again show the downward trend for interpretator use, but the slopes for both verbs turn out considerably less steep than in the long-term model. The diminished rate of change can at least partly be put down to the fact that the model now focuses on American English as the more conservative variety in the relevant respect, and includes data from the more formal corpus components: It is obvious that the informal usage that we observed in the macro-genre 'fiction' (in Section 4.2) is the driving force in the change, while non-fiction turns out to be less progressive. This underscores our assumption to the effect that the loss of interpretators is a change from below, spreading from informal registers upwards.

After neutralizing the transitivity-reducing predictors, a comparison of the two verbs in American English suggests that *delude* is lagging behind *deceive* in the omission of interpretators. Recall that the estimates in Section 4.2 suggested the opposite order for British English and no clear difference for American English. A comparison will be made in Section 4.4.

As for the effects of contextual factors reducing the transitivity (and discourse prominence) of a clause, most of our expectations are met and the striking parallels between *deceive* and *delude* lend credence to the observed tendencies: The estimates for non-negated and (broadly defined) negated hits indicate that negation is compatible with the incoming reductive pattern, while absence of negation disfavors it. In other words, acts of deceiving and deluding that are merely conceived but not implemented seem to facilitate the omission of an interpretator.

Among the three constructional types distinguished in terms of valency, it turns out that reflexives (involving one and the same participant as subject and object, engaged in an act of self-deception) represent the strongest contextual factor promoting the omission of interpretators. While this was expected, the limited effect of passivization as a transitivity-reducing context came as a surprise. A potential account for this effect will be provided in the discussion (Section 6).

In sum, the model depicted in Figure 3 suggests that the loss of interpreting expressions can still be described as incipient in formal American English. In these disfavoring conditions, it is however promoted by the discourse-backgrounding factors of negation and reflexivity. Finally, the verbs investigated so far accommodate the trend at different rates.

4.4 Short-term diachronic perspective: Integrating a newcomer

Our analysis of factors promoting the loss of interpretators culminates in the third step, a short-term perspective spanning only thirty years, but sufficiently populated with data to allow all predictors to be played out. What is more, compared to *deceive* and *delude*, which remain at rather low levels of occurrence, the frequency of the verb *fool* skyrockets from a mere 86 occurrences in the relevant construction up to the year 1989 to as many as 1,284 occurrences from 1990 to 2019, thus outdistancing its long-established forerunners by far. We ran three regression models, examining to what extent the previously introduced extra- and intralinguistic predictors carry over to the newcomer to the construction. As before, the outcome variable depicted in Figure 4 is the percentage of interpreted *that*-clauses.

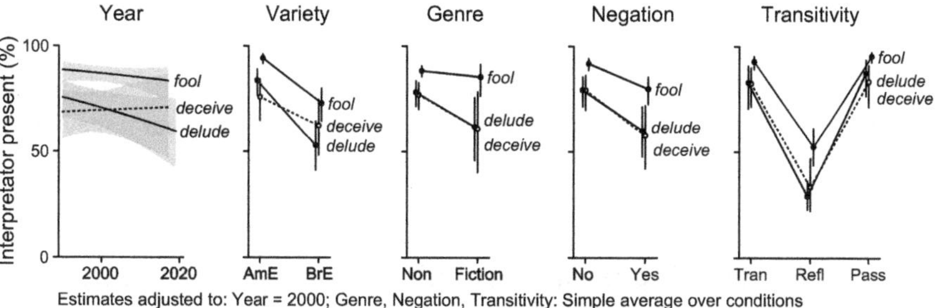

Figure 4: Partial effects of the factors 'verb', 'year', 'variety', 'genre', 'negation' and 'transitivity' on the presence of interpretators from 1990 onwards. Error bars denote 95% uncertainty intervals. Model specifications and coefficients can be found in the Appendix (Table 10).

First off, as all of the pre-1990 data have been cut off, the estimated diachronic trends are now surrounded by rather wide uncertainty bands. For *deceive*, the confidence interval easily accommodates the basic downward trend that has been established in the long-term picture. Thus, the opposite trend indicated in the leftmost panel presents no cogent reason to revise the assumption of a diachronic loss. In contrast, the verb *fool* provides sufficient evidence to warrant a slight downward slope across the thirty-year period, although it lags markedly behind the development for *deceive* and *delude*. We are thus witnessing the initiation of a change that has already gained ground with semantically related lexical verbs, extending to a novel member of the constructional class.

Intriguingly, all other model estimates provide strong support for the effects previously noted. British English is leading the change; the variety difference is consistent across all three verbs. At a closer look, we now see more evidence for what has been conjectured in Sections 4.2 and 4.3: In British English, the trend towards the abandonment of interpretators is more advanced for *delude*, while in American English it is more advanced for *deceive*. We also note that for *fool*, the dropping of interpretators is at present virtually restricted to British English. As shown above, informal usage, seen in the macro-genre 'fiction' here, is heading the change from below, even though *fool* does not exhibit a strong genre effect.

Intralinguistic factors fostering the reductive change are, as above, most prominently reflexive uses, and in the second place also various negated contexts. In contrast, passivization once again does not produce the expected effect. For *fool*, it even appears to increase the proportion of interpreted cases significantly above the level of fully transitive uses, giving rise to a post-hoc consideration that we will discuss in Section 6.

All in all, not only the size, but also the consistency of effects of external and context-dependent factors across all three verbs under scrutiny, lend credence to the conclusion that the increasing omissibility of interpreting expressions is fostered by informal usage in British English as well as by the pragmatic backgrounding of propositional content through negation and reflexivization, but it may affect individual exponents of the lexical class at different rates.

4.5 Ensuing developments: Dropping of complementizers

The reductive changes undergone by the syntactic patterns associated with *deceive*, *delude* and *fool* have been viewed as concomitants of an underlying process of grammaticalization, taking place in syntactic niches that are shielded from speakers' attention and endowing the verbs with a novel argument structure. Further to these changes, the loss of phonological and morphological bulk in the form of the complementizer *that* might provide additional evidence in favor of grammaticalization.

The dropping of the complementizer *that* is first and foremost dependent on the presence of an interpretator. In the present context, interpretive nouns as well as verbs can serve as heads of *that*-clause complements, and the heads retain a major influence on the use or omission of *that*. In the case of nominal heads as in examples (10), (12) and (13) above, omission of *that* is liable to ambiguity with *that*-less relative clauses and almost categorically excluded (3% out of a total of 304 examples, see Table 11 in the Appendix).

In the case of verbal heads, however, *that*-omission is found in roughly half of our observations (52% out of 2119 examples). By far the most frequent verbal interpretator is *think*, which generally happens to be among the most common verbs taking complement clauses (along with *believe*) and one of the two most likely to omit the complementizer (Biber et al. 2021: 656, 661, 674–675). In our entire dataset, 57% of the 1397 tokens of interpretators involving *think* come without *that*,[7] 43% of the 655 interpretators involving *believe*,[8] and only 22% of the small minority of 67 cases of other verbal interpretators. In addition to the specific verb, the omission rate can be assumed to depend on well-known factors such as register (with informal language dropping optional function words more readily), variety (with American English

---

7 *into thinking, in thinking, by thinking, to thinking, with thinking, thinking, to think, so far as to think*
8 *into believing, in believing, by believing, believing, to believe, as to believe*

typically being more economic) and syntactic complexity (as in the case of negation, which can be compensated by the retention of function words).[9] The model estimates for verbal interpretators shown in Figure 5 confirm these expectations. Above all, the tendency to drop the interpretator grows stronger with time.

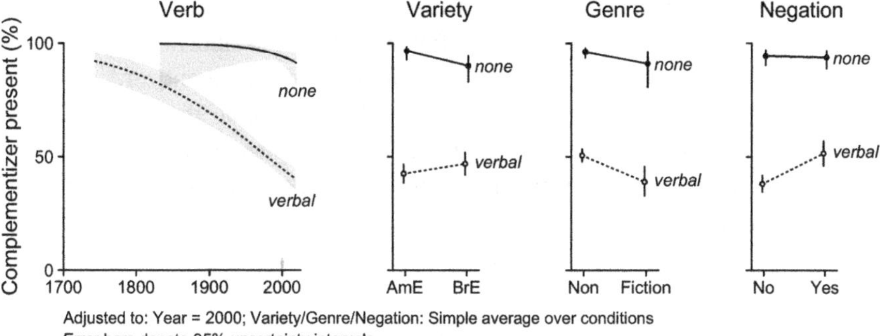

Figure 5: Partial effects of the factors 'year', 'variety', 'genre' and 'negation' on the presence of complementizer *that* with 'verbal' interpretators and without interpretators ('none'). Error bars denote 95% uncertainty intervals. Model specifications and coefficients can be found in the Appendix (Table 11).

While the conditional omission of the complementizer after mental verbs like *think* and *believe* comes as little surprise and would hardly deserve mention here, what is investigated in the last part of our analysis is the possibility to drop *that* in the novel uninterpreted construction type after *deceive, delude* and *fool*. Instances without *that*, illustrated in example (15) above, do occur, but are so far extremely infrequent (5% out of a total of 651 instances). Dropping *that* after *deceive, delude* and *fool* is thus on a completely different level than dropping *that* after *think, believe* and other common verbs of cognition. Figure 5 includes model estimates for the set of uninterpreted complement clauses (labelled 'none') for the same predictors as we have seen at work with the verbal interpretators.

In this model, effect sizes are small due to the infrequency of *that*-less constructions. The timeline however suggests that we may be witnessing the onset of a loss over the last few decades. In addition, the genre labelled 'fiction' shows a high concentration of these rare cases, pointing to the beginnings of the reductive

---

9 For the frequent omission of function words in informal language see, e.g., Rohdenburg (2008: 317–318) and Biber et al. (2021: 674); for variety differences see, e.g., Kövecses (2002: 203–217); for negation as a complexity factor see, e.g., Erdmann (1980: 125). For more data on the omission of complementizer *that* after verbs, see Biber et al. (2021: 673–676).

process in informal usage. Unlike with verbal interpretators, the first signs of the change appear in British English, where uninterpreted clauses are already more common. We observe no effect of negation.

After the reduction of interpreting expressions, the incipient tendency to drop the complementizer lends additional support to our view that complement clauses become increasingly grammaticalized in the valency patterns of the verbs *deceive*, *delude* and *fool*, to the point of following better-established matrix verbs (like *think*, *believe* and others) in the omission of the complementizer.[10] As far as we can judge, the predictors promoting this loss resemble those relevant for other matrix verbs. In the long run, a probabilistic complementizer use after transitive verbs of deception may come to characterize the ultimate stage in the current grammaticalization process.

5 Supplementary observations

This section lists preliminary results from a few spot-checks connected with our main topic, pointing to four additional effects. The factors investigated have not been fully annotated for all verbs or all text databases and have therefore not been included in the regression modelling of the main study. Many of the results are statistically insufficient and at best suggestive; yet we note that reflexive objects exhibit a special attraction to the construction under investigation (Section 5.1), that a more fine-grained categorization of object expressions in terms of transitivity degrees (Section 5.2) will prove worthwhile, that the use of interpretators might correlate with the length and complexity of sentence constituents (Section 5.3), and that the binary distinction of levels of formality employed in our analysis could be refined (Section 5.4).

5.1 The role of reflexive objects

For a start, further insights are afforded by a comparison of the relative frequencies of reflexive objects in the constructions under discussion, i.e. those with a *that*-clause complement, compared to other transitive uses of the same verb, here

---

10 It would be interesting, but outside the scope of this study, to compare the frequency of complementizer omission with other suasive verbs taking direct objects followed by complement clauses, such as *advise, convince, inform, let X know, notify, promise, remind, reassure, tell* and *warn*. The data in Biber et al. (2021: 673–676) offer little detail in this respect, beyond the observation that objects between the head verb and the complement clause render *that*-dropping less likely.

exemplified by *delude*. The analysis in Figure 6[11] indicates that beginning in the first half of the nineteenth century – and possibly owing to text type and stylistic changes – the reflexive object in sentences without *that*-clauses as complements steadily raises its share of the object category to reach more than two thirds of all instances by the late twentieth century. Crucially, however, the proportion of the reflexive object in combination with *that*-complement clauses turns out to be much higher in every subperiod. This is also true of the twentieth century reflexives, stemming from the narrative domain of the BNC, where nine out of ten *that*-clause complements involve the directly linked type.

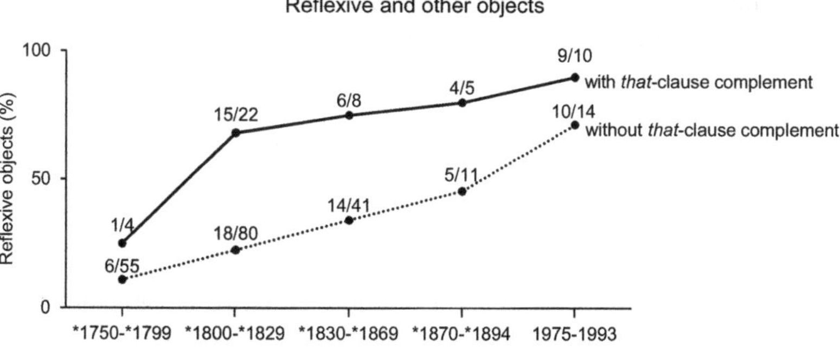

Figure 6: Reflexive and other objects associated with the verb *delude* in a series of (mostly narrative) British texts. Details on the database can be found in the online appendix at https://osf.io/h8325.

5.2 The role of object individuation

A further aspect of transitivity distinguished by Hopper and Thompson (1980: 253, see our Section 2) relates to the individuation of the class of non-reflexive objects. We draw on the Individuation Hierarchy proposed by Timberlake (1977: 162), which consists of the noun phrase parameters listed as (a)-(f).

a) proper
b) human
c) concrete
d) singular
e) count
f) definite (referential)

---

11 Coordinations of *delude* and some other verb are included in the count. The type *He has been easy to delude* is disregarded.

With a view to distinguishing clearly between two quantifiable categories of objects, we adopt the following classification: 'Individuated objects' possess all of the properties in (b) to (f) and may potentially bear a proper name. The remaining parameters and their combinations are then assigned to the class of 'non-individuated objects'. Thus, in the case of personal pronouns, it is only *me, you* (when referring to one person), *him* and *her* that may function as individuated objects. Furthermore, (superficially) definite noun phrases like *the reader* in (22), which do not single out one particular person, have been assigned to the class of non-individuated objects.

(22)   These thinkers . . . abuse the terms and theories of modern science to **deceive** the reader **into thinking** that they are thinking when in fact they are doing no such thing. (*The Times*, 1998)

In line with our previous findings, we expected directly linked *that*-clauses to display a lower percentage of individuated objects than their interpreted counterparts. Figure 7 shows that this is indeed the case for both British and American newspapers, and also for the conflation of the two varieties. However, the contrast between the two types of clausal variants is far from significant. Notice that with both types of *that*-clauses, the vast majority of objects turn out to be non-individuated.

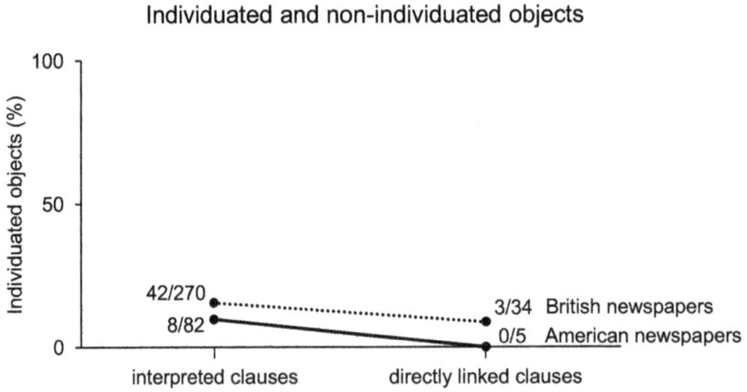

Figure 7: The role of the two *that*-clause variants in constraining the distribution of individuated and non-individuated objects after *deceive* in British and American newspapers. Details on the database can be found in the online appendix at https://osf.io/h8325.

5.3 The role of argument complexity

This section takes a brief look at potential effects of the phonological bulk and semantic precision contributed by the presence of interpreting expressions. An intriguing tendency involving the subject expressions in the two *that*-clause variants is illustrated in (23) and (24).

(23)   ... the naïve treasurers who **delude** themselves **into believing** that <u>they</u> are financial wizards, ... (*Los Angeles Times*, 1994)

(24)   ... the young women in 19th century novels who **delude** themselves Ø that <u>a glance from</u> <u>a man</u> could only mean he intends marriage. (*Los Angeles Times*, 1994)

One basic difference between the two variants concerns the portion stretching from the object of the deception verb to the subject of the *that*-clause complement: The sequence is less complex in the directly linked variant as in (24) than that in the interpreted case as in (23). Consider now the data in Figure 8, which distinguishes between simple subject expressions (containing 1 to 2 words) and more complex ones. It is apparent that the increase in subject complexity correlates with a striking decline of the interpreted *that*-clause variant. In other words, the choice of the shorter sequence between the object of the deception verb and the subject of the *that*-clause as in (24) tends to coincide with the use of a longer subject expression. Interestingly, the increased inclination of the directly linked *that*-clause towards greater subject complexity and the lowered occurrence of the interpretator seem to accord with the theory of information density championed by, e.g., Jaeger (2011) and Crocker et al. (2016). Basically, the theory assumes that languages strive to distribute evenly across a given utterance the amount of information conveyed by comparable linguistic elements.

Incidentally, the ability of interpretators to function as explicit markers in the case of complex constructions deserves further scrutiny. For one, more explicit structures may be triggered by the processing complexity generated by passivization. For another, we have occasionally observed cases of complex object expressions where the interpretator seems to establish an explicit link with the superordinate verb, as in (25).

(25)   "You can have a lot of fun by colouring white wine red and giving them to wine experts. It depends on the wine, but with many wines you can **fool** <u>wine</u> <u>experts who are tasting a £ 20-£ 30 bottle of white wine that has been coloured</u> <u>red</u> **into thinking** that it smells like a red wine." (*The Guardian*, 2005)

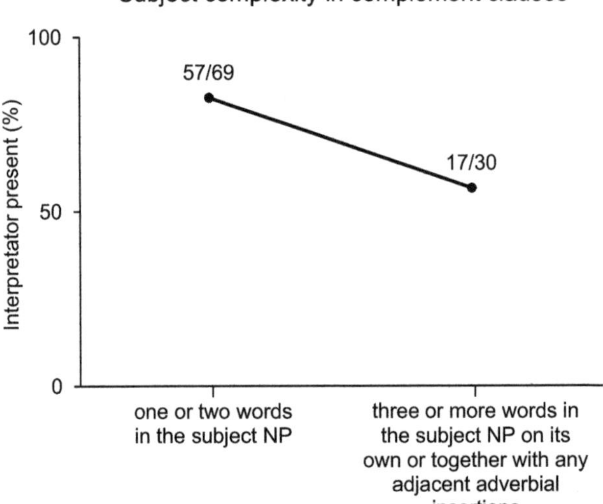

Figure 8: The role of subject complexity in directly linked and interpreted *that*-clauses after the verb *delude* in American newspapers. Details on the database can be found in the online appendix at https://osf.io/h8325.

5.4 The role of direct speech

In the models outlined in Section 4, a simplified binary genre division, for convenience labelled 'fiction' vs. 'non-fiction', has been used as a proxy for the distinction between informal and formal language, and the demise of interpretators has been identified as a change from below. Newspaper language, classified as 'non-fiction', however contains a sizeable number of quotations from direct speech (indicated mainly by the use of relevant punctuation marks), which allows us to implement a finer differentiation. For the American newspapers and the verb *delude*, we found the formality difference clearly reflected in the fact that the share of interpreted variants is much lower in quoted speech than elsewhere (see Figure 9).

6 Discussion

By way of summary, the study has investigated a (three-step) reductive change affecting three exemplary verbs: *deceive, delude* and *fool*. All of them seem to have progressed from a) unadorned/basic transitive verb constellations (S-V-O), via b)

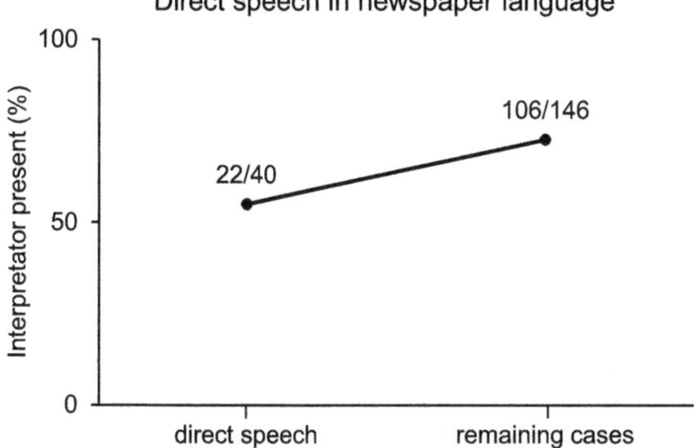

Figure 9: The role of direct speech in directly linked and interpreted *that*-clauses after the verb *delude* in American newspapers. Details on the database can be found in the online appendix at https://osf.io/h8325.

newly gained nominal or gerundial adjuncts specifying the content of the deceptive mindset phrased as a dependent *that*-clause, to reach c) the stage of directly linked *that*-clause complements. Two classes of expressions that arguably serve to endow subordinated propositions with semantic interpretations and syntactic integration have been shown to compete with each other (with the verbal class ousting the nominal class in the course of the nineteenth and twentieth centuries), only to be made redundant themselves and replaced by directly linked, uninterpreted complement clauses (a change that is currently ongoing). As a result, *deceive* and *delude* as matrix verbs increasingly accept a novel class of clausal complements. These, in turn, begin to shed the complementizer *that*, thus joining a large class of transitive verbs of communication, most of which have preserved a centuries-old *that*-clause pattern. Buttressing the relevance of the factors involved in the change, the newcomer *fool* integrates into this paradigm, yet demonstrating that its time of entry codetermines the options available as constructional patterns and leads to a delay in the loss of interpretators.

Reductive changes like these can be perspectivized with reference to a number of overarching considerations. As we have seen, gerundial linkers like *thinking* and *believing* have become desemanticized from their original sense of 'holding the respective ideas and beliefs'. To the extent that they now apply to inanimate experiencers, their function has contracted from a semantico-syntactic one to a primarily syntactic one, turning them into grammatical functors. This finding, their increasing absence from the constructions dependent on verbs of deception and the subsequent loss of complementizers can be accounted for by an erosive grammaticalization process wearing away the morphophonological and syntactic bulk of the construction.

Unsurprisingly, the separation of our textual data into more or less formal genres has indicated that we are dealing with a change from below, with more speech-like registers in the lead and stylistically more elaborate ones following at a distance. This aligns well with a large number of observations supporting a general colloquialization tendency in the English language (e.g. Mair 2006: 181–199).

Perhaps surprisingly, however, the constructional innovation has clearly turned out to be driven by British English, which is often described as having more formal leanings – including in its grammar – than the American variety (cf. Kövecses 2002: 235–246, Rohdenburg and Schlüter 2009: 421) and as having been more conservative recently than the latter (cf. Algeo 2001; for a critical assessment see Rohdenburg and Schlüter 2009: 364–423 and several chapters in that edited volume). Conversely, it has been suggested that recently editorial policies have been stricter and that academic writing has been more subject to stylistic prescriptivism in the US than in Britain (Tottie 2005, Denison 2009: 163). This would agree with our finding that formal American English provides the stronghold of interpreted complement clauses. Reiterating a conclusion from the collection of analyses in Rohdenburg and Schlüter (2009: 421), we propose that each grammatical phenomenon deserves to be studied in its own right rather than in terms of preconceived generalizations.

On several occasions in our discussion, reference has been made to Denison's (2018) pioneering study, which focuses on the incidence of the patterns 'V + shell noun + *that*-clause' and 'V + *that*-clause' after a large set of verbs in the recent history of English, as exemplified in (26). Denison points out that writers less familiar with the diction of academic writing tend to introduce or favor simpler verb-dependent *that*-clauses over the established ones containing an additional shell noun.

(26)   This observation **highlights (the fact)** <u>that</u> we are dealing here with a unique case.

Our data on the progressive expansion of uninterpreted *that*-clauses from informal to formal text types parallel and underscore Denison's conclusions. Going beyond the author's (necessarily) quantitative orientation, we would recommend including a qualitative aspect distinguishing between specific verbs and their associated *that*-clauses with or without a specific shell noun. Such an approach was sketched above in connection with *rule out* and *possibility* (see Section 2). Preliminary observations concerning a set of related negative implicative verbs (*exclude, overlook, ignore* and *preclude*) suggest that – with these items – the omission of a shell noun like *possibility* might, in particular, be subject to the same detransitivization tendency as that found with *rule out*: the retreat of the shell noun in a clause involving its own (syntactic) negator. Assuming that this is the case, clause negation could be regarded as promoting two kinds of *that*-clauses: a) the derived pattern V + *that*-clause after certain negative implicative verbs, and b) the directly linked *that*-clause after transitive uses of *delude, deceive* and *fool*.

In a more theoretically-oriented perspective, we have thus found that negation as well as other detransitivizing strategies can be used to pragmatically background a clause, which helps innovative constructions to sneak in by the back door (cf. Hopper and Thompson 1980: 284, quoted in Section 2). Gauging the influence of a variety of transitivity-related factors, we found that matrix clauses involving highly transitive direct-object constructions ("cardinal transitivity" in the sense of Hopper and Thompson 1980: 253) are the most resistant to the demise of interpreting expressions, while reflexive objects (as exponents of "de-transitive voice" in the sense of Givón 2001: 91–94) accommodate them most readily. This much was expected and confirmed.

The other exponent of low transitivity, the passive, has turned out to be less easily reconciled with our assumptions about the mitigating effects of backgrounding, as the high share of interpreted subordinate clauses does not differ markedly from that of fully transitive clauses. Reconsidering examples like (18) and (19), a post-hoc explanation suggests itself: Since the experiencer NP appears in subject position, the passivized verb of deception is as a rule immediately followed by the questionable *that*-clause – except in the case of intervening elements as in (17), which can serve as buffers similar to the object expressions in the canonical word order. This constellation appears more objectionable than corresponding active constructions; a sense of incompatibility or repulsion between the verb and a directly linked complement clause seems to persist. We predict that this avoidance will disappear as *that*-clauses become more and more established, but perhaps no sooner than in cardinal transitive contexts.

To conclude, let us widen our perspective to changes in English complementation patterns more globally. There has recently been an increase in the number of cases involving the rivalry between finite complement clauses and other syntactic alternatives. The last few centuries have witnessed a general, though not exceptionless, decline of *that*-clause complements in favor of gerundial and infinitival constructions (see, e.g., Rudanko 2000, Vosberg 2006, Iyeiri 2010). The topic addressed in this paper concerns contrary and hitherto ignored developments undergone by (at least) three verbs of deception. Interestingly, the tendency to delete interpretators in the area treated in this article can be shown to be reversed in several other environments. Thus, in its recent history, English has evolved a number of constructions where a directly linked complement clause has increasingly been replaced by one including an additional verbal interpretator (Rohdenburg 1998). To begin with, it has been noted that certain types of dependent interrogative clauses tend to be expanded by mental verbs like *see* or *know* as in (27). Furthermore, there is an increasing range of unstable *that*-clause complements – associated with a variety of superordinate verbs and nouns – which have been extended by the addition of basic verbs of communication like *say* as in (28). Again, such developments seem to be favored by informal registers.

(27)   I was at a loss **to know** what you were feeling. (BNC, fiction, 1992)

(28)   I got a letter **to say** Dad was in hospital . . . (BNC, spoken/scripted)

In addition, both the replacement of the nominal interpretator by the verbal one and the subsequent dropping of the interpretator itself could simply be interpreted as an extension of the (more) nominal to the (more) clausal domain. The history of English provides a number of further examples illustrating this type of change. For instance, the emergence of a prepositional gerundial complement on the basis of an existing prepositional phrase has been noted in several studies (see e.g. Kjellmer 1980, De Smet 2010, Rudanko 2015: 25).

In this larger context, future work will have to examine the question as to which environments are susceptible to the addition or the deletion of interpretators and to what extent these tendencies can be accounted for in terms of general evolutionary trends.

Appendix

Table 5: Overview of data selected and factors modelled in the regression analysis (see Section 4).

section	period	verbs	subset	factors	outcome variable
4.1	1725–2019	*deceive, delude*	fiction	year, variety	interpretator type (nominal/verbal)
4.2	1725–2019	*deceive, delude*	fiction	year, variety	presence/absence of interpretator
4.3	1810–2019	*deceive, delude*	AmE	year, genre, negation, transitivity	presence/absence of interpretator
4.4	1990–2019	*deceive, delude, fool*	all data	year, variety, genre, negation, transitivity	presence/absence of interpretator
4.5	1725–2019	*deceive, delude, fool*	all data	year, variety, genre, negation	presence/absence of complementizer

Table 6: Logistic regression models (R function glm, family = binomial).

section	model specification
4.1	interpretator verbal ~ year_c + variety
4.2	interpretator present ~ year_c + variety
4.3	interpretator present ~ year_c + genre_binary + transitivity + negation
4.4	interpretator present ~ year_c + genre_binary + transitivity + negation
4.5	interpretator present ~ year_c + variety + negation + genre_binary

Table 7: Predictor coding for the logistic regression analysis (see Section 4).

predictor	coding	meaning (on the logit scale) of:	
		coefficient	**model intercept**
year	(year − 2000)/50	difference between two time points 50 years apart	estimate for the year 2000
variety	BrE −1; AmE +1	half the difference between the varieties	simple average over varieties
genre	fiction −1; non-fiction +1	half the difference between the genres	simple average over genres
negation	yes −1 (= negated); no +1	half the difference between negated and non-negated cases	simple average over negation
transitivity	sum contrasts: (1) trans +1; refl 0; pass −1 (2) trans 0; refl +1; pass −1	difference between (1) transitive cases and the average over all three types; (2) reflexive cases and the average over all three types	simple average over transitivity types

Table 8: Logistic regression for interpretator types in fiction (see Section 4.1). Predicted outcome: verbal interpretator.

	deceive (n = 233)		*delude* (n = 146)	
	estimate	**SE**	**estimate**	**SE**
(intercept)	3.71	0.56	2.44	0.59
year	1.26	0.19	1.54	0.26
variety	−0.55	0.18	−0.29	0.26
C score	0.79		0.85	
Condition number kappa	5.3		4.6	

Table 9: Logistic regression for long-term loss of interpretators in fiction (see Section 4.2). Predicted outcome: interpretator present.

	deceive (n = 265)		*delude* (n = 193)	
	estimate	**SE**	**estimate**	**SE**
(intercept)	−0.16	0.36	−0.77	0.34
year	−1.28	0.21	−1.56	0.24
variety	−0.05	0.26	0.28	0.28
C score	0.87		0.88	
Condition number kappa	4.5		3.5	

Table 10: Logistic regression for mid-term loss of interpretators in American English from 1810 onwards (see Section 4.3). Predicted outcome: interpretator present.

	deceive (n = 448)		*delude* (n = 530)	
	estimate	**SE**	**estimate**	**SE**
(intercept)	0.88	0.23	1.45	0.27
year	−1.10	0.20	−1.02	0.18
genre	0.47	0.18	0.41	0.13
negation	0.52	0.17	0.33	0.12
transitivity1	0.90	0.27	0.96	0.43
transitivity2	−1.16	0.22	−1.58	0.26
C score	0.83		0.80	
Condition number kappa	3.5		3.3	

Table 11: Logistic regression for short-term loss of interpretators from 1990 onwards (see Section 4.4). Predicted outcome: interpretator present.

	deceive (n = 413)		*delude* (n = 693)		*fool* (n = 1284)	
	estimate	**SE**	**estimate**	**SE**	**estimate**	**SE**
(intercept)	0.83	0.24	0.88	0.21	1.90	0.16
year	0.19	1.16	−1.28	0.73	−0.81	0.80
variety	0.32	0.15	0.76	0.10	0.91	0.12
genre	0.38	0.22	0.40	0.16	0.13	0.16
negation	0.51	0.16	0.47	0.10	0.52	0.11
transitivity1	0.72	0.20	0.70	0.25	0.66	0.15
transitivity2	−1.51	0.20	−1.77	0.18	−1.80	0.14
C score	0.82		0.83		0.84	
Condition number kappa	4.0		4.4		3.4	

Table 12: Logistic regression for long-term loss of complementizer *that* (see Section 4.5). Predicted outcome: complementizer present.

	nominal (n = 304)		verbal (n = 2118)		none (n = 651)	
	estimate	SE	estimate	SE	estimate	SE
(intercept)	4.28	0.94	−0.21	0.08	2.76	0.25
year	0.30	0.32	−0.51	0.08	−1.11	0.80
variety	0.71	0.37	−0.09	0.05	0.56	0.25
genre	−0.09	0.49	0.24	0.07	0.45	0.28
negation	−0.07	0.41	−0.27	0.05	0.06	0.18
C score	0.69		0.61		0.65	
Condition number kappa	6.3		3.4		2.8	

Databases

See the online appendix at https://osf.io/h8325.

References

Algeo, John. 2001. External history. In John Algeo (ed.), *The Cambridge history of the English language.* Volume 6: *English in North America*, 1–58. Cambridge: Cambridge University Press.

Biber, Douglas, Stig Johansson, Geoffrey Leech, Susan Conrad & Edward Finegan. 2021. *Grammar of spoken and written English*. Amsterdam & Philadelphia: Benjamins.

Bolinger, Dwight. 1967. Apparent constituents in surface structure. *Word* 23. 47–56.

Crocker, Matthew W., Vera Demberg & Elke Teich. 2016. Information density and linguistic encoding (IDEAL). *Künstliche Intelligenz* 30. 77–81.

Davies, Mark & Jong-Bok Kim. 2018. Semantic and lexical shifts with the "*into*-causative" construction in American English. In Hubert Cuyckens, Hendrik De Smet, Liesbet Heyvaert & Charlotte Maekelberghe (eds.), *Explorations in English historical syntax*, 159–178. Amsterdam & Philadelphia: Benjamins.

Denison, David. 2009. Argument structure. In Günter Rohdenburg & Julia Schlüter (eds.), *One language, two grammars? Differences between British and American English*, 149–165. Cambridge: Cambridge University Press.

Denison, David. 2018. *That*-clauses as complements of verbs or nouns. In Elena Seoane, Carlos Acuña Fariña & Ignacio Palacios-Martinez (eds.), *Subordination in English: Synchronic and diachronic perspectives*, 61–84. Berlin & Boston: De Gruyter.

De Smet, Hendrik. 2010. English -*ing* clauses and their problems: The structure of grammatical categories. *Linguistics* 48. 1153–1193.

Duffley, Patrick J. 2018. *Talk into* vs *convince to*: Talking as a cause leading to containment, convincing as a cause leading to a result. In Mark Kaunisto, Mikko Höglund & Paul Rickman (eds.),

Changing structures: Studies in constructions and complementation, 15–30. (Studies in Language Companion Series 195). Amsterdam & Philadelphia: Benjamins.

Erdmann, Peter. 1980. Der Konjunktiv im britischen und amerikanischen Englisch. In Peter Kunsmann & Ortwin Kuhn (eds.), *Weltsprache Englisch in Forschung und Lehre. Festschrift für Kurt Wächter*, 110–131. Berlin: Schmidt.

Flach, Susanne. 2021. From movement into action to manner of causation: Changes in argument mapping in the *into*-causative. *Linguistics* 59(1). 247–283.

Fox, John & Sanford Weisberg. 2018. Visualizing fit and lack of fit in complex regression models with predictor effect plots and partial residuals. *Journal of Statistical Software* 87 (9). 1–27. https://www.jstatsoft.org/article/view/v087i09.

Fox, John & Sanford Weisberg. 2019. *An {R} companion to applied regression.* Third edition. Thousand Oaks, CA: Sage. https://socialsciences.mcmaster.ca/jfox/Books/Companion/.

Givón, Talmy. 2001. *Syntax.* Volume II. Amsterdam & Philadelphia: Benjamins.

Hopper, Paul J. & Sandra A. Thompson. 1980. Transitivity in grammar and discourse. *Language* 56. 251–299.

Iyeiri, Yoko. 2010. *Verbs of implicit negation and their complements in the history of English.* Amsterdam & Philadelphia: Benjamins; Tokyo: Yushoda Press.

Jaeger, T. Florian. 2011. Corpus-based research and language production: Information density and reducible subject relatives. In Emily M. Bender & Jennifer E. Arnold (eds.), *Language from a cognitive perspective: Grammar, usage and processing. Studies in honor of Thomas Wasow*, 161–197. Stanford: CSLI Publications.

Kjellmer, Göran. 1980. Accustomed to swim: Accustomed to swimming. On verbal forms after *to*. In Jens Allwood & Magnus Lund (eds.), *ALVAR: A linguistically varied assortment of readings. Studies presented to Alvar Ellegård on the occasion of his 60th birthday*, 75–99. Stockholm: University of Stockholm.

Kövecses, Zoltán. 2002. *American English: An introduction.* Peterborough, Ontario: Broadview Press.

Lüdtke, Jens. 1984. *Sprache und Interpretation: Semantik und Syntax reflexiver Strukturen im Französischen.* (Tübinger Beiträge zur Linguistik). Tübingen: Narr.

Mair, Christian. 2006. *Twentieth century English: History, variation, and standardization.* Cambridge: Cambridge University Press.

Mondorf, Britta & Ulrike Schneider. 2016. Detransitivisation as a support strategy for causative *bring*. *English Language and Linguistics* 20(3). 439–462.

OED (*Oxford English Dictionary*). Oxford: Oxford University Press. https://www.oed.com.

R Development Core Team. 2021. R: A language and environment for statistical computing. R Foundation for Statistical Computing, Vienna, Austria. http://www.R-project.org.

Rickman, Paul & Mark Kaunisto. 2018. Aspects of the use of the transitive *into -ing* pattern in New Zealand English. In Mark Kaunisto, Mikko Höglund & Paul Rickman (eds.), *Changing structures: Studies in constructions and complementation*, 71–87. (Studies in Language Companion Series 195). Amsterdam & Philadelphia: Benjamins.

Rohdenburg, Günter. 1998. Subordinate clauses introduced by interpretative verbs in English and their less explicit counterparts in German. In Wolfgang Börner & Klaus Vogel (eds.), *Kontrast und Äquivalenz: Beiträge zu Sprachvergleich und Übersetzung*, 233–249. Tübingen: Narr.

Rohdenburg, Günter. 2008. On the history and present behaviour of subordinating *that* with adverbial conjunctions in English. In Elena Seoane & María José López-Couso (eds.), *Theoretical and empirical issues in grammaticalization*, 315–331. Amsterdam & Philadelphia: Benjamins.

Rohdenburg, Günter. 2014. The changing status of *that*-clauses. In Marianne Hundt (ed.), *Late Modern English Syntax*, 155–181. (Studies in English language). Cambridge: Cambridge University Press.

Rohdenburg, Günter. 2020. The replacement of direct objects and directly linked gerunds by prepositional ones after *shirk, refrain* and *lack* in Modern English, with special reference to clause negation. *Anglia* 138(4). 561–585.

Rohdenburg, Günter & Julia Schlüter (eds.). 2009. *One language, two grammars? Differences between British and American English*. Cambridge: Cambridge University Press.

Rudanko, Juhani. 2000. *Corpus and complementation: Tracing sentential complementation patterns of nouns, adjectives and verbs over the last three centuries*. Oxford: University Press of America.

Rudanko, Juhani. 2015. *Linking form and meaning: Studies on selected control patterns in recent English*. Basingstoke: Palgrave Macmillan.

Sarkar, Deepayan. 2008. *Lattice: Multivariate data visualization with R*. New York: Springer.

Schmid, Hans-Jörg. 2012. *English abstract nouns as conceptual shells: From corpus to cognition*. (Topics in English linguistics 34). Berlin: De Gruyter Mouton.

Schneider, Ulrike. 2021. Loss of intersective gradience as the lifeboat of a dying construction: An analysis of the diachronic change of causative *bring*. *Folia Linguistica* 55 (s42–s2). 429–459.

Stempel, Philipp. 2019. *A constructional reanalysis of semantic prosody*. Doctoral thesis, Houston, TX: Rice University.

Timberlake, Alan. 1977. Reanalysis and actualization in syntactic change. In Charles Lee (ed.), *Mechanisms of syntactic change*, 141–180. Austin: University of Texas Press.

Tottie, Gunnel. 2005. On substituting *with* for *for* with *substitute* (and some other prepositions as well). In Kevin McCafferty, Tove Bull & Kristin Killie (eds.), *Contexts – historical, social, linguistic. Studies in celebration of Toril Swan*, 203–223. Bern: Lang.

Vosberg, Uwe. 2006. *Die große Komplementverschiebung: Außersemantische Einflüsse auf die Entwicklung satzwertiger Ergänzungen im Neuenglischen*. Tübingen: Narr.

Paul Rickman and Juhani Rudanko

10 Straddling a syntactic divide

Tracking sentential complements of *promise* and *threaten* in CLMET3.0

Abstract: This paper investigates sentential complementation patterns of the matrix verbs *promise* and *threaten* over the course of 210 years in recent British English, using data drawn from the Corpus of Late Modern English Texts, version 3.0. The focus is on subject control and subject to subject raising constructions with both verbs when a *to* infinitive complement is selected. Documented evidence suggests that the subject control construction is the older, more established syntactic arrangement for both *promise* and *threaten*, with subject to subject raising a more recent development, possibly beginning during the early period of the CLMET3.0 data. The fact that these verbs can appear in both syntactic environments puts them in a restricted class of verbs that straddle the syntactic divide between control and raising. The paper documents the evolution of the raising version, and explains it within the context of grammaticalization. The authentic data examined here allow the suggestion that the grammaticalization process took place during this time period at a significantly faster rate with *threaten* than it did with *promise*. Two possible reasons are put forward for this, highlighting differences between the two semantically related verbs that have not yet received much attention in the literature.

Keywords: *promise*, *threaten*, subject to subject raising, subject control, grammaticalization, complementation, CLMET3.0

1 Introduction

One of the most important insights gained by generative grammarians in the area of non-finite sentential complementation concerns the setting up of a systematic distinction between control and raising (NP movement) in the analysis of matrix verbs and adjectives. For instance, consider the difference between a control verb such as *swear* and a raising verb such as *seem*, as in (1a–b), which are both from the CLMET3.0.

https://doi.org/10.1515/9783110753059-010

(1) a. They swore to spill their blood [. . .] (1842, George Borrow, *The Bible in Spain*)

  b. She seemed to believe him. (1847, Emily Brontë, *Wuthering Heights*)

There is an infinitival complement in both (1a) and (1b). It is assumed here that in both sentences the infinitival complement is sentential. This assumption makes it possible to describe the argument structures of the verbs of the lower clauses in a straightforward way. It is assumed further that in both sentences the lower clause has an understood or covert subject, even though no such subject is overtly present. The notion of an understood subject is found in the work of traditional grammarians (e.g. Jespersen [1940] 1961: 140), and in much current work, for instance, in Chomsky (1986: 119–132).

However, it is a widely accepted assumption that there is a sharp syntactic difference between the two types of constructions. The key difference is that sentence (1b) involves movement, whereas there is no such movement in (1a). In (1b) the higher subject is generated as an empty NP, which does not receive a theta role from *seem* and is not an argument of the verb. The movement consists in the subject of the lower clause moving into that non-theta position. The NP node is left behind by the movement, together with the symbol t, for trace, which is coindexed with the NP moved. The label "subject to subject raising" describes the nature of the movement rule in question well. Since the choice of construction depends on the higher verb, it is customary to say that *seem* can be a subject to subject raising verb. In (1b) it selects only one argument, which is the lower clause.

By contrast, the higher subject of sentence (1a) is generated by phrase structure rules, without movement, in the subject position and the NP is then an argument of the higher verb and receives a theta role from the verb. Thus *swear* in (1a) has two arguments: the higher subject and the lower clause. The lower subject in the control construction is a pronominal NP without phonological realization. In current work the symbol PRO is used for the empty NP. Since PRO in (1a) is coreferential with the higher subject, it is customary to refer to the construction as one of subject control and to say that *swear*, the higher verb, can be a subject control verb in English.

The sentences in (1a) and (1b) may then be minimally bracketed as in (1a′) and (1b′).

(1) a.′ [[They]$_{NP}$ swore [[PRO]$_{NP}$ [to]$_{Aux}$ [spill their blood]$_{VP}$]$_{S2}$]$_{S1}$

  b.′ [[She]$_{NP}$ seemed [[t]$_{NP}$ [to]$_{Aux}$ [believe him]$_{VP}$]$_{S2}$]$_{S1}$

There are syntactic differences between the two types of constructions that motivate the distinction between control and raising. They include a difference relating to selectionally restricted NPs, such as *there* and *advantage*. For instance, consider (2a–b).

(2)   a. *There swore to be several people present.
       b. There seemed to be several people present.

The contrast between (2a) and (2b) is explained by the analysis: existential *there* can occur as the subject of existential clauses, such as the lower clause of (2b), and it is then raised into the higher subject position. On the other hand, existential *there* cannot occur as the subject of a verb such as *swear*. *Swear* assigns a theta role to its subject, and an NP such as *there* cannot carry a theta role.

The syntactic difference between the two patterns is clear enough and there is a difference in their structural representations, as is clear when (1a') is compared to (1b'). Many verbs and adjectives are also similar to *swear* and to *seem* in that they only permit one of the two patterns. However, linguistic categories can be permeable and there are some higher verbs that permit both types of structures. The verbs *promise* and *threaten* are of this type. This fact about these common verbs has been noted for instance by Davies and Dubinsky (2004: 9–10), who have pointed out that the sentences in (3a–b) and those in (4a–b) are all well-formed.

(3)   a. The boy promises to be a good musician.
       b. The boy promised to pick up a quart of milk on the way home.

(4)   a. Several downtown businesses threaten to go bankrupt.
       b. Several downtown businesses have threatened to take the city to court over the new parking regulations.

As Davies and Dubinsky note, (3b), which involves subject control, has a paraphrase of the type "the boy has made a verbal commitment to perform a task," whereas in (3a), which involves raising, it "describes someone's assessment of whether or not the boy will become a gifted musician" (Davies and Dubinsky 2004: 10). A difference that is analogous in relevant respects holds for the pair of sentences with *threaten* in (4a–b). As Davies and Dubinsky also note, the "volitional uses of *promise* and *threaten* are control constructions and the non-volitional uses are raising constructions."

The difference between the control and raising constructions is also reflected in two different senses of the matrix verb. The two senses have been recognized in major dictionaries, and they can be associated with the different syntactic structures.

For instance, in the *Oxford English Dictionary*[1] the sense of *promise* linked to the control structure includes the glosses 'to make a promise of (something), to give verbal assurance of' (from the glosses of sense 1), and the sense linked to the raising structure includes the sense 'to give strong or reasonable grounds for expecting (future achievements or good results)' (sense 5). As for *threaten*, the sense linked to the control construction includes the glosses 'to hold out or offer (some injury) by way of a threat; to declare one's intention of inflicting' (sense 3) and the sense linked to the raising construction is 'to appear likely *to do* some evil' (sense 4.b). The paraphrases are in line with the statement made by Davies and Dubinsky about *promise* and *threaten* that when the "subject [of the verb] is agentive, the verb takes two arguments," which is the control variant, and when the "subject is non-agentive, the verb takes a single argument" (Davies and Dubinsky 2004: 9), with the single argument being the lower clause in cases of sentential complements.

Illustrations of the four usages[2] in the *OED* include the examples in (5a–d), with the syntactic analyses spelled out by the present authors.

(5)   a. The Baronet promised to take charge of the lad at school. (1847, Thackeray) (sense 1.a of *promise* in the *OED*; subject control)

        b. He..promis'd to be stout when grown up. (1863, Defoe) (sense 5.a of *promise* in the *OED*; raising)

        c. Thretning to murder all who should oppose them. (1748, Robin and Walter) (sense 3.a of *threaten* in the *OED*; subject control)

        d. I am sometimes..frightened with dangers that threaten to diminish it [my estate]. (1780 *Mirror*) (sense 4.b of *threaten* in the *OED*; raising)

An additional observation relating to the argument structure of *promise* also emerges from the *OED* treatment of the verb. This is that under sense 1.a, which is the sense involving subject control, the verb may select a third argument. For instance, the *OED* illustrates sense 1.a with the example *I had promised Sarah to take 1000mg of VitC+Zinc every night if I went drinking* (1997, Hawes). In this sentence the NP *Sarah* is an argument of *promise* with a theta role, that of Recipient or Goal, expressing the addressee of an act of communication. For present purposes, it may

---

1 The *OED* online entries for *promise* and *threaten* were both modified in the latter months of 2021. The data for this chapter were retrieved in June 2021, and the relevant information taken from the *OED* is unchanged. We thank an anonymous reviewer for pointing this out.

2 The complementation possibilities with *promise* and *threaten* discussed here are of course not the only possibilities. Both verbs are flexible in their complement selection range, taking both sentential and non-sentential arguments of different types in a variety of combinations. For comprehensive lists, see e.g. Herbst et al. (2004).

be noted that this sentence, with a third argument, also involves subject control and is therefore relevant to this study. As regards the status of the third argument today, it has been noted in the literature that the inclusion of the Recipient argument with a following *to* infinitive is not universally accepted in Present-day English (see, for example, Dixon 1991: 148; Huddleston and Pullum 2002: 1229–1230). For *threaten*, an NP seems less likely between *threaten* and a following *to* infinitive complement – indeed, Egan (2006: 2) believes that *promise* is unique in this respect – but the construction is discussed further in Section 2.

The glosses of the senses of *promise* and *threaten*, quoted from the *OED* and initially illustrated with examples from the same source, also make it possible to argue that in each case one of them is more lexical, and the other one is more grammaticalized. Thus comparing 'to give verbal assurance of' with 'to give strong or reasonable grounds for expecting' for *promise*, the former has more lexical content meaning and specificity and the latter is more general and bleached (see Traugott and Dasher 2002: 84), with less lexical content meaning. Because the latter has less lexical content meaning, it can also be expected to be compatible with a broader range of subjects, and it is the more grammaticalized sense. (For the loss of lexical content meaning and other parameters of grammaticalization, cf. Brinton and Traugott 2005: 29–30.) The former will be called the lexical sense of the verb, and the latter the grammaticalized sense of the verb. As for *threaten*, the sense 'to declare one's intention of inflicting' is also clearly more lexical than the broader and more general sense 'to appear likely to do some evil'. The former will again be termed the lexical sense, the latter the grammaticalized sense.

Regarding the dates of the examples of each type with *to* infinitive complements in the *OED*, the earliest example of the lexical sense of *promise*, of the type of (5a), is from as early as 1430, while the first example of the grammaticalized sense, of the type shown in (5b), is from 1723. As for *threaten*, the earliest token with the lexical sense is from as early as 1297, and the earliest example of the verb with the grammaticalized sense is the one reproduced as (5d), from 1780. The fact that the earliest tokens of the lexical type clearly predate the earliest tokens of the grammaticalized type is in line with the general direction of grammaticalization.

With the background information given above taken for granted, it is possible to define the topic of this study. It is to investigate the recent history of the two types of complement constructions in CLMET3.0, including any trends of change in their incidence. Whether or not the grammaticalized sense of the verb, and with it the raising construction, might have become more prominent in recent centuries in relation to the lexical sense, and the control construction, is an obvious research task in this connection. The comparison of the two verbs in respect of the process of the spread of the grammaticalization is another question to be addressed in this study. The incidence of constructions with a third argument, with the Recipient role, is also investigated because, as noted, it appears (in the case of *promise*) that that construction goes together with the control pattern, and is not found with the raising derivation.

Regarding the structure of this study, section 2 begins with comments on the early history of *promise* and *threaten* and then turns to the three periods of CLMET3.0 in the subsequent subsections. Each verb is examined and illustrated in each period to identify trends of continuity and change in the incidence of subject control and subject to subject raising constructions it selects. This method of proceeding makes it possible also to pay attention to analytic issues that deserve further discussion. Comments are then offered to shed light on possible reasons for the trends observed.

2 Control and Raising Constructions with *promise* and *threaten* in CLMET3.0

As a preliminary to analyzing the data, it is helpful to take account of Traugott's (1993, 1996) pioneering work on *promise* and *threaten*. With respect to *promise*, borrowed from French into Middle English, she notes that "[f]rom the beginning it is performative, a verbal commitment to do something, and so the subject must be animate and able to perform an illocutionary act" (Traugott 1996: 186). As for *threaten*, it occurred even in Old English and from then on it "is not necessarily performative or commissive." She analyzes its meaning as to "'signal intention of inflicting something negative', verbally or otherwise, with or without commitment," adding that its "subject must be sentient and have the ability to intend" (Traugott 1996: 186). Regarding the origin of the epistemic – that is, subject to subject raising – uses of the verbs, she relates their emergence to both verbs selecting NP complements with the sense of 'portend, presage' (Traugott 1996: 187; for illustrations, see below).

CLMET3.0, the source of corpus data in this study, is divided into three periods: the first from 1710 to 1780 (10,480,431 words), the second from 1780 to 1850 (11,285,587 words), and the third from 1850 to 1920 (12,620,207 words). It is thus a sizeable corpus covering a lengthy stretch of the Late Modern English period, from 1710 to 1920, it contains texts from different text types, including narrative fiction and nonfiction, drama, and letters, and it seems a suitable source of data for a study of this type. The earliest tokens involving raising in the *OED* illustrations are rather close to, or indeed later than, the earliest decade covered by CLMET3.0, and this corpus is selected for examination here because a systematic study of this corpus covers a key period in the evolution of the two types of *to* infinitive complements selected by the two verbs (see e.g. Traugott 1993: 349–355) and can therefore be expected to shed fresh light on the history of the two constructions with these verbs.

Regarding the search string used, the present authors opted not to make use of the part-of-speech tagging in CLMET3.0, and instead used the simple search string "promis* to" for *promise* and "threaten* to" for *threaten*.[3] The huge majority[4] of the tokens derived with the search string are relevant, but there are some tokens where the constituent that follows *to* is an NP, not a clausal complement, as in (6a). More frequently, the word *promise* is an NP itself, as in (6b). Both types are easy enough to exclude from further analysis. As for *threaten*, again, most of the tokens retrieved are relevant and exceptions such as (6c) are rare.

(6)   a.   What I promised to thee, that I will give, [. . .] (1834, Bulwer-Lytton, *The Last Days of Pompeii*)
   b.   The time is come for the fulfilment of your promise to me. (1843, Ainsworth, *Windsor Castle*)
   c.   [. . .] the mountain scenery made him very threatening to her brother. (1898, Meredith, *The Amazing Marriage*)

The simple search string given is supplemented with two other search strings. These are "promis*/threaten** to" and "promis*/threaten*** to." These permit one or two words to intervene between the higher verb and the following *to*. The data were retrieved using AntConc concordancing software.

In analyzing the relevant tokens, it is generally fairly easy to distinguish control constructions from raising ones. It is possible to consider the sense of the verb, as discussed above, and it is also possible to consider the nature of the higher subject. Here the question is whether in the absence of movement that subject is an argument of *promise* or *threaten* and whether the subject receives a theta role from these verbs. If it does receive a theta role from *promise* or *threaten* in the absence of movement, it is a subject argument of the verb, and we are dealing with a subject control structure. If it does not, the default assumption is that we are dealing with a raising structure.

Regarding the structure of this section, the three periods of the corpus are investigated chronologically. This makes it possible to compare the complementation

---

3 Spelling variation in the matrix verbs, such as that seen in example (5c) from the *OED*, *Thretning to murder all who should oppose them*, is extremely rare in CLMET3.0, and no additional searches, aside from searches for the more obvious variants, were carried out for these tokens.
4 In the case of *promise*, the proportion of irrelevant tokens ranged from 16–18 percent of the total across the three CLMET3.0 time periods, while in the case of *threaten*, irrelevant tokens were around 13 percent in all three periods.

of each verb during each of the periods investigated. *Promise* is discussed first in each subsection, followed by comments on *threaten.*

2.1 CLMET3.0, Period 1

Beginning with *promise* in period 1 of CLMET3.0, almost 600 tokens are retrieved with the search strings. Almost all of them are constructions with complements of the subject control type, but the investigator still needs to be alert to tokens where the *to* infinitive clause is an adjunct. Only one example of the latter type was found and it is given in (7)

(7)   He promised only to betray, he flattered only to ruin; [. . .] (1776, Gibbon, *The Decline and Fall of the Roman Empire*)

Sentence (7) does involve subject control, but the *to* infinitive that follows *promise* is an adjunct of purpose or result, not a complement of *promise* in this case.

Turning to complements, the search strings retrieved 565 tokens of the verb involving subject control in the first part of the corpus and 26 tokens involving subject to subject raising. Table 1 provides a summary of the numbers of control and raising tokens identified in period 1 of CLMET3.0.

Table 1: Subject control and subject to subject raising tokens with *promise* and *threaten* in the period from 1710 to 1780 in CLMET3.0 (numbers in parentheses represent frequencies per million words).

	Subject control	S to S raising	Totals
Promise	565 (53.91)	26 (2.48)	591 (56.39)
Threaten	113 (10.78)	17 (1.62)	130 (12.40)

The examples in (8a–b) are illustrations of subject control and (9a–b) of subject to subject raising.

(8)   a.   They came to visit her, and promised to serve her. (1753, Cibber, *The Lives of the Poets of Great Britain*)

       b.   He promised to be governed by me in every thing. (1748, Samuel Richardson, *Clarissa*)

(9)   a. This piece was poorly performed, otherwise it promised to have given great satisfaction. (1776, Gibbon, *The Decline and Fall of the Roman Empire*)

       b. Fox's ministry does not as yet promise to be of long duration. (1735–1769, Walpole, *Letters*)

The control construction is thus over 20 times more frequent than the raising construction in the first part of the corpus.

Among the tokens with subject control, there are as many as 38 with three arguments, with an NP with the theta role of Recipient, between *promise* and the *to* infinitive. Two examples are given in (10a–b).

(10)   a. I promised Allworthy already to give up half my estate [. . .] (1763, Henry Brooke, *The History of Lady Julia Mandeville*)

       b. [. . .] my Dairy-house, as it used to be called, where once I promised myself to be happy in you. (1748, Samuel Richardson, *Clarissa*)

There is also one token where the Recipient is expressed with the prepositional phrase *to* + NP. This is given in (11).

(11)   [. . .] they instructed me in no science by which men may promise to themselves to acquire the least riches or worldly power, [. . .] (1749, Henry Fielding, *The History of Tom Jones, a Foundling*)

Turning to raising constructions governed by *promise*, Traugott's postulation of an intermediate stage of incipient grammaticalization in their emergence, where the main verb took on the sense of 'portend, presage', and the complement was an NP, leads us to expect such uses in the present data. This expectation is borne out, as in (12a–b).

(12)   a. [. . .] the principle part of personal beauty is an air of health and vigour, and such a construction of members as promises strength and activity. (1739–40, David Hume, *A Treatise of Human Nature*)

       b. It is a general remark, that those we call good women's men, who have either signalized themselves by their amorous exploits, or whose make of body promises any extraordinary vigour of that kind, are well received by the fair sex, [. . .] (1739–40, David Hume, *A Treatise of Human Nature*)

The subject of *promise* in (12a), for instance, is the NP *such a construction of members*, suggesting something "that leads to an expectation of the proposition coming into being," to quote Traugott (1996: 188).

While (12a–b) represent an intermediate stage in grammaticalization, there are also some raising constructions selected by *promise* in the first period of the corpus. Two further examples are given in (13a–b).

(13) a. I cannot blame you for rejoicing in a match which promises to be advantageous to her, [. . .] (1749, Henry Fielding, *The History of Tom Jones, a Foundling*)

    b. [. . .] though I have had sharp pain and terrible nights, this codicil to my gout promises to be of much shorter duration than what I had in England, [. . .] (1735–1769, Horace Walpole, *Letters*)

To consider (13a), for instance, the subject of *promise* refers to the NP *a match*, and the sentence suggests that there is something about the match in question that raises the expectation that it promises to be advantageous to her. (13a) is also close to a variant where the complement of *promise* is an NP, as in *I cannot blame you for rejoicing in a match which promises advantages to her*, which lends further support for postulating the intermediate step in the grammaticalization process.

Overall, it appears that the assumption, also pointed out by Davies and Dubinsky (2004: 10), that the semantic role of the Agent is associated with the control reading and that the lack of agency or agentivity can be linked to the raising construction serves to characterize the two readings. Davies and Dubinsky (2004) did not engage in a more detailed discussion of the notion of Agent, but the definition based on semantic features that has recently been used in the investigation of grammatical variation and change in recent English (see Rickman and Rudanko 2018; Gentens and Rudanko 2019; Ruohonen and Rudanko 2021) seems likewise appropriate for defining the agentivity, or the lack of it, of the higher subject in the present case. That definition is based on the three features of volitional involvement, control over the action predicated by the lower verb, and responsibility. Thus, for instance, in *They promised to serve her* in (8a), which involves control, the event or state of affairs expressed by the sentence is conceptualized as encoding volitional involvement on the part of the referent of the higher subject *they* (coreferential with the lower subject PRO) in the event or state of affairs, and the referent is further conceptualized as having a degree of control over the event or state of affairs and as being responsible for it. These three features are absent from the interpretation of the higher subject in the raising case. Thus, for instance, in (13a) the referent of the abstract NP *a match* is not volitionally involved in anything. Nor does it denote something that is in control of the event or state of affairs expressed by the sentence. Nor is it possible to ascribe responsibility to it for the event or state of affairs.

Turning to the interpretation of *to* infinitive constructions with *threaten*, their overall number is considerably lower than the corresponding number for *promise*. No adjuncts were encountered among them, and they are thus all complements. However, not all of them are immediately relevant to the present investigation of subject control and subject to subject raising. Consider the tokens in (14a–b).

(14) a. [. . .] she went to pay her duty to him, at his lodgings at Piccadilly, where she was received with many scurvy compellations too coarse to be repeated, and was even threatened to be kicked out of doors. (1749, Henry Fielding, *The History of Tom Jones, a Foundling*)

   b. The relation he gave of his own seizure, was, that he rambled into the woods, at some distance from the barricadoe where he had first attempted to pass, but had been stopt and threatened to be punished; that his principal view was to gather a quantity of limes for his master's stores; [. . .] (1773–1774, Henry David, *An Historical Account of All the Voyages Round the World, Performed by English Navigators*)

There are two other tokens similar to (14a–b) in the first period. The *to* infinitive clauses in (14a–b) are certainly sentential complements of the matrix verb *threaten*. However, the subject of *threaten* in each of them has been moved into the subject position by the NP Movement rule of Passivization, and subject control is therefore not relevant, since the subject in each case was not generated in the subject position and did not receive its theta role in that position. That is, the NP moved in each sentence receives its theta role in the indirect object position of the matrix sentence, and an NP trace, coreferential with the NP moved, is left in that original position when the movement rule applies, with that NP trace controlling the reference of PRO in (14a–b). The sentences in (14a–b) do not involve subject control. (Note that sentences of the type of *John was persuaded to remain silent* also do not involve subject control.) The derived subjects of (14a) and (14b), *she* in (14a) and *he* in (14b), designate the addressees of acts of communication and they are assigned theta roles by the matrix verb *threaten*. The sentences in (14a–b) are therefore most appropriately analyzed as being derived by object control – or, more precisely, indirect object control – since the derived subject represents an indirect object of the matrix clause, and they are set aside in the present study because of its focus on comparing subject control and subject to subject raising constructions with *threaten*.

Regarding subject control and subject to subject raising constructions with *threaten*, control constructions clearly predominate in the present segment, by a ratio of approximately seven to one. The precise numbers are 113 control constructions and 17 raising constructions.

Among the 113 control constructions, the present authors also included three tokens where there is an NP between the higher verb and the following *to* infinitive complement, with *threaten* thus selecting three arguments. Two of the three are given in (15a–b). Each of them needs more context than is normally required.

(15) a. [. . .] we are giving ourselves airs, and sending a secret expedition against France; we don't indeed own that it is in favour of the Chevalier William Courtenay who, you know, claims the crown of France, and whom King William threatened them to proclaim, when they proclaimed the Pretender; [. . .] (1735–1769, Walpole, *Letters*)

     b. There are no acts, no menaces, which the Opposition do not practice. They have threatened one gentleman to have a reversion cut off from his son, unless he will vote for them. (1735–69, Horace Walpole, *Letters*)

When analyzing sentences of the type of (15a–b), it is necessary to bear in mind the conclusion reached with respect to (14a–b), namely, that the verb *threaten* was found with indirect object control during the first period of the corpus. However, in sentence (15b), it seems clear that the NP *they*, the higher subject, at the beginning of the second sentence refers to (members of) the opposition, and the example gives an example of what the opposition may be prepared to do. That is, it is the opposition who may be cutting off the son's reversion. If this interpretation is correct, the sentence exemplifies subject control, and is relevant to the present discussion. A similar interpretation also seems salient in (15a). Overall, the examples illustrate some of the complexities that may sometimes arise in the analysis of even fairly recent data. However, they also suggest that *threaten*, similarly to *promise*, permitted an argument with the theta role of Recipient in eighteenth-century English. As in the case of *promise*, such sentences when they are in the active voice with a Recipient argument are subject control constructions.

Two examples that are less complex as instances of subject control are given in (16a–b).

(16) a. He was desperately angry, and threatened to throw her out of the window. (1740, Samuel Richardson, *Pamela*)

     b. But indeed his threatening to see me most sensibly alarms and shocks me. (1748, Samuel Richardson, *Clarissa*)

Sentence (16b) illustrates the presence of a *Poss -ing* complementizer as part of the sentential subject of the main clause (for *Poss -ing*, see Rosenbaum 1967), with the possessive NP *his* controlling the PRO one level down. In both (16a) and (16b) the higher subject is an Agent, and the referent of the NP has the three features identified above as criterial for agentivity.

Turning to epistemic usages of *threaten*, we may again begin by illustrating tokens of the intermediate type. The first period of the corpus offers numerous examples of incipient grammaticalization, where constructions of *threaten* with NP objects represent epistemic and non-intentional usages. Two examples are given in (17a–b).

(17) a. [. . .] on a sudden the cold became so very intense, as to threaten the most direful effects. (1773–1774, Henry David, *An Historical Account of All the Voyages Round the World, Performed by English Navigators*)
      b. [. . .] the progress of this metaphysical controversy seemed to threaten a public and lasting division of the Greek and Latin churches. (1776, Edward Gibbon, *The Decline and Fall of the Roman Empire*)

It is again only a short step from (17a), for instance, to a sentence with subject to subject raising, as in *on a sudden the cold became so very intense, as to threaten to produce/cause the most direful effects*.

As for subject to subject raising constructions with *threaten*, three illustrations are given in (18a–c).

(18) a. The animosities of the palace, by irritating the ambition and alarming the fears of Plautianus, threatened to produce a revolution, [. . .] (1776, Gibbon, *The Decline and Fall of the Roman Empire*)
      b. Mrs Deborah had made a discovery, which, in its event, threatened at least to prove more fatal to poor Tommy than all the reasonings of the captain. (1749, Henry Fielding, *The History of Tom Jones, a Foundling*)
      c. [. . .] an hurricane which every moment threatens to blow your house down. (1758, Samuel Richardson, *Clarissa*)

The referents of the abstract NPs *the animosities of the palace* and *a discovery* cannot be volitionally involved in an event or a state of affairs. Nor can they be thought of as being in control of anything. Nor can the referent of the NP *an hurricane*. The subjects are not Agents, confirming the salience of agentivity to the two interpretations once more.

From the perspective of grammaticalization, as is expected, the grammaticalized variant is the minority variant with both verbs, but in the case of *threaten* the ratio of grammaticalized tokens to lexical tokens is much higher than is evident with *promise*. It was noted above that the earliest examples in the OED of the grammaticalized variant with both matrix verbs are from the eighteenth century – *promise* in 1723, and *threaten* in 1780 – which suggests that grammaticalization may have begun with both predicates at roughly the same time. There may well be earlier examples of the grammaticalized sense with both verbs to be found – indeed, the *threaten* tokens of this type found in the first period of CLMET3.0 data are all earlier than 1780, with the earliest from 1748 – but judging by the numbers given in Table 1 alone, it is possible to suggest that the grammaticalization process may be progressing more quickly with *threaten.*

2.2 CLMET3.0, Period 2

Moving on to period 2 of CLMET3.0, covering the years 1780 to 1850, the search strings for *promise* retrieve 542 examples of the subject control complement, and 44 examples of subject to subject raising. The first thing to note is that the subject control complement still greatly outnumbers the raising complement, and the overall picture is not too different to that seen in the earlier period of the corpus, but there is a noticeable rise in the share of the raising tokens. From the point of view of statistical significance, this is a significant difference at $p < 0.05$ (chi-squared value 4.54).

The numbers as they stand as we turn to the second period of CLMET3.0 are laid out in Table 2 below.

Table 2: Subject control and subject to subject raising tokens with *promise* and *threaten* in the period from 1780 to 1850 in CLMET3.0 (numbers in parentheses represent frequencies per million words).

	Subject control	S to S raising	Totals
Promise	542 (48.03)	44 (3.9)	586 (51.92)
Threaten	65 (5.76)	63 (5.58)	128 (11.34)

(19a–b) below give examples of control, and (20a–b) give raising examples with *promise* from this period of CLMET3.0.

(19) a. The old man had promised to admit them when he had completed his task, but not before [. . .] (1837, Benjamin Disraeli, *Venetia*)
      b. [. . .] I will agree to wait a little – if you promise at last to let me see the book, [. . .] (1845–6, Elizabeth & Robert Browning, *The letters of Robert Browning and Elizabeth Barrett Barrett, Vol. 1*)

(20) a. Entering also into creek after creek which promised to be the entrance of the bay we were seeking, [. . .] (1796, Mary Wollstonecraft, *Letters on Sweden, Norway and Denmark*)
      b. The children of your village are happier, more orderly, more obedient, promise to be wiser and better men in their own station of life, [. . .] (1838, Edward George Bulwer-Lytton, *Alice*)

As was noted in relation to the period 1 data, the higher subjects of the raising types can be either [–Human] or (non-agentive) [+Human], with both types shown here in (20a–b), but the [–Human] examples are by far the more common subjects found with *promise*. When the subject is [+Human], more often than not, the lower verb describes a human quality that one does not usually have control over, such as physical and mental attributes (height, beauty, intelligence, wisdom etc.), or a station in life that is not always predictable (success, prosperity and the like) as in (20b).

Among the 542 subject control tokens, the number of tokens with a third argument, a Recipient, is still relatively high, at 31 (examples of this type were given in (10a–b) above). It was noted above that this type of pattern with *promise* is not universally accepted in Present-day English, but the present dataset is evidence of a fairly consistent appearance in British English during the period under discussion, and even a slight rise in its use as we move into the nineteenth century.

Moving on to *threaten* in period 2 of CLMET3.0, the first thing to note is the appearance of two examples of the indirect object control structure that were noted in the period 1 data, and, while of some interest, are not relevant to the present study. One of the tokens is given in (21).

(21) For which free speeches he was once or twice threatened to be whipped. (1807, Charles and Mary Lamb, *Tales from Shakespeare*)

One further token from period 2 that is of theoretical interest yet outside the scope of the present investigation is given in (22).

(22) It kept him waking upon his safe and commodious bed; was sure to recur with every misfortune by which he was threatened to make his fears still stronger, [. . .] (1796, Elizabeth Inchbald, *Nature and Art*)

Here, the *to* infinitive following *threatened* is not an argument of the verb; rather it is better analyzed as an adjunct of result. This type of pattern is rare – the example given here is the only one found in the entire dataset used for this study.

The number of subject control tokens retrieved is 65, while the raising variant is now becoming something of a serious competitor, with the number of tokens now as high as 63. Two examples of each are given in (23a–b) and (24a–b).

(23) a. the Under-Sheriff actually threatened to take Lord Cochrane and myself into custody, [. . .] (1820–2, Henry Hunt, *Memoirs of Henry Hunt*)

b. In short, finding that all further motive of action and object of concern or of love, here below, were forever removed from him, he abandoned himself to despair, and threatened to go down to the grave with his son. (1824, James Hogg, *Private Memoirs and Confessions of a Justified Sinner*)

(24) a. May you, my young madam, escape that frivolity which threatens universally to pervade the minds and manners of fashionable life [. . .] (1780–96, Robert Burns, *Letters 1780–96*)

b. [. . .] and the clouds are gathering, and threaten to discharge themselves in hail! (1844, Charles Dickens, *Dombey and Son*)

While classifying the *threaten* data, one often comes across tokens of the type shown in (23b), where the default, or the most likely interpretation, is that of control. Unlike *promise*, clear non-agentive [+Human] subjects in raising structures with *threaten* are rare in the present dataset, and we therefore work on the assumption that, even though it may be possible to make a case for a raising interpretation in an example like (23b), they are best seen as control structures in the absence of any clear indication that they should be interpreted otherwise. That is, in (23b), the more probable interpretation is that *he* was alive and well, and declared his intention of taking his own life while grieving over his dead son, rather than it looking to an observer as though *he* was about to die. One of the few clear examples in the *threaten* data of the [+Human] subject with raising is given in (25), which serves as an illustrative counterpart to the example just discussed.

(25) [. . .] his wife was now daily declining, and threatening to follow her aged partner to the grave. (1834, Katherine Grace Frances Gore, *Theresa Marchmont, or the Maid of Honour: A Tale*)

Here the raising interpretation seems uncontroversial; *his wife* does not appear to be volitionally involved in making the threat, with the action described by the lower verb out of her control, and in this case there is additional support from the previous description of her condition, *was now daily declining.*

It seems to be characteristic of *threaten,* unlike *promise,* that there are quite often cases, such as (23b), that are not easy to firmly classify as either control or raising structures without paying attention to the larger context, which may extend beyond sentence boundaries. Consider (26a–b) as a further case in point.

(26) a. From Ireland Lady Caroline continued the siege, threatening to follow him into Herefordshire, demanding interviews, and writing about him to Lady Oxford. (1810–3, George Lord Byron, *Letters*)

     b. Who has not heard of Alonzo Guzman the faithful, who allowed his only son to be crucified before the walls of the town rather than submit to the ignominy of delivering up the keys to the Moorish monarch, who, with a host which is said to have amounted to nearly half a million of men, had landed on the shores of Andalusia, and threatened to bring all Spain once more beneath the Moslem yoke? (1842, George Borrow, *The Bible in Spain*)

The present investigators classified (26a–b) as control and raising, respectively. In (26a) it is the *-ing* clauses following the *to* infinitive that seem to point the reader towards a control interpretation, but in (26b) there are less obvious clues as to whether the Moorish monarch declared his intention of bringing Spain beneath the Muslim yoke, or whether it was the evaluation of the author of the text. The use of the word *yoke* is perhaps one factor that suggests an outsider's perspective, and therefore a raising interpretation. In addition, as (26b) quite nicely illustrates, it may be that one factor promoting the use of the raising variant with *threaten* is that it affords a handy and unobtrusive way of conveying a negative stance toward the content of a lower clause. In the construction the proposition of the sentential complement is framed in a negative way by the author's use of the matrix verb *threaten.* (See Gray and Biber 2014: 220–222 on how a lexical item can frame the proposition of a complement.) Such a negative stance is also in line with the author's use of the word *yoke.*

The overall number of *threaten* tokens remains roughly the same as it was in period 1, but the actual usage has seen a pronounced shift towards the raising variant, or the grammaticalized sense. As in the case of *promise,* the increase in the share of *threaten* tokens taken up by the raising type is statistically significant at $p < 0.0001$ (chi-squared value 37.71).

2.3 CLMET3.0, Period 3

The discussion now turns to the final period of CLMET3.0, covering the seventy years from 1850 to 1920. Beginning with *promise*, the number of subject control tokens in this period is 433, while the number of raising tokens is 67. Table 3 provides the numbers of control and raising tokens.

Table 3: Subject control and subject to subject raising tokens with *promise* and *threaten* in the period from 1850 to 1920 in CLMET3.0 (numbers in parentheses represent frequencies per million words).

	Subject control	S to S raising	Totals
Promise	433 (34.31)	67 (5.31)	500 (39.62)
Threaten	59 (4.68)	71 (5.63)	130 (10.30)

Table 3 suggests that while *promise* continues frequently to select *to* infinitive complements in the third period, its use has dropped slightly from the early years of the Late Modern English period; compare the normalized frequency of 56.39 in the earliest period with 39.62 in the third period. (27a–b) give examples of control, and (28a–b) give raising examples with *promise* from this period of CLMET3.0.

(27) a. I have a picture to finish, and I have just promised to do a portrait to which I must give all my spare time. (1852, author unknown, *Chambers's Edinburgh Journal, n°418–462*)

b. You've promised not to breathe a word to any living soul. (1908, Henry Arthur Jones, *Dolly Reforming Herself*)

(28) a. Your daughter promised to be a pretty girl, Betteredge, and she has kept her promise. (1868, Wilkie Collins, *The Moonstone*)

b. But nevertheless, things are better than they were, and promise still to mend. (1903, Herbert George Wells, *Mankind in the Making*)

Control examples are, by and large, similar to those seen in the earlier periods, and are characterized by little in the way of ambiguity or difficulty in interpretation. It has been stated that search strings were employed in this study to retrieve tokens with up to two intervening words between *promise* and the *to* infinitive clause, and it can be noted that, third argument NPs notwithstanding, the negative particles *never* and *not* are by far the most common elements found in this slot, giving a structure of the type shown in (27b). This is typical across all three periods of the corpus, with little apparent variation.

With the grammaticalized sense having become fairly well established by now and its use becoming significantly more frequent, it is of interest to note the occurrence of tokens such as (28a), which show how an author can play with the grammatical distinction between the control and raising structures for communicative purposes. As the subject of a raising structure, the daughter obviously did not declare her intention of becoming beautiful, thus the additional comment in the following clause *she has kept her promise* sets up the suggestion that the matrix verb *promise* was intended to be interpreted in the older, lexical sense, rather than the grammaticalized sense, and lends an element of humour to the passage. Interestingly, the same type of juxtaposition of the two readings occurs twice in the data from period 3, and both are from the same work, and occur within a few paragraphs of each other. The other token is given in (29).

(29) To make matters worse, he had promised to be tall, and had not kept his promise. He was neat, and slim, and well made; but he wasn't by an inch or two up to the middle height. (1868, Wilkie Collins, *The Moonstone*)

This example occurs first in the passage, as part of the inner monologue of the first-person narrator. The second occurrence, in (28a), comes several paragraphs later, and is spoken by a different character.

Regarding the ratio of control to raising tokens with *promise* in the three periods, it is clear from Table 3 above that the preponderance of control constructions is just over 6:1 in the most recent period. Comparing this ratio to those of the previous two periods (21:1 in period 1; 12:1 in period 2) there is a clear increase in the share of the raising variant. The difference between period 2 and period 3 is significant at $p < 0.01$, (chi-squared value 9.57) and the difference between period 1 and period 3 is significant at $p < 0.0001$ (chi-squared value 27.00). The subject control pattern still holds a clear majority even in period 3, but the proportion of the raising tokens has gone up considerably.

The subject control structure with the third argument is still very much in use during this period, with 30 tokens identified, that is, a ratio of roughly one to 14 with the standard two-argument control structure. This is, in fact, something of an increase: during the second period of the corpus the ratio was approximately one to 18. Two examples from period 3 are given in (30a–b).

(30) a. I had promised Etherell to breakfast with him. (1870, George Meredith, *The Adventures of Harry Richmond*)

b. I promised you not to behave as other wives would do. (1918, James Matthew Barrie, *What Every Woman Knows*)

The reflexive pronoun occurs as the third argument in three of the 30 cases, so it can be seen as a relatively uncommon choice in this structure.

As for *threaten*, the situation shows a remarkable change in the frequency of each pattern, with control tokens now numbering 59, and subject to subject raising 71. Thus, the grammaticalized use now outnumbers the older, lexical use of this verb. Frequency-wise, the picture is interesting: in each section the overall frequencies of *threaten*, both senses, taken together, remain fairly close. They were at their highest in period 1 (130 tokens, 12.4 w.p.m.), dropping slightly in period 2 (131 tokens, 11.61 w.p.m.), and in period 3 (130 tokens, 10.3 w.p.m.). Despite the lack of any significant change in overall numbers, language users have carried out a steady replacement of the lexical sense with the grammaticalized sense across the entire period covered by the corpus. The difference in the ratios of control to raising examples between periods is highly significant between periods 1–2 ($p < 0.0001$, chi-squared value 37.71), and periods 1–3 ($p < 0.0001$, chi-squared value 48.25), but not between periods 2–3. Examples of control tokens are given in (31a–b), and raising tokens in (32a–b).

(31) a. Then they all cursed him for a pig and an infidel, and threatened to put him ashore and leave him for his vile conduct towards noble Hareem. (1866–9, Lucie Duff Gordon, *Letters from Egypt*)

b. Lyell had been threatening to publish a book on the geological history of Man, [. . .] (1907, Edmund Gosse, *Father and Son*)

(32) a. Constance grew more serious. The discussion threatened to be warm. Suddenly Cyril yielded. (1908, Arnold Bennett, *The Old Wives' Tale*)

b. This huge library, growing into unwieldiness, threatening to become a trackless desert of print [. . .] (1891, George Gissing, *New Grub Street*)

The grammaticalized use of *threaten* provides the possibility to personify the inanimate in a very colourful way, and the variety of raised subjects seen among the data is one of its most striking features. All subjects in the period 3 data are [–Human], and range from the meteorological and the elemental (*the winter, the November rains, the surf, a fire, a suddenly gathered storm*) to the highly descriptive and picturesque (*that laisser-aller policy of his, a hoarse bronchial crying, my accursed want of money*). Two such examples are given in (33a–b). In (33a) the pronoun *that*, the subject of *threaten*, stands for the NP *my accursed want of money*.

(33) a. All that's wrong is my accursed want of money. But that threatens to be such a fearful wrong, that I begin to wish I had died before my marriage-day. (1891, George Gissing, *New Grub Street*)

b. The perilous sweetness of that look threatened to upset my equanimity for good and all. (1885, Mathilde Blind, *Tarantella*)

The attractiveness of this picturesque use of *threaten* to writers may well be part of the reason, in addition to the possibility, discussed above, of marking negative stance, for the relatively quick rise of the raising pattern.

3 Conclusion

In the system of English predicate complementation, the distinction between subject control verbs and adjectives, on the one hand, and those involving subject to subject raising, on the other, constitutes one of the basic dividing lines of matrix predicates selecting non-finite complements. Most higher verbs and adjectives to which the distinction is relevant belong to either one category or the other. *Promise* and its "evil twin" *threaten* (Culicover and Jackendoff 2005: 437), merit investigation because they have straddled the divide between the two grammatical constructions in relatively recent English. The two syntactic structures can be linked to different senses of the two verbs, with the lexical sense being associated with the control structure and the grammaticalized sense linked to the subject to subject raising construction.

The study offers a practical demonstration of how a grammatical distinction can be applied in a body of authentic texts. It is suggested that the distinction between subject control and subject to subject raising tends to be relatively easy to implement for *promise*. As for *threaten*, careful attention often needs to be paid to the context of the token, in order to determine whether a particular token represents an instance of subject control or subject to subject raising. The authors also make the proposal that, for *threaten*, object control constructions need to be recognized. With respect to grammaticalization, the authors illustrate how both verbs displayed the sense of 'portend', 'presage' in the eighteenth century, when raising constructions were emerging.

Perhaps the most striking finding of this study concerns the spread of the grammaticalized senses of the verbs in environments when they select *to* infinitive complements. For both verbs, the proportion of the grammaticalized sense rises in relation the lexical sense from the first period of CLMET3.0 to the second, and again from the second period to the third. However, for *threaten* the increase is dramatic.[5] In the first period only every sixth token, approximately, of *threaten* was of the grammaticalized type, but in the most recent period, tokens where *threaten* has its lexical sense are actually a minority. By contrast, with *promise*, the rise in the relative frequency of the grammaticalized sense is much more modest. *Promise* is of course much more frequent with infinitival complements than *threaten*, which was reflected in the high frequency of the lexical sense of the verb in the first period, and the sheer frequency of the sense may have been a factor protecting it. By contrast, *threaten* was found much less frequently with *to* infinitives in the period investigated, permitting the grammaticalized sense to spread more rapidly. Additionally, it was suggested that the grammaticalized use of *threaten* offers possibilities of apparent personifications and it can also offer an unobtrusive way for the speaker to convey a negative stance towards the proposition of the lower clause, and that such possibilities may have enhanced its appeal to writers.

The present study covers over two centuries of the Late Modern English period, with a systematic investigation of data from a corpus that includes several different text types. It naturally invites follow-up work on the two verbs in earlier English, for while the present study brought to light tokens of the grammaticalized sense of *threaten* that predate those in the *OED*, it may be presumed that even earlier examples may be found. The default assumption for such a study is that the proportion of the grammaticalized sense in such earlier tokens with both verbs is lower than what was found in period 1 of the present corpus. Naturally, work on more recent trends of change will also be desirable, perhaps on the basis of the NOW Corpus and of additional text types. A comparison of British and American English is another project for future study.

References

Brinton, Laurel & Elizabeth Traugott. 2005. *Lexicalization and language change*. Cambridge: Cambridge University Press.
Chomsky, Noam. 1986. *Knowledge of language: Its nature, origin and use*. New York: Praeger.
Cornillie, Bert. 2019. On the pace of syntactic elaboration from Latin calques. Evidence from Spanish, Dutch and English. *Belgian Journal of Linguistics* 33. 81–106.
Cornillie, Bert. 2022. Syntactic complexity in Standard Average European: language contact and discourse traditions in the domain of communicative distance. In Esme Winter-Froemel &

---

5 For another perspective, emphasizing the development of the grammaticalization of *threaten* against the backdrop of European language contact, see Cornillie (2019, 2022).

Álvaro S. Octavio de Toledo y Huerta (eds.), *Manual of discourse traditions in Romance*, 721–738. Berlin & New York: De Gruyter.

Culicover, Peter & Ray Jackendoff. 2005. *Simpler syntax*. Oxford: Oxford University Press.

Davies, William & Stanley Dubinsky. 2004. *The grammar of raising and control*. Malden, MA: Blackwell.

Dixon, Robert M. W. 1991. *A new approach to English grammar, on semantic principles*. Oxford: Oxford University Press.

Egan, Thomas. 2006. Did John really promise Mary to leave? *Constructions* 2. 1–32.

Gentens, Caroline & Juhani Rudanko. 2019. The Great Complement Shift and the role of understood subjects: the case of *fearful. Folia Linguistica* 53(1). 51–86.

Gray, Bethany & Douglas Biber. 2014. Stance markers. In Karin Aijmer & Christoph Rühlemann (eds.), *Corpus pragmatics: A handbook*, 219–246. Cambridge: Cambridge University Press.

Herbst, Thomas, David Heath, Dieter Götz & Ian Roe. 2004. *A valency dictionary of English*. Berlin & New York: De Gruyter.

Huddleston, Rodney & Geoffrey Pullum. 2002. *The Cambridge grammar of the English language*. Cambridge: Cambridge University Press.

Jespersen, Otto. [1940] 1961. *A modern English grammar on historical principles*. Part V: Syntax (Vol. IV). London: Allen and Unwin.

Oxford English Dictionary. 2nd ed. 1989. OED online. Available from http://:www.oed.com. [Accessed June 2021] Oxford: Oxford University Press.

Rickman, Paul & Juhani Rudanko. 2018. *Corpus-based studies on non-finite complements in recent English*. London: Palgrave Macmillan.

Rosenbaum, Peter. 1967. *The grammar of English predicate complement constructions*. Cambridge: MIT Press.

Ruohonen, Juho & Juhani Rudanko. 2021. *Infinitival vs gerundial complementation with* afraid, accustomed, *and* prone: *Multivariate corpus studies*. Cham: Palgrave Macmillan.

Traugott, Elizabeth C. 1993. The conflict promises/threatens to escalate into war. In Joshua Guenter, Barbara Kaiser & Cheryl Zoll (eds.), *Proceedings of the nineteenth annual meeting of the Berkeley linguistics society: general session and parasession on semantic typology and semantic universals*, 348–358. Berkeley: The Berkeley Linguistics Society.

Traugott, Elizabeth C. 1996. Subjectification and the development of epistemic meaning: the case of *promise* and *threaten*. In Toril Swan & Olaf Westvik (eds.), *Modality in Germanic languages: Historical and comparative perspectives*, 185–210. Berlin: Mouton de Gruyter.

Traugott, Elizabeth & Richard Dasher. 2002. *Regularity in semantic change*. Cambridge: Cambridge University Press.

Bettelou Los and Thijs Lubbers

11 The development of prose style in English horse manuals

Interpreting stylometric findings

Abstract: This paper explores data-driven, stylometric methodologies in order to see whether their findings would reflect stylistic developments from Early Modern English to the present day, on the basis of a small corpus of 13 texts representing the same register (horse manuals) and the same topic (feeding a horse) from 1565 to 2009. The corpus was POS-tagged, and then stripped of its lexical material, leaving only the tags. Sequences of tags were then input to a correspondence analysis and subjected to a procedure to create an association plot. Interpreting the results is a particular challenge of data-driven methods, which requires a mixture of quantitative and qualitative analysis, and differently-sized samples. The assumption that the results would not be driven by syntactic change was confirmed, so that the chronological progression that emerged in the data had to be explained by changing styles. Horse manuals contain at least two text types, to varying degrees: instructional/procedural "cookery book" writing and the logical-argumentative text type of scientific writing. The latter has been known to exhibit higher frequencies of passivization and a more nominal style (Halliday 2004); this is also evident in these texts. The data further suggest that the flow of given to new information is not adhered to as strictly in the earlier texts than in the later texts; in the earlier texts, pronouns are found more frequently in end-focus position, and the strategy of using the by-phrase of the "long passive" to manoeuvre a new agent into end-focus position is only found in the later texts.

Keywords: stylistic variation, information structure, Early Modern English, Late Modern English, modification, horse manuals

1 Introduction

After the Middle English period, English syntax as we know it is largely in place, with *do*-support (Ellegård 1953), the gerund (Fanego 1996, De Smet 2013), the *for*-NP-*to*-VP-complement (Cuyckens and De Smet 2007) and the loss of *be*-perfects (Rydén and Brorström 1987) being some of the most obvious innovations in Early Modern English. Other changes in that period tend to be labelled stylistic – a matter of changes in frequencies of existing structures rather than new developments. "Since

https://doi.org/10.1515/9783110753059-011

relatively few categorical losses or innovations have occurred in the last two centuries, syntactic change has more often been statistical in nature, with a given construction occurring throughout the period and either becoming more or less common generally or in particular registers. The overall, rather elusive effect can seem more a matter of stylistic than syntactic change" (Denison 1998: 93). Beal et al., quoting Denison, confirm the truth of this claim, arguing only that the elusiveness detected by Denison can be dismantled by careful data collection and analysis, which will uncover trends in these changing patterns (Beal, Fitzmaurice and Hodson 2012: 204). The challenge with developments in Early (and Late) Modern English is how to interpret what drives the frequency patterns that we see; a statistical analysis requires sufficiently large corpora, but interpreting any significant rises or falls in frequencies calls for a close examination of the data, which is generally not possible with large data sets.

An example is the passive, where we see a general rise in frequencies overall from the Early Modern period onwards (Toyota 2008 and references therein). The connection between the passive and scientific writing has been explained as a growing preference for a more impersonal style (Seoane 2013); see also (Halliday 2004; Biber, et al. 1999; Huddleston 1971). In this light, Seoane's (2013) findings of a marked decline in the use of the passive in Late Modern English on the basis of a large historical corpus is intriguing. Seoane's interpretation that this means that the passive is losing some of its pragmatic functions is challenged by Banks (2017), on the basis of a small but focused corpus – papers in two series of journals – which allows a more detailed investigation. Banks also sees a decline, but much more marked in one than in the other journal, and he concludes that the decline could well be topic-driven rather than a new characteristic of the genre. In his much smaller corpus, the decline was most marked in papers on topics requiring a discussion of mathematical computation, which required the use of active verbs with first person pronoun subjects, with the verb often "a mental process rather than material process . . . in articles based on mathematical modeling, as opposed to experimental reports" (Banks 2017: 13).

A similar challenge as the one faced by Seoane is a quantitative study by Lubbers and Los (2020). That paper presents various visualizations (correspondence analysis, an association plot analysis and dendrograms) of a historical corpus of English, from the Early Modern period to the present day. In spite of the fact that the principle underlying the various operations (performing repeated chi-squaring of groups of cells in a contingency table) is sound and well-tested, the resulting visualizations of patterns and trends has the "feel" of a black box because it is difficult to interpret the results. The present paper will complement these findings by a much more detailed discussion of the findings.

2 Methodology

2.1 Corpus

As we saw in the previous section in the study by Banks (2017), texts may not only differ because they reflect historical developments but also because they reflect different genres or different subject matter. Focusing on texts from the same register, characterised by the same text types, and dealing with the same topic should allow us to isolate changes that are most likely to reflect historical developments, which is why Lubbers and Los (2020) selected texts from the same genre and about a single topic. As genre, horse manuals were chosen because they have been popular throughout these periods; the horse fulfilled a role not unlike that of the car today, and similarly represented a valuable asset that needed looking after, so every century has its share of horse manuals. The texts for the corpus were obtained from the digital repository of early English printed publications, *Early English Books Online* (EEBO), freely accessible web repositories and other sources in the public domain (like http://www.archive.org/ and the Google Books project, http://books.google.com). The texts are listed in Table 1. Within those texts, Lubbers and Los (2020) selected samples that dealt with one particular feature of horse care: feeding.

Table 1: Descriptive statistics of the texts of the corpus based on (Lubbers and Los 2020).

Date	Author/text	Sample size (words)	Utterances (*n*)	Mean utterance length (words)	Source
1565	Blundeville, Thomas	4209	127	33.99	EEBO
1585	Clifford, Christopher	4639	89	52.96	EEBO
1607	Markham, Gervais	4439	100	45.31	EEBO
1618	Baret, Michael	4386	102	43.92	EEBO
1697	Speed, A.	4652	161	29.74	EEBO
1721	Gibson, William	5028	195	26.7	EEBO
1796	Hunter, J.	4480	130	35.28	EEBO
1823	Kirby, Jeremiah (Encycl. Brit.)	4457	200	23.58	online
c1840	Skeavington, George	4507	187	24.87	EEBO
1886	Fleming, George	4437	193	23.74	EEBO
1921	Matheson, Darley	4599	193	24.57	online
1977	Leighton-Hardman, A.C.	4588	217	21.6	publ. libr.
2009	Davies, Zoe	4308	273	16.13	publ. libr.

2.2 Visualizing style by POS-tag trigrams

The procedures in Lubbers and Los (2020) followed a method to visualize historical styles pioneered by Ernestus, van Mulken and Baayen (2006) which uses samples of Part-of-Speech (POS) tagged corpora that have been stripped of lexical content, so are represented by series of POS tags. These sequences are snipped into overlapping sequences of n POS tags ("n-grammed"), where n can be any number, but for these purposes is usually three ("trigrams"). Trigrams have been reported to strike an optimal balance between linguistic interpretability, statistical power and computational costs (Gries, Newman and Shaoul 2011). The underlying assumption for working with POS-tags rather than lexical material is that such recurring bundles of three successive elements, even when they are part of more complex grammatical clusters, indicate the rate of occurrence of frequently used constructions and habitual patterns of language use (and, in the case of POS-tags, of structure). All string processing and statistical analyses reported in this paper were carried out using the statistical environment R (R Core Team 2014). For more details of the methodology underlying the data-driven processes in this paper, see Lubbers and Los (2020).

2.3 Spelling normalization, POS Tagging and trigram generation

After manually entering the data and some minor cleaning (lower casing, expansion of abbreviations like y^t, &c. into *that* and *etcetera*, deletion of illegible sections, of punctuation markers around roman and arabic numerals), the texts were standardised for spelling using the Variant Detector VARD 2 (Baron and Rayson 2008). The resulting texts still required a large amount of manual correction.

After normalisation, the online CLAWS4 tagger in combination with the CLAWS-5 tagset (60+ tags)[1] was used to enrich the data with POS tags (for an overview of the CLAWS-5 tagset, see http://ucrel.lancs.ac.uk/claws5tags.html). The restricted number of tags in the CLAWS-5 tagset avoids the fine-grained tagging errors of more elaborate tagsets and boosts frequency counts, which increases statistical reliability of the results.[2] For some of the texts, a cross-check was

---

1 See http://ucrel.lancs.ac.uk/claws5tags.html/.
2 For comparison, the same data was also tagged using two other taggers (the CLAWS-7 and the Penn-Treebank NLP tagger available through Python and the Apache OpenNLP tagger in R, package "OpenNLP"), but the CLAWS-5 tagset produced the most robust results in consecutive statistical processing.

available in the form of manually annotated POS-files in the Penn-Helsinki corpus, which revealed only minor deviations.[3] Because the punctuation systems in the earlier texts differed too much from modern punctuation to be able to distinguish sentence-medial from sentence-final punctuation, all punctuation marks apart from quotation marks and brackets, which were removed from the corpus, were assigned a single tag PUN, as per the standard CLAWS-5 tagset. The remaining tagset had exactly 60 possible POS categories. The next step was to remove lexical material, so that only sequences of POS-tags remained.

To be able to allow a direct comparison of the n-gram frequencies in our samples, each sample was trimmed at exactly 4,000 tokens (i.e. POS tags). The selection of 4,000 tokens per text was taken from the beginnings of the sections on feeding, so includes topic introductions but not necessarily equal amounts of closing sections. This was found to be an acceptable sacrifice, since it would maximally result in one incomplete clause per text sample. We would have liked to balance the section length of subtopics, like "hay" and "watering", but this proved impossible – the size of these sections varied too much per text.

Example (1a-d), taken from the Baret text (1618), illustrates the various steps of the procedure.

(1)   a. [after cleaning special characters]
          Now whereas it hath bene a custome to water a running Horse in the house, and to have him drinke but once a day, and likewise to put Liquoras, or such like, into the water to helpe his winde, all these I doe except against, and why?

    b. [VARD spelling regularisation]
          now whereas it has been a custom to water a running horse in the house, and to have him drink but once a day, and likewise to put liquorice, or such like, into the water to help his wind, all these I do except against, and why?

    c. [CLAWS5 tagging]
          now_AV0 whereas_CJS it_PNP has_VHZ been_VBN a_AT0 custom_NN1 to_TO0 water_VVI a_AT0 running_AJ0 horse_NN1 in_PRP the_AT0 house_NN1,_PUN and_CJC to_TO0 have_VHI him_PNP drink_VVB but_CJC once_AV0 a_AT0 day_NN1,_PUN and_CJC likewise_AV0 to_TO0 put_VVI liquorice_NN0,_PUN or_CJC such_DT0 like_AJ0,_PUN into_PRP the_AT0

      water_NN1 to_TO0 help_VVI his_DPS wind_NN1,_PUN all_DT0 these_DT0
      I_PNP do_VDB except_VVB against_PRP,_PUN and_CJC why_AVQ ?_PUN
  d. [removing lexical material, leaving only POS tags]
      AV0 CJS PNP VHZ VBN AT0 NN1 TO0 VVI AT0 AJ0 NN1 PRP AT0 NN1 PUN
      CJC TO0VHI PNP VVB CJC AV0 AT0 NN1 PUN CJC AV0 TO0 VVI NN0 PUN
      CJC DT0 AJ0 PUNPRP AT0 NN1 TO0 VVI DPS NN1 PUN DT0 DT0 PNP VDB
      VVB PRP PUN CJC AVQ PUN

The resulting strings of POS tags served as the basis for the calculation of POS frequency averages as well as the generation of n-grams (i.e., POS grams). N-gram generation was carried out in R using the RWeka library (Hornik, et al. 2007). Trigram generation results in overlapping strings, as exemplified for the string AV0 CJS PNP VHZ VBN AT0 NN1 in (2).

(2)   AV0 CJS PNP – CJS PNP VHZ – PNP VHZ VBN – VHZ VBN AT0 – VBN AT0 NN1

The trigrams generated can be grouped and tabulated by frequency. The rows of trigrams and columns of the texts they occur in can then become input to various statistical techniques.

3 The correspondence analysis

3.1 Introduction

A cumulative list of the POS-trigram frequencies found across these 13 texts served as the basis for a correspondence analysis (cf. Benzécri 1973; Greenacre 1984; Greenacre 2017; Murtagh 2005). After computing the distances between rows and columns in a contingency table, a correspondence analysis visualizes associations between these rows and columns. As a multidimensional scaling technique, correspondence analysis aims to reduce the information in the contingency table to factors (dimensions) that can account for the distance between data points. The dimensions that account for most of the variation in the data are then placed along the x-axis and the y-axis of a two-dimensional plot, and the rows and columns of the contingency table positioned according to their scores/ coordinates on these new dimensions. The plot thus reduces the information in the data to overarching 'dimensions', which then require interpretation based on our knowledge of the data; i.e., how can we best make sense of (a) the distances between rows (e.g. texts) and columns (e.g. POS-trigram frequencies), and (b) describe the meaning of these overarching dimensions based on these distances between data points.

3.2 Result

Figure 1 shows one of the correspondence plots from Lubbers and Los (2020), with the POS-trigrams, which would otherwise obscure the names of the texts (in blue), replaced by red triangles in order to present a less cluttered picture. The labels of the axes show the "dimensions" and how much of the total variation between the texts they account for, which is 13.9% + 34.8% = 48.7%. Note that Figure 1 has arranged the texts in a chronological progression, even though the dates of the texts were not part of the input. This means that the method has picked out differences in style between the texts that apparently correlate with their relative

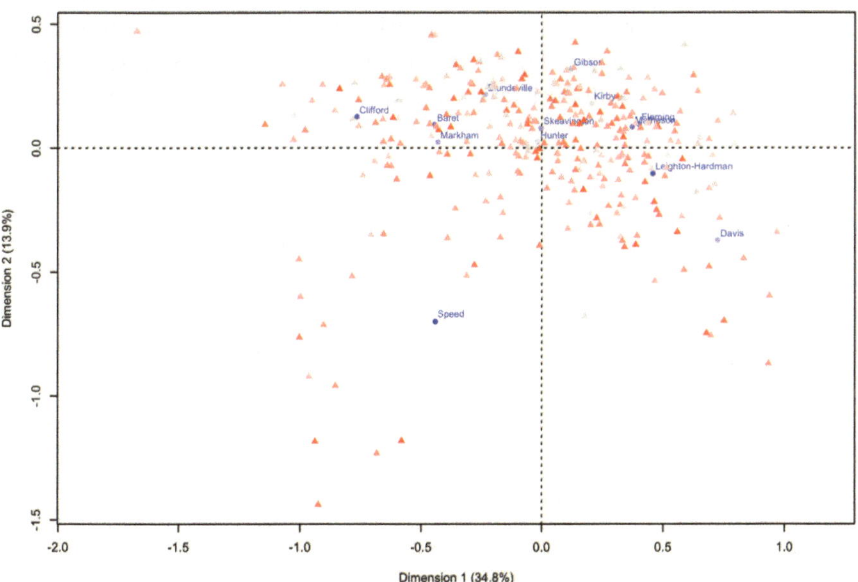

Figure 1: Symmetric plot of trigrams and texts (50% of tokens).

chronology, and may well represent a historical development. The 16th- and 17th-century texts cluster in the upper left quadrant, the 18th- and 19th-century texts in the centre near the origin, and the contemporary text (Davies' text, from 2009) shows up on the far right. This slope is not perfect, however: the Blundeville text from 1565 is positioned near the centre of the plot, away from its contemporaries, and the mid-19th-century text by Skeavington is similarly displaced. For plots showing the trigrams, and more explanation of the various decisions underlying the correspondence analyses (e.g. why the most frequent 309 POS-trigrams were selected for Figure 1, rather than more reduced sets), see Lubbers and Los (2020); this paper also contains discussions of all the dimensions that are relevant for accounting for the variation, not just the first two shown here in Figure 1. In this paper we will limit the discussion to just one "dimension", dimension 1, which is the dimension in the plot that accounts for the chronological progression.

Table 2 shows the highest POS trigram correlations on dimension 1. The "quality" score indicates the degree of certainty that the position of the data point (the POS-trigram) is being represented accurately by the dimensions chosen; a score of over 500 corresponds to more than 50% certainty. A high "correlation" means that the POS trigram is strongly associated with the dimension (this is also indicated by the shading in Figure 1). "Coordinates" indicate whether the POS-trigram is associated with the later (+) or rather the earlier (-) texts of the corpus.

Table 2: Highest POS trigram correlations on dimension 1 (in permille).

#	POS trigram	Quality	Correlation	Coordinate
23	PRP-DPS-NN1	839	826	−569
58	TO0-VVI-PNP	829	783	−571
72	VM0-VVI-PNP	945	817	−1012
12	DPS-NN1-PUN	821	803	−657
125	CJS-PNP-VBI	830	754	−980
31	VVN-PRP-AT0	877	840	+480
133	VBZ-VVN-PRP	792	785	+530
253	NN2-PUN-AT0	820	763	+569
206	VVN-PRP-AJ0	762	742	+725
28	AJ0-NN1-PRF	732	721	+562

3.3 Discussion of dimension 1

One of the limitations of this method is that we cannot recover these POS tags together with the lexical items that they derive from – this is the "black box" problem mentioned in the introduction. We have to search for these sequences in the unstripped input. We will try to discover in the original corpus what it was in these texts that caused the features in Table 2 to bubble up as significant markers of the early period versus the later one.

We will start with the features that characterize the earlier texts, i.e. the five trigrams with negative coordinates in Table 2, and then discuss the five trigrams with positive coordinates that identify them as typical of the later texts.

3.3.1 Preposition – possessive – noun – punctuation

The first POS trigram in the negative domain indicates the combination of a preposition (other than *of*), a possessive determiner and a singular noun (#23: PRP-DPS-NN1). This POS trigram and the fourth combination, #12: DPS-NN1-PUN, also in the negative domain, both represent occurrences of the string PRP-DPS-NN1-PUN, so that they are both generated by the phrases in bold in example (3a-b), from the earlier period, and (4a-d), from the later:

(3)   a. Moreover Camerarius thinketh it a greate deale better for horses to be watered abroade then in the stable unles some greate necessitie do otherwyse requyre, and then he exhorteth the keper to be carefull, that the water which he offreth **unto his horse,** be swete and pure, without any motes or strawes, and when so ever his horse hath laboured, and is whotte, he would not haue him to drincke, untill he hath stalyd, and be throughely dryed of his sweat. (Blundeville, 1565)

        b. for sure I am, that to their houes it doth no good, & to lye moist & wet, must nedes be hurtful **to their body.** (Blundeville, 1565)

(4)   a. But if your Horse be already fat, you ought to observe diligently what Quantity of Food, and what Degrees of Exercise are sufficient to keep up the same Order and Oeconomy **in his Body,** and likewise the same Degree of Activity and Spirit; and the way to know this is, **by his Dung,** his staling, and principally when you ride him abroad to give him Exercise. (Gibson, 1721)

        b. standing with your face opposite to the horse's, hold the left cheek of his head stall in your left hand; and curry him with a good strong hand,

    from the root of his ears, **along his neck,** and **to his shoulders,** then go
    over the other parts of his body, but more lightly; (Hunter, 1796)
  c. It will obviously occur to most people, that the quantity and quality of a
    horse's food should be proportioned **to his labour:** (Kirby, 1823)

A look at all the occurrences of *his* and *their* – which are the most frequent possessives in the corpus – in the original corpus suggests that the earlier texts have a tendency to position information in end-focus position (i.e. the end of a clause, where it will be likely to be followed by a punctuation mark) that is already given and highly "accessible" in the context; this is the case with *unto the horse* in (3a) which occurs in the middle of a passage wholly given over to watering the horse, and also with *their barley* mentioned in (3b). The four-gram may also have been given a boost by the dialogic format of one early text, which leads to some repetition of the same structure:

(5)   Kingdon.
    I pray you shewe me in what place **of their bodies,** these horses let themselues bloud.

    Clifford.
    Upon their shoulders most commonly so high, as is possible for them to reach **towardes their withers,** they will also let themselues bloud on their buttockes a little beneath the buckle bone, but this last use not halve so common as the first note, that these horses will alwaies let themselues bloud so neere the place where the griefe or sicknesse is as is possible for them to reache **wyth their mouthes.** (Clifford, 1585)

Example (5) also suggests a different possibility, i.e. that the more practical advice that is interspersed among the information about the horse's food in the earlier texts causes more references to the horse's body parts, and that it is this that boosts the counts of these trigrams; the later texts are not entirely free of this either, however (cf. (4b)), and even the 1977 text by Leighton-Hardman is structured along similar lines.

3.3.2 Infinitive – pronoun

The second POS trigram with a negative coordinate in the list represents the use of an infinitive marker, an infinitive of a lexical verb and a personal pronoun: TO0-VVI-PNP (#58). An example is (6):

(6) you shall adde to his Oates Beanes; for they will increase strength and lust, and so keepe him till you intend **to hunt him**; . . . (Baret, 1618)

The third trigram in the list that characterizes the early texts is #72: VM0-VVI-PNP, which is the combination of a modal verb, the infinitive form of a lexical verb and a personal pronoun. This trigram is generated from examples as in (7):

(7) Even so do I wishe also that the heye, strawe, or garbage, whereof the horse feedyth all the daye, be gyven hym by lytle and lytle, even as he dothe spende it, and not to be layde before him all at once, for that **will lothe him**, and take away his appetyte, . . . (Blundeville, 1565)

What these items have in common is the fact that the object is a pronoun. The higher frequencies of this configuration in the earlier texts is probably connected to the suggestion made in the previous section, i.e. the fact that the later texts adhere more strictly to the idea that end-focus should contain new information, and that the earlier texts are more likely to position given rather than new information there. This is indeed a clear difference between the early and the later texts, as we will see in section 3.3.4.

3.3.3 Conjunction – pronoun – BE

Another POS trigram in the early texts is the combination #125: CJS-PNP-VBI: a subordinating conjunction, a personal pronoun and the infinitive form of *be*. This turned out to be generated not by the infinitive *be* but by the present subjunctive form *be*, a finite form – a mistagging. Not unexpectedly, the subjunctive is more frequent in the earlier period. Although the subjunctive is still around in Present-Day English, there are certain features that betray it being something of an artificial resurrection: although officially a finite form, it appears to be analysed by speakers as an infinitive, witness its behaviour with negation, where we do not get *do*-support. The position of the negation, after the subjunctive form, is also reminiscent of non-finite behaviour (see Aarts 2012); for the historical development of the subjunctive, see Moessner (2020).

(8) a. But Aristotle saythe, that a horse delighteth rather to dryncke of that water
which is somewhat troubled and thicke, in so muche as **if it be** to cleare,
he will not drincke thereof, untill he hath sturryd, or troubled it with his
foote. (Blundeville, 1565)

   b. **if he be** laid downe, you shal not onelie your selfe refraine from com-
ming unto him, but also have care no noise or tumult be neare the stable,
. . . (Markham, 1607)

The last text to have *be* as a present subjunctive is *Gibson 1721*. But it is not just
the subjunctive form that is responsible for the higher frequency of this trigram
in the earlier text; a search through the original corpus for forms of *if* shows that
conditional clauses are slightly more frequent in the earlier part of the corpus.

3.3.4 Passives

On the positive end of the scale, we find trigrams that are identified as more characteristic of the later period. Three of the five contain past participles of lexical
verbs (VVN): #31: VVN-PRP-AT0: a past participle (VVN), a preposition other than
of (PRP) and an article (AT0), as in (9):

(9) a. problems can arise if they are **brought into a** stuffy loose-box on a hot sum-
mer evening (Leighton-Hardman, 1977)

   b. organic fertilisers are **released at a** slower rate than artificial fertilisers
(Leighton-Hardman, 1977)

   c. Free water or that **contained in a** feedstuff releases varying amounts of
water. (Davies, 2009)

The second one is #133: VBZ-VVN-PRP: the 3rd present sg of the verb *be*, a past
participle form of a lexical verb and a preposition other than *of*, as in (10a-b):

(10) a. Water **is lost from** the horse's body via urine, feces, sweat and evaporation
from the lungs and skin. (Davies, 2009)

   b. Haylage **is preferred for** horses in hard work or with known respiratory
conditions (Davies, 2009)

The third POS trigram containing a past participle is #206: VVN-PRP-AJ0: a past
participle form of a lexical verb, a preposition other than *of* and an unmarked
adjective (i.e. not a comparative or superlative), as in (11a-c):

(11) a. Should an excess of this material be given for any length of time, and no requirement for it be **created by corresponding** increase of work, disease must result. (Fleming, 1884)

b. but all this superfluous flesh has to be got rid of by about the end of October, being **substituted by hard** muscles for soft ones (Matheson, 1921)

c. Minerals are **required in different** amounts by different horses. (Leighton-Hardman, 1977)

What we are seeing here is the higher frequency of passive constructions, a well-known feature of contemporary informative prose, particularly scientific writing, as we noticed in the introduction. The "long" passive (i.e. the passive that is accompanied by a *by*-phrase containing the "demoted" agent) as in (11a-c) is also present in the earlier texts, but less frequently, 4 times on average versus 8 in the later texts. This may be one reason why #206: VVN-PRP-AJ0 emerges as more characteristic of the later texts, but there is an additional reason: the *by*-phrase needs to be positioned at the end of the clause to generate #206: VVN-PRP-AJ0. So instances like (12) will not contribute to that trigram:

(12) so **by early and late Airings** the foulness will be deminished, and the gross Humours dispersed (Speed, 1697)

The earlier texts not only have fewer by-phrases, they also do not position them in end-focus position. It is the later texts that are more geared to using the long passive in order to manoeuvre new information into clause-final position, supporting the finding that the later texts observe the flow of given to new information more diligently than the earlier texts.

3.3.5 Nominal style

The fifth POS trigram highlighted as characteristic of the later texts by dimension 1 is #28: AJ0-NN1-PRF: an unmarked adjective, a singular noun and the preposition *of*. Examples are given in (13a-d):

(13) a. This causes a breakdown of the air-cells in the lungs, reducing the area through which the **normal exchange of** gasses takes place. (Leighton-Hardman, 1977)

b. Nutrition has long been recognised as a vital and **integral part of** horse care and is known to be important for horse health, reproduction, performance and general well being. (Davies, 2009)

c. The comparatively **small size of** a horse's stomach, and the short time that food remains within it, clearly indicate that this animal requires to be fed at fairly short intervals (Matheson, 1921)

d. The **vast array of** commercial products available for feeding to horses does not help this situation, and overfeeding and oversupplementation with resulting health and performance problems are becoming more common. (Davies, 2009)

As we noticed in the introduction, the rise of such complex noun phrases has been noticed and discussed in the literature, including Halliday (2004), who contextualises it as one of the markers of the transition from a "Doric" style to an "Attic" style of science writing; see Schneider (2021) for a quantitative account. The "Attic" style is dense and has a high information content; the rise of the gerund in Early Modern English contributed to the development of this style, as any verb could be turned into a gerund (cf. *overfeeding* in (13d)) so that the writer is not at the mercy of what nominalizations the language makes available; derivational morphology typically attaches to only a subset of a major category, and it is not a given that there is a nominalization available for every verb. Another development that facilitated the "Attic" style in this way was the increasingly available option of conversion (cf. *exchange* in (13a)). The "Doric" style of the earlier manuals illustrate what has been called a "continuative" style (Burnley 1986), with long sentences and a high frequency of conjunctions, either coordinating or subordinating. The fact that the earlier texts exhibit the continuative style is supported by the variation in "mean length of utterances" of the texts in Table 1 – the earlier texts have longer sentences. An example is the single sentence in (14), with all elements that introduce finite clauses marked in bold:

(14)   Now for the propertie of the foodes; first the Grasse questionlesse is nourishing during the time of sommer, **whilest** the strength of the Sun abides within it, **and** is food good inough for ordinary trauelling horses, **but** for sto[. . .] horses of great pride and courage it is somewhat too cold and moyst, **and** therefore onely to be giuen phisically, as for a month together in the beginning of sommer, only to scowre them, **which** is called the soyle time, **and if when** you giue them grasse, you giue them blades of greene corne, it is passing good also. (Markham, 1607)

Note in particular the nested conjunctions at the end: [₁*and* [₂ *if* [₃*when you giue them grasse*]₃, *you giue them blades of greene corne*]₂, *it is passing good also*]₁.

3.3.6 Noun – punctuation – article

The final trigram to discuss is #253: NN2-PUN-AT0, i.e. a plural noun, a punctuation marker and an article. This is the sequence in bold in example (15):

(15)   Unless the food contains a sufficient proportion of these **substances, the** body must be inefficiently nourished, . . . (Fleming, 1884)

The reason that this trigram bubbles up appears to be that the early texts have remarkably few sentences starting with a definite article, and none starting with an indefinite article (AT0 stands for definite as well as indefinite articles); the sentences in the texts in the early period tend to start with an adjunct rather than with the subject. This can be linked to the phenomenon that phrasal (as opposed to clausal) adjuncts preceding the subject in the main clause become less frequent in the history of English, quite probably as a consequence of the loss of verb second in the 15th Century. After that period, it is the subject that makes the link to the previous discourse rather than an adjunct (Los and Dreschler 2012), so the subject will tend to be definite (i.e. "given" information); indefinite subjects can be expected to have been uncommon in all periods. The frequency of sentences starting with a subject rather than a (clausal or phrasal) adjunct is low in the early period, and the chance that the last word of the previous clause is a plural noun (NN2) is a minority pattern anyway (in all periods), and it is this combination that leads to this trigram having such a low frequency in the earlier texts that the correspondence analysis picks it up as a significant feature of the later texts, and marks it with a +. So although this trigram is marked by a + in Table 2, which points to an association with the later rather than the earlier texts of the corpus, in this case it is best interpreted as proceeding from a feature of the earlier texts – the high frequency of a presubject constituent.

3.4 Conclusion

This section has tried to break open the black box of the findings of the correspondence analysis using a POS-tagged corpus from which all the lexical material had been stripped. Two clear differences emerged between early and late texts: a higher frequency of complex nouns and passives. It is well-known that the frequencies of these constructions increase in the Early and Late Modern periods, so the increase is not unexpected. The increase marks the manuals as containing the logical-argumentative text type of scientific writing; apart from the very earliest horse manuals, which seem more akin to the cookery book genre with their lists of remedies,[4] almost all manuals give rationales for why certain foodstuffs should be given to certain horses, and whether the information is couched in terms of the thickness of the air[5] or in terms of the amounts of nitrogen in the soil,[6] the language used is "the language of science".

The correspondence analysis also throws up a point of style that is less obvious, and does not seem to have come to the same attention in the literature as the nominal style and passives, and that is the patterns discussed in sections 3.3.1, 3.3.2 and 3.3.4 – the flow of information, which in the earlier text is not as strictly from given to new as in the later texts. Section 3.3.6 reported the surprising finding that the earlier texts in the original corpus rarely start new clauses with a (singular) subject requiring a definite or indefinite article; this could be because subjects that start a clause are plural, or pronouns, or that subjects tend to be preceded by other material (which is expected as part of the continuative style).

4 Association plot

4.1 Rationale and method

Another way to visualize the degree to which trigrams are associated with individual texts is by means of an association plot. For this procedure, the number of POS trigram types was greatly reduced, to only the 10 most frequent POS trigrams. These 10 most frequent POS trigrams together account for approximately 8.77% of all trigram tokens in the data.

Association plots do not visualize the absolute frequencies of trigrams per text but rather their residuals, i.e. the difference between the observed and expected frequencies, as calculated on the basis of the row and column totals. A bar

---

4 An example of such a text is a 15th-century treatise known under various labels (MS Sloane 2584, Horse Leechynge, A Late Middle English Treatise on Horses) and has been included in the Helsinki Corpus of as *CMHorses*, and it was excluded from Lubbers and Los (2020) for that reason. We will encounter another Late Middle English text on horse care, MS Harley 6398 or *The Boke of Marchalsi* (Odenstedt 1973), also excluded from Lubbers and Los (2020) for the same reason, in section 4.

5 ". . .we are remote from the Influence of the Sun in Winter, so our Grass at that time is very Weak, and affords but little Nourishment; besides that, our Grounds are wet and miry in many Places, because of the Thickness of the Air, which would greatly expose all such Horses as have been delicately kept." (Gibson, 1721).

6 "To get the best value from the grass, the land must be well drained and the soil in good condition – that is, there must not be any deficiency of lime, nitrogen, phosphate or potash." (Leighton-Hardman, 1977).

in green above the centre line of the association plot of Figure 2 indicates that a trigram's residual is positive: it has more occurrences in a particular text than would be expected based on the average across the corpus ("overuse"). A bar below the centre line in red indicates that there are fewer occurrences than expected ("underuse"). Table 3 provides more detail than could be supplied in the legend of Figure 2, as well as absolute frequencies for these 10 POS trigrams.[7]

4.2 The continuative style

Like the correspondence analysis, the association plot also appears to identify a chronological progression. The signal observed for the second trigram from the top, NN1-PUN-CJC (singular noun, punctuation mark, and coordinate conjunction) shows a remarkably positive association (blue bars) with the earlier texts of the corpus and a negative association (red bars) with the later texts. The strength of this signal may come as a surprise, as the absolute figures in Table 2 indicate that this POS trigram is frequently used throughout the corpus; but note that the trigram is connected to the four-gram discussed in section 3.3.1, many of which could in fact be part of a five-gram PRP-DPS-NN1-PUN-CJC or PRF-DPS-NN1-PUN-CJC like **in his Body, and** in (4a), **of his body, but** in (4b) and **of their food, and** in (4d); the Claws5-tagset distinguishes *of* (PRF) from other prepositions (PRP), a distinction that may not be helpful in the case of our texts, because it fragments the frequency of an n-gram that might otherwise have "bubbled up" as a feature associated to texts of a particular period – in this case, the continuative style of the earlier texts (see section 3.3.5); an example is (16), from *Markham 1607*. Instances of the trigram NN1-PUN-CJC are in bold.

---

7 A chi-squared test was carried out on this table, which indicates that there is an association between these trigrams and text samples (χ^2= 422.57, df=108, p < 0.001). However, this result should probably be taken with a pinch of salt given that the counts for the trigrams shown here can hardly be assumed to be independent (an assumption for the chi-squared test), since it can be observed that more than one trigram in this table may overlap with other trigrams listed. Note also that these 10 trigram cell frequencies and their row and column totals are a subset of a larger contingency table, and the computation of a correct chi-squared statistic for such a subtable is less straightforward than might appear at first sight (see Gries 2014: 376), including a reference to the sub.table function for R used to compute the statistic above).

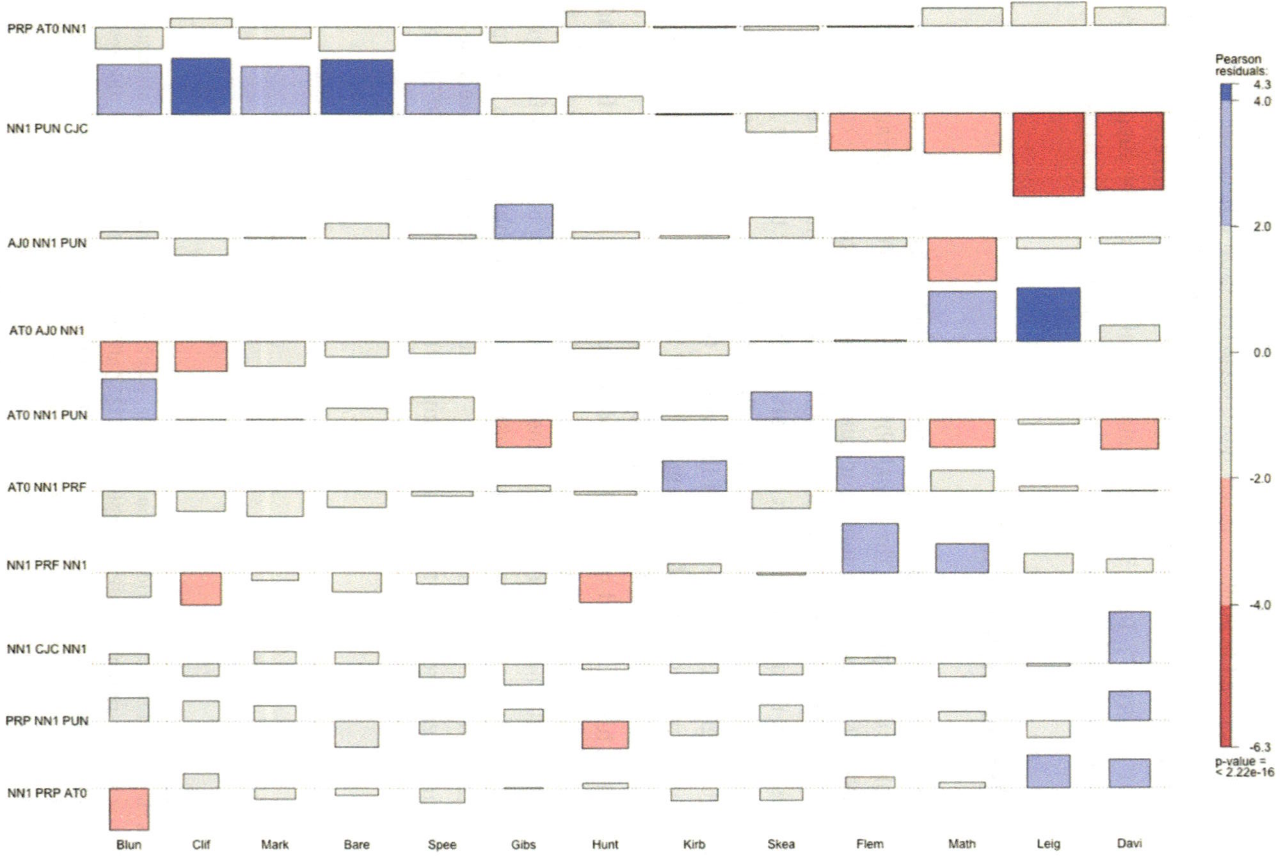

Figure 2: Association plot of 10 most frequent POS trigrams and sources.

Table 3: 10 most frequent POS trigrams in the corpus (*n*).

POS trigram	Blun	Clif	Mark	Bare	Spee	Gibs	Hunt	Kirb	Skea	Flem	Math	Leig	Davi
PRP-AT0-NN1	36	44	47	45	59	40	74	68	56	75	78	72	62
NN1-PUN-CJC	67	61	73	83	75	51	68	61	42	45	37	7	7
AJ0-NN1-PUN	37	22	39	50	48	50	50	51	52	50	26	37	35
AT0-AJ0-NN1	20	16	26	34	39	34	42	41	41	54	73	67	44
AT0-NN1-PUN	48	26	35	44	53	20	46	47	51	38	30	36	21
AT0-NN1-PRF	19	17	22	29	37	32	38	57	28	64	51	38	32
NN1-PRF-NN1	12	7	20	18	23	17	16	33	24	53	40	32	27
NN1-CJC-NN1	19	10	22	24	17	10	20	20	16	28	18	19	34
PRP-NN1-PUN	23	19	23	11	17	20	12	18	25	20	26	14	27
NN1-PRP-AT0	3	17	14	17	16	16	23	18	15	29	24	30	26
Total *n*	284	239	321	355	384	290	389	414	350	456	403	352	315

(16) and in this manner of **trayning, and** with this gentle exercise, you shall bring him to a good state of **bodie, &** to be able to indure some reasonable extremity, which you may knowe by the cleannesse of his neather chappes, the thinnesse of his **ribbe, and** the emptinesse of his flanke (Markham, 1607)

The fact that the tagging system distinguishes between PRF (the preposition *of*) and PRP (prepositions other than *of*) means that the frequencies of n-grams containing these tags will be lower than would have been the case if only a single tag would have been used to cover all prepositions.

5 Limitations of the tagset

The findings of the stylometric explorations of the previous section showed some alignment with what we know about changing styles from the literature, mostly with respect what changes in the later period: passives and noun phrases can be picked up with the claws5-tagset. The features of the earlier period that appeared to be picked up were, possibly, the continuative style, and, more clearly, the pronominal objects at clause endings, i.e. "given" information in end-focus position, a combination that is not optimal from the perspective of PDE. Passives and a more nominal style can be argued to reflect the logical-argumentative side of the genre, the rationales provided by the authors as a justification for the procedures they advocate. The features of the instructive text type do not seem to come to the fore at all in the Correspondence Analysis. To get a steer for what the data-driven investigations might be missing, we provide a "snapshot" of the various styles of the manuals in Table 4. It is

Table 4: subjects/imperatives in the qualitative corpus – main clauses and reason clauses. Bold clausal postmodifiers. Capital letters indicate first position in clause; totals of subjects and imperatives in first position indicated in the last column.

year	text or author	subjects and imperatives in main clauses and reason-clauses	first /total
1425	*The Boke of Marchalsi*	imp – he – he – thu – the horse – that – milk – imp – he – imp – non hors – thu – imp – that – that – that – imp – imp – imp – he	0/20
1565	Blundeville	The moste naturall kynds of meates, **wherewith horses ought to be fedde, accordyng to russius** – Some (people) – Grasse – Sweet heye – it – Strawe – it – they – they – Barlie – it – it – we – it – I–i – it	7/17
1585	Clifford	I – imp – thou – you – he – I – i – Imp – imp – imp – imp – Imp – imp – twelve times as much Oates **as you can take up in your two handes**	4/14
1607	Markham	the foodes **which belong to horses** – the grasse – it – it – Hay – it – it	1/7
1609	Morgan	imp – Imp – Imp – imp – imp – imp – imp – imp – imp – imp – imp – imp – imp – imp – he – the chiefe danger	2/16
1618	Baret	you – hee – they – the strength of the beanes – they – they – some horses – many (people) – they – I – the meale – they – they – the land – that – you – it – they	1/18
1697	Speed	imp – Imp – imp – imp – Imp – imp – Imp – imp – imp – imp – imp – imp – he – imp – imp – imp – imp – Imp – imp – imp – imp – imp – imp – imp – imp – imp	4/26
1721	Gibson	it(dummy) – those things – there – ease and full feeding alone – we – you – the way **to know this**	0/7
1796	Hunter	Imp – imp – imp – imp – imp – imp – you – It (dummy) – it – horses – Many horses – the barley **when thus given** – The water	4/13

1823	Kirby	It (dummy) – It (dummy) – these diseases – this – Horses – his diet – All horses **that are fed on grass and hay alone** – A moderate quantity of corn or other hard food	5/8
1840s	Skeavington	Water – Some (owners) – this plan of watering – Soft water – rivers and running streams – springs **that supply ponds, where the water gets impregnated and softened by a loomy or chalky soil** – The quantity in this – Some horses – others (horses) – Such (horses) – water – some horses – they – It – a horse – It – nothing	8/17
1921	Matheson	Horses – they – Anything from half to one gallon – Another fallacious notion in the watering of sick horses – cold water – Another matter **which should never be lost sight of by attendants on horses** – This – The best forage – it (dummy) – A good horse-master – it (dummy) – it – the matter – Every class of the community – such unscrupulousness – It (dummy) – A conscientious horse keeper – he	10/18
1977	Leighton-Hardman	it – Any hay – It (dummy) – The easiest way **to do this** – The tar – You – Imp – imp – imp – imp – imp – imp – The water in the trough – imp – Mashes – all dry feeds apart from horse cubes – Only enough water – The final consistency	10/18
2009	Davies	The subject of horse nutrition – There – This often quite technical subject – Nutrition – This book – Malnutrition of horses – The vast array of commercial products **available for feeding to horses** – overfeeding and oversupplementation with resulting health and performance problems – Nutrition – Horses – There – Pasture – Pasture – Spring pasture – Horses – It (dummy) – High quality, permanent pasture	16/17

always difficult to provide a visualisation of larger stretches of text, so what we have done here is to extract two paragraphs of every text, averaging 284 words. To keep the content of these fragments as similar as we could, paragraphs were selected, if possible, that linked the kind of feed the horse should receive to the level of activity or work that was required of it. Table 4 presents a snapshot of the main clauses in these fragments by giving the subject of that clause; if the subject is given with a capital letter, that indicates that the subject is also the first constituent of the clause. Such subjects are expected to be a feature of the later texts. Some main clauses could not be represented by a subject because they contained an imperative, in which case the clause is represented by the label *Imp* (if the imperative is first in the clause) or *imp* (if it isn't). We also included reason-clauses, as these are very main-clause-like, particularly in the earlier texts, where phrases like *for the which cause* (Blundeville, 1565) or *Wherefore* (Baret, 1618) appear to be syntactically equivalent to *therefore*.[8] Reason-clauses are here taken to include purpose and result, because these are the means by which writers provide explanations – why they are advocating certain procedures. Table 4 includes two texts that are not included in the original corpus, *The Boke of Marchalsi* (Odenstedt 1973), and *The Perfection of Horse-manship, Drawne from Nature; Arte, and Practise*, by N. Morgan (1609) (excluded from the n-gramming in order to restrict the number of texts per century to two) for interest.

Imperatives are of course clear markers of the instructive, procedural text type, so it is not surprising to find them here; but they do not have their own label in the Claws5-tagset, being subsumed with the base form of lexical verbs (except the infinitive) as "VVB". The Claws5-tagset was selected because it is not extensive and hence will lead to higher n-gram frequencies; but the downside is that it turns out to be not sufficiently fine-grained to single out this particular feature which is so characteristic of instruction. Table 4 shows that imperatives tend to become scarcer as time goes on. A closer look at the larger corpus shows that the reason is not because the texts become less instructive, but because there are other ways to direct the reader, e.g. by addressing the reader by *you*, followed by a modal of obligation (*should* or *must*), or, more indirectly, by impersonal phrases that introduce directive sublauses containing *should*, like *It is to be noted, that the*

---

8 Reason-clauses are syntactically subordinate, but their strong sense of assertion make them good candidates for encoding foregrounded events, occasionally leading to main-clause behaviour. In PDE, for example, reason-clauses can be questioned by a tag-question, as in (i), from (Chafe 1976, 439), quoted in Cristofaro (2003: 35) – tag–questions normally only question main clauses. In Cristofaro's (2003) typological overview, reason-clauses are positioned at the main-clause-like pole of a continuum.

(i) a. I decided to buy it, because it has such a big memory.

   b. I decided to buy it, because it has such a big memory, hasn't it?

barley for this purpose should be fresh ground every day (Hunter, 1796) or *It will obviously occur to most people that the quantity and quality of a horse's food should be proportioned to his labour* (Kirby, 1823); most of the dummy-*its* in Table 4 are of this type (for more discussion, see Lubbers 2016). Another way of expressing a directive less directly is by outlining good practice, by means of third person subjects followed by the auxiliary *will*: *A good horse-master* or *A conscientious horse keeper* (both in *Matheson 1921*).

Speed's text (1697) – already marked out by the correspondence analysis as an outlier, see Figure 1 – is clearly the most extreme, with all but one main clause of the fragment from this text being in the imperative. All but one paragraph of Speed's text in the larger, original corpus is of this kind (subordination conjunctions are in italics, imperatives are in bold).

(17) [Directions to Order him after the taking this.] *When* you have given the Horse this Scowring, **rub** him well all over with Whisps and a Curry-comb; **follow** these with a Brush, and **dust** him well, then **rub** him with a dry Cloath till no Sweat appears; **put** his Cloath on again, and **truss** under the Cloath warm Wisps, **let** him fast for the space of two Hours, and **keep** him in continual motion *that* he sleep not, *that* the Humours may disperse and evacuate, then **give** him a handful of Wheat-ears: *If* upon handling him under the Ears and near the Heart, you perceive no more Sweat arises, but *if* he be faint or sickish, after the expiration of the time, **toss up** his Litter, **take off** his Bridle, and **let** him rest for the space of two Hours, and he will be well again, then **give** him Wheatears gradually, and **rub** him down; after that, **let** him feed on Hay out of your Hand, and an hour after **crum** three shivers of the Bread mentioned, with a quart of Oats and a pint of split Beans; **let** him rest after this three Hours; that expired, **Visit** him again, and *before* you Dress him, **give** him a like quantity of Oats, Beans and Bread, then **Ride** him, his Cloathing being on, a little way, but **suffer** him not to Water till about an hour and an half after; then **wash** a pint of Oats in Beer and **give** them to Cool him, and in so ordering **leave** him till Morning with a little Hay, and **continue** after, his usual Feedings and gentle Breathings. [265 words] (Speed, 1697)

The reason for Speed being an outlier is that he is the only author who just reports his own practices, without commenting – or critiquing – the practices of others; the clauses introduced by *that* 'so that' in line 4 are in fact the only occasions where he gives some kind of rationale.

The non-finite temporal clause *that expired* 'once that (= the 'three hours' of the previous clause) has expired' in Speed's text in (17) also alerts us to an area where the Claws5-tagset makes distinctions between categories which it might have been more useful to merge. There is no tag for non-finite clauses as they do not have complementizers, so that each clause is only being marked by the form of its non-finite verb (VVG for *-ing* forms, VVI for infinitives or VVN for past participles). Fewer distinctions between non-finite clauses might have caused particular n-grams to bubble up as significant, but unlike the preposition-tag-set (PRF and PRP) where there is a similar problem (see section 5.2), merging the non-finite tags successfully requires parsing as well as tagging, in order to distinguish non-finite verbs that are part of a verbal periphrasis from non-finite verbs that head their own clause. The non-finites are a reminder of the kind of constructions that are impossible to detect by means of POS-trigrams, but may nevertheless be very characteristic of the earlier texts.

Imperatives or subjects starting with a capital letter in Table 4 mark that they are the first element in the clause and it is clear from the right-hand column that subjects are much more likely to be the first element in the clause in the later texts; this is the reason that the earlier texts in the original corpus are rarely found with the trigram #253: NN2-PUN-AT0 (see section 3.3.6). After the loss of verb-second syntax, phrasal (as opposed to clausal) adjuncts preceding the subject in the main clause become less frequent (Los and Dreschler 2012). The subjects also appear to be longer in the later texts than in the earlier ones, as they contain postmodifiers of some length (including relative clauses). It is tempting to connect these longer noun phrases with Halliday's "Attic" style, possibly as a response to a change in the type of referents that need to be tracked in the discourse: from protagonists like horses and their human carers, to scientific processes describing horse digestion and crop production, but the only one that stands out in this small sample is yet another "off-record" instruction: *Another matter which should never be lost sight of by attendants on horses* (Matheson, 1921).

6 Conclusions

This paper investigated a corpus of texts of the same genre and topic – horse manuals – when subjected to data-driven stylometric methods. The idea was to see whether its findings can be interpreted, and if possible aligned by what is known from the literature about changing styles. The texts turn out to be mixtures of the instructive text type and the logical-argumentative type: the authors describe procedures (instructive) but also give rationales for them (logical–argumentative). What is interesting is that both of these show gradual shift over the years – instruction can be relayed by imperatives and by expressions containing modals of obligation, but also by less "on-record" instruction in terms of outlining good practice or using phrases like *It will obviously occur to most people*. The logical-argumentative rationales to justify the advice exhibits increasing use of passivization and a more nominal style, the same shifts that have been noted for the evolution of scientific texts. The horse manuals share these developments because the procedures they describe tend to be given scientific explanations, although the degree in which this happens differs per text. A particular outlier here was *Speed 1697*, with very little explanation, or reference to (and critique of) alternative methods. As a result, that text is almost purely instructive, proceeding from the author's aim to give a detailed account of his own practice, as an example for others to follow.

We pointed out some potentially significant differences between the early and the later texts that were not picked up: frequencies of non-finite subclauses, for instance, could have been expected to emerge as characteristic of the earlier texts, but they were assigned too many different POS-tag labels to "bubble up" as significant. This is particularly the case for the non-finite subclauses, as they are not introduced by a dedicated element like a subordinate conjunction. There was a similar issue with the tagging of prepositions being fragmented by different tags for *of* (PRF) and prepositions other than *of* (PRP), but in the latter case, the signal was still strong enough to make it to the top of the frequency list. Once noted, such fragmentation can be addressed by merging tagging labels, but the whole point of the exercise was to see what would bubble up in an analysis that was purely data-driven.

We also explored some shortcuts to understanding stylistic variation by considering the type and length of subjects, and whether they started their clause or were preceded by other constituents; presubject constituents is a feature of the earlier texts, and aligns with findings in the literature that the frequency of presubject phrasal adjuncts, in particular, declines (Los et al. forthcoming). What did "bubble up" in the stylometric investigations were signs that the flow of given to new information is more strictly adhered to in the later than in the earlier texts; in the earlier texts, pronouns are found more frequently in end-focus position, and the strategy of using the by-phrase of the "long passive" to manoeuvre a new agent into end-focus position is a feature of the later texts.

References

Aarts, Bas. 2012. The subjunctive conundrum. *Folia Linguistica* 46(1). 1–20.
Banks, David. 2017. The extent to which the passive voice is used in the scientific journal article, 1985-2015. *Functional Linguistics* 4(1). 1–17.

Baron, Alistair & Paul Rayson. 2008. VARD 2: a tool for dealing with spelling variation in historical corpora. *Proceedings of the postgraduate conference in corpus linguistics.* <http://citeseerx.ist.psu.edu/viewdoc/summary?doi=10.1.1.151.798>.

Beal, Joan C., Susan Fitzmaurice & Jana Hodson. 2012. Introduction: Late Modern English – the state of the art. *English Language and Linguistics* 16(2). 201–207.

Benzécri, J. P. 1973. *L'analyse des données.* Paris: Dunod

Biber, Douglas, Stig Johansson, Geoffrey Leech, Susan Conrad & Edward Finegan. 1999. *Longman Grammar of Spoken and Written English.* Harlow: Longman.

Burnley, J.D. 1986. Curial prose in England. *Speculum* 61. 593–614. <https://www.jstor.org/stable/2851597>.

Chafe, Wallace. 1976. Givenness, contrastiveness, definiteness, subjects, topics and point of view. In Charles N. Li (ed.), *Subject and Topic,* 27–55 New York: Academic Press.

Cristofaro, Sonia. 2003. *Subordination (Oxford Studies in Typology and Linguistic Theory).* Oxford: Oxford University Press.

Cuyckens, Hubert & Hendrik De Smet. 2007. For . . . to-infinitives from Early to Late Modern English. In Javier Pérez-Guerra, Dolores González-Álvarez & Jorge L. Bueno Alonso (eds.), *"Of varying language and opposing creed": New insights into Late Modern English,* 77–102. Frankfurt: Peter Lang.

De Smet, Hendrik. 2013. *Spreading Patterns: Diffusional Change in the English System of Complementation.* New York: Oxford University Press.

Denison, David. 1998. Syntax. In Suzanne Romaine (ed.), *The Cambridge history of the English language,* Vol. 4: 1776–1997, 92–329. Cambridge: Cambridge University Press.

Ellegård, Alvar. 1953. *The Auxiliary Do: The Establishment and Regulation of its Use in English.* Stockholm: Almqvist & Wiksell,

Ernestus, Mirjam, Margot van Mulken & R. Harald Baayen. 2006. Ridders en heiligen in tijd en ruimte: Moderne stylometrische technieken toegepast op Oud-Franse teksten. *Taal & Tongval* 58. 70–83.

Fanego, Teresa. 1996. The gerund in Early Modern English: evidence from the Helsinki Corpus. *Folia Linguistica Historica* 17. 97–152.

Greenacre, Michael J. 2017. *Correspondence Analysis in Practice.* Boca Raton: CRC Press.

Greenacre, Michael J. 1984. *Theory and applications of correspondence analysis.* London: Academic Press.

Gries, Stefan T. 2014. Frequency tables, effect sizes, and explorations. In Dylan Glynn & Justyna Robinson. *Corpus methods for semantics: Quantitative studies in polysemy and synonymy,* 365–389. Amsterdam: John Benjamins.

Gries, Stefan T., John Newman & Cyrus Shaoul. 2011. N-grams and the clustering of registers. *Empirical Language Research Journal* 5.1.

Halliday, Michael A.K. 2004. The language of science. In Jonathan Webster (ed.), *Collected works of M.A.K. Halliday Vol. 5.* London: Continuum.

Hornik, Kurt, Christian Buchta, Torsten Hothorn, Alexandros Karatzoglou, David Meyer & Achim Zeileis. 2007. R Weka: An R Interface to Weka. *R package version* 0.4-34. <https://CRAN.R-project.org/package=RWeka>.

Huddleston, Rodney D. 1971. *The sentence in written English: A syntactic study based on an analysis of scientific texts.* London: Cambridge University Press.

Los, Bettelou & Gea Dreschler. 2012. The loss of local anchoring: From adverbial local anchors to permissive subjects. In Terttu Nevalainen & Elizabeth C. Traugott, *Rethinking Approaches to the History of English,* 859–871 New York: Oxford University Press.

Los, Bettelou, Gea Dreschler, Ans Van Kemenade, Erwin Komen & Stefano Coretta. 2023. The decline of local anchoring: A quantitative investigation. *English Language and Linguistics*. 10.1017/S1360674323000047.

Lubbers, Thijs & Bettelou Los. 2020. Visualizing the development of prose styles in Horse Manuals from Early Modern English to Present-Day English. Consulted on 28 July 2021. <https://jdmdh.episciences.org/7003>.

Lubbers, Thijs. 2016. *Towards Profiles of Periodic Style: Discourse organisation in modern English instructional writing*. Edinburgh: PhD, University of Edinburgh.

Moessner, Lilo. 2020. *The History of the Present English Subjunctive. A Corpus-based Study of Mood and Modality*. Edinburgh: Edinburgh University Press.

Murtagh, Fionn. 2005. *Correspondence analysis and data coding with Java and R*. Boca Raton: CRC Press.

Odenstedt, Bengt. 1973. *The boke of marchalsi: a 15th century treatise on horse-breeding and veterinary medicine: Edited from ms. harley 6398*. Stockholm: PhD Stockholm University

Parkes, Malcolm B. 1992. *Pause and effect: An introduction to the history of punctuation in the West*. Aldershot: Scolar Press.

R Core Team. 2014. R Core Team. R: A language and environment for statistical computing. *R Foundation for Statistical Computing*, Vienna, Austria. Consulted on 16 12 2020. <http://www.R-project.org>.

Rydén, Mats & Sverker Brorström. 1987. The *Be/Have Variation with Intransitives in English, with Special Reference to the Late Modern Period*. Stockholm: Almqvist and Wiksell.

Schneider, Gerold. 2021. Syntactic changes in verbal clauses and noun phrases from 1500 onwards. In Bettelou Los, Claire Cowie, Patrick Honeybone & Graeme Trousdale (eds.), *English Historical Linguistics: Change in Structure and Meaning. Papers from the XXth ICEHL*, Vol. 1, 163–200. Amsterdam: John Benjamins.

Seoane, Elena. 2013. On the conventionalisation and loss of pragmatic function of the passive in Late Modern English scientific discourse. *Journal of Historical Pragmatics* 14(1). 70–99.

Toyota, Junichi. 2008. *Diachronic change in the English passive*. Basingstoke: Palgrave Macmillan.

Index

https://doi.org/10.1515/9783110753059-012